Great Priest Imhotep

10

MAKOTO
MORISHITA

SCROLL **36** 03 WAIT FOR US,
YOU BIG BUFFOON

SCROLL **37** 43 THE PURE
WHITE YOUTH

SCROLL **38** 87 THOSE WHO WERE
ONCE PHARAOHS

SCROLL **39** 131 THE HOPE LEFT
BY DESPAIR

Great Priest Imhotep

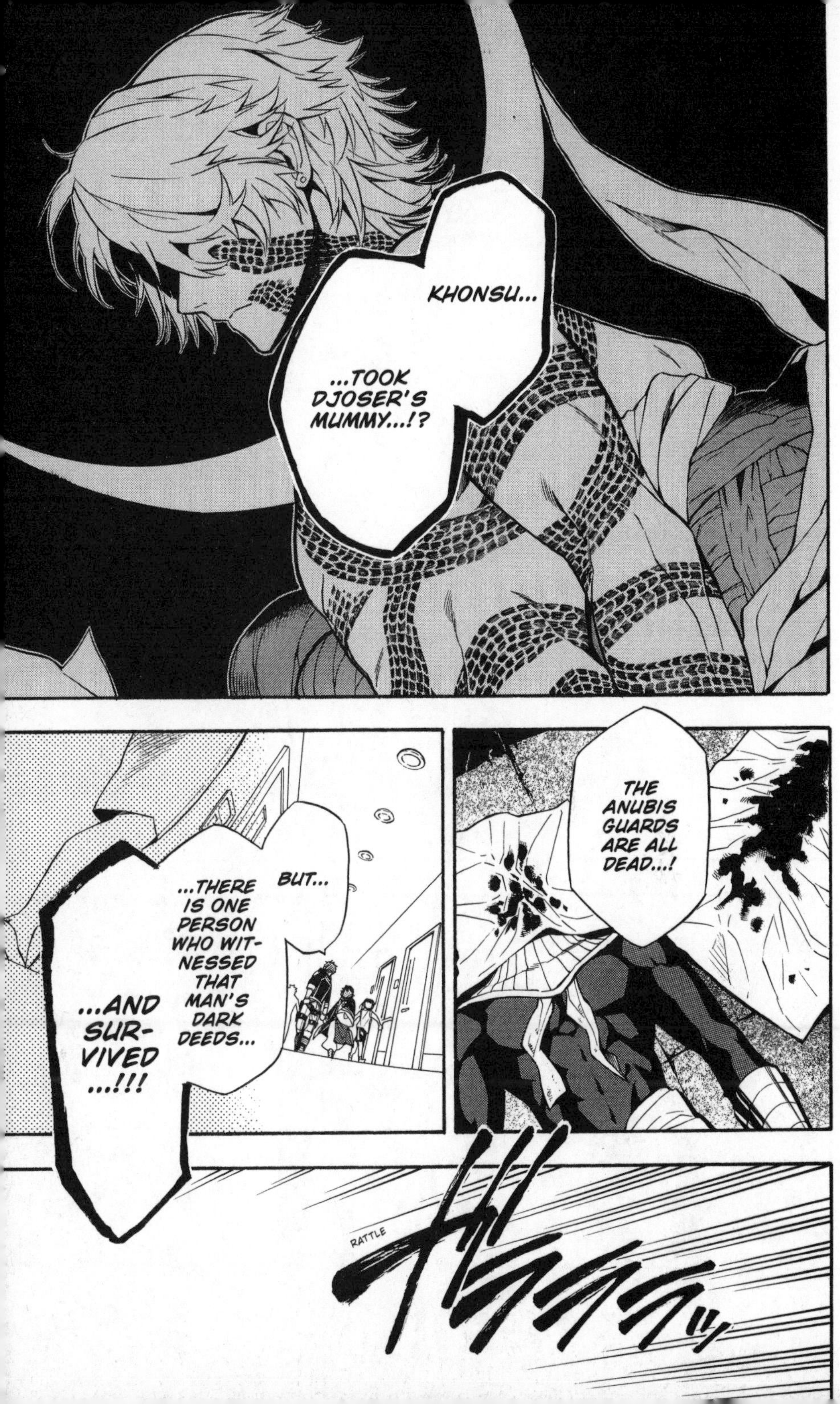
KHONSU...
...TOOK DJOSER'S MUMMY...!?
THE ANUBIS GUARDS ARE ALL DEAD...!
BUT...
...THERE IS ONE PERSON WHO WIT-NESSED THAT MAN'S DARK DEEDS...
...AND SUR-VIVED ...!!!
RATTLE

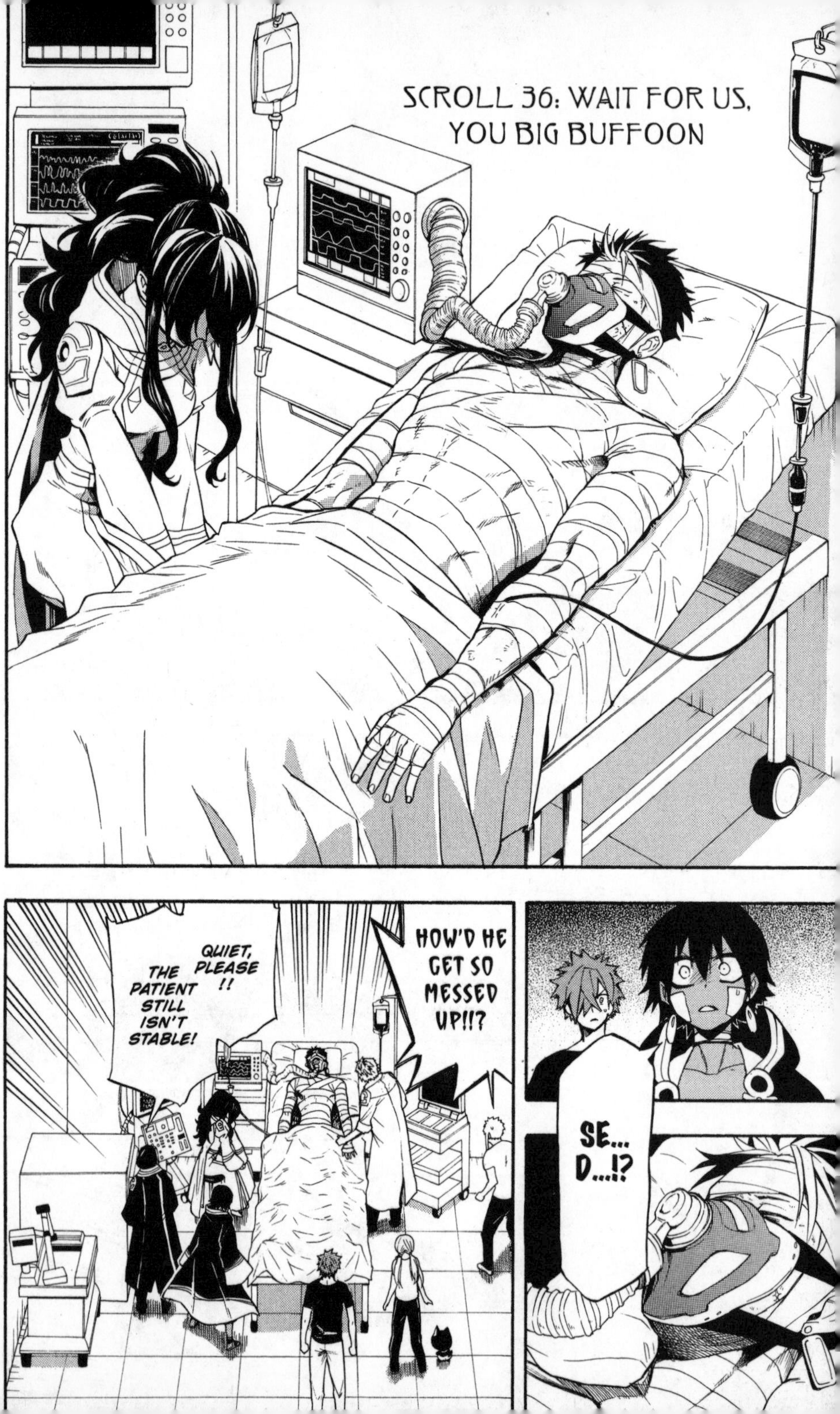
SCROLL 36: WAIT FOR US, YOU BIG BUFFOON
SE... D...!?
HOW'D HE GET SO MESSED UP!!?
QUIET, PLEASE!!
THE PATIENT STILL ISN'T STABLE!

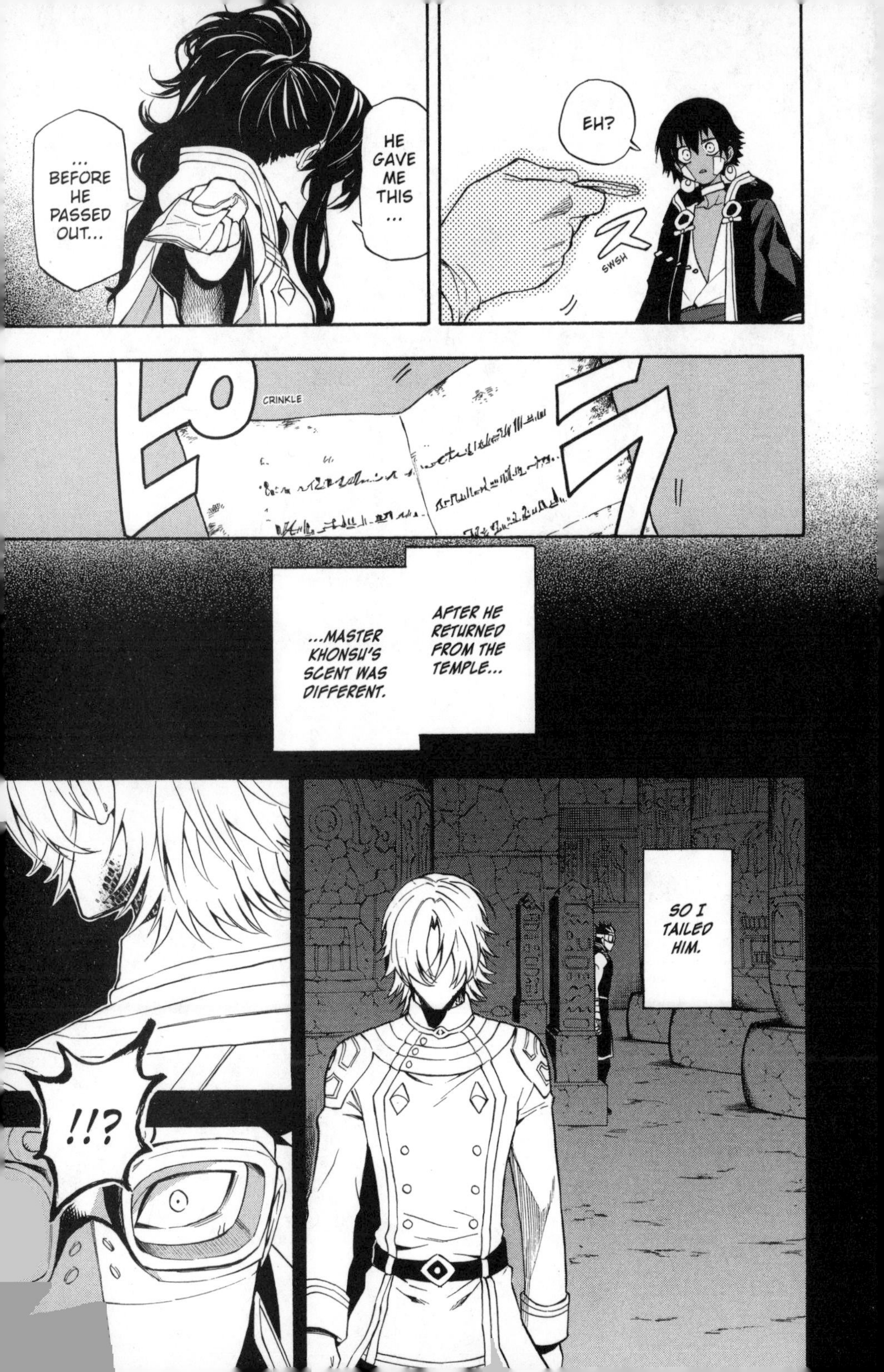
EH?
SWSH
HE GAVE ME THIS...
...BEFORE HE PASSED OUT...
CRINKLE
AFTER HE RETURNED FROM THE TEMPLE...
...MASTER KHONSU'S SCENT WAS DIFFERENT.
SO I TAILED HIM.
!!?

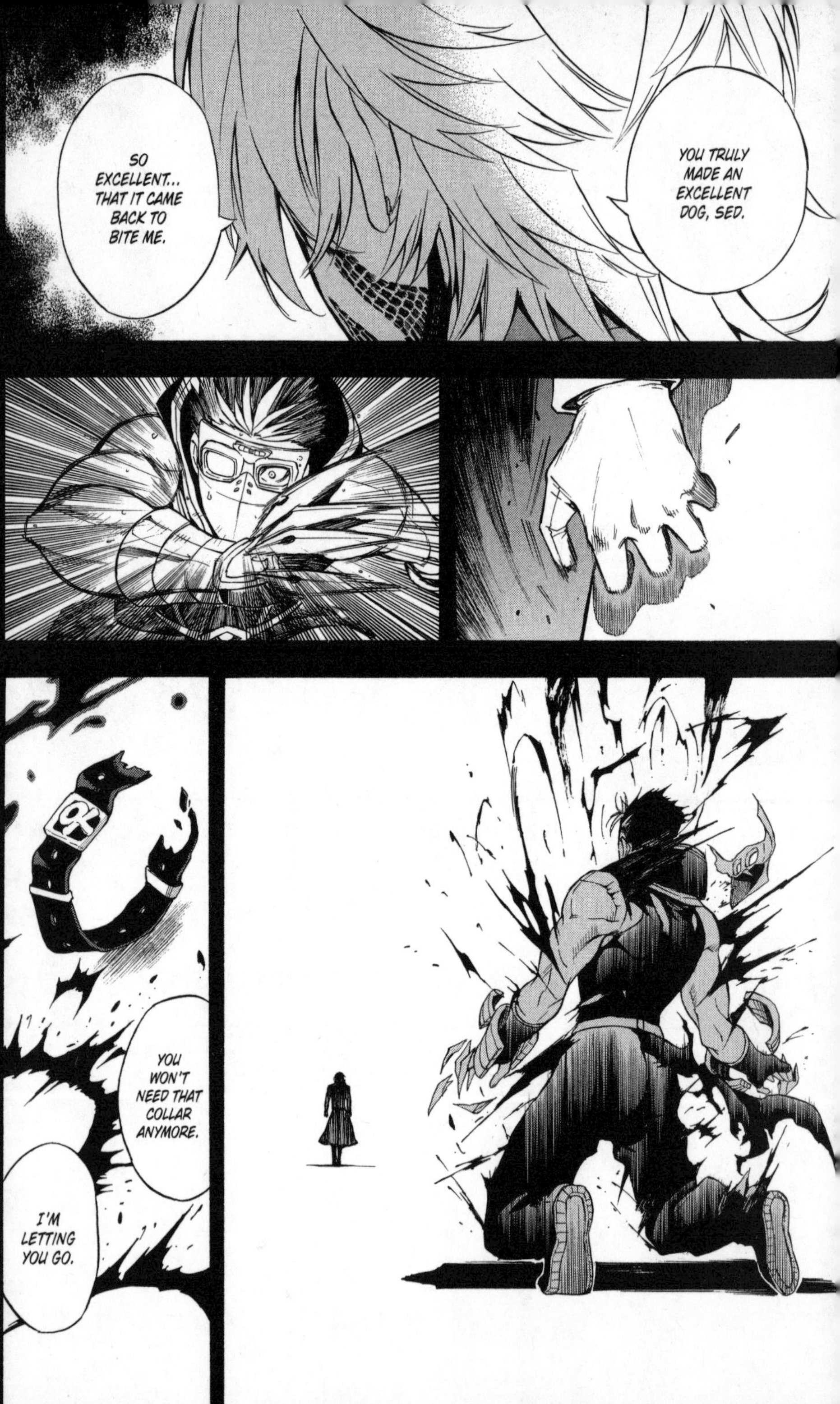
YOU TRULY MADE AN EXCELLENT DOG, SED.
SO EXCELLENT... THAT IT CAME BACK TO BITE ME.
YOU WON'T NEED THAT COLLAR ANYMORE.
I'M LETTING YOU GO.

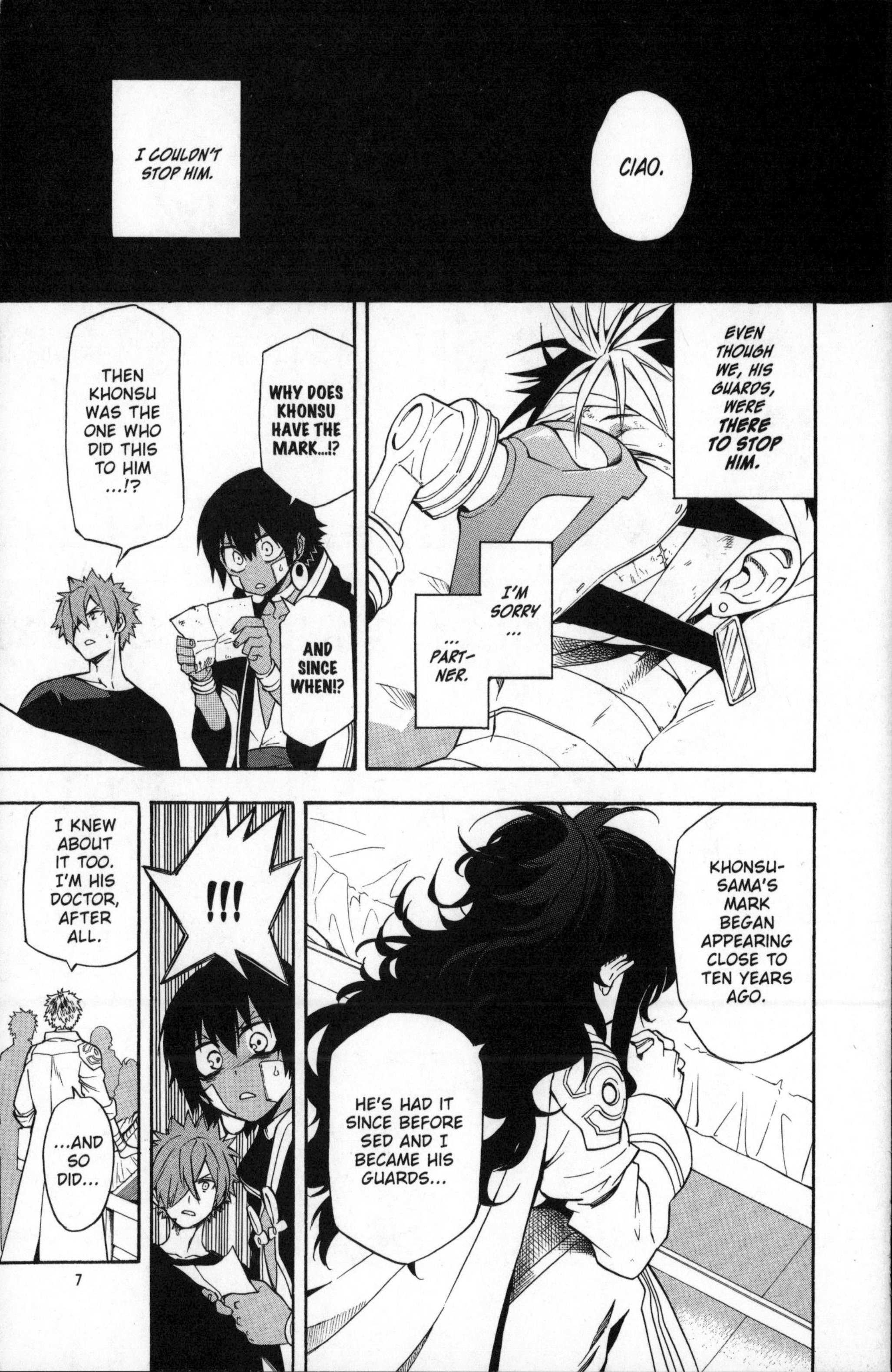
CIAO.
I COULDN'T STOP HIM.
EVEN THOUGH WE, HIS GUARDS, WERE THERE TO STOP HIM.
I'M SORRY...
...PART-NER.
WHY DOES KHONSU HAVE THE MARK...!?
AND SINCE WHEN!?
THEN KHONSU WAS THE ONE WHO DID THIS TO HIM ...!?
KHONSU-SAMA'S MARK BEGAN APPEARING CLOSE TO TEN YEARS AGO.
HE'S HAD IT SINCE BEFORE SED AND I BECAME HIS GUARDS...
!!!
I KNEW ABOUT IT TOO. I'M HIS DOCTOR, AFTER ALL.
...AND SO DID...

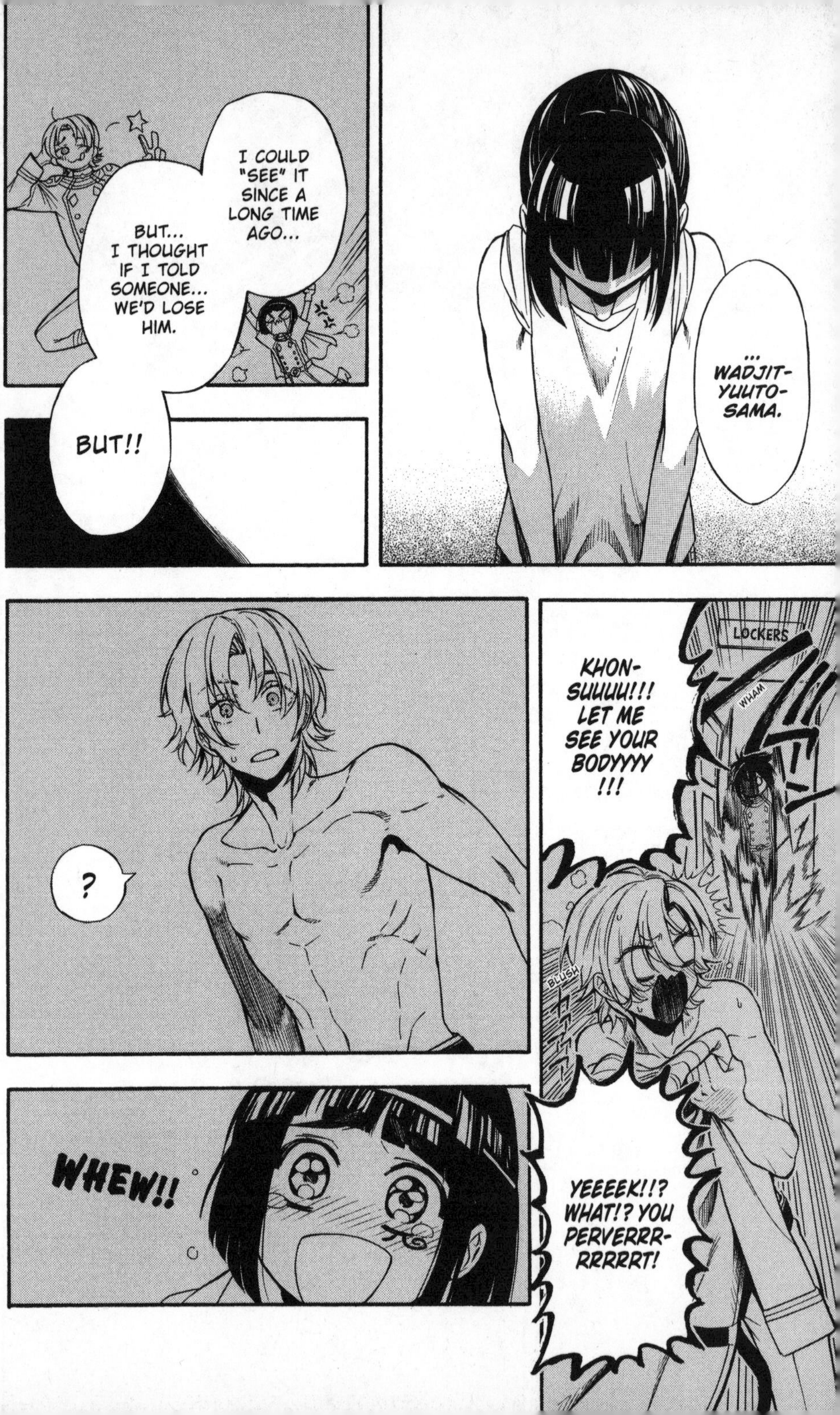
...WADJIT-YUUTO-SAMA.
I COULD "SEE" IT SINCE A LONG TIME AGO...
BUT... I THOUGHT IF I TOLD SOMEONE... WE'D LOSE HIM.
BUT!!
LOCKERS
KHONSUUUU!!! LET ME SEE YOUR BODYYYY!!!
WHAM
BLUSH
YEEEEK!!? WHAT!? YOU PERVERRR-RRRRRT!
?
WHEW!!

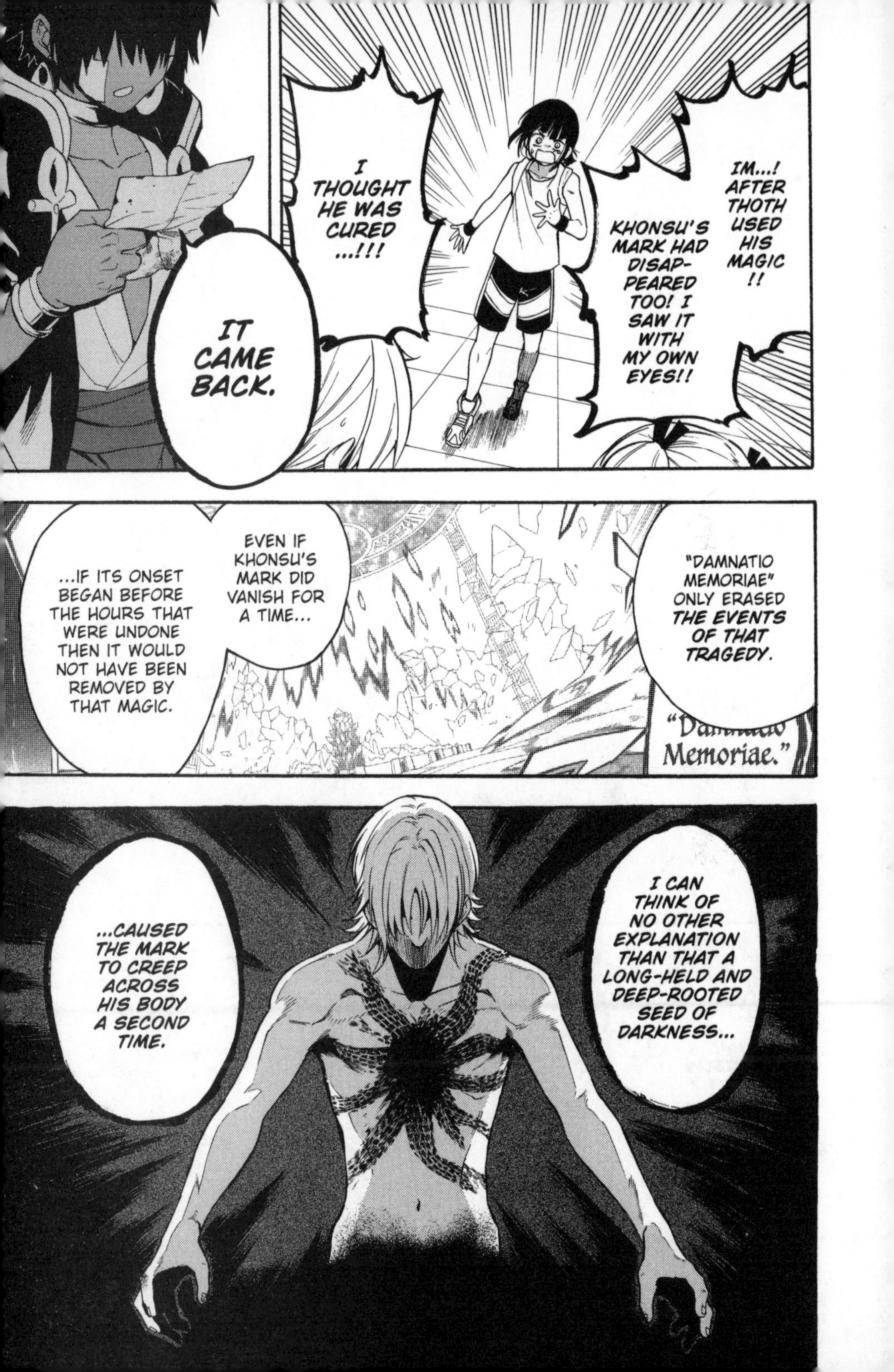
IM...! AFTER THOTH USED HIS MAGIC!!
KHONSU'S MARK HAD DISAPPEARED TOO! I SAW IT WITH MY OWN EYES!!
I THOUGHT HE WAS CURED...!!!
IT CAME BACK.
"DAMNATIO MEMORIAE" ONLY ERASED THE EVENTS OF THAT TRAGEDY.
“Damnatio Memoriae.”
EVEN IF KHONSU'S MARK DID VANISH FOR A TIME...
...IF ITS ONSET BEGAN BEFORE THE HOURS THAT WERE UNDONE THEN IT WOULD NOT HAVE BEEN REMOVED BY THAT MAGIC.
I CAN THINK OF NO OTHER EXPLANATION THAN THAT A LONG-HELD AND DEEP-ROOTED SEED OF DARKNESS...
...CAUSED THE MARK TO CREEP ACROSS HIS BODY A SECOND TIME.

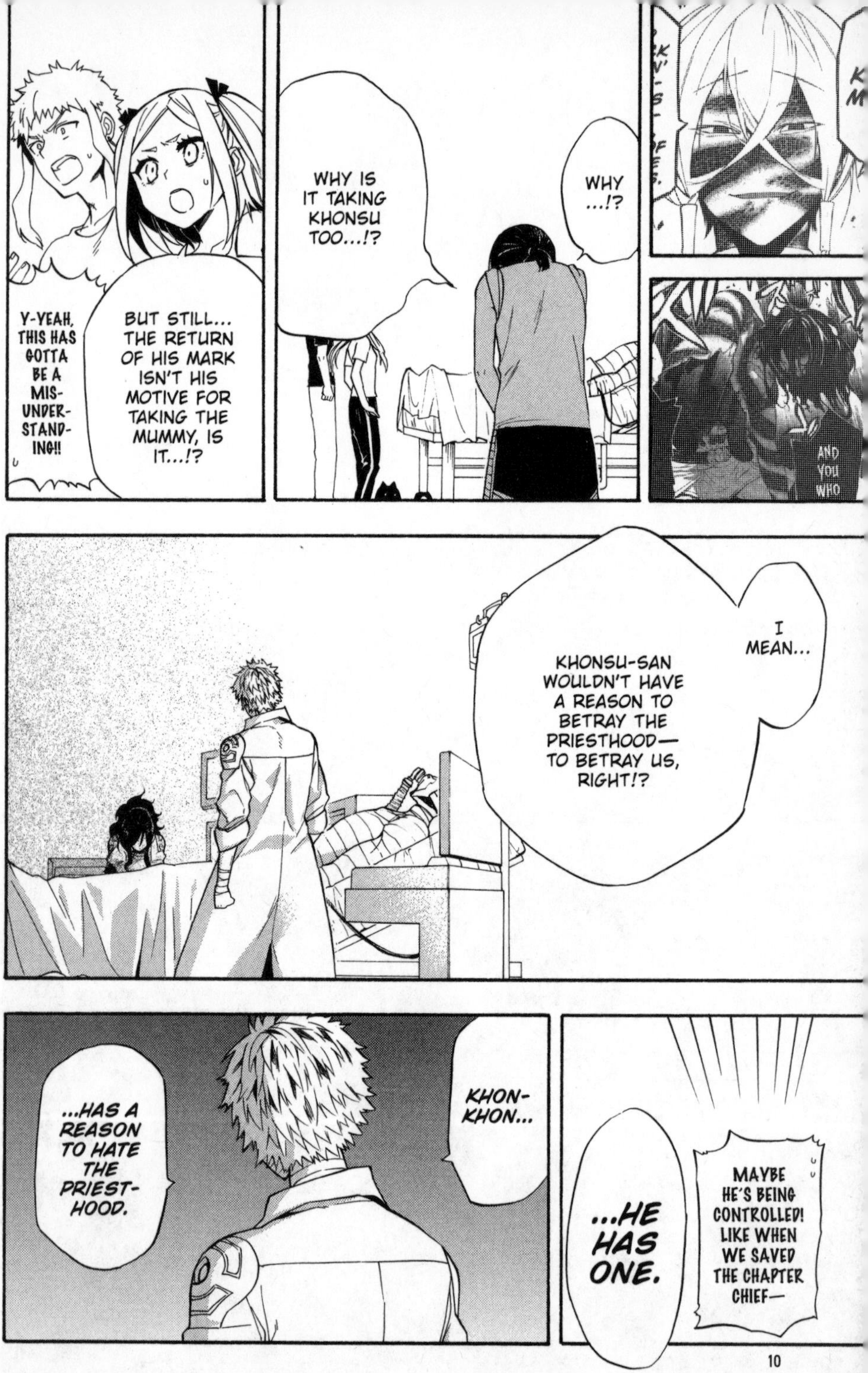
AND YOU WHO
WHY ...!?
WHY IS IT TAKING KHONSU TOO...!?
BUT STILL... THE RETURN OF HIS MARK ISN'T HIS MOTIVE FOR TAKING THE MUMMY, IS IT...!?
Y-YEAH, THIS HAS GOTTA BE A MISUNDERSTANDING!!
I MEAN...
KHONSU-SAN WOULDN'T HAVE A REASON TO BETRAY THE PRIESTHOOD—TO BETRAY US, RIGHT!?
MAYBE HE'S BEING CONTROLLED! LIKE WHEN WE SAVED THE CHAPTER CHIEF—
...HE HAS ONE.
KHON-KHON...
...HAS A REASON TO HATE THE PRIESTHOOD.

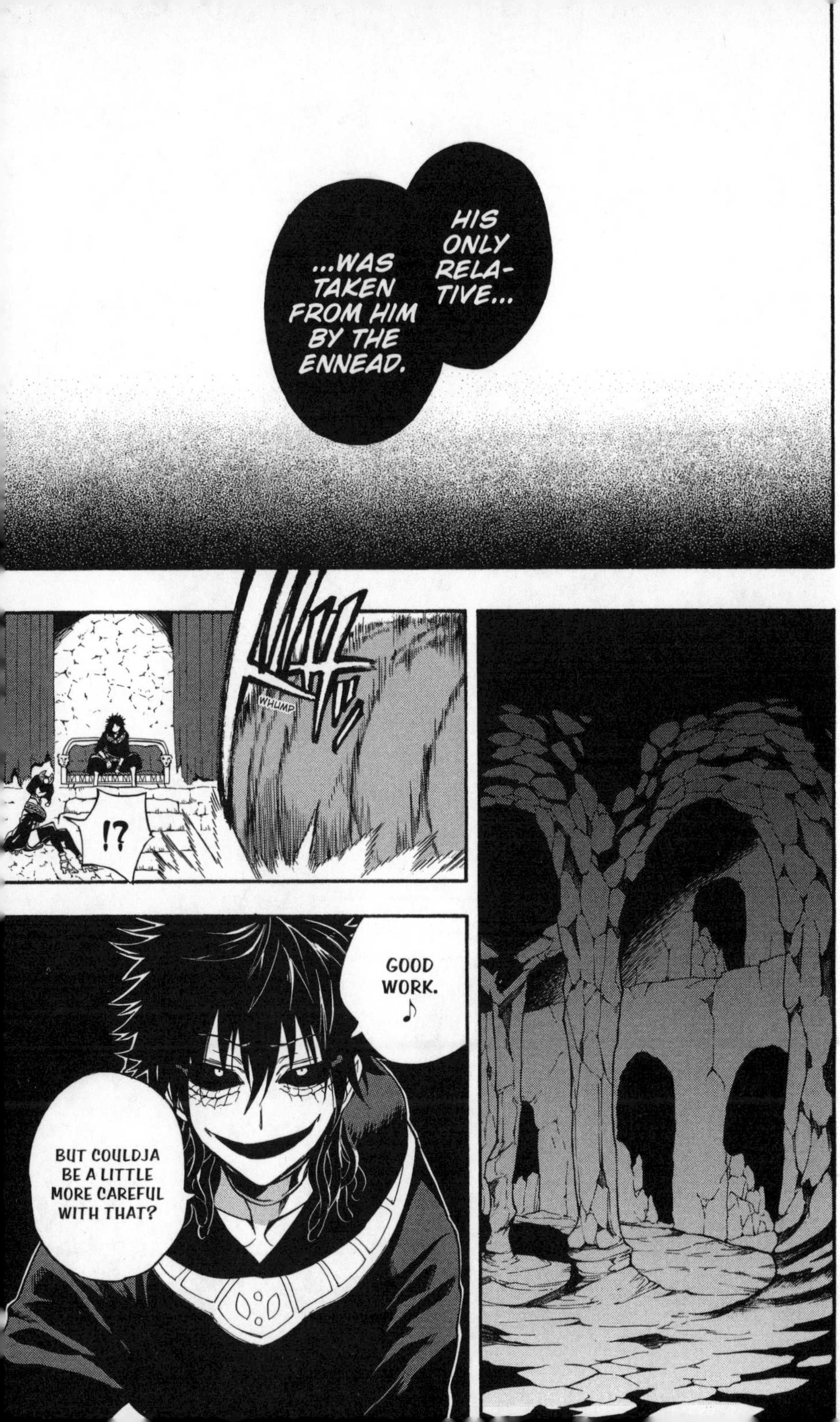
HIS ONLY RELA-TIVE...
...WAS TAKEN FROM HIM BY THE ENNEAD.
WHUMP
!?
GOOD WORK. ♪
BUT COULDJA BE A LITTLE MORE CAREFUL WITH THAT?

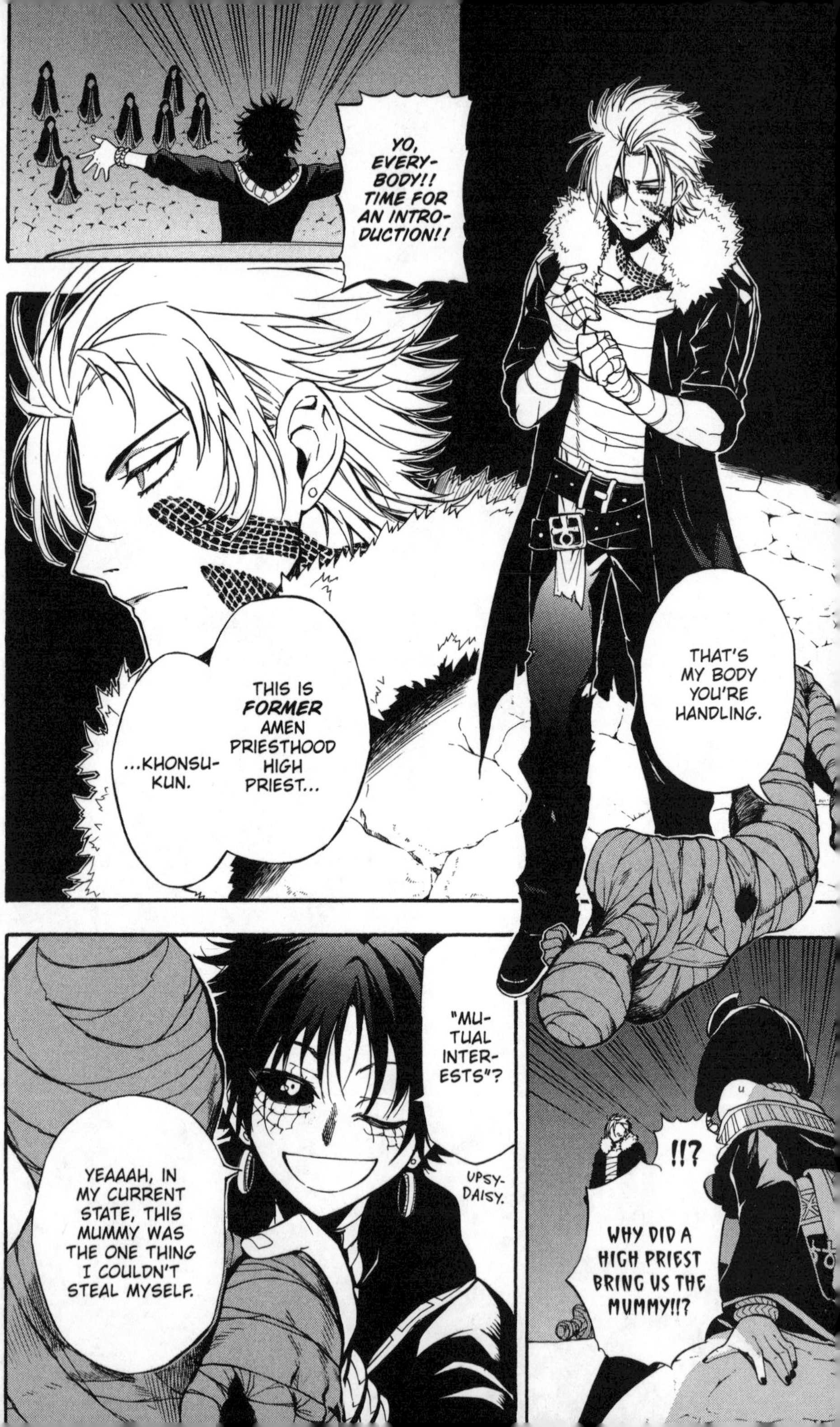
YO, EVERY-BODY!! TIME FOR AN INTRO-DUCTION!!
THIS IS FORMER AMEN PRIESTHOOD HIGH PRIEST...
...KHONSU-KUN.
THAT'S MY BODY YOU'RE HANDLING.
!!?
WHY DID A HIGH PRIEST BRING US THE MUMMY!!?
"MU-TUAL INTER-ESTS"?
UPSY-DAISY.
YEAAAH, IN MY CURRENT STATE, THIS MUMMY WAS THE ONE THING I COULDN'T STEAL MYSELF.

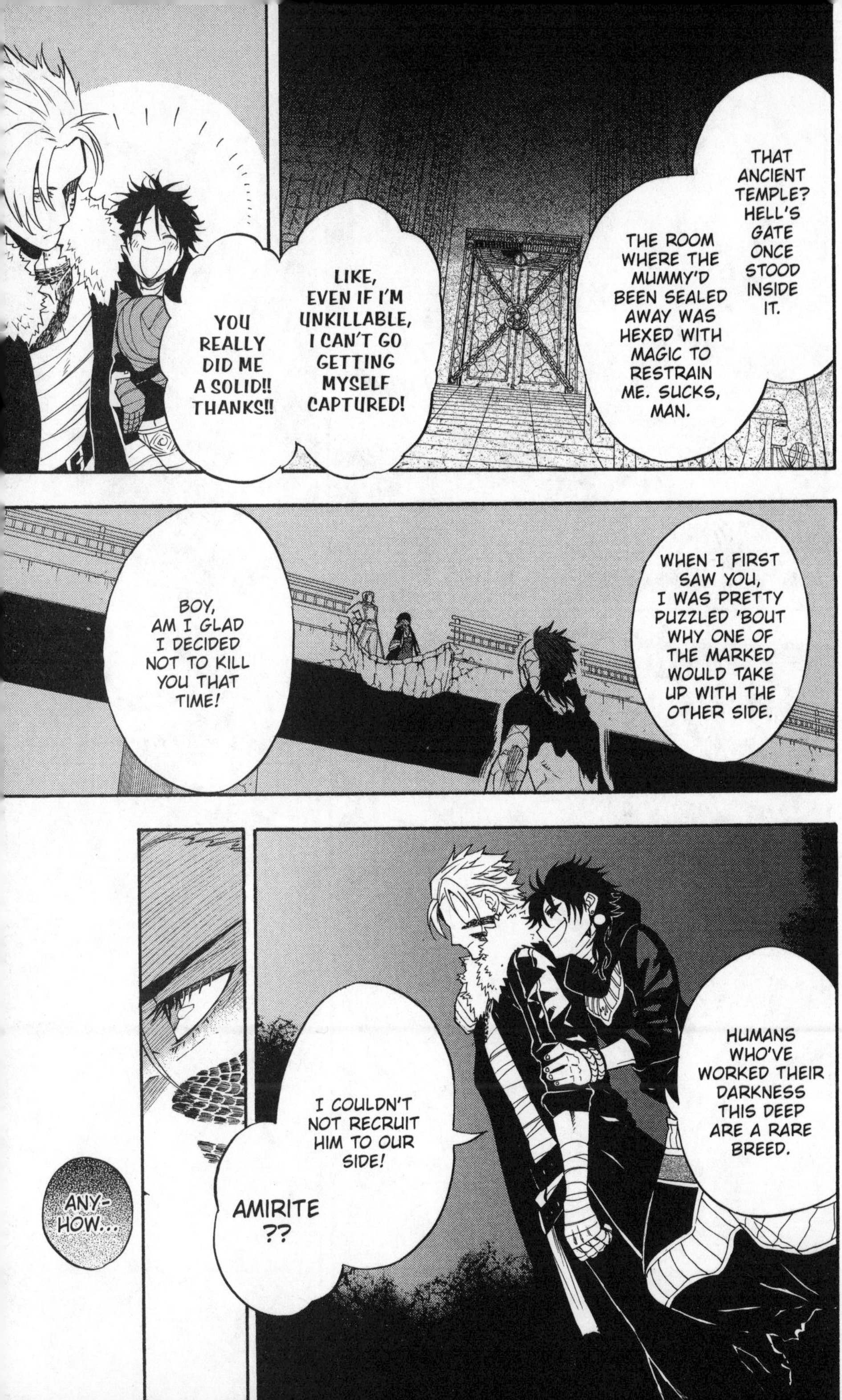
THAT ANCIENT TEMPLE? HELL'S GATE ONCE STOOD INSIDE IT.
THE ROOM WHERE THE MUMMY'D BEEN SEALED AWAY WAS HEXED WITH MAGIC TO RESTRAIN ME. SUCKS, MAN.
LIKE, EVEN IF I'M UNKILLABLE, I CAN'T GO GETTING MYSELF CAPTURED!
YOU REALLY DID ME A SOLID!! THANKS!!
WHEN I FIRST SAW YOU, I WAS PRETTY PUZZLED 'BOUT WHY ONE OF THE MARKED WOULD TAKE UP WITH THE OTHER SIDE.
BOY, AM I GLAD I DECIDED NOT TO KILL YOU THAT TIME!
HUMANS WHO'VE WORKED THEIR DARKNESS THIS DEEP ARE A RARE BREED.
I COULDN'T NOT RECRUIT HIM TO OUR SIDE!
AMIRITE ??
ANY-HOW...

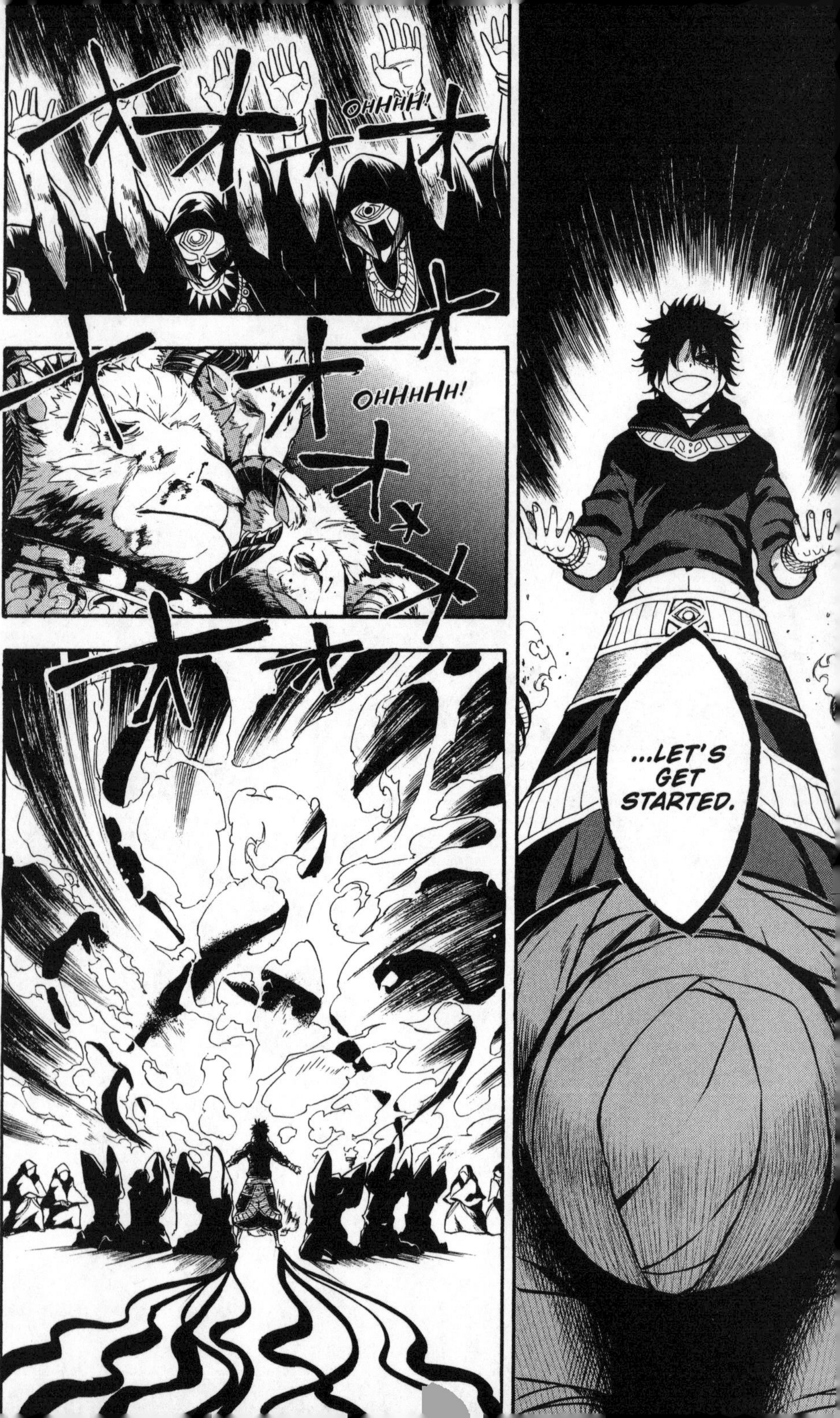
...LET'S GET STARTED.
OHHHH!
OHHHHH!

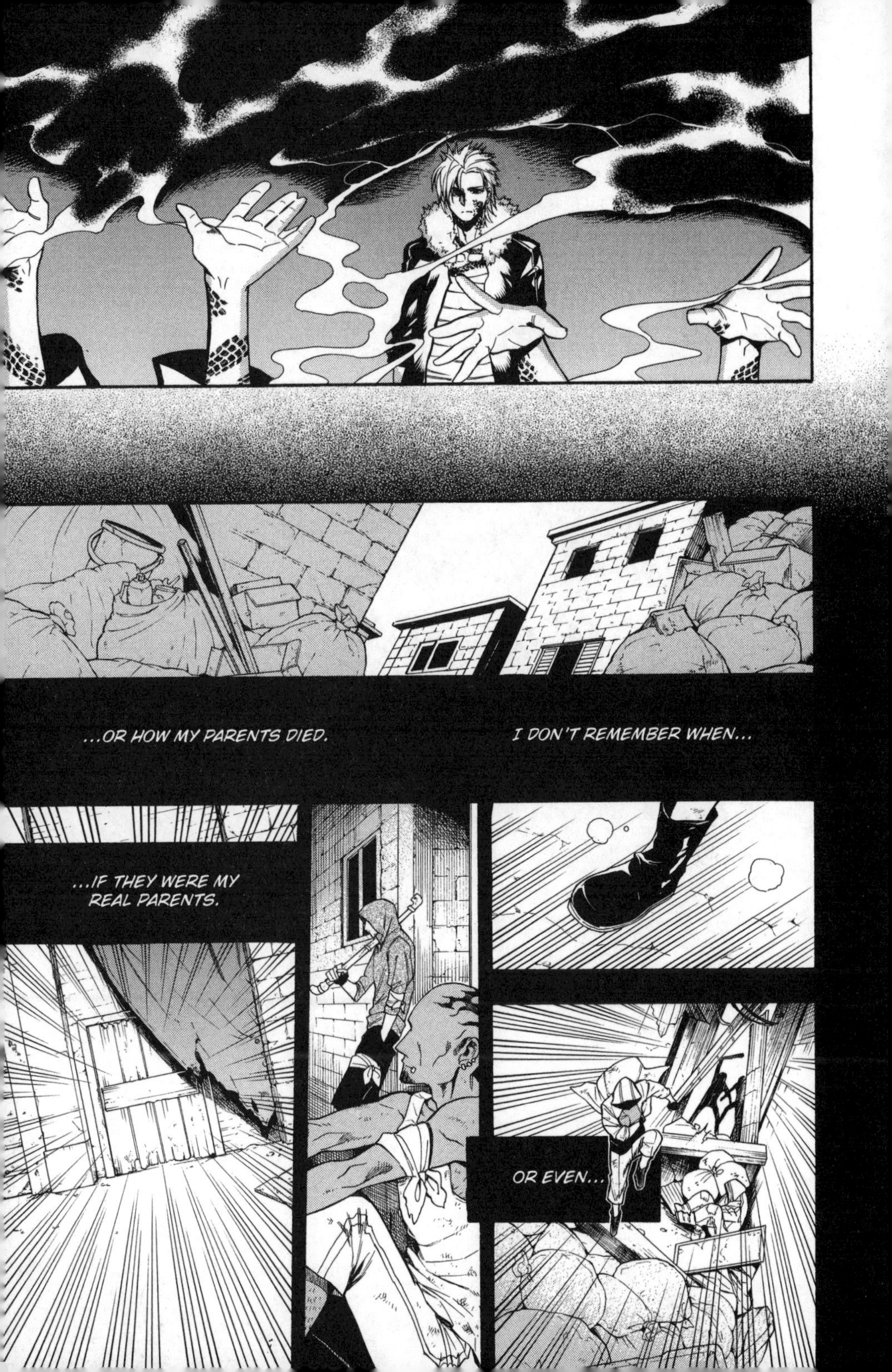
I DON'T REMEMBER WHEN...
...OR HOW MY PARENTS DIED.
OR EVEN...
...IF THEY WERE MY REAL PARENTS.

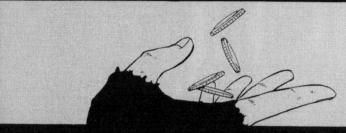

I DID ANYTHING IT TOOK TO SURVIVE.

I'M BACK!

BAM

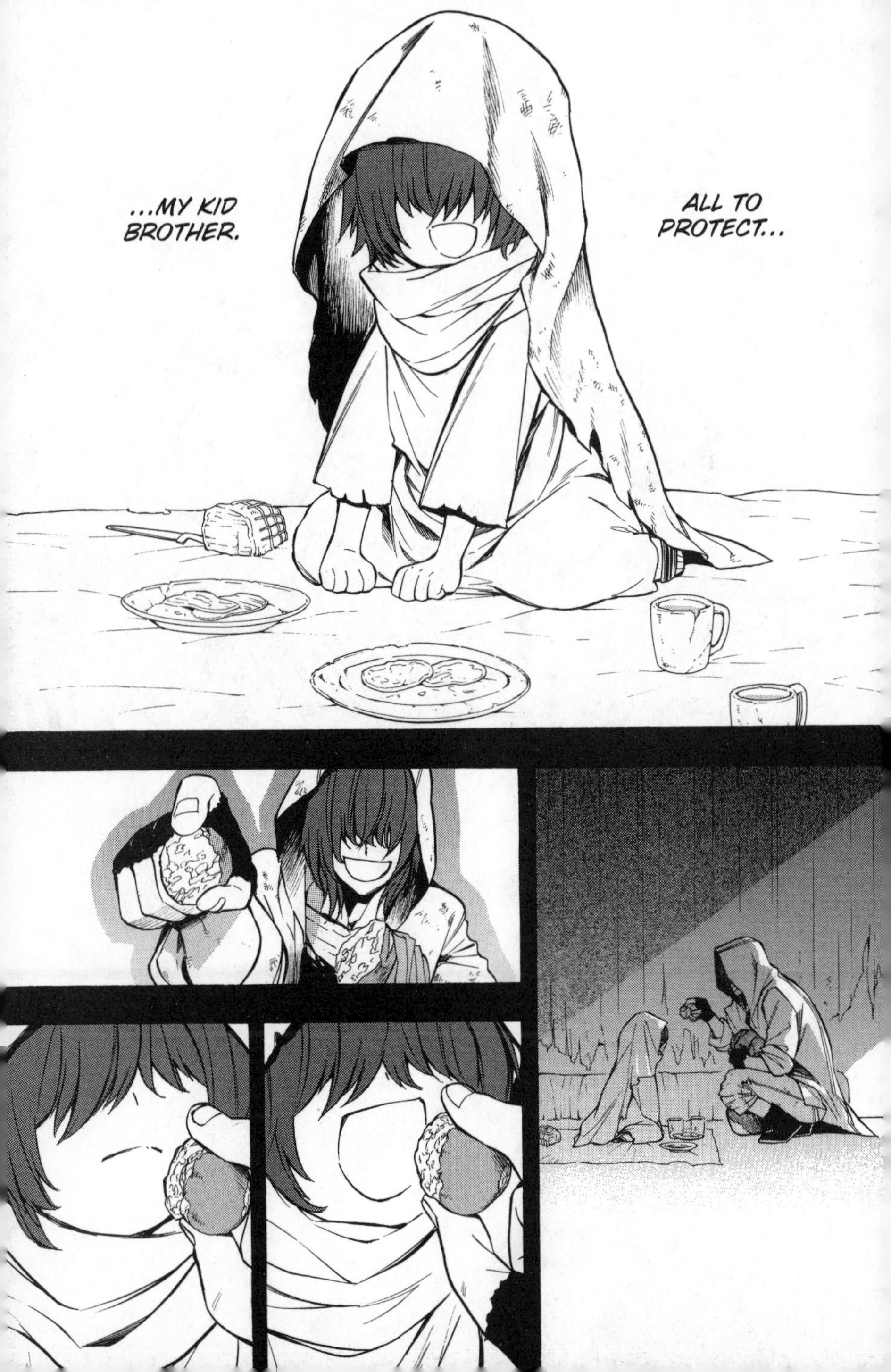
ALL TO PROTECT...
...MY KID BROTHER.

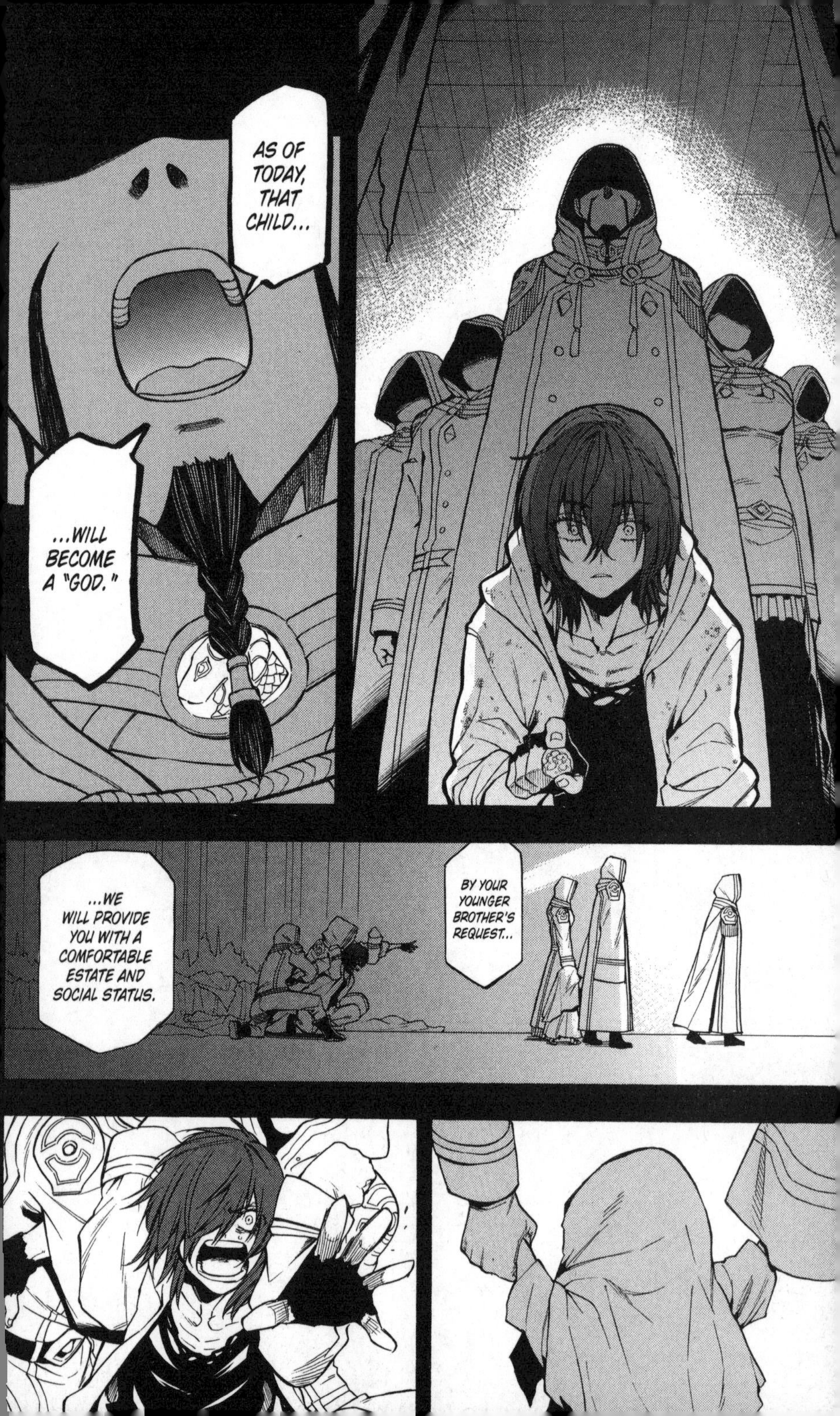
AS OF TODAY, THAT CHILD...
...WILL BECOME A "GOD."
BY YOUR YOUNGER BROTHER'S REQUEST...
...WE WILL PROVIDE YOU WITH A COMFORTABLE ESTATE AND SOCIAL STATUS.

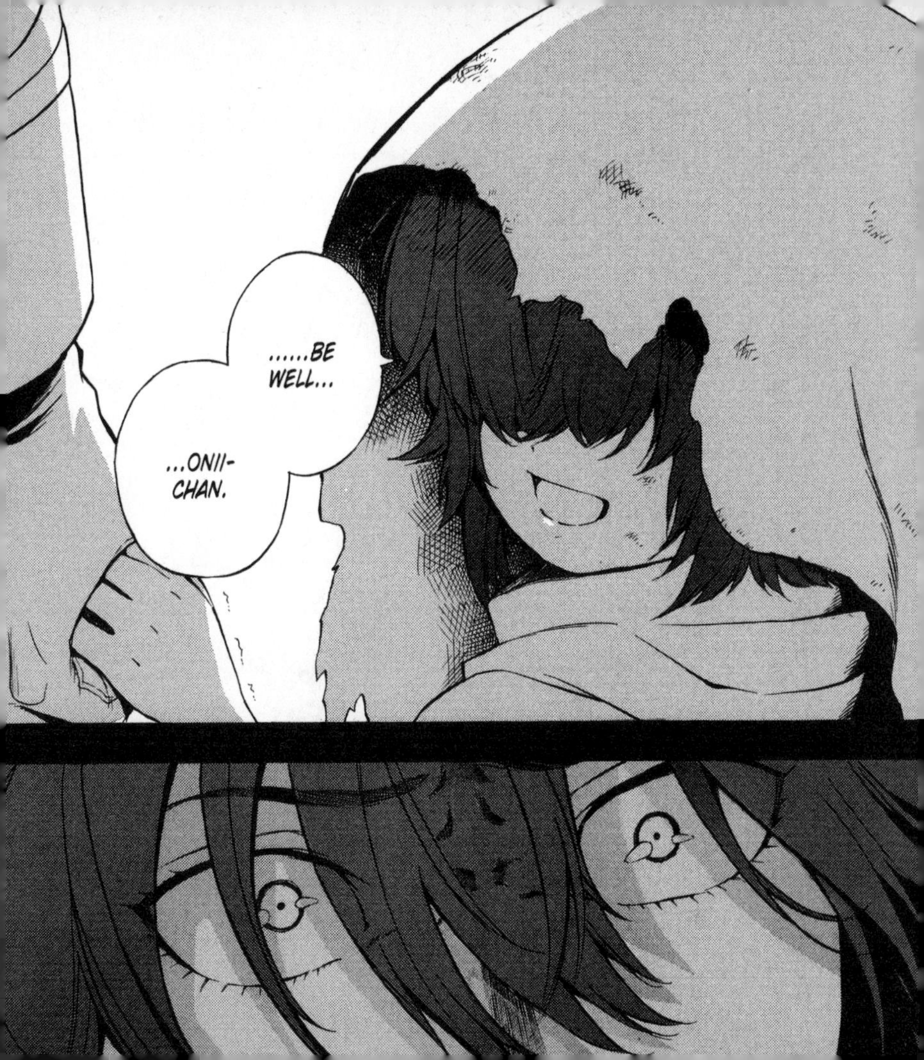
......BE WELL...
...ONII-CHAN.

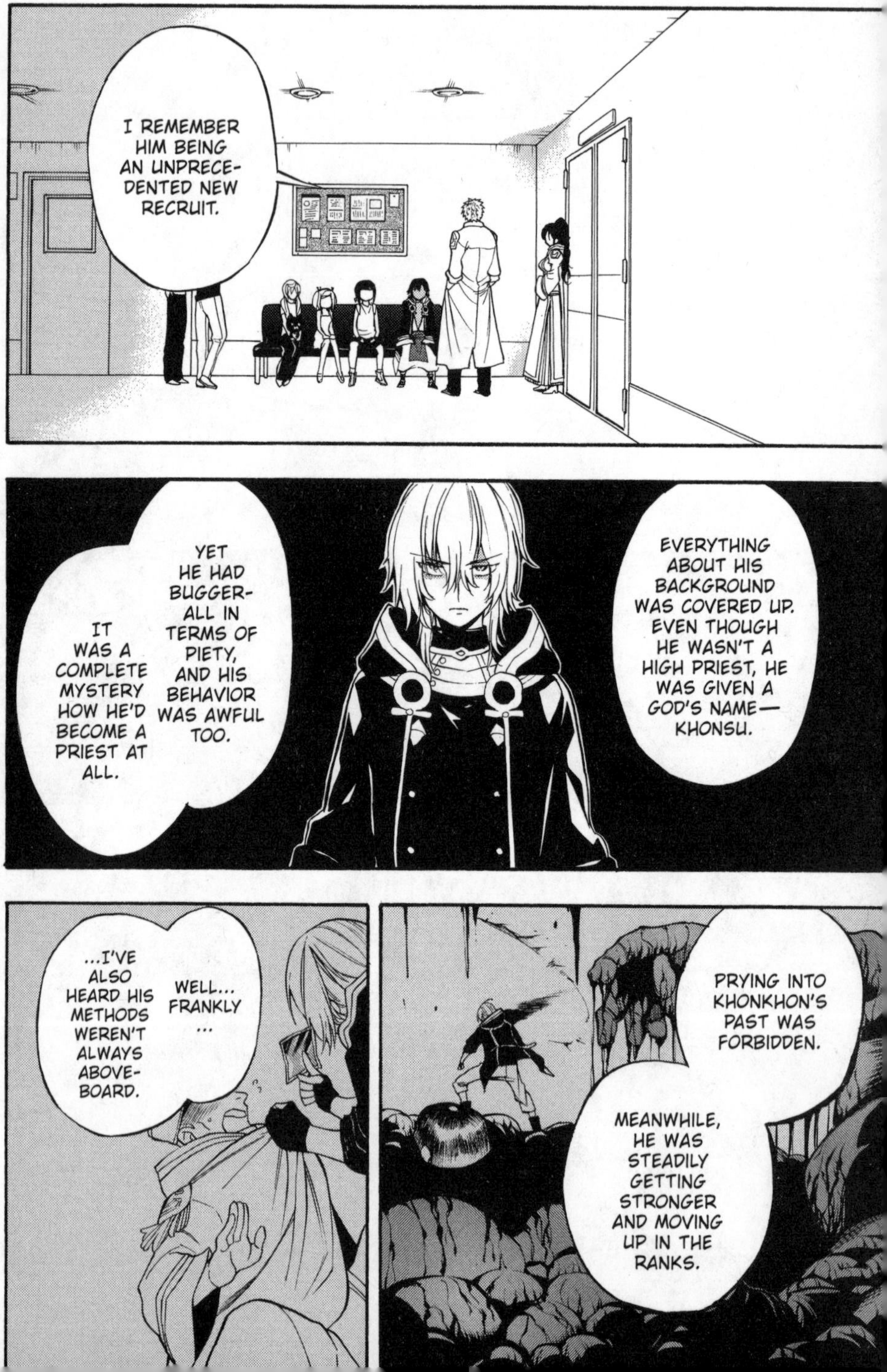
I REMEMBER HIM BEING AN UNPRECE-DENTED NEW RECRUIT.
EVERYTHING ABOUT HIS BACKGROUND WAS COVERED UP. EVEN THOUGH HE WASN'T A HIGH PRIEST, HE WAS GIVEN A GOD'S NAME—KHONSU.
YET HE HAD BUGGER-ALL IN TERMS OF PIETY, AND HIS BEHAVIOR WAS AWFUL TOO.
IT WAS A COMPLETE MYSTERY HOW HE'D BECOME A PRIEST AT ALL.
PRYING INTO KHONKHON'S PAST WAS FORBIDDEN.
MEANWHILE, HE WAS STEADILY GETTING STRONGER AND MOVING UP IN THE RANKS.
WELL... FRANKLY...
...I'VE ALSO HEARD HIS METHODS WEREN'T ALWAYS ABOVE-BOARD.

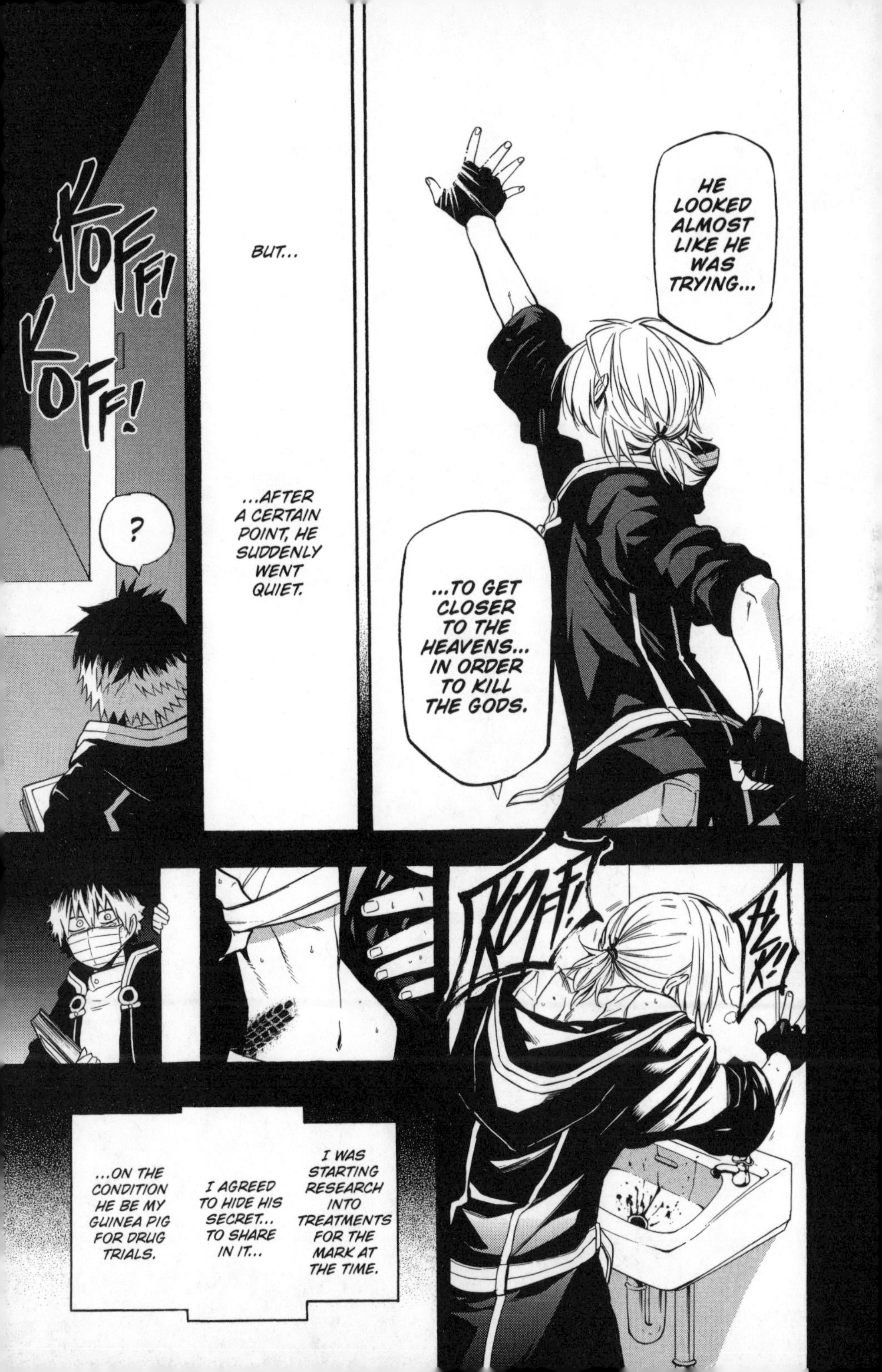
HE LOOKED ALMOST LIKE HE WAS TRYING...
...TO GET CLOSER TO THE HEAVENS... IN ORDER TO KILL THE GODS.
BUT...
...AFTER A CERTAIN POINT, HE SUDDENLY WENT QUIET.
KOFF! KOFF!
?
KOFF!
I WAS STARTING RESEARCH INTO TREATMENTS FOR THE MARK AT THE TIME.
I AGREED TO HIDE HIS SECRET... TO SHARE IN IT...
...ON THE CONDITION HE BE MY GUINEA PIG FOR DRUG TRIALS.

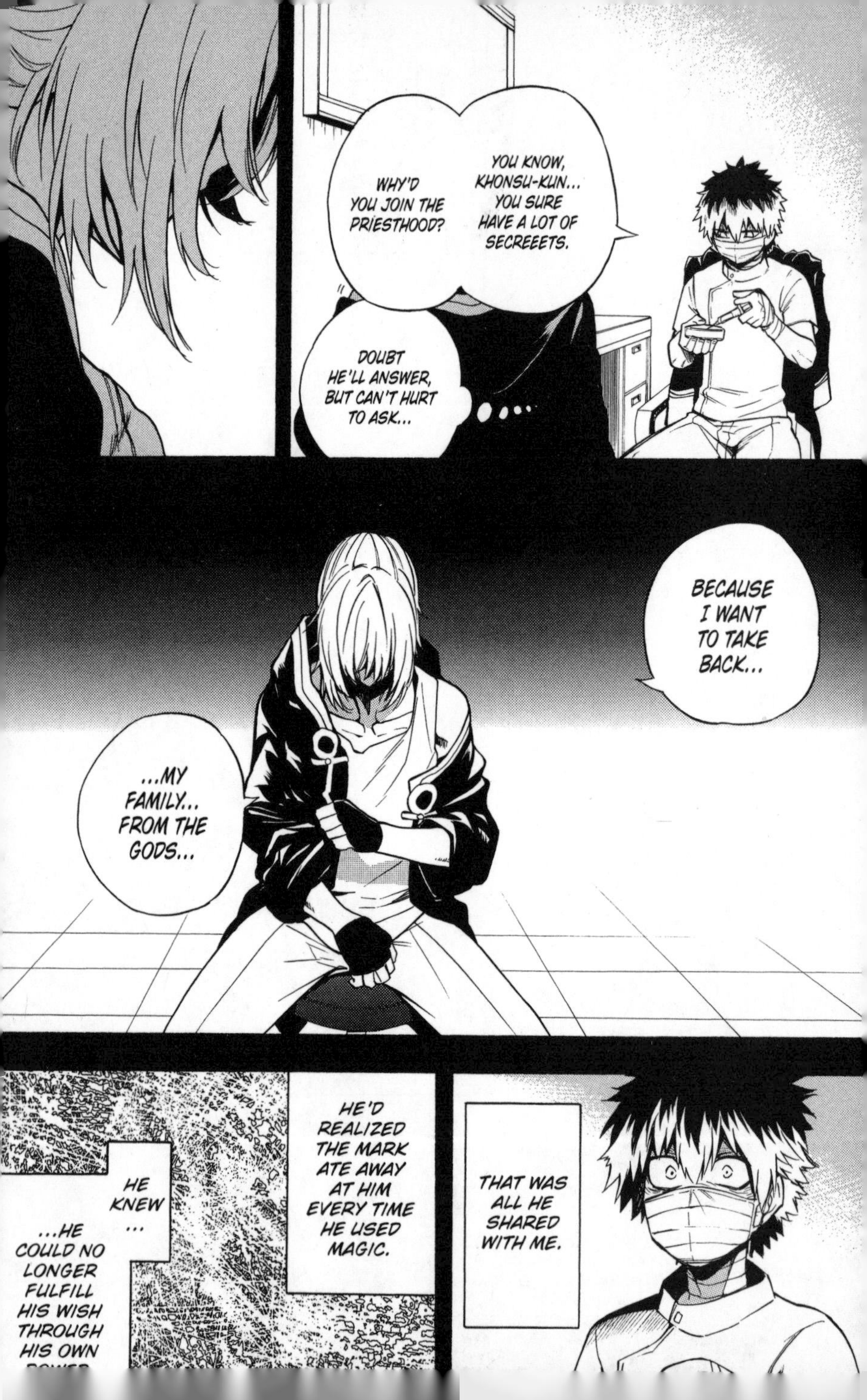
YOU KNOW, KHONSU-KUN... YOU SURE HAVE A LOT OF SECREEETS.
WHY'D YOU JOIN THE PRIESTHOOD?
DOUBT HE'LL ANSWER, BUT CAN'T HURT TO ASK...
BECAUSE I WANT TO TAKE BACK...
...MY FAMILY... FROM THE GODS...
THAT WAS ALL HE SHARED WITH ME.
HE'D REALIZED THE MARK ATE AWAY AT HIM EVERY TIME HE USED MAGIC.
HE KNEW...
...HE COULD NO LONGER FULFILL HIS WISH THROUGH HIS OWN

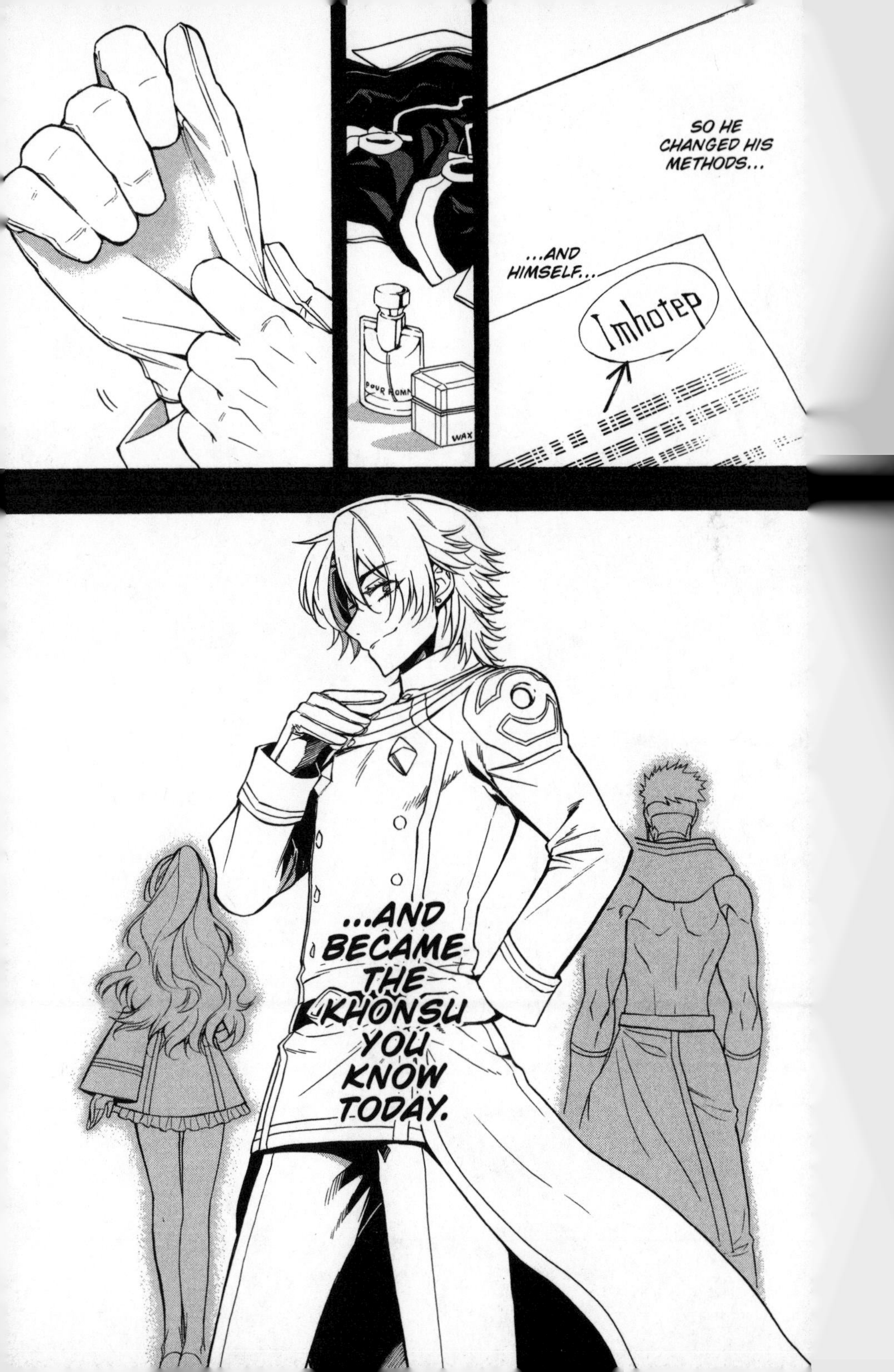
SO HE CHANGED HIS METHODS...
...AND HIMSELF...
Imhotep
POUR HOMM
WAX
...AND BECAME THE KHONSU YOU KNOW TODAY.

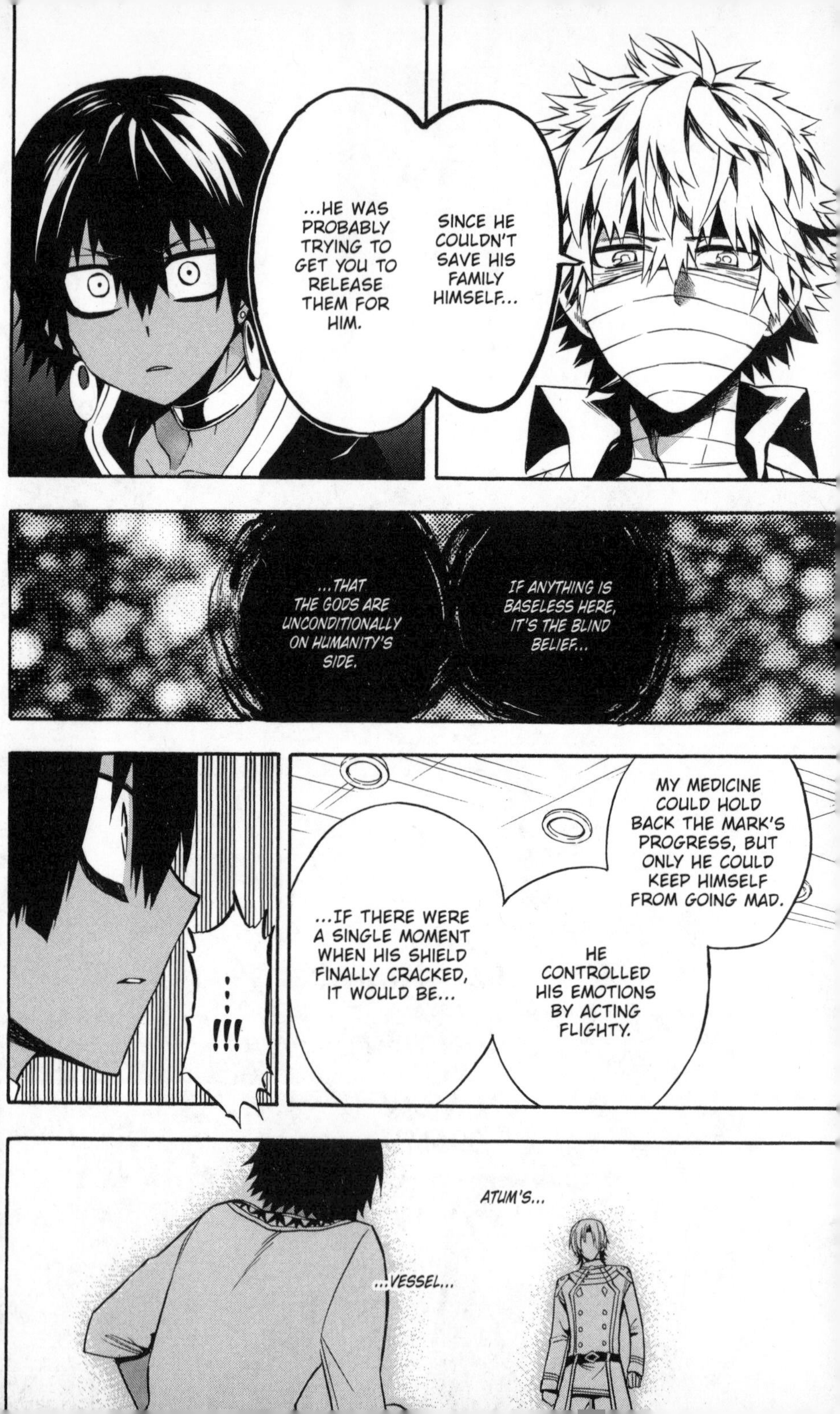
SINCE HE COULDN'T SAVE HIS FAMILY HIMSELF...
...HE WAS PROBABLY TRYING TO GET YOU TO RELEASE THEM FOR HIM.
IF ANYTHING IS BASELESS HERE, IT'S THE BLIND BELIEF...
...THAT THE GODS ARE UNCONDITIONALLY ON HUMANITY'S SIDE.
MY MEDICINE COULD HOLD BACK THE MARK'S PROGRESS, BUT ONLY HE COULD KEEP HIMSELF FROM GOING MAD.
HE CONTROLLED HIS EMOTIONS BY ACTING FLIGHTY.
...IF THERE WERE A SINGLE MOMENT WHEN HIS SHIELD FINALLY CRACKED, IT WOULD BE...
...!!!
ATUM'S...
...VESSEL...

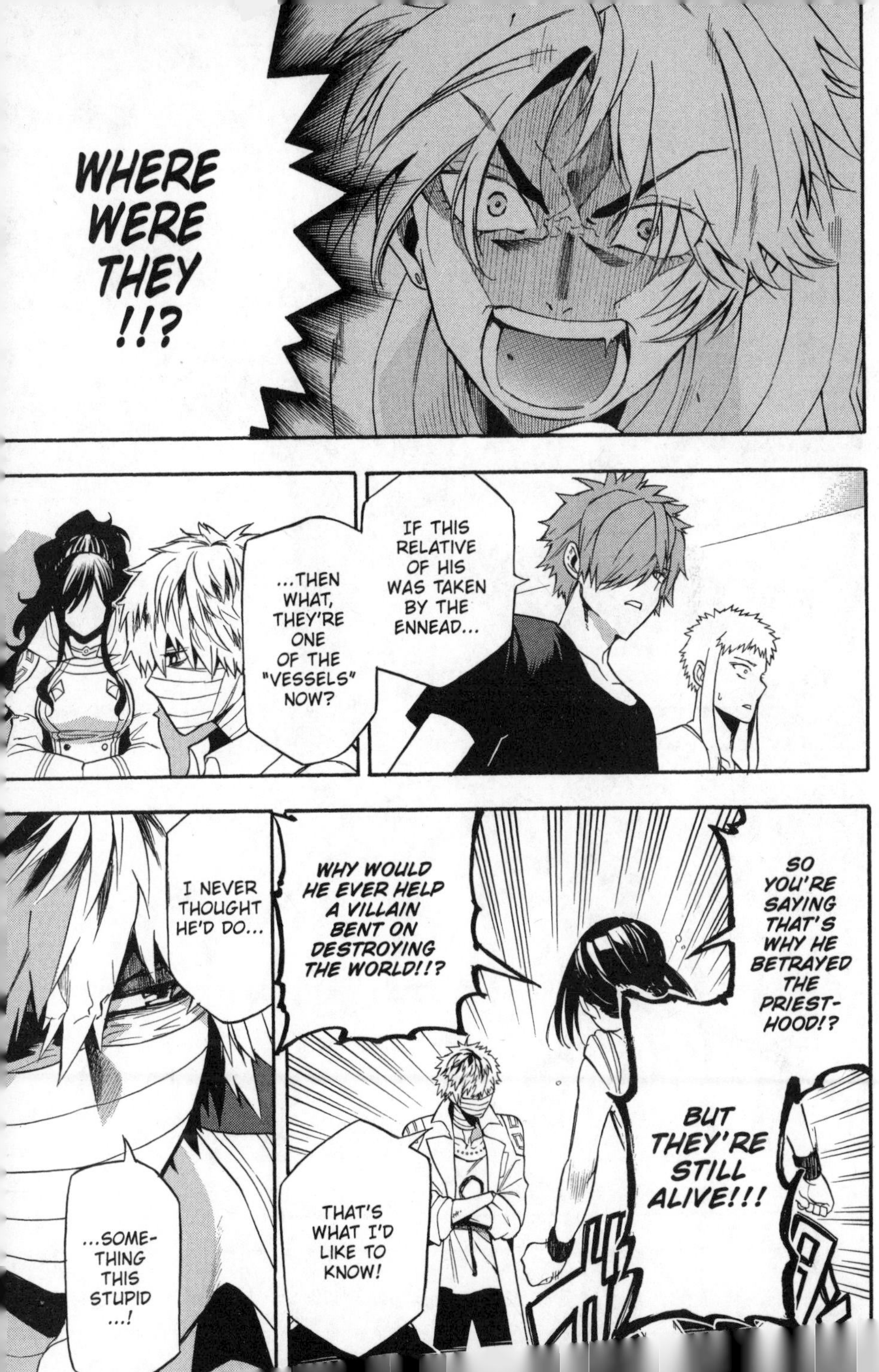
WHERE WERE THEY !!?
IF THIS RELATIVE OF HIS WAS TAKEN BY THE ENNEAD...
...THEN WHAT, THEY'RE ONE OF THE "VESSELS" NOW?
SO YOU'RE SAYING THAT'S WHY HE BETRAYED THE PRIEST-HOOD!?
BUT THEY'RE STILL ALIVE!!!
WHY WOULD HE EVER HELP A VILLAIN BENT ON DESTROYING THE WORLD!!?
THAT'S WHAT I'D LIKE TO KNOW!
I NEVER THOUGHT HE'D DO...
...SOME-THING THIS STUPID ...!

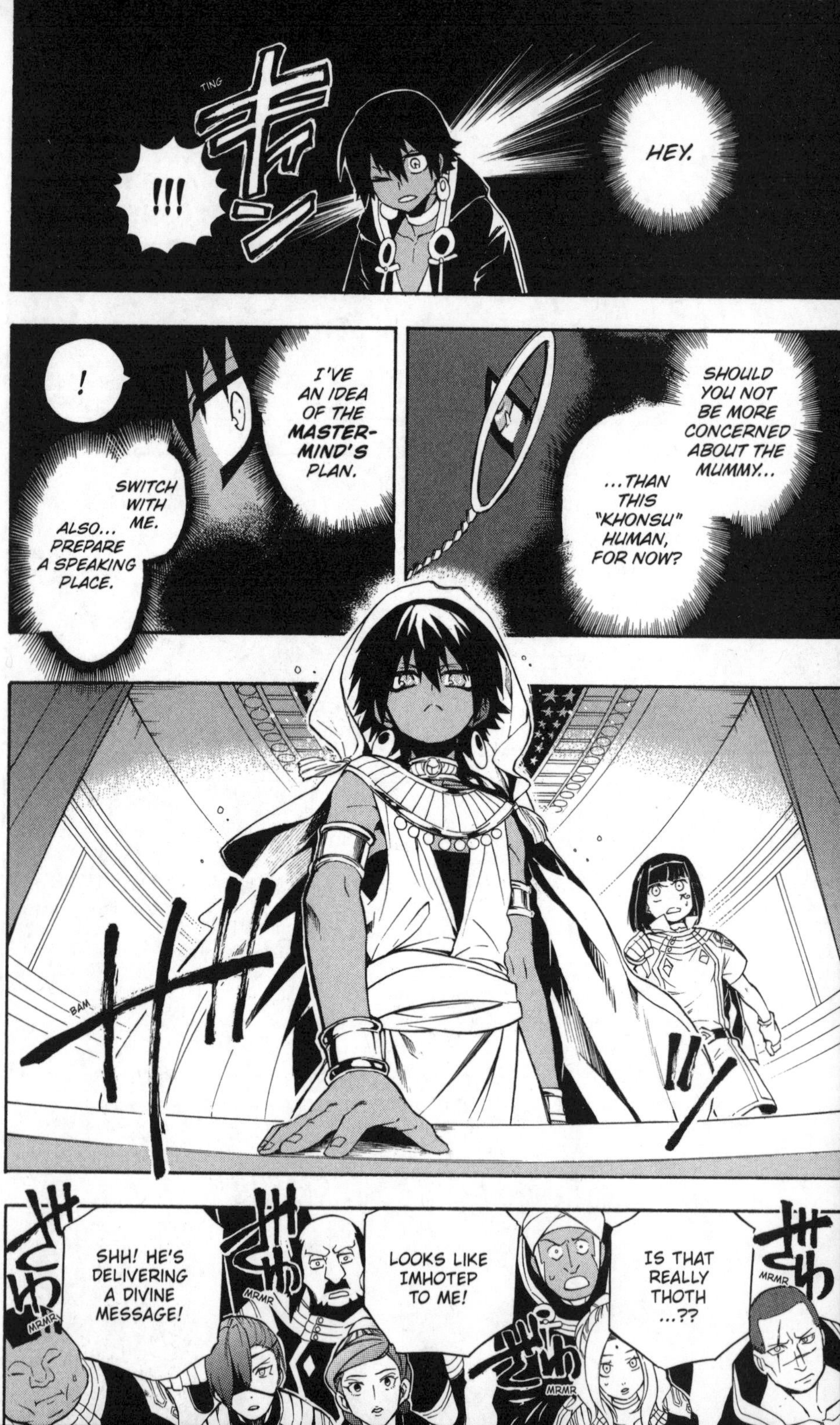
HEY.
TING
!!!
SHOULD YOU NOT BE MORE CONCERNED ABOUT THE MUMMY...
...THAN THIS "KHONSU" HUMAN, FOR NOW?
I'VE AN IDEA OF THE MASTERMIND'S PLAN.
!
SWITCH WITH ME.
ALSO... PREPARE A SPEAKING PLACE.
BAM
MRMR
IS THAT REALLY THOTH ...??
LOOKS LIKE IMHOTEP TO ME!
MRMR
MRMR
SHH! HE'S DELIVERING A DIVINE MESSAGE!
MRMR

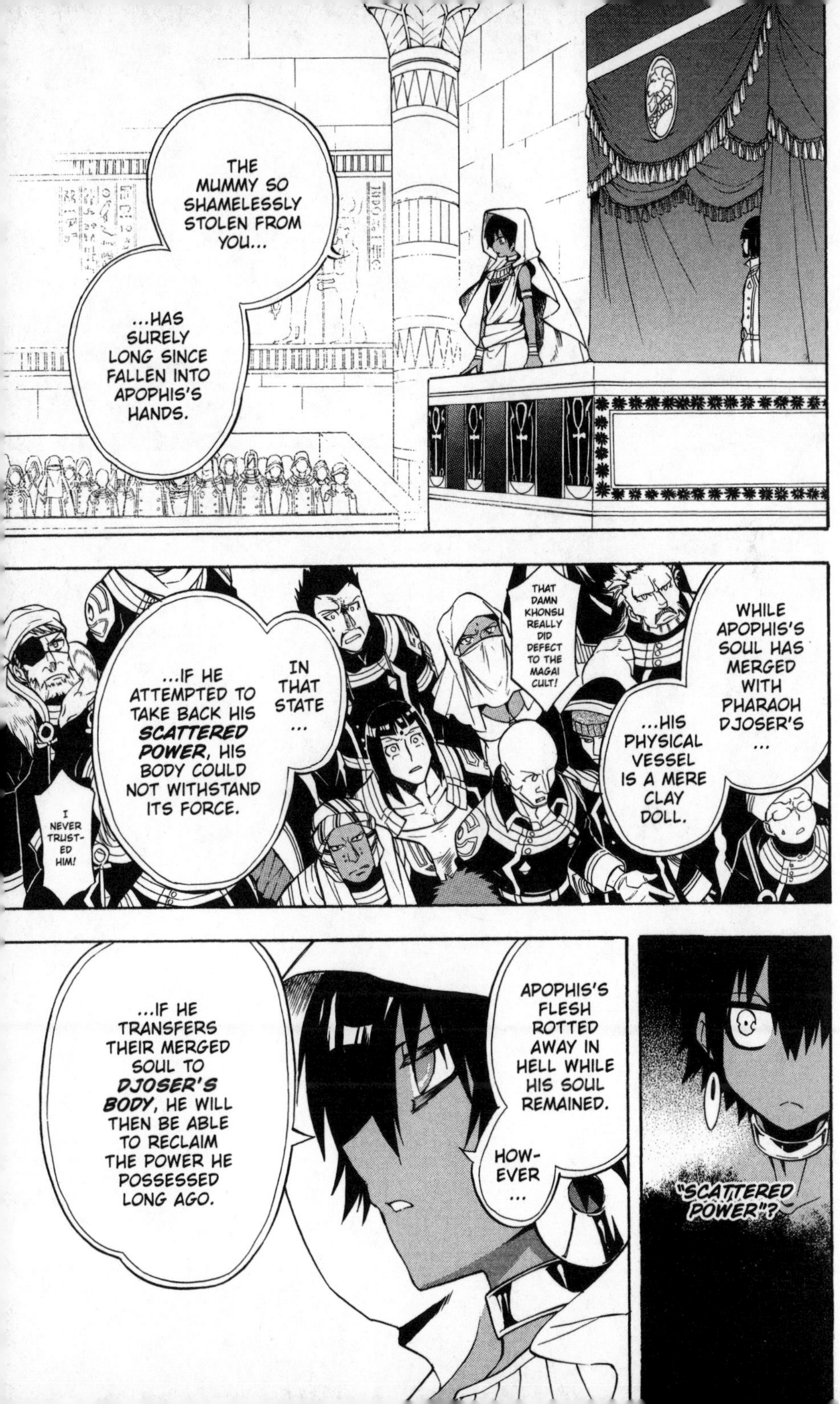
THE MUMMY SO SHAMELESSLY STOLEN FROM YOU...
...HAS SURELY LONG SINCE FALLEN INTO APOPHIS'S HANDS.
WHILE APOPHIS'S SOUL HAS MERGED WITH PHARAOH DJOSER'S...
...HIS PHYSICAL VESSEL IS A MERE CLAY DOLL.
THAT DAMN KHONSU REALLY DID DEFECT TO THE MAGAI CULT!
IN THAT STATE...
...IF HE ATTEMPTED TO TAKE BACK HIS ***SCATTERED POWER***, HIS BODY COULD NOT WITHSTAND ITS FORCE.
I NEVER TRUST-ED HIM!
"SCATTERED POWER"?
APOPHIS'S FLESH ROTTED AWAY IN HELL WHILE HIS SOUL REMAINED.
HOW-EVER...
...IF HE TRANSFERS THEIR MERGED SOUL TO ***DJOSER'S BODY***, HE WILL THEN BE ABLE TO RECLAIM THE POWER HE POSSESSED LONG AGO.

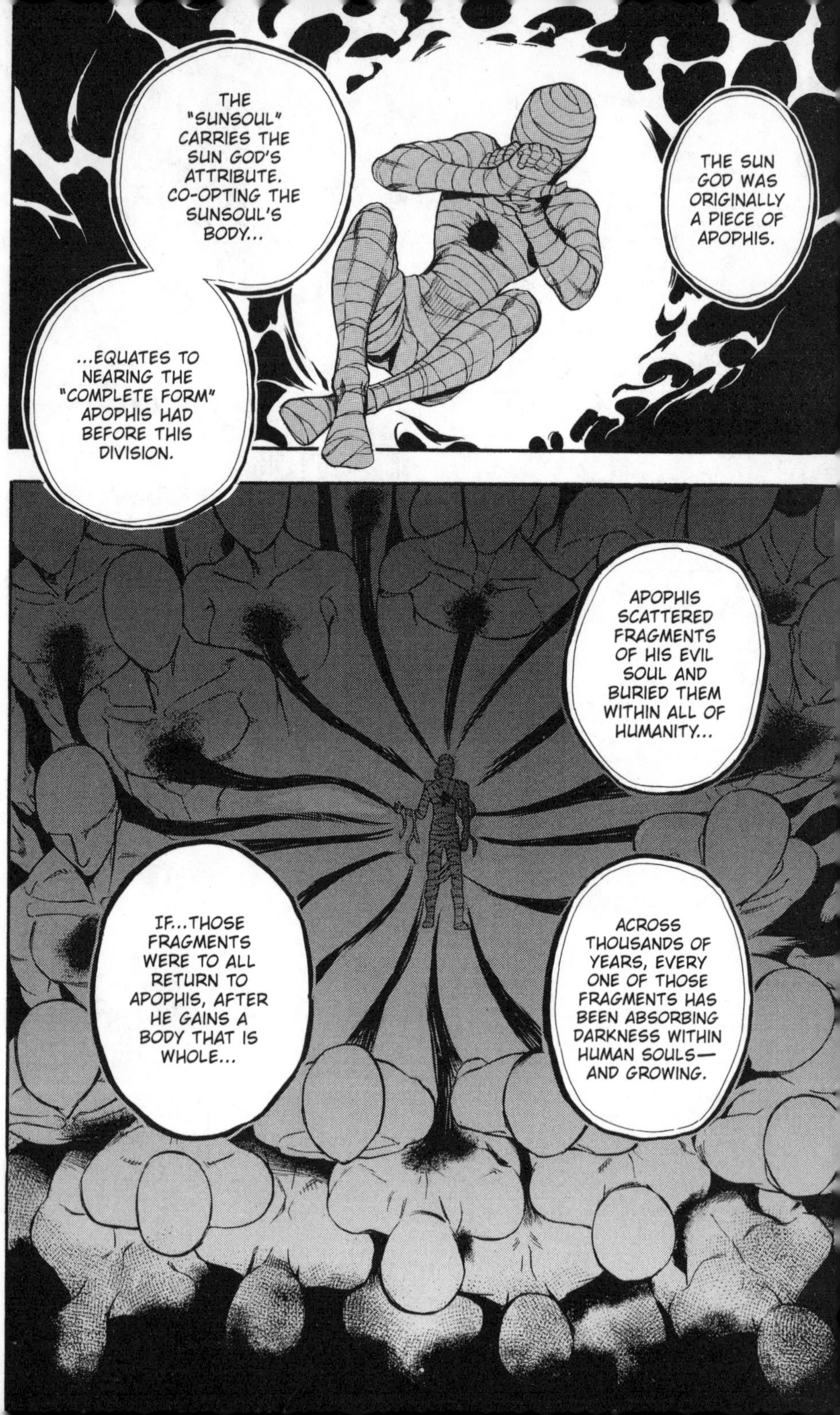
THE SUN GOD WAS ORIGINALLY A PIECE OF APOPHIS.
THE "SUNSOUL" CARRIES THE SUN GOD'S ATTRIBUTE. CO-OPTING THE SUNSOUL'S BODY...
...EQUATES TO NEARING THE "COMPLETE FORM" APOPHIS HAD BEFORE THIS DIVISION.
APOPHIS SCATTERED FRAGMENTS OF HIS EVIL SOUL AND BURIED THEM WITHIN ALL OF HUMANITY...
ACROSS THOUSANDS OF YEARS, EVERY ONE OF THOSE FRAGMENTS HAS BEEN ABSORBING DARKNESS WITHIN HUMAN SOULS—AND GROWING.
IF...THOSE FRAGMENTS WERE TO ALL RETURN TO APOPHIS, AFTER HE GAINS A BODY THAT IS WHOLE...

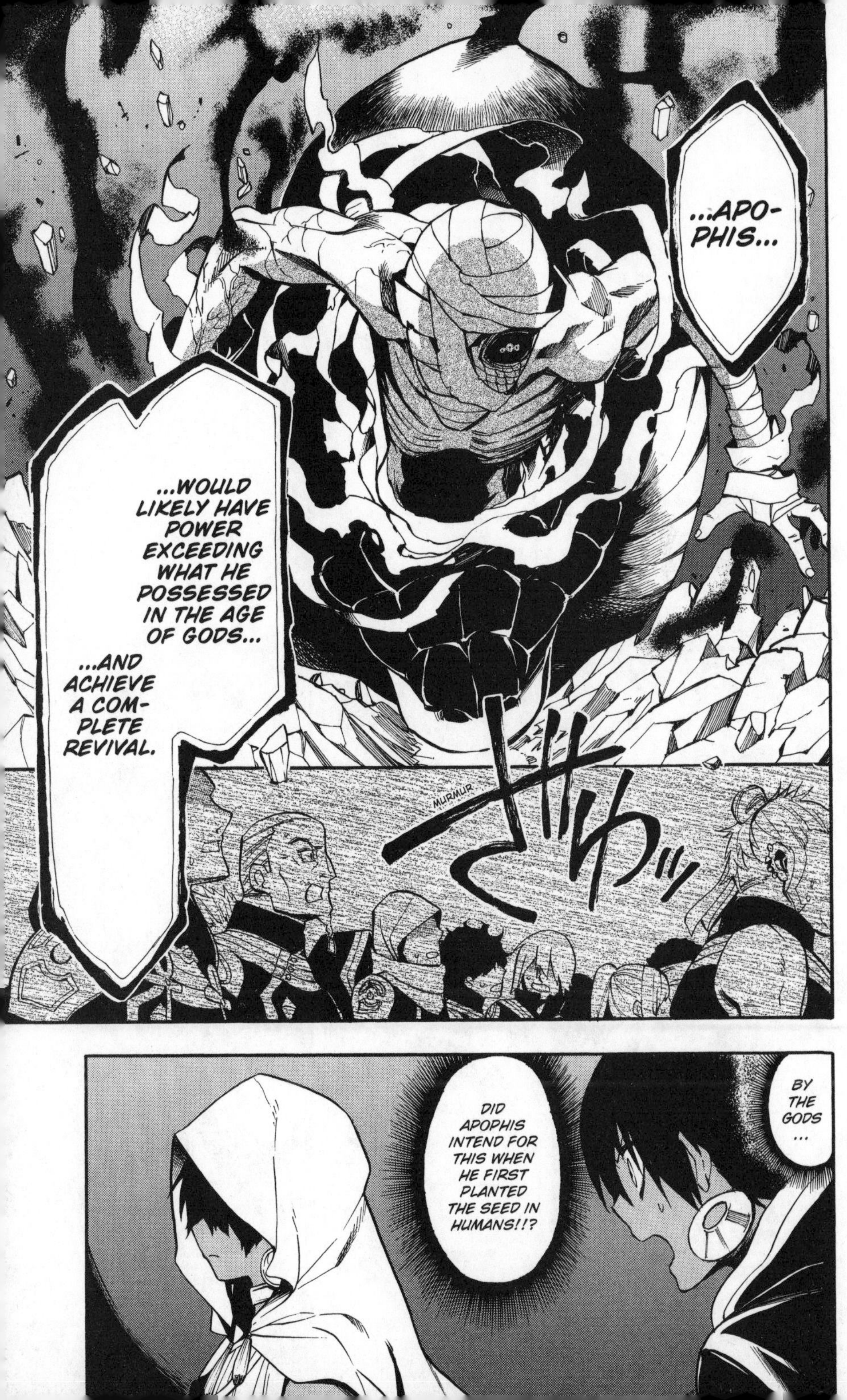
...APO-PHIS...
...WOULD LIKELY HAVE POWER EXCEEDING WHAT HE POSSESSED IN THE AGE OF GODS... ...AND ACHIEVE A COM-PLETE REVIVAL.
MURMUR
BY THE GODS ...
DID APOPHIS INTEND FOR THIS WHEN HE FIRST PLANTED THE SEED IN HUMANS!!?

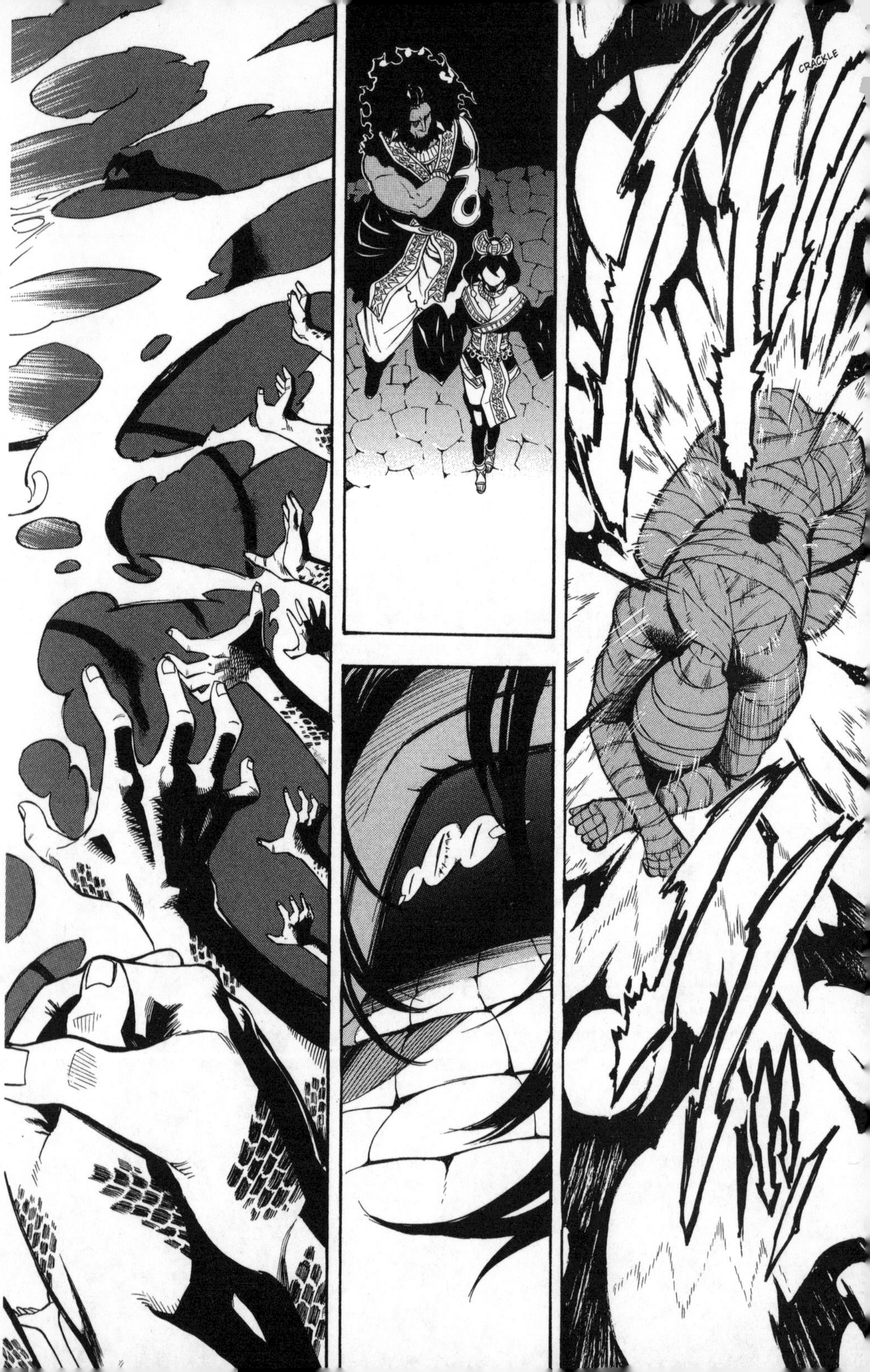
CRACKLE

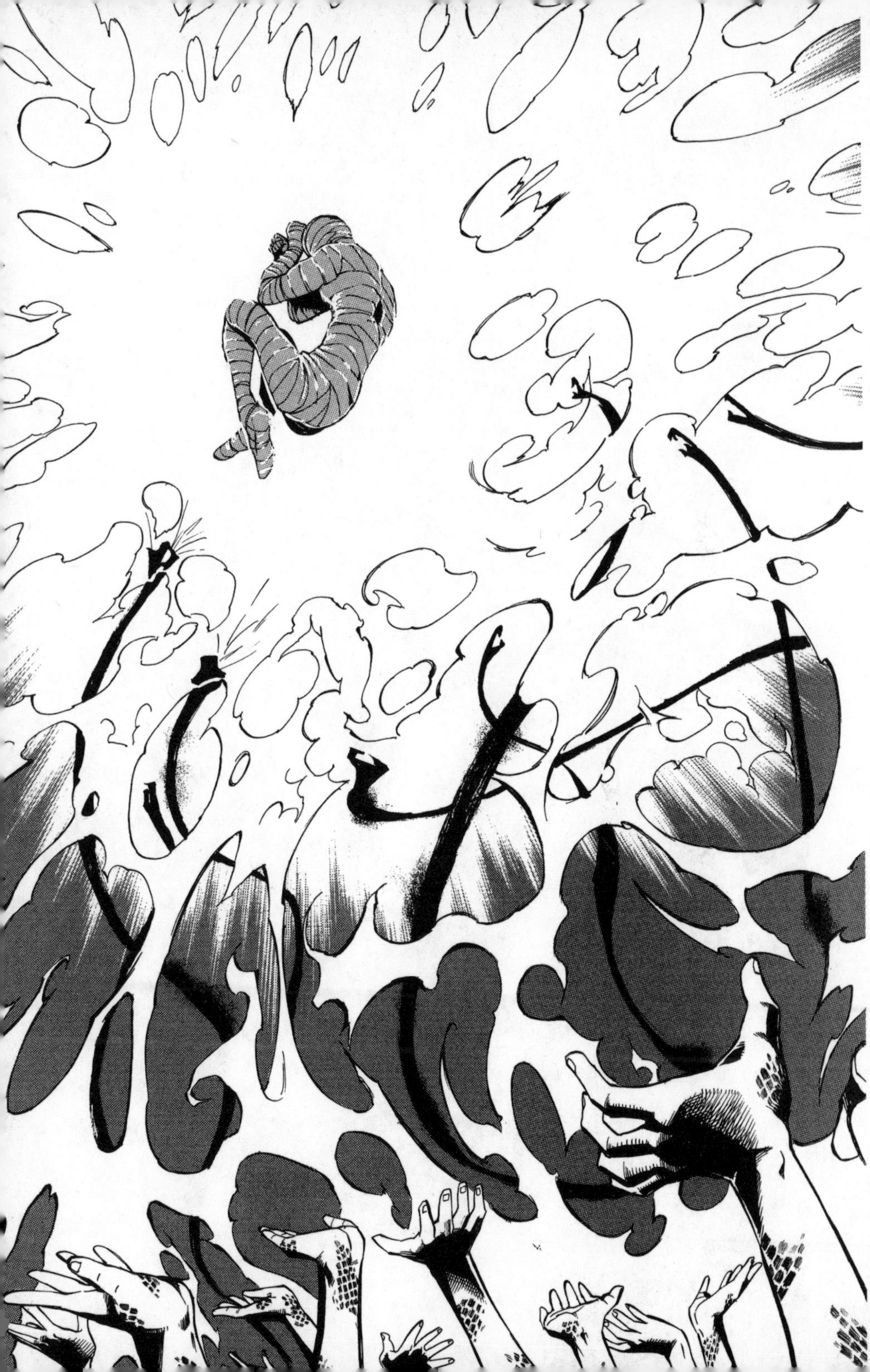

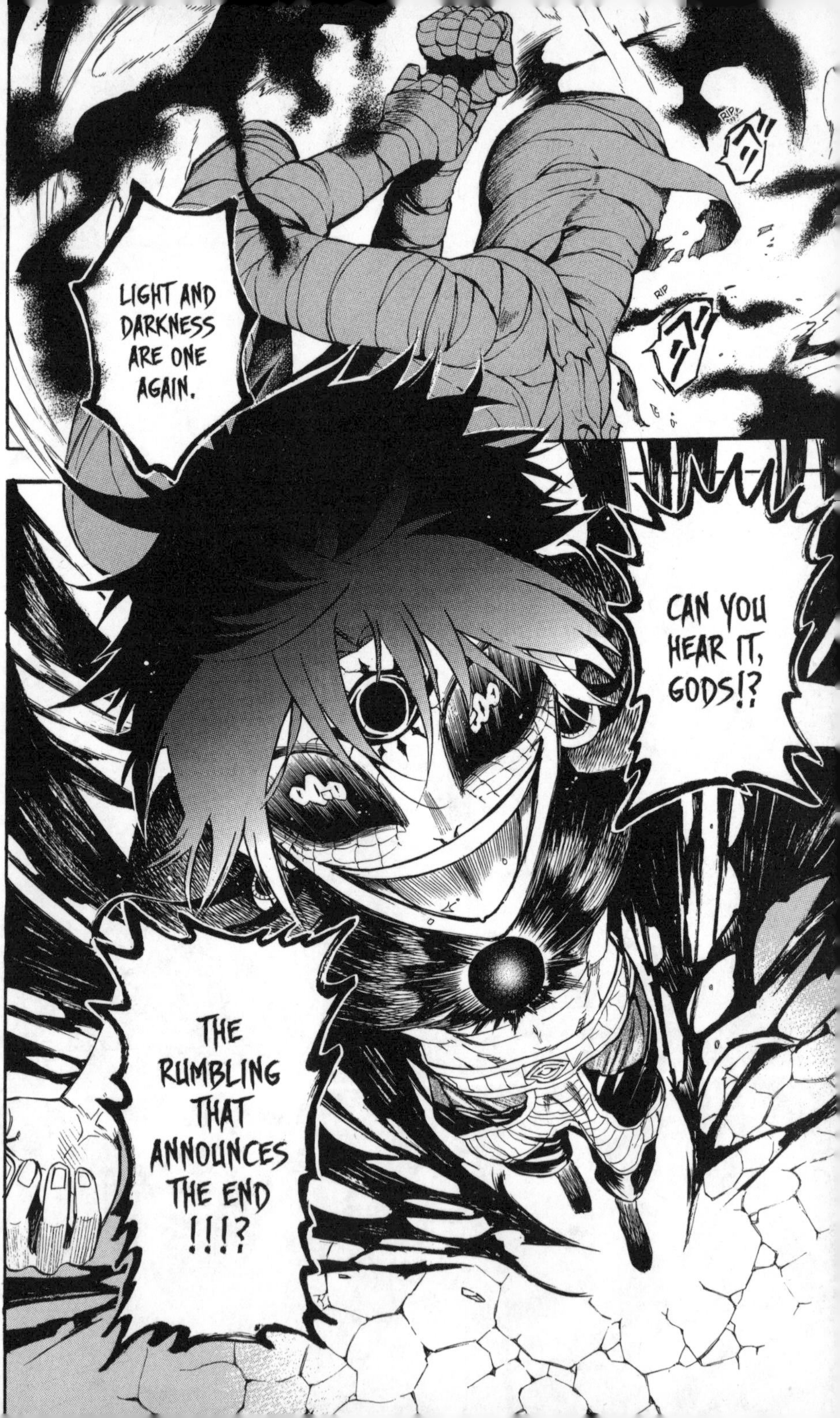
RIP
RIP
LIGHT AND DARKNESS ARE ONE AGAIN.
CAN YOU HEAR IT, GODS!?
THE RUMBLING THAT ANNOUNCES THE END !!!?

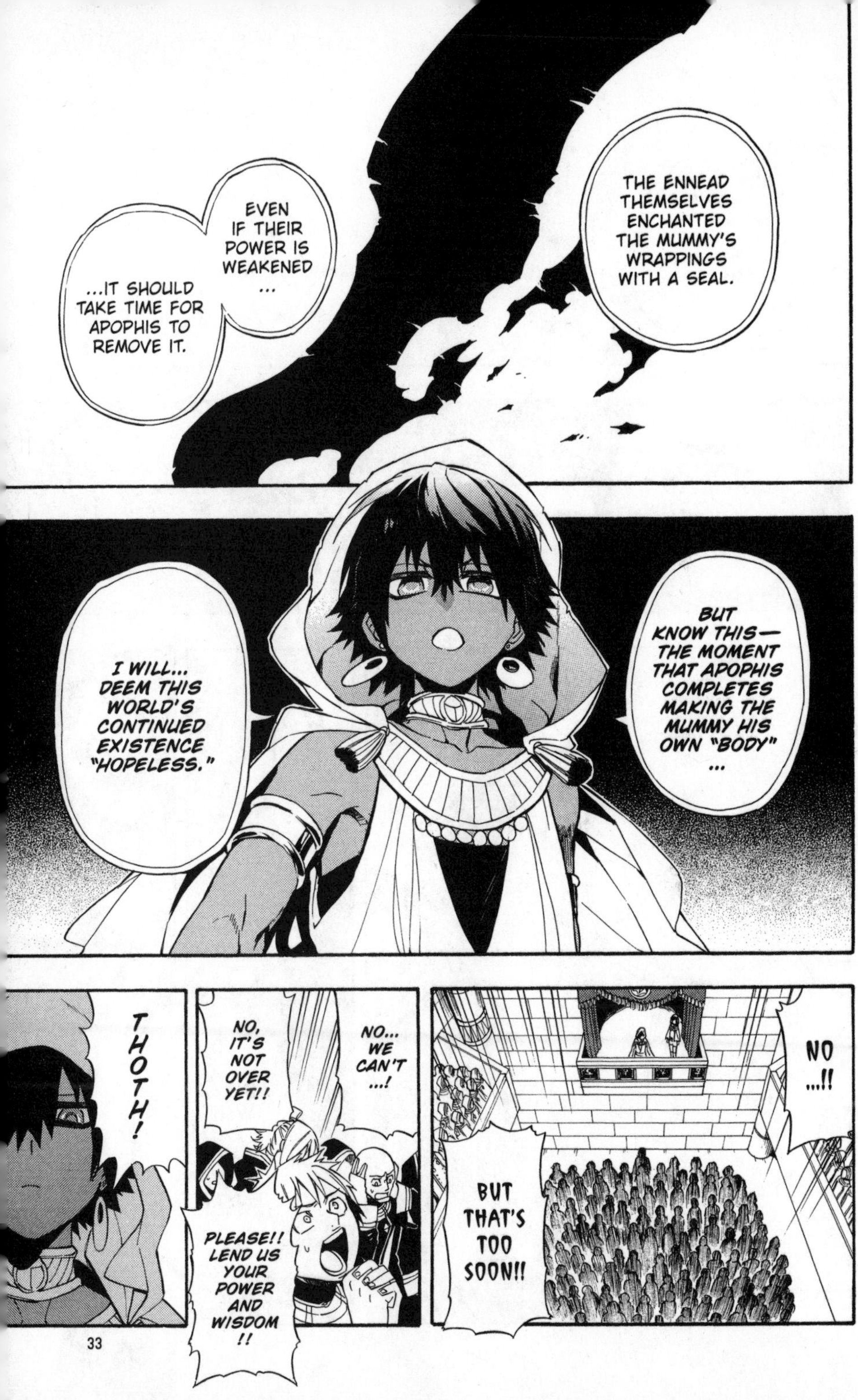
THE ENNEAD THEMSELVES ENCHANTED THE MUMMY'S WRAPPINGS WITH A SEAL.
EVEN IF THEIR POWER IS WEAKENED ...
...IT SHOULD TAKE TIME FOR APOPHIS TO REMOVE IT.
BUT KNOW THIS— THE MOMENT THAT APOPHIS COMPLETES MAKING THE MUMMY HIS OWN "BODY" ...
I WILL... DEEM THIS WORLD'S CONTINUED EXISTENCE "HOPELESS."
NO ...!!
BUT THAT'S TOO SOON!!
NO... WE CAN'T ...!
NO, IT'S NOT OVER YET!!
PLEASE!! LEND US YOUR POWER AND WISDOM !!
THOTH!

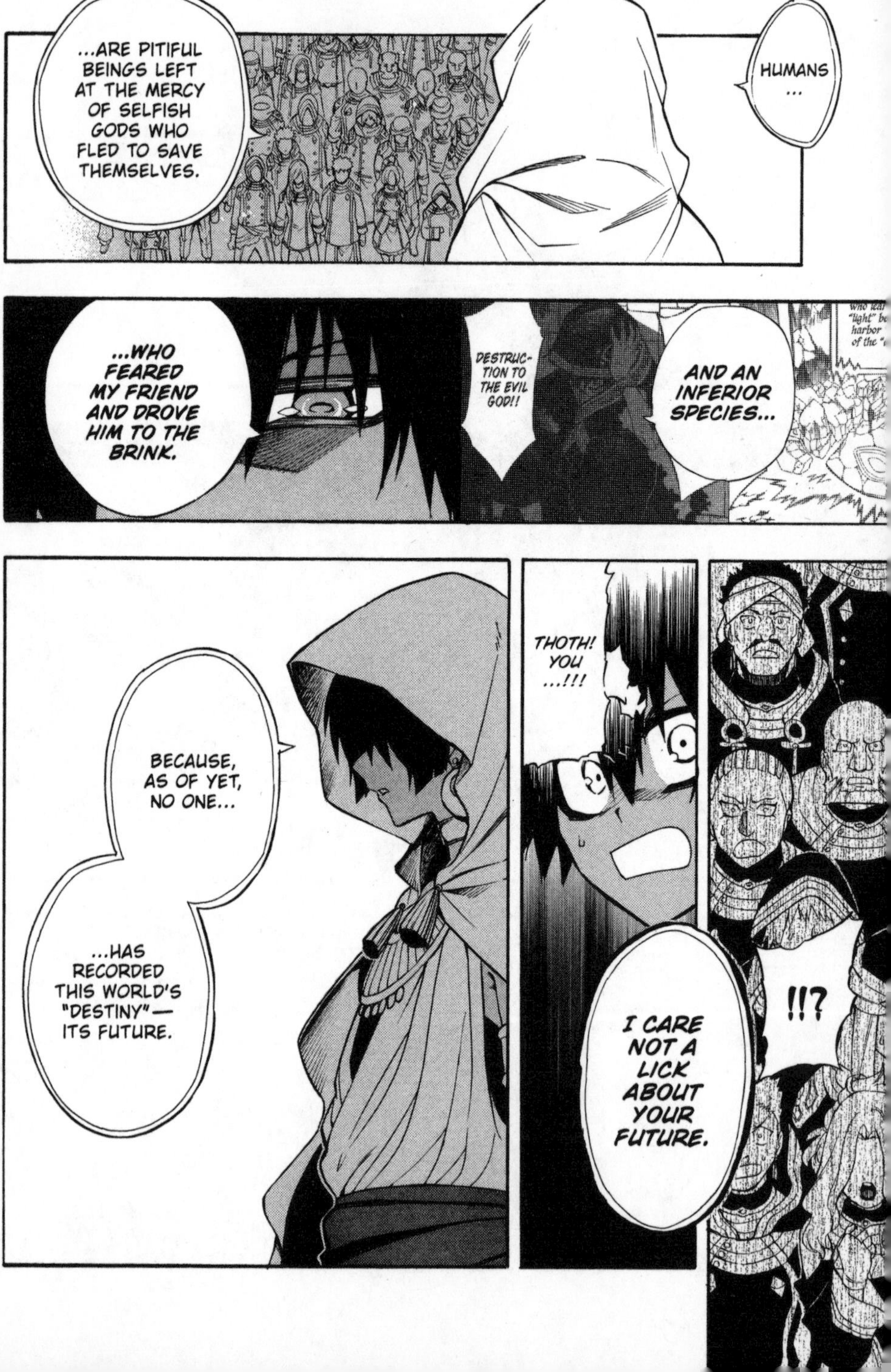
HUMANS ...
...ARE PITIFUL BEINGS LEFT AT THE MERCY OF SELFISH GODS WHO FLED TO SAVE THEMSELVES.
AND AN INFERIOR SPECIES...
DESTRUCTION TO THE EVIL GOD!!
...WHO FEARED MY FRIEND AND DROVE HIM TO THE BRINK.
I CARE NOT A LICK ABOUT YOUR FUTURE.
!!?
THOTH! YOU ...!!!
BECAUSE, AS OF YET, NO ONE...
...HAS RECORDED THIS WORLD'S "DESTINY"— ITS FUTURE.

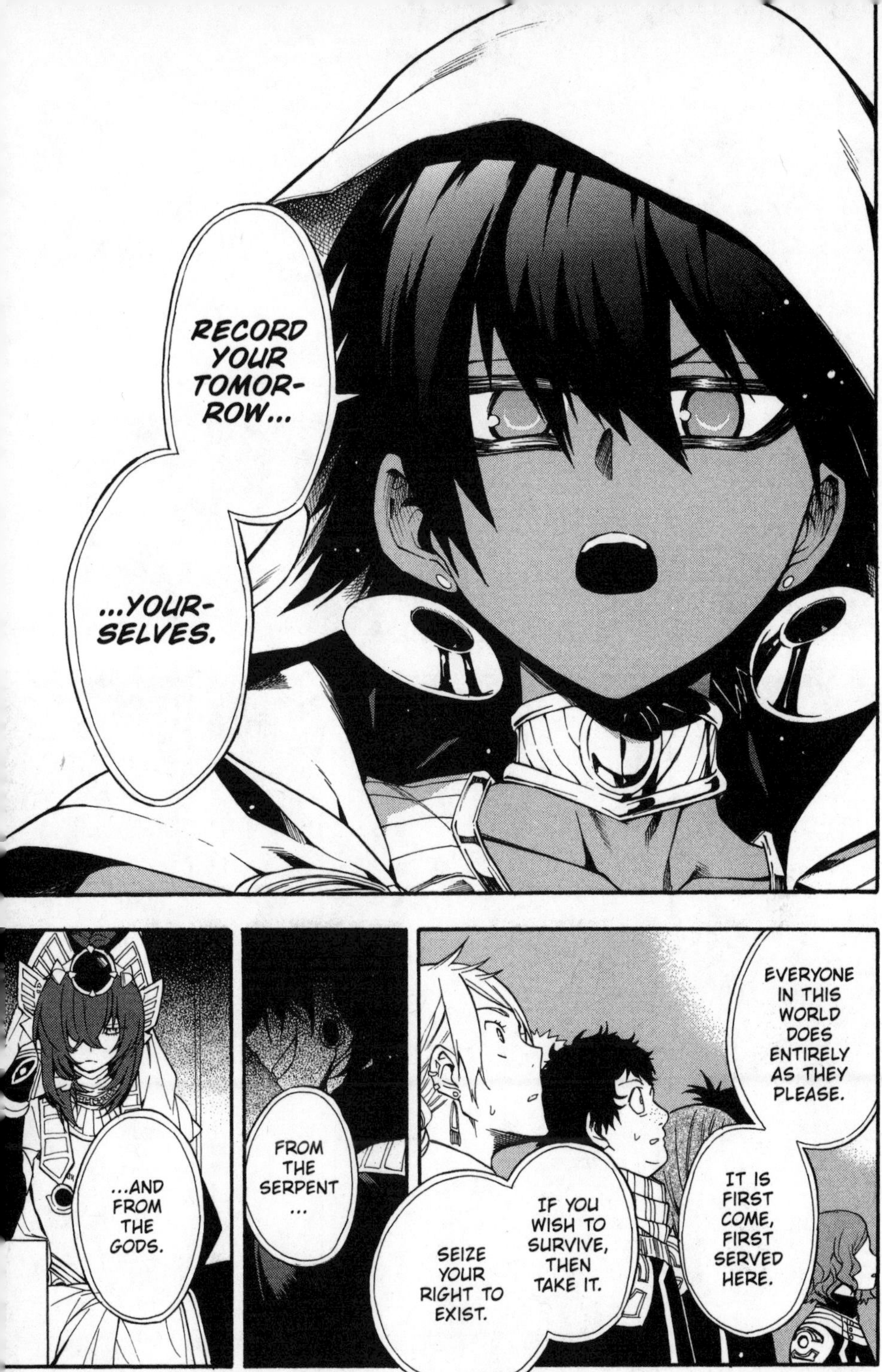
RECORD YOUR TOMOR-ROW...
...YOUR-SELVES.
EVERYONE IN THIS WORLD DOES ENTIRELY AS THEY PLEASE.
IT IS FIRST COME, FIRST SERVED HERE.
IF YOU WISH TO SURVIVE, THEN TAKE IT.
SEIZE YOUR RIGHT TO EXIST.
FROM THE SERPENT...
...AND FROM THE GODS.

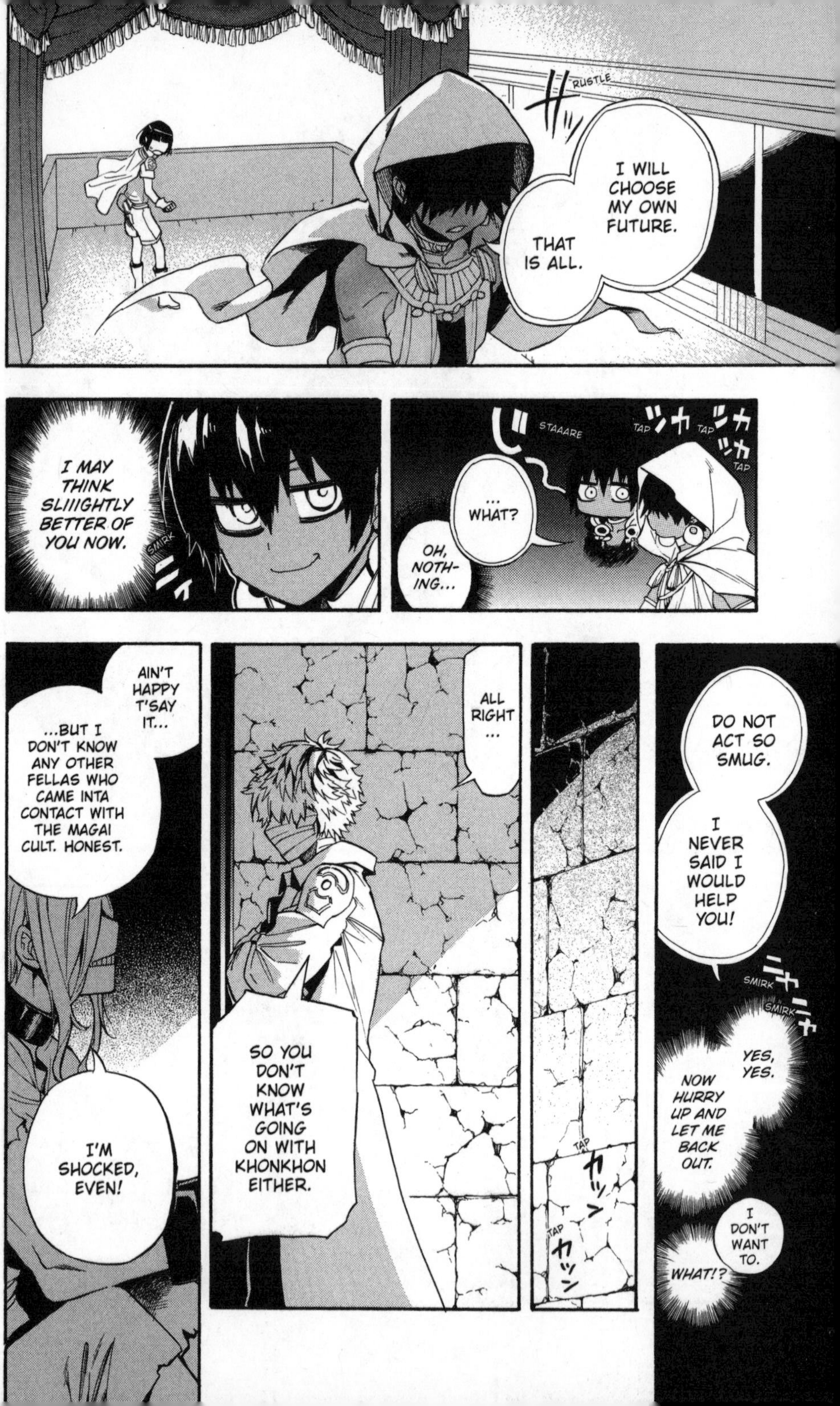
RUSTLE
I WILL CHOOSE MY OWN FUTURE.
THAT IS ALL.
STAAARE
TAP TAP TAP
...WHAT?
OH, NOTHING...
I MAY THINK SLIIIGHTLY BETTER OF YOU NOW.
SMIRK
DO NOT ACT SO SMUG.
I NEVER SAID I WOULD HELP YOU!
SMIRK SMIRK
YES, YES.
NOW HURRY UP AND LET ME BACK OUT.
I DON'T WANT TO.
WHAT!?
TAP
TAP
ALL RIGHT...
SO YOU DON'T KNOW WHAT'S GOING ON WITH KHONKHON EITHER.
AIN'T HAPPY T'SAY IT...
...BUT I DON'T KNOW ANY OTHER FELLAS WHO CAME INTA CONTACT WITH THE MAGAI CULT. HONEST.
I'M SHOCKED, EVEN!

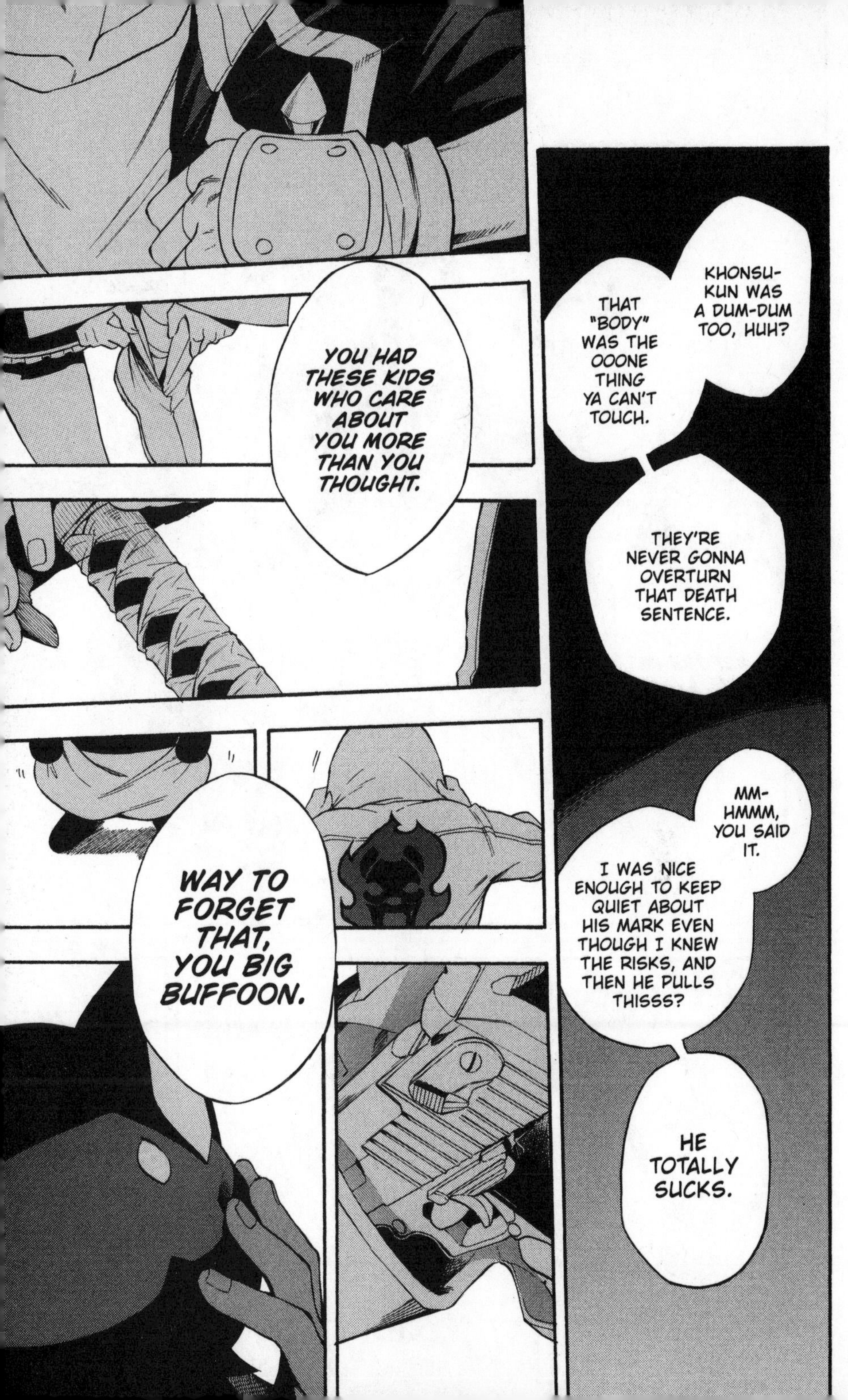
KHONSU-KUN WAS A DUM-DUM TOO, HUH?
THAT "BODY" WAS THE OOONE THING YA CAN'T TOUCH.
THEY'RE NEVER GONNA OVERTURN THAT DEATH SENTENCE.
MM-HMMM, YOU SAID IT.
I WAS NICE ENOUGH TO KEEP QUIET ABOUT HIS MARK EVEN THOUGH I KNEW THE RISKS, AND THEN HE PULLS THISSS?
HE TOTALLY SUCKS.
YOU HAD THESE KIDS WHO CARE ABOUT YOU MORE THAN YOU THOUGHT.
WAY TO FORGET THAT, YOU BIG BUFFOON.

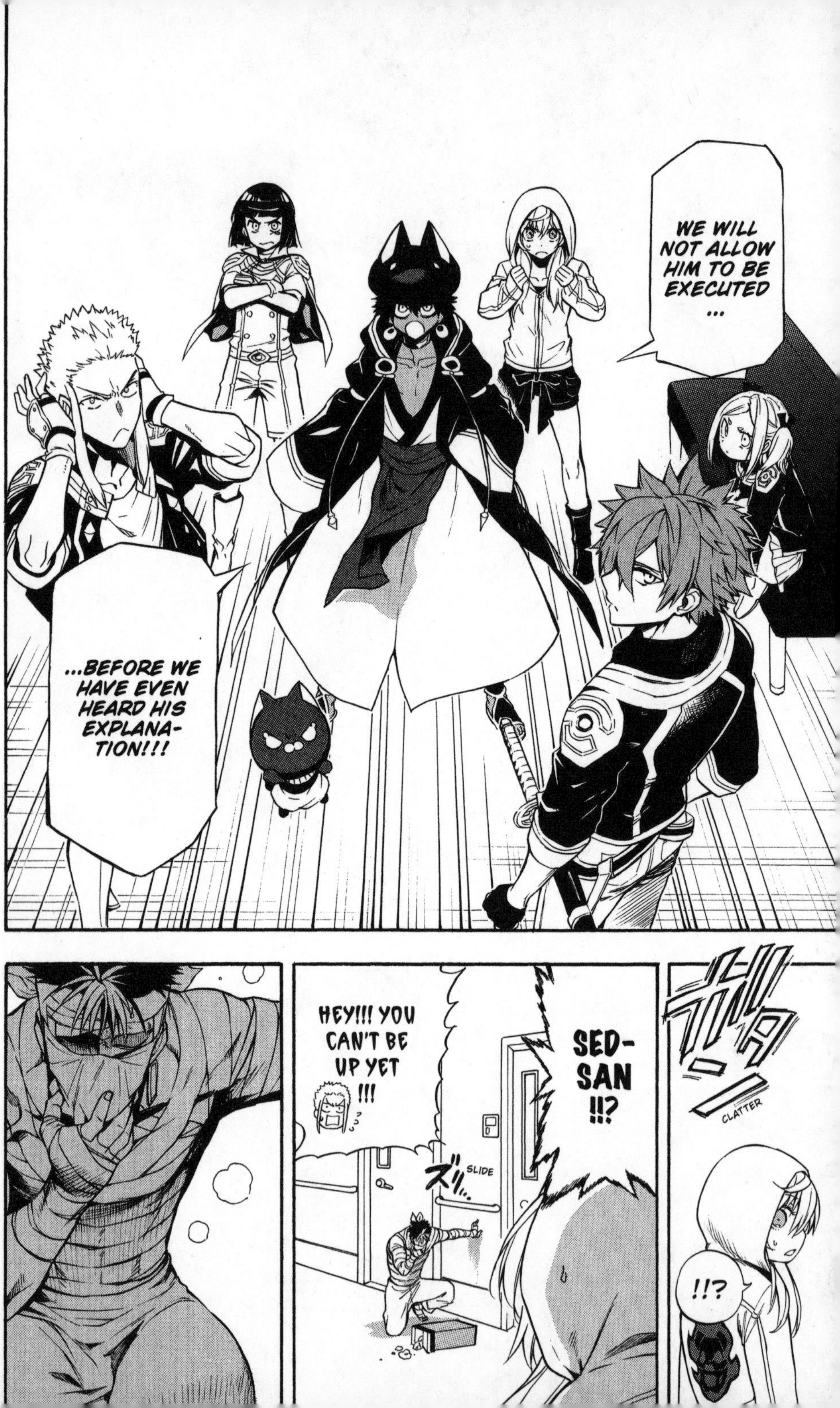
WE WILL NOT ALLOW HIM TO BE EXECUTED ...
...BEFORE WE HAVE EVEN HEARD HIS EXPLANATION!!!
CLATTER
!!?
SED-SAN!!?
HEY!!! YOU CAN'T BE UP YET!!!
SLIDE

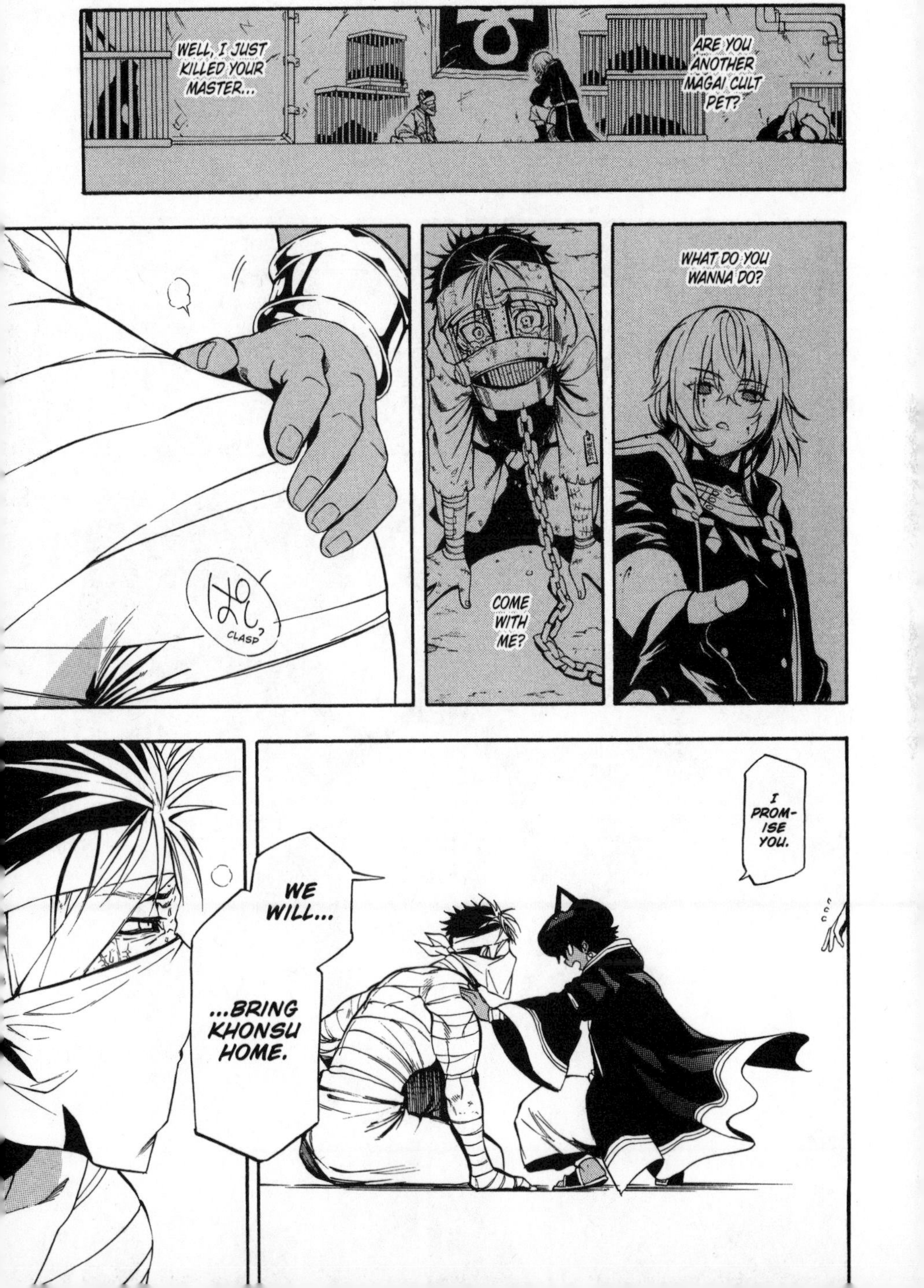
ARE YOU ANOTHER MAGAI CULT PET?
WELL, I JUST KILLED YOUR MASTER...
WHAT DO YOU WANNA DO?
COME WITH ME?
CLASP
I PROMISE YOU.
WE WILL...
...BRING KHONSU HOME.

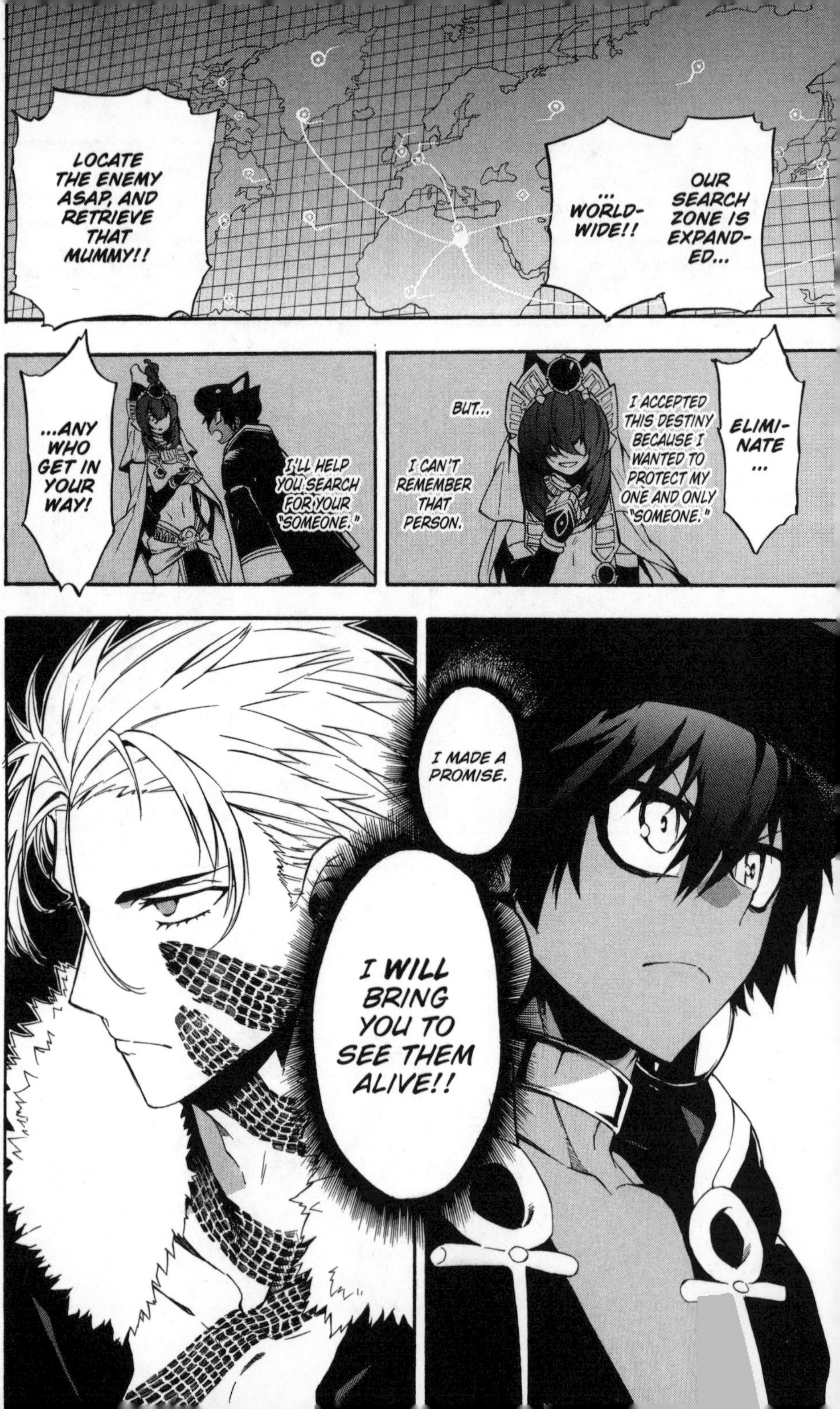
OUR SEARCH ZONE IS EXPAND-ED...
... WORLD-WIDE!!
LOCATE THE ENEMY ASAP, AND RETRIEVE THAT MUMMY!!
ELIMI-NATE ...
I ACCEPTED THIS DESTINY BECAUSE I WANTED TO PROTECT MY ONE AND ONLY "SOMEONE."
BUT...
I CAN'T REMEMBER THAT PERSON.
...ANY WHO GET IN YOUR WAY!
I'LL HELP YOU SEARCH FOR YOUR "SOMEONE."
I MADE A PROMISE.
I WILL BRING YOU TO SEE THEM ALIVE!!

Great Priest Imhotep

Great Priest Imhotep

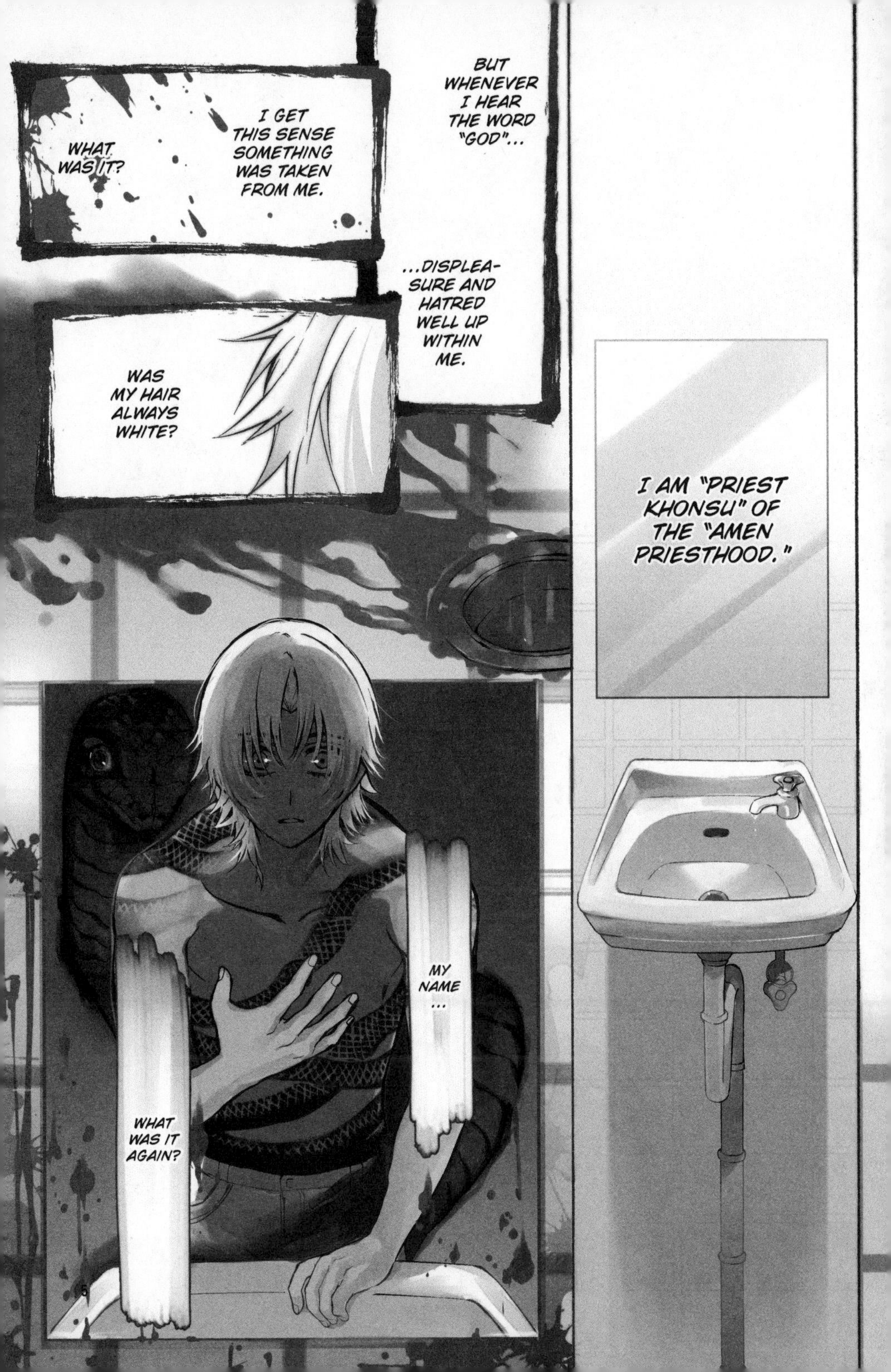
I AM "PRIEST KHONSU" OF THE "AMEN PRIESTHOOD."
BUT WHENEVER I HEAR THE WORD "GOD"...
I GET THIS SENSE SOMETHING WAS TAKEN FROM ME.
WHAT WAS IT?
...DISPLEA-SURE AND HATRED WELL UP WITHIN ME.
WAS MY HAIR ALWAYS WHITE?
MY NAME ...
WHAT WAS IT AGAIN?

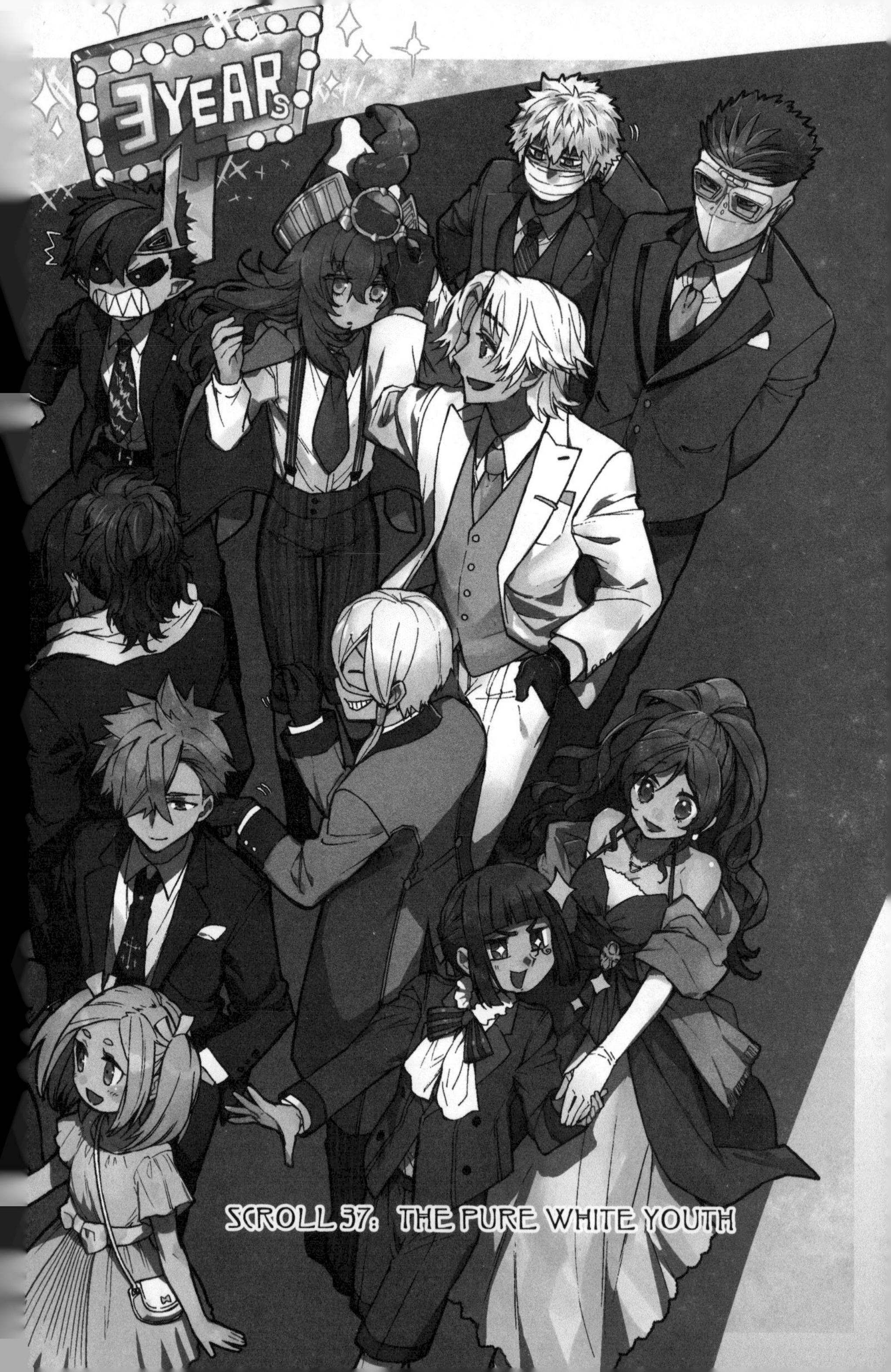
3 YEARS
SCROLL 37: THE PURE WHITE YOUTH

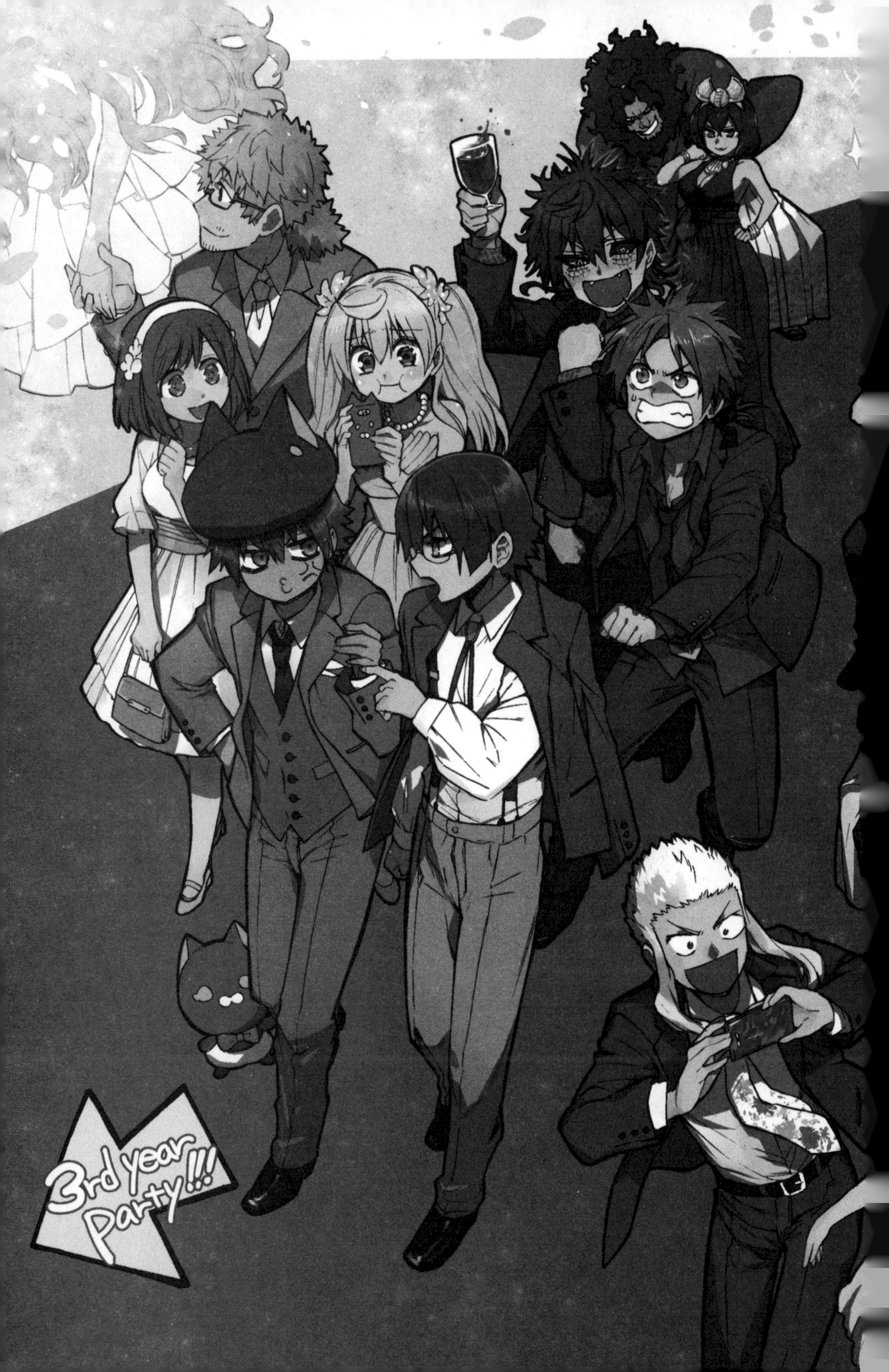
3rd year
party!!!

Great Priest Imhotep

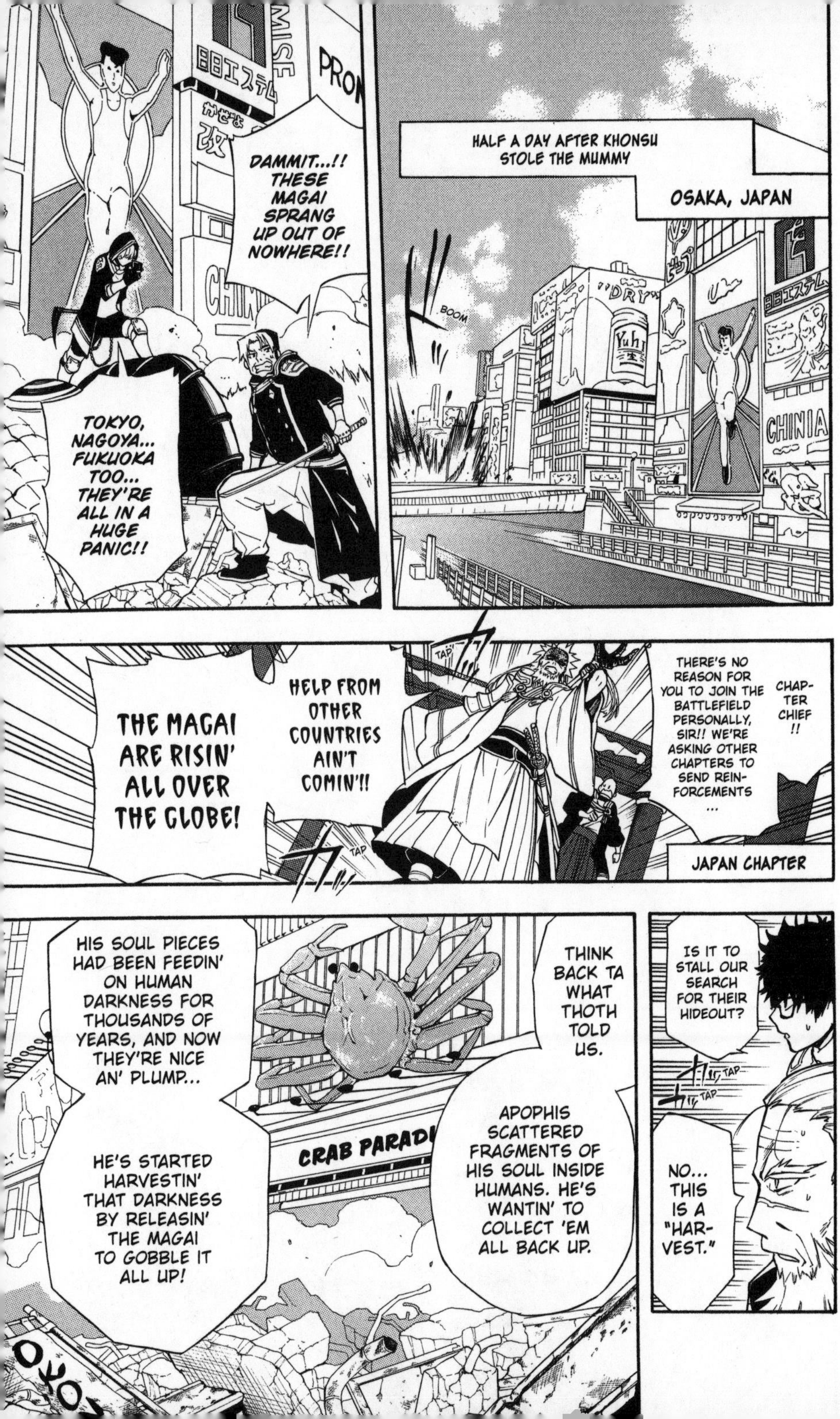
HALF A DAY AFTER KHONSU STOLE THE MUMMY
OSAKA, JAPAN
BOOM
"DRY"
CHINIA
DAMMIT...!! THESE MAGAI SPRANG UP OUT OF NOWHERE!!
TOKYO, NAGOYA... FUKUOKA TOO... THEY'RE ALL IN A HUGE PANIC!!
CHAPTER CHIEF!!
THERE'S NO REASON FOR YOU TO JOIN THE BATTLEFIELD PERSONALLY, SIR!! WE'RE ASKING OTHER CHAPTERS TO SEND REIN-FORCEMENTS...
TAP
HELP FROM OTHER COUNTRIES AIN'T COMIN'!!
THE MAGAI ARE RISIN' ALL OVER THE GLOBE!
JAPAN CHAPTER
TAP
IS IT TO STALL OUR SEARCH FOR THEIR HIDEOUT?
TAP
TAP
NO... THIS IS A "HAR-VEST."
THINK BACK TA WHAT THOTH TOLD US.
APOPHIS SCATTERED FRAGMENTS OF HIS SOUL INSIDE HUMANS. HE'S WANTIN' TO COLLECT 'EM ALL BACK UP.
HIS SOUL PIECES HAD BEEN FEEDIN' ON HUMAN DARKNESS FOR THOUSANDS OF YEARS, AND NOW THEY'RE NICE AN' PLUMP...
HE'S STARTED HARVESTIN' THAT DARKNESS BY RELEASIN' THE MAGAI TO GOBBLE IT ALL UP!
CRAB PARADI

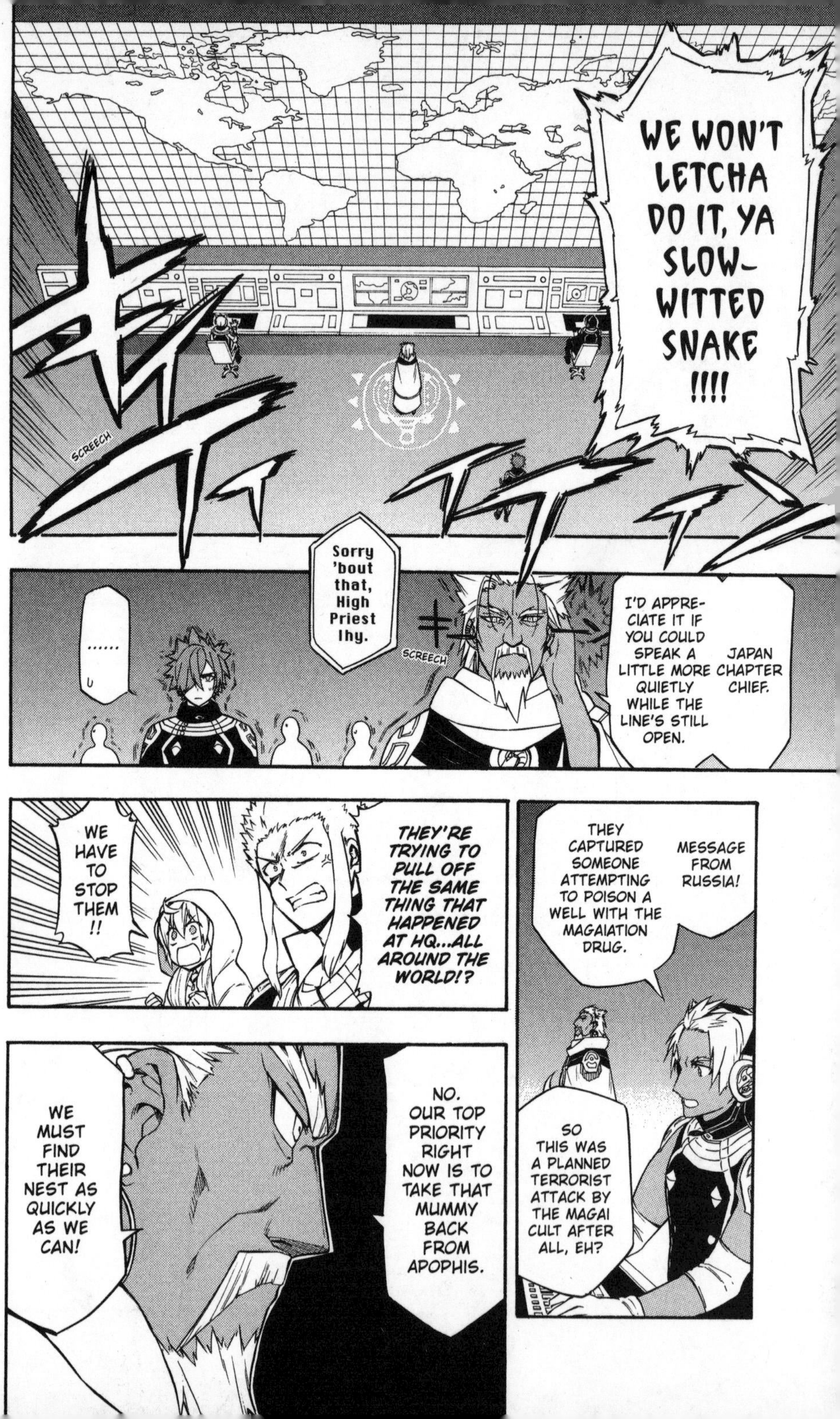
WE WON'T LETCHA DO IT, YA SLOW-WITTED SNAKE !!!!
SCREECH
I'D APPRECIATE IT IF YOU COULD SPEAK A LITTLE MORE QUIETLY WHILE THE LINE'S STILL OPEN. JAPAN CHAPTER CHIEF.
SCREECH
Sorry 'bout that, High Priest Ihy.
......
MESSAGE FROM RUSSIA!
THEY CAPTURED SOMEONE ATTEMPTING TO POISON A WELL WITH THE MAGAIATION DRUG.
SO THIS WAS A PLANNED TERRORIST ATTACK BY THE MAGAI CULT AFTER ALL, EH?
THEY'RE TRYING TO PULL OFF THE SAME THING THAT HAPPENED AT HQ...ALL AROUND THE WORLD!?
WE HAVE TO STOP THEM !!
NO. OUR TOP PRIORITY RIGHT NOW IS TO TAKE THAT MUMMY BACK FROM APOPHIS.
WE MUST FIND THEIR NEST AS QUICKLY AS WE CAN!

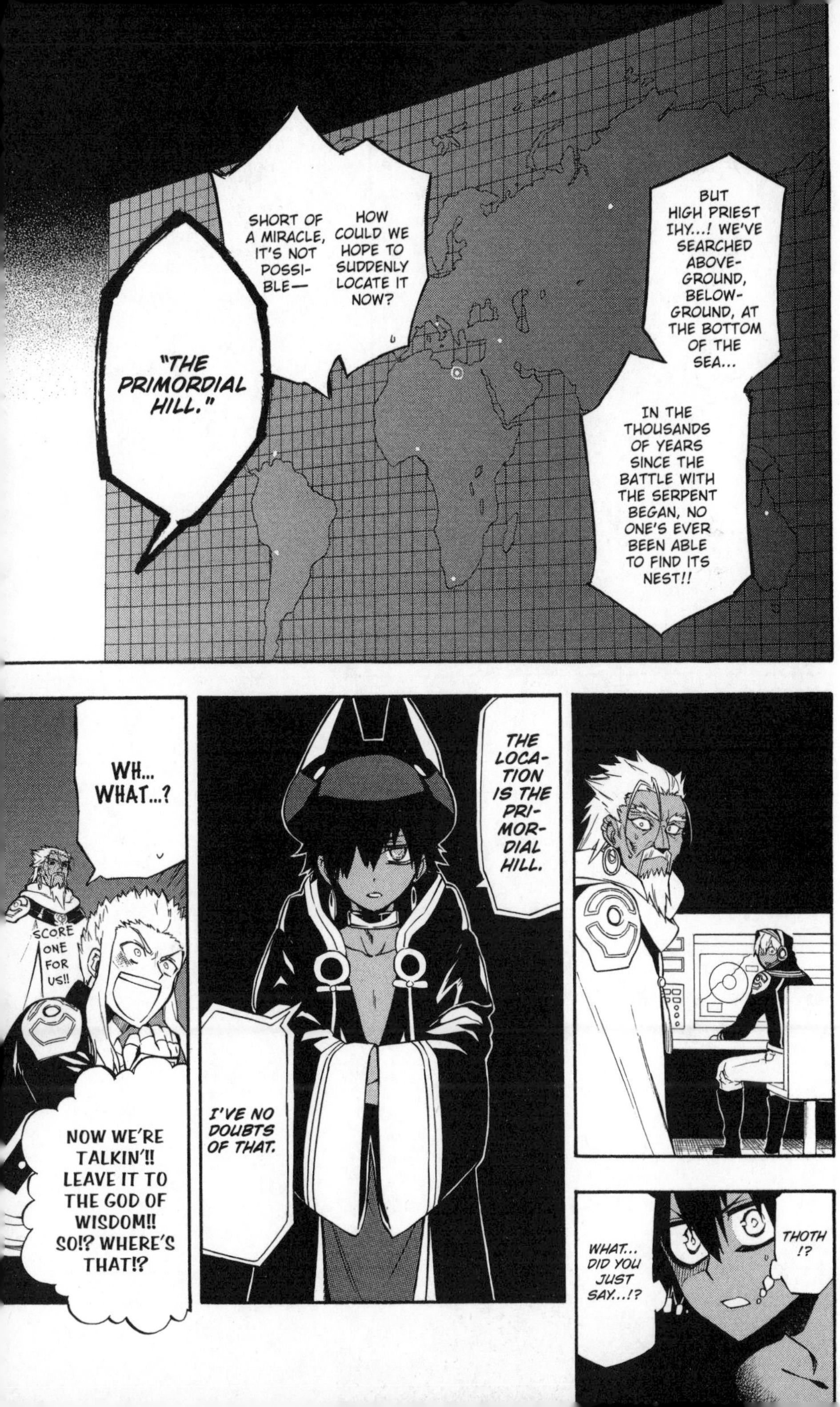
BUT HIGH PRIEST IHY...! WE'VE SEARCHED ABOVE-GROUND, BELOW-GROUND, AT THE BOTTOM OF THE SEA...
IN THE THOUSANDS OF YEARS SINCE THE BATTLE WITH THE SERPENT BEGAN, NO ONE'S EVER BEEN ABLE TO FIND ITS NEST!!
HOW COULD WE HOPE TO SUDDENLY LOCATE IT NOW?
SHORT OF A MIRACLE, IT'S NOT POSSI-BLE—
"THE PRIMORDIAL HILL."
THOTH !?
WHAT... DID YOU JUST SAY...!?
THE LOCA-TION IS THE PRI-MOR-DIAL HILL.
I'VE NO DOUBTS OF THAT.
WH... WHAT...?
SCORE ONE FOR US!!
NOW WE'RE TALKIN'!! LEAVE IT TO THE GOD OF WISDOM!! SO!? WHERE'S THAT!?

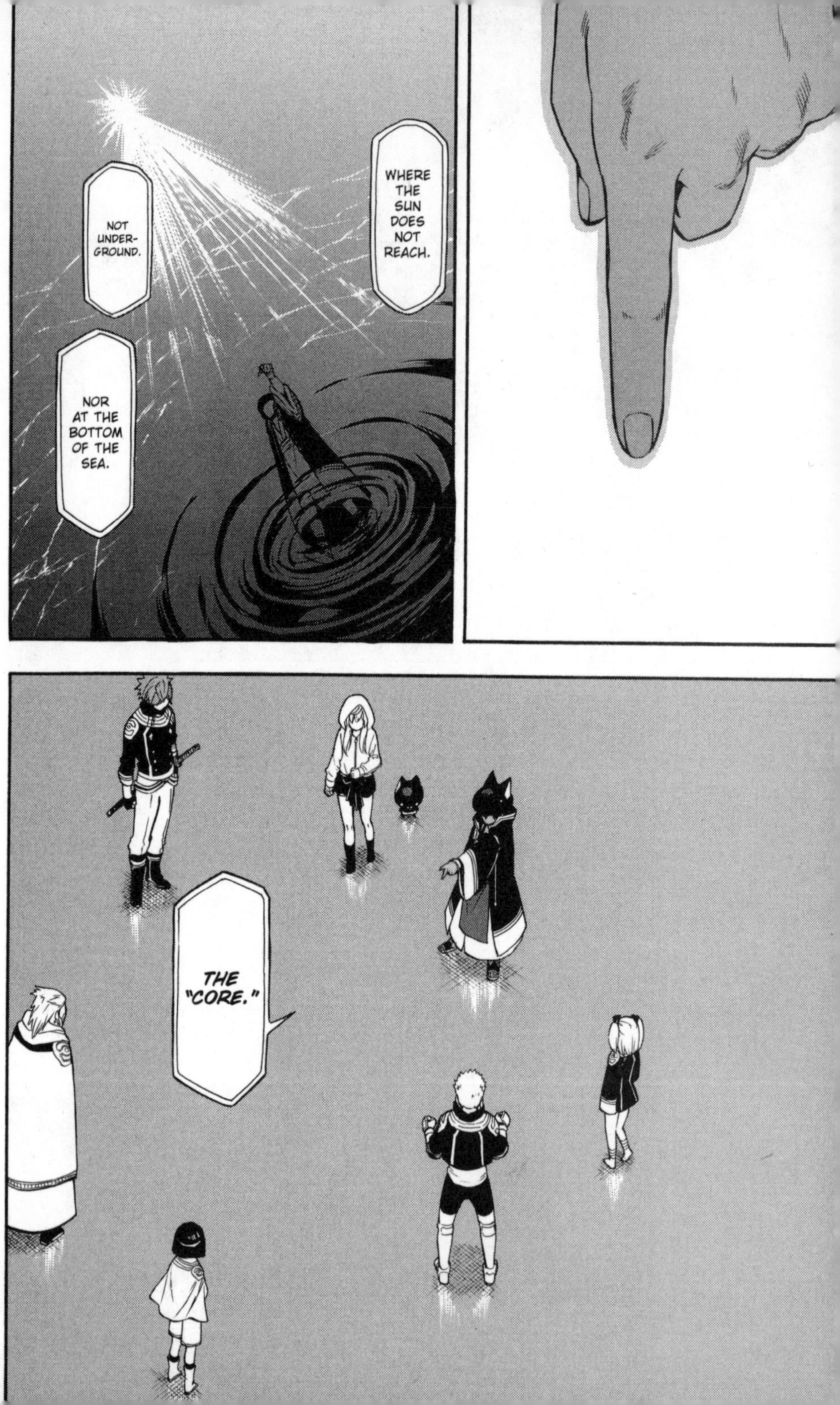
WHERE THE SUN DOES NOT REACH.
NOT UNDERGROUND.
NOR AT THE BOTTOM OF THE SEA.
THE "CORE."

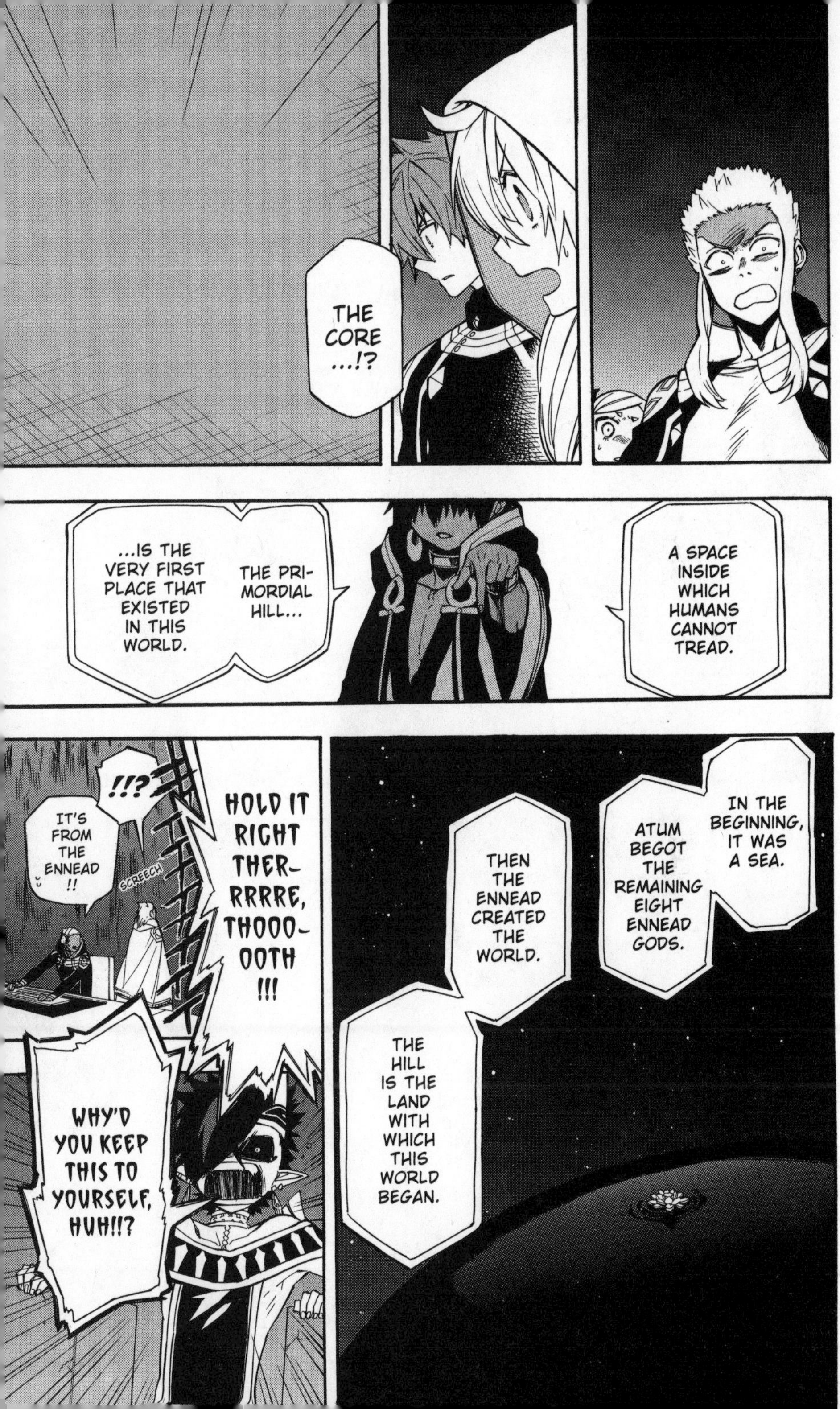
THE CORE ...!?
A SPACE INSIDE WHICH HUMANS CANNOT TREAD.
THE PRI-MORDIAL HILL...
...IS THE VERY FIRST PLACE THAT EXISTED IN THIS WORLD.
IN THE BEGINNING, IT WAS A SEA.
ATUM BEGOT THE REMAINING EIGHT ENNEAD GODS.
THEN THE ENNEAD CREATED THE WORLD.
THE HILL IS THE LAND WITH WHICH THIS WORLD BEGAN.
HOLD IT RIGHT THER-RRRRE, THOOO-OOTH !!!
!!?
IT'S FROM THE ENNEAD !!
SCREECH
WHY'D YOU KEEP THIS TO YOURSELF, HUH!!?

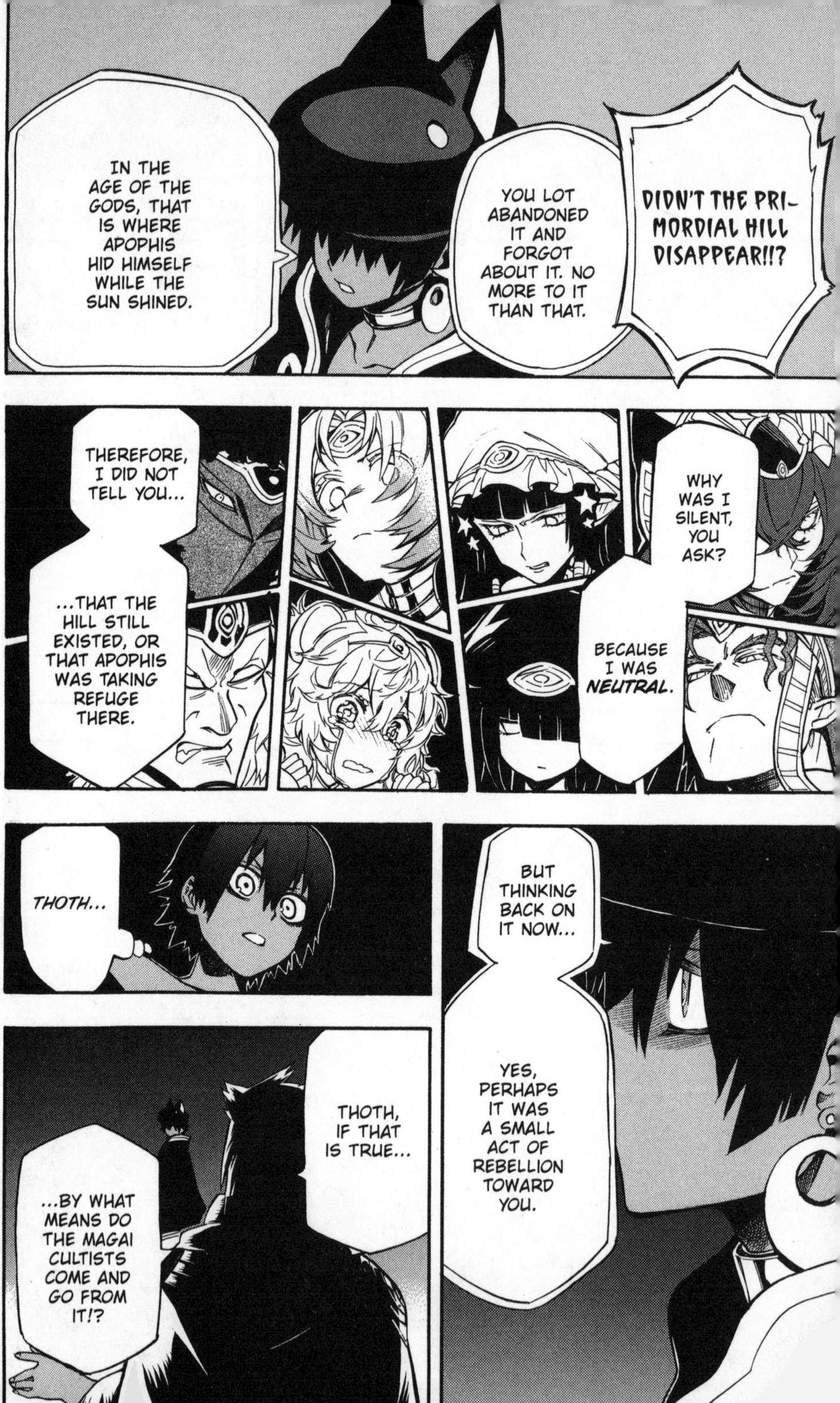
DIDN'T THE PRIMORDIAL HILL DISAPPEAR!!?
YOU LOT ABANDONED IT AND FORGOT ABOUT IT. NO MORE TO IT THAN THAT.
IN THE AGE OF THE GODS, THAT IS WHERE APOPHIS HID HIMSELF WHILE THE SUN SHINED.
WHY WAS I SILENT, YOU ASK?
BECAUSE I WAS *NEUTRAL*.
THEREFORE, I DID NOT TELL YOU...
...THAT THE HILL STILL EXISTED, OR THAT APOPHIS WAS TAKING REFUGE THERE.
BUT THINKING BACK ON IT NOW...
YES, PERHAPS IT WAS A SMALL ACT OF REBELLION TOWARD YOU.
THOTH...
THOTH, IF THAT IS TRUE...
...BY WHAT MEANS DO THE MAGAI CULTISTS COME AND GO FROM IT!?

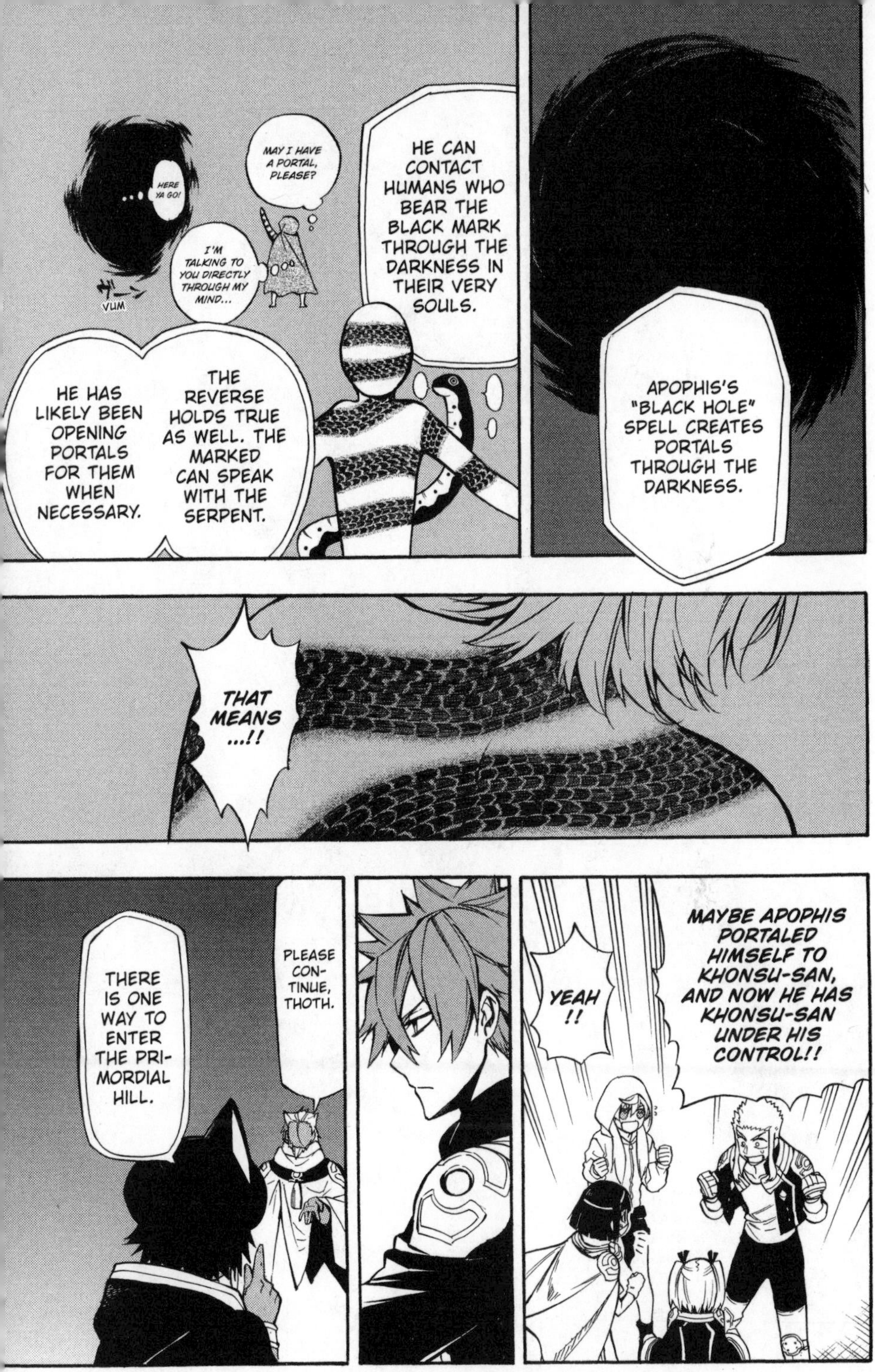

APOPHIS'S "BLACK HOLE" SPELL CREATES PORTALS THROUGH THE DARKNESS.
HE CAN CONTACT HUMANS WHO BEAR THE BLACK MARK THROUGH THE DARKNESS IN THEIR VERY SOULS.
MAY I HAVE A PORTAL, PLEASE?
HERE YA GO!
I'M TALKING TO YOU DIRECTLY THROUGH MY MIND...
ザーン
VUM
THE REVERSE HOLDS TRUE AS WELL. THE MARKED CAN SPEAK WITH THE SERPENT.
HE HAS LIKELY BEEN OPENING PORTALS FOR THEM WHEN NECESSARY.
THAT MEANS ...!!
MAYBE APOPHIS PORTALED HIMSELF TO KHONSU-SAN, AND NOW HE HAS KHONSU-SAN UNDER HIS CONTROL!!
YEAH !!
PLEASE CON-TINUE, THOTH.
THERE IS ONE WAY TO ENTER THE PRI-MORDIAL HILL.

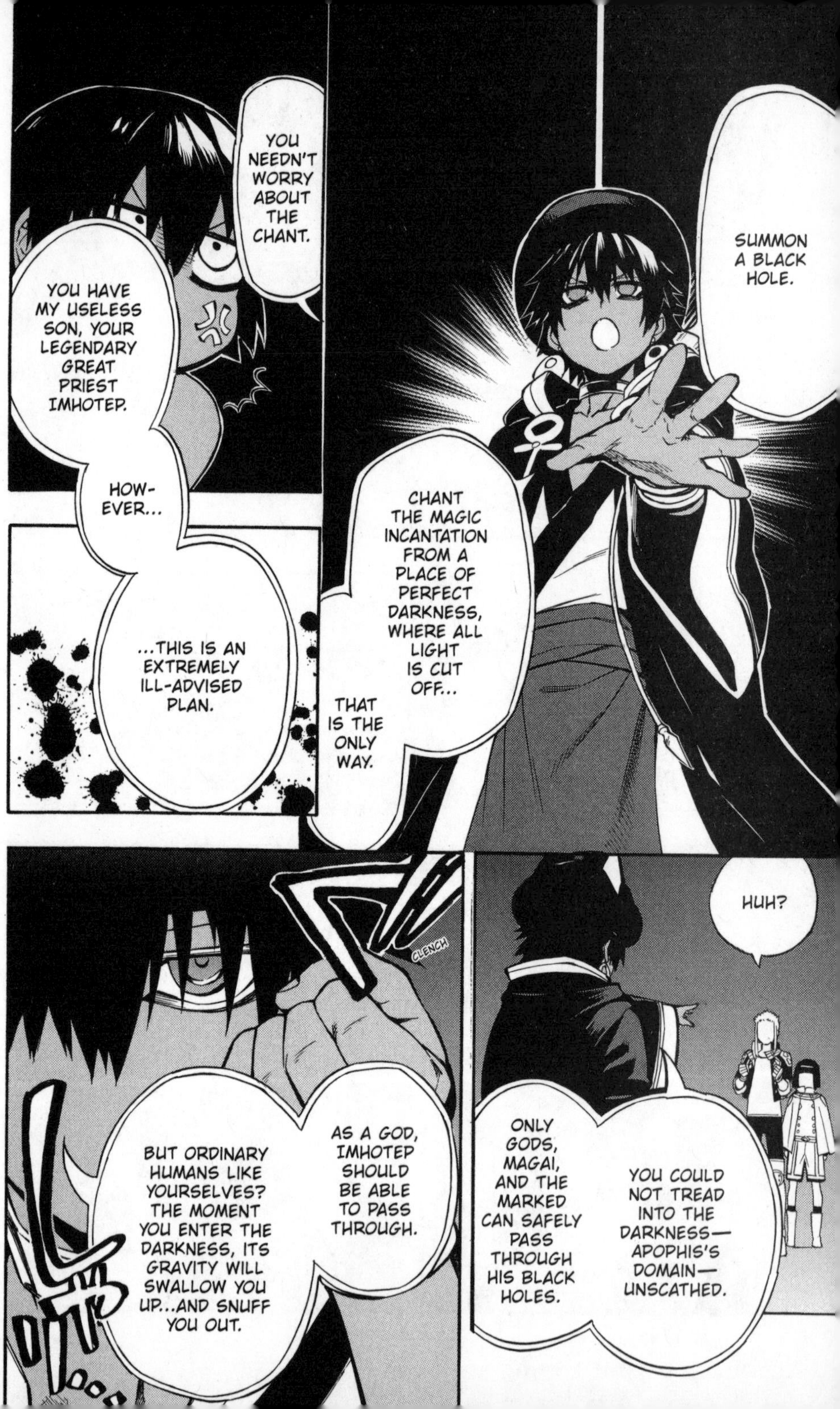
SUMMON A BLACK HOLE.
CHANT THE MAGIC INCANTATION FROM A PLACE OF PERFECT DARKNESS, WHERE ALL LIGHT IS CUT OFF...
THAT IS THE ONLY WAY.
YOU NEEDN'T WORRY ABOUT THE CHANT.
YOU HAVE MY USELESS SON, YOUR LEGENDARY GREAT PRIEST IMHOTEP.
HOW-EVER...
...THIS IS AN EXTREMELY ILL-ADVISED PLAN.
HUH?
YOU COULD NOT TREAD INTO THE DARKNESS—APOPHIS'S DOMAIN—UNSCATHED.
ONLY GODS, MAGAI, AND THE MARKED CAN SAFELY PASS THROUGH HIS BLACK HOLES.
CLENCH
AS A GOD, IMHOTEP SHOULD BE ABLE TO PASS THROUGH.
BUT ORDINARY HUMANS LIKE YOURSELVES? THE MOMENT YOU ENTER THE DARKNESS, ITS GRAVITY WILL SWALLOW YOU UP...AND SNUFF YOU OUT.

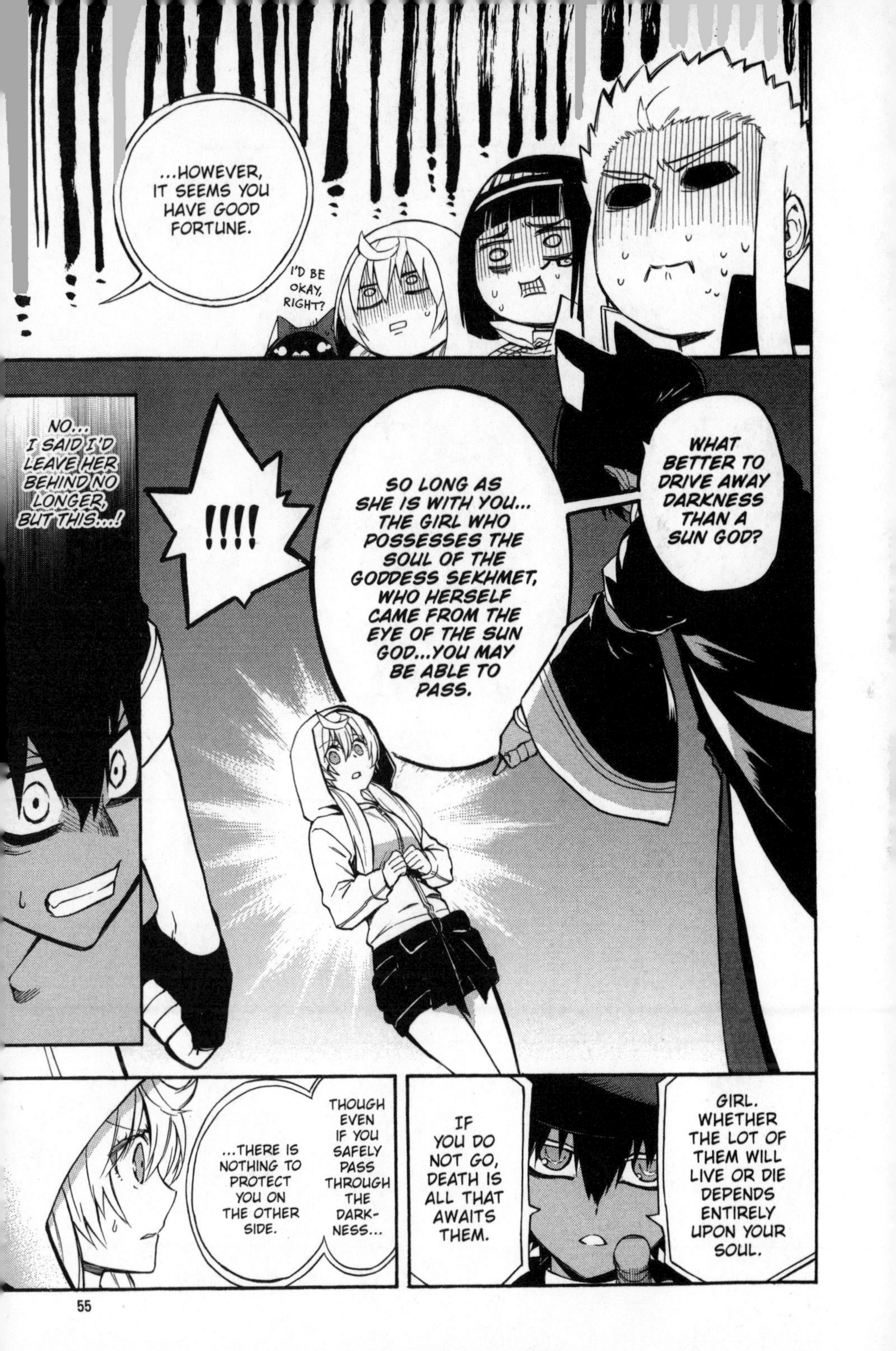
...HOWEVER, IT SEEMS YOU HAVE GOOD FORTUNE.
I'D BE OKAY, RIGHT?
WHAT BETTER TO DRIVE AWAY DARKNESS THAN A SUN GOD?
SO LONG AS SHE IS WITH YOU... THE GIRL WHO POSSESSES THE SOUL OF THE GODDESS SEKHMET, WHO HERSELF CAME FROM THE EYE OF THE SUN GOD...YOU MAY BE ABLE TO PASS.
!!!!
NO... I SAID I'D LEAVE HER BEHIND NO LONGER, BUT THIS...!
GIRL. WHETHER THE LOT OF THEM WILL LIVE OR DIE DEPENDS ENTIRELY UPON YOUR SOUL.
IF YOU DO NOT GO, DEATH IS ALL THAT AWAITS THEM.
THOUGH EVEN IF YOU SAFELY PASS THROUGH THE DARK-NESS...
...THERE IS NOTHING TO PROTECT YOU ON THE OTHER SIDE.

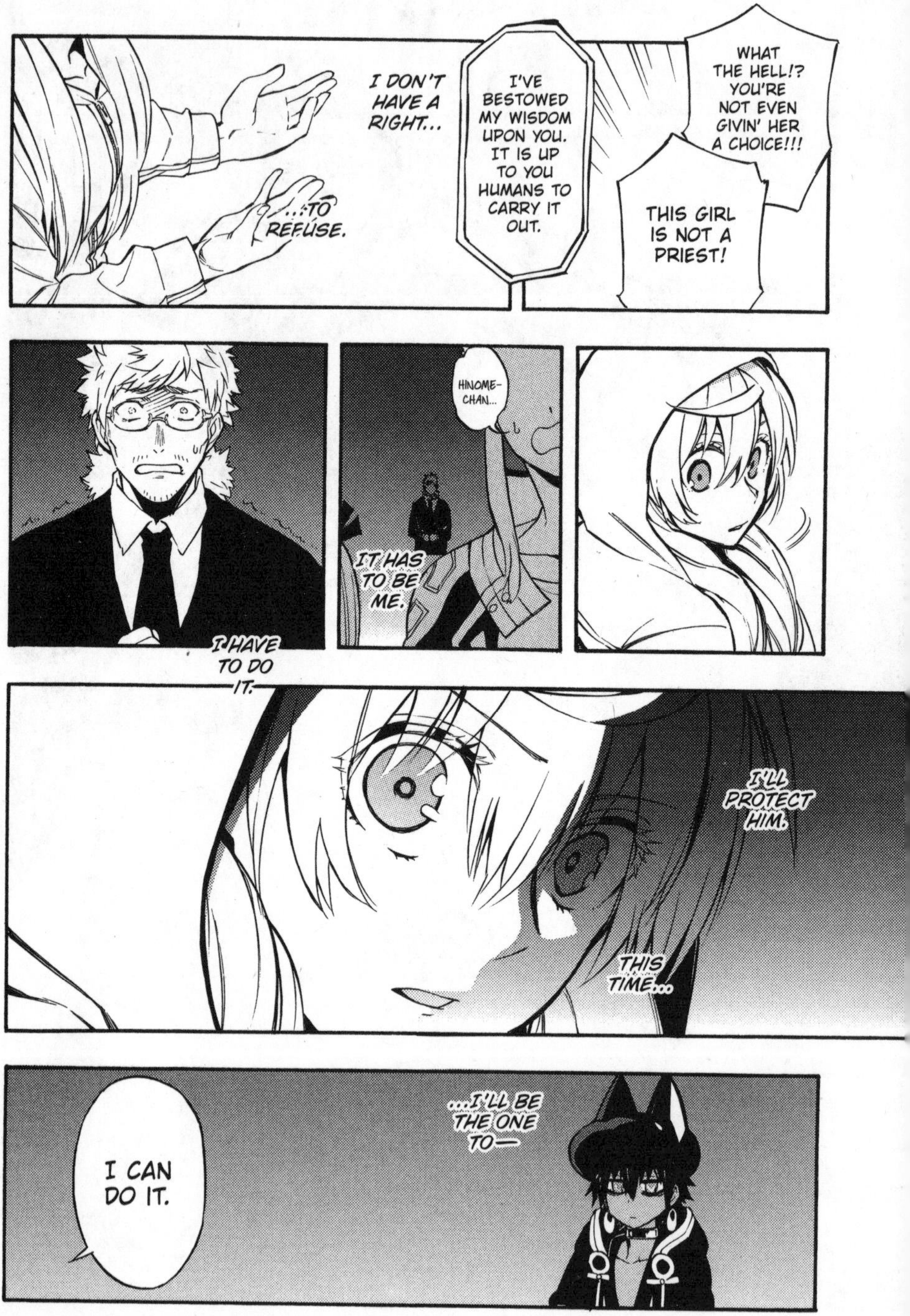
WHAT THE HELL!? YOU'RE NOT EVEN GIVIN' HER A CHOICE!!!
THIS GIRL IS NOT A PRIEST!
I'VE BESTOWED MY WISDOM UPON YOU. IT IS UP TO YOU HUMANS TO CARRY IT OUT.
I DON'T HAVE A RIGHT...
...TO REFUSE.
HINOME-CHAN...
IT HAS TO BE ME.
I HAVE TO DO IT.
I'LL PROTECT HIM.
THIS TIME...
...I'LL BE THE ONE TO—
I CAN DO IT.

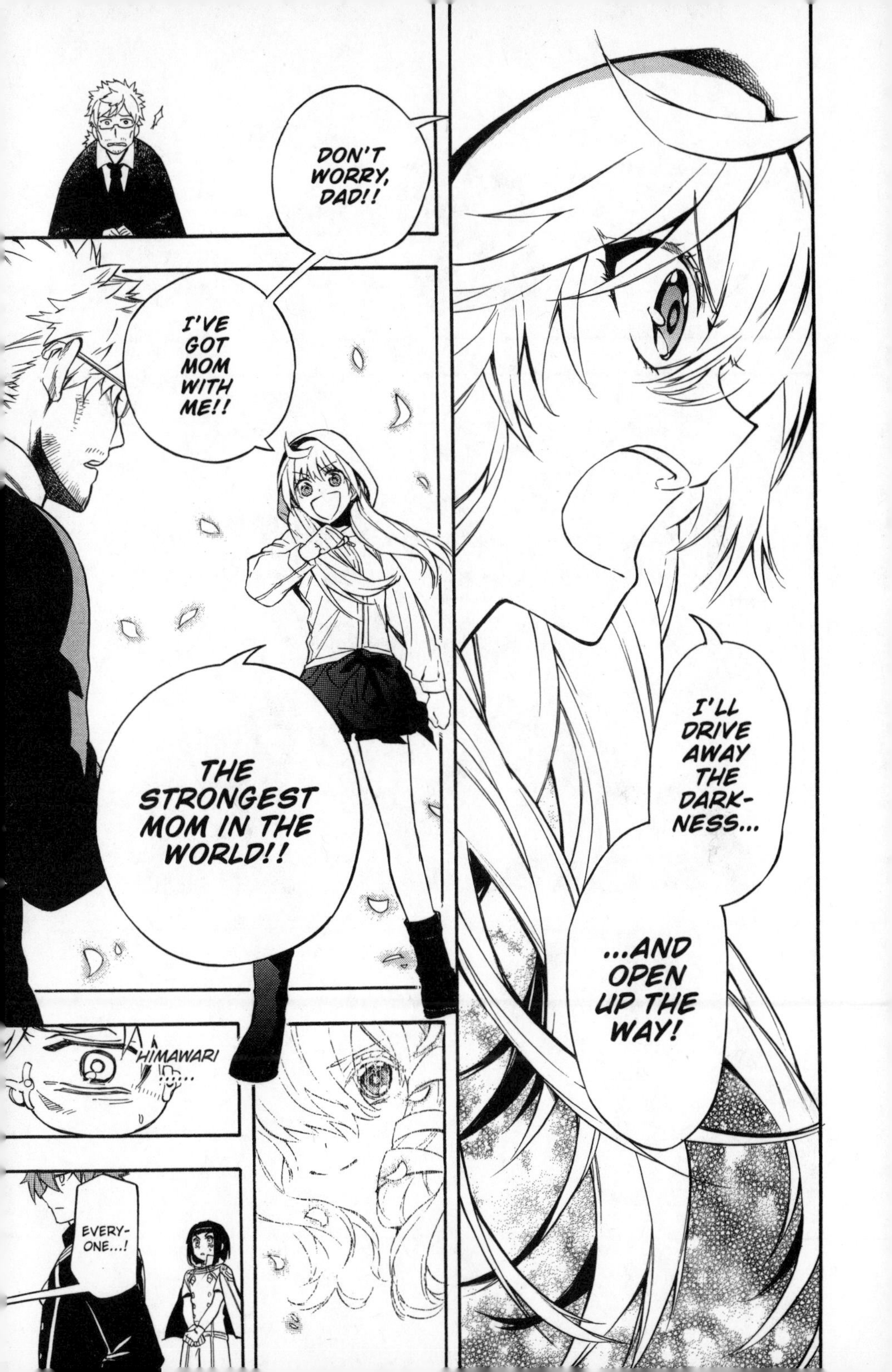
I'LL DRIVE AWAY THE DARK-NESS...
...AND OPEN UP THE WAY!
DON'T WORRY, DAD!!
I'VE GOT MOM WITH ME!!
THE STRONGEST MOM IN THE WORLD!!
HIMAWARI......
EVERY-ONE...!

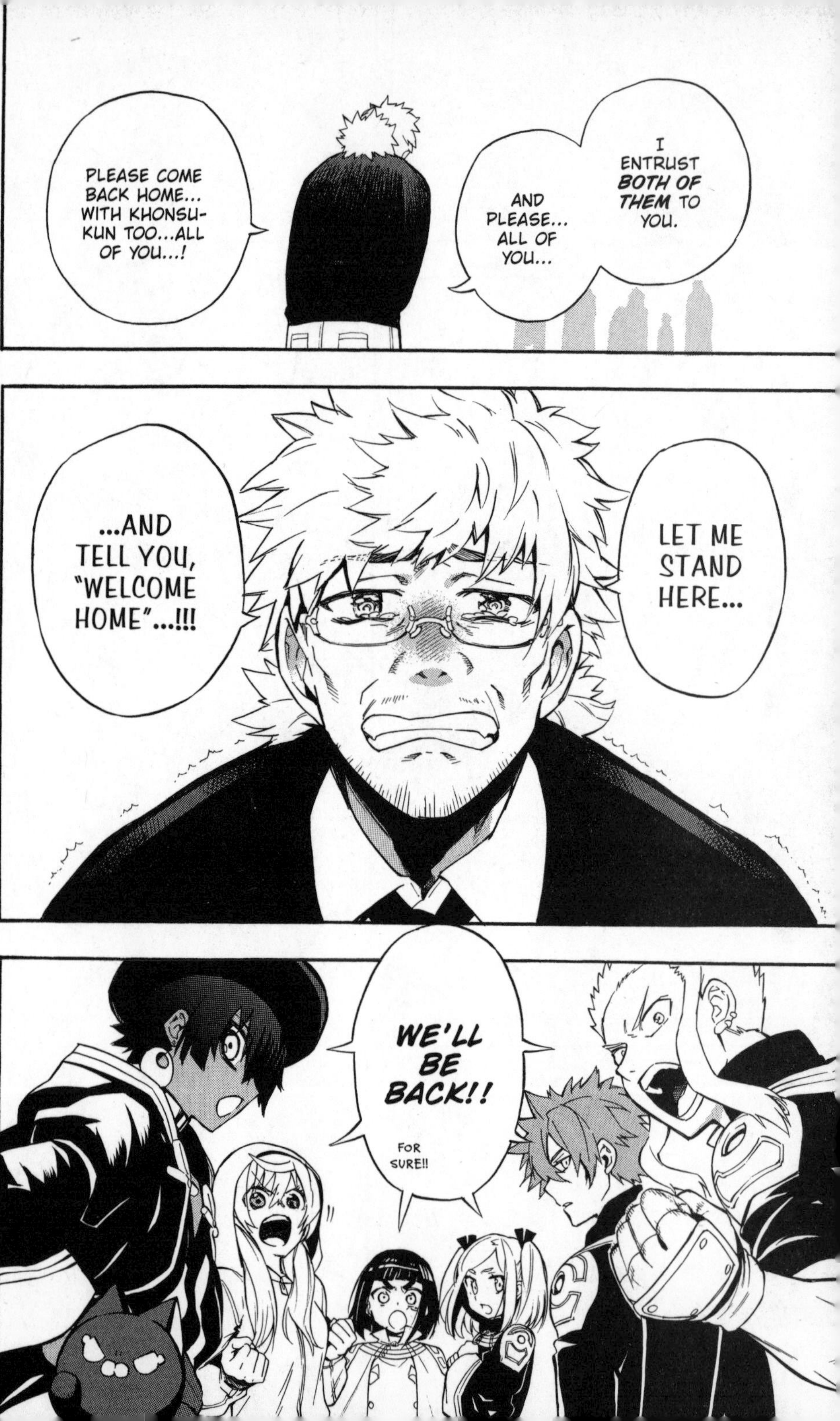
I ENTRUST BOTH OF THEM TO YOU.
AND PLEASE... ALL OF YOU...
PLEASE COME BACK HOME... WITH KHONSU-KUN TOO...ALL OF YOU...!
LET ME STAND HERE...
...AND TELL YOU, "WELCOME HOME"...!!!
WE'LL BE BACK!!
FOR SURE!!

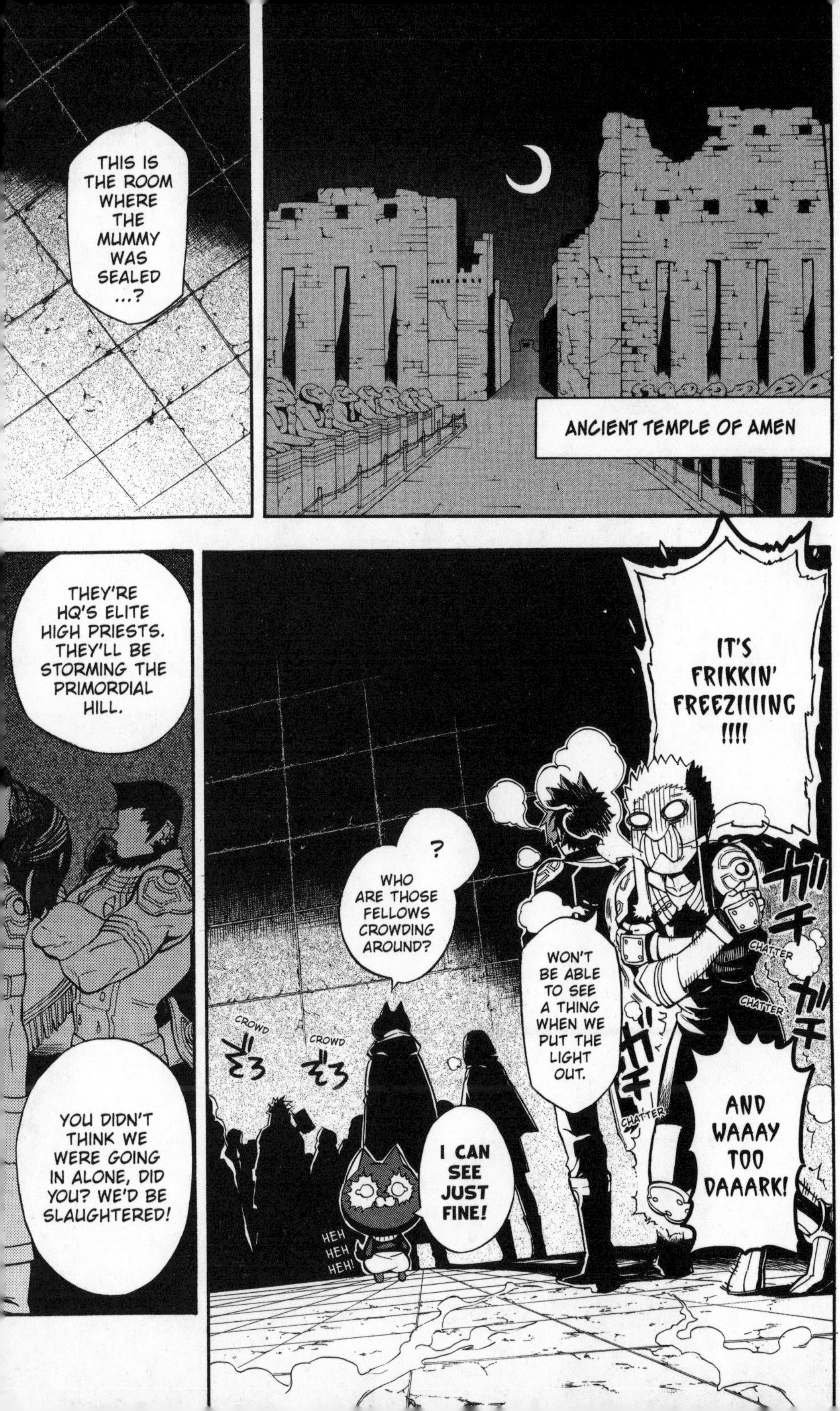
ANCIENT TEMPLE OF AMEN
THIS IS THE ROOM WHERE THE MUMMY WAS SEALED ...?
IT'S FRIKKIN' FREEZIIIING !!!!
CHATTER
CHATTER
AND WAAAY TOO DAAARK!
WON'T BE ABLE TO SEE A THING WHEN WE PUT THE LIGHT OUT.
CHATTER
? WHO ARE THOSE FELLOWS CROWDING AROUND?
I CAN SEE JUST FINE!
HEH HEH HEH!
CROWD
CROWD
THEY'RE HQ'S ELITE HIGH PRIESTS. THEY'LL BE STORMING THE PRIMORDIAL HILL.
YOU DIDN'T THINK WE WERE GOING IN ALONE, DID YOU? WE'D BE SLAUGHTERED!

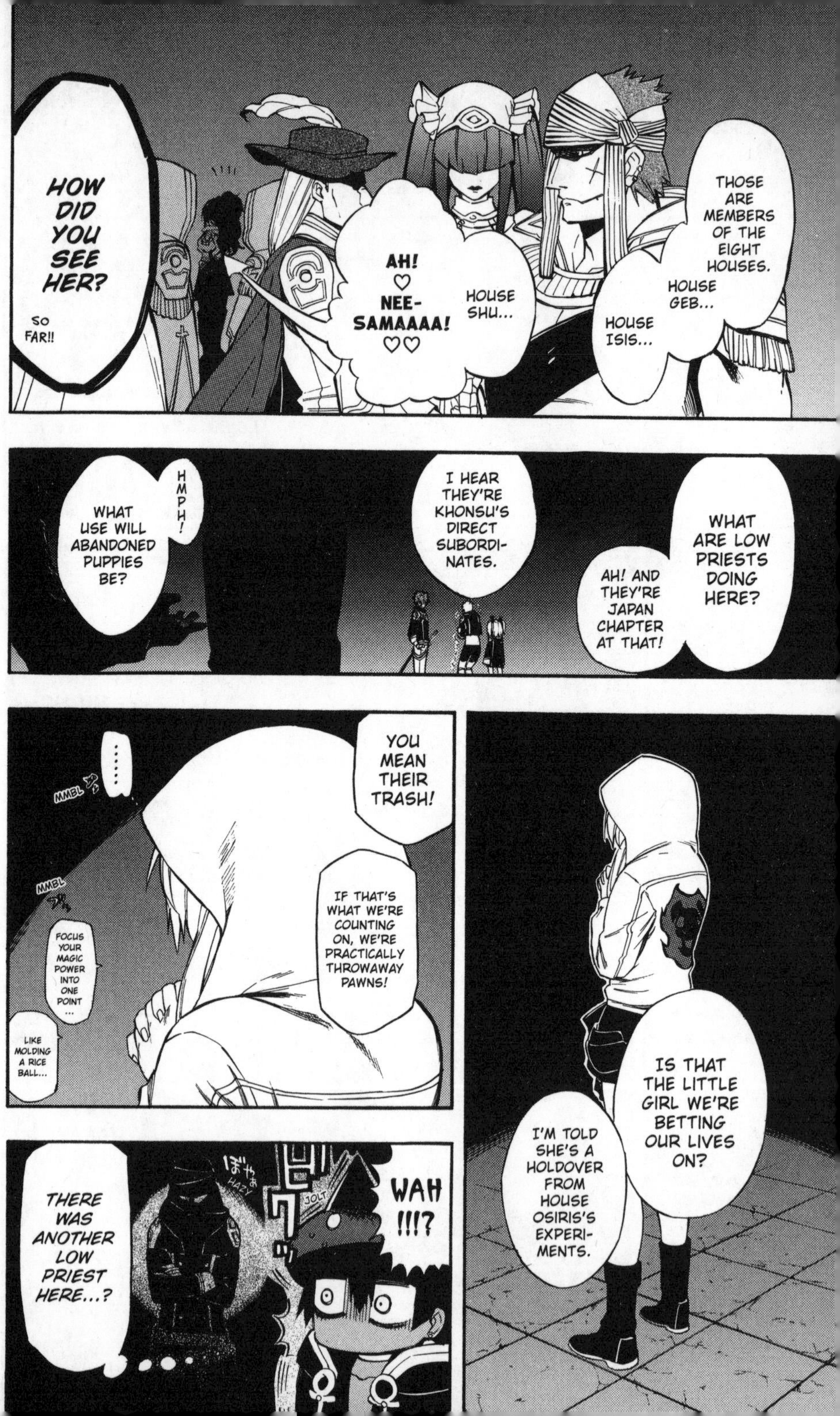
THOSE ARE MEMBERS OF THE EIGHT HOUSES.
HOUSE GEB...
HOUSE ISIS...
HOUSE SHU...
AH! ♡ NEE-SAMAAAAA! ♡♡
HOW DID YOU SEE HER?
SO FAR!!
WHAT ARE LOW PRIESTS DOING HERE?
AH! AND THEY'RE JAPAN CHAPTER AT THAT!
I HEAR THEY'RE KHONSU'S DIRECT SUBORDINATES.
HMPH!
WHAT USE WILL ABANDONED PUPPIES BE?
IS THAT THE LITTLE GIRL WE'RE BETTING OUR LIVES ON?
I'M TOLD SHE'S A HOLDOVER FROM HOUSE OSIRIS'S EXPERIMENTS.
YOU MEAN THEIR TRASH!
IF THAT'S WHAT WE'RE COUNTING ON, WE'RE PRACTICALLY THROWAWAY PAWNS!
......
MMBL
MMBL
FOCUS YOUR MAGIC POWER INTO ONE POINT...
LIKE MOLDING A RICE BALL...
WAH!!!?
JOLT
ぼやぁ HAZY
THERE WAS ANOTHER LOW PRIEST HERE...?
....

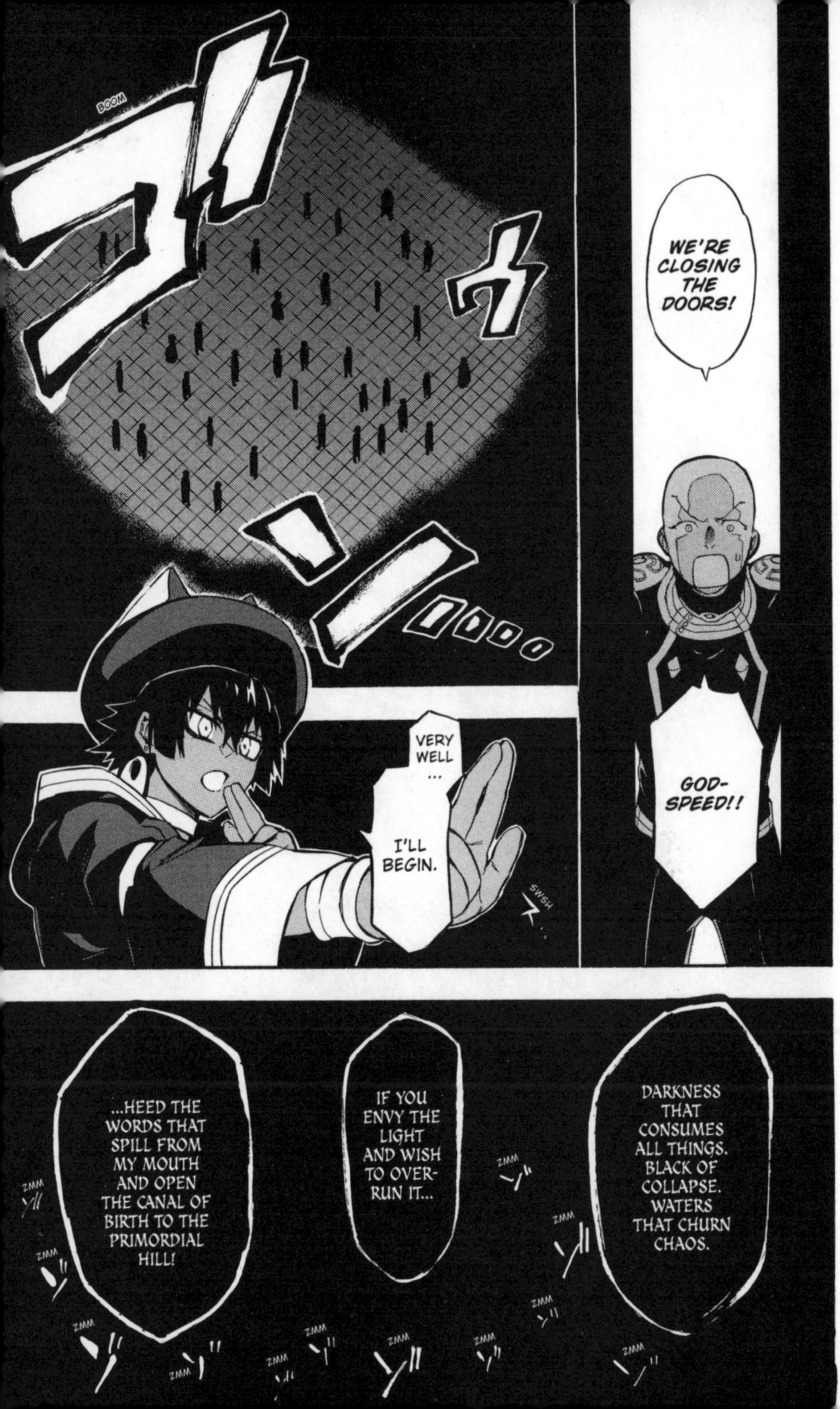
WE'RE CLOSING THE DOORS!
GOD-SPEED!!
BOOM
VERY WELL...
I'LL BEGIN.
SWSH
DARKNESS THAT CONSUMES ALL THINGS. BLACK OF COLLAPSE. WATERS THAT CHURN CHAOS.
IF YOU ENVY THE LIGHT AND WISH TO OVER-RUN IT...
...HEED THE WORDS THAT SPILL FROM MY MOUTH AND OPEN THE CANAL OF BIRTH TO THE PRIMORDIAL HILL!
ZMM

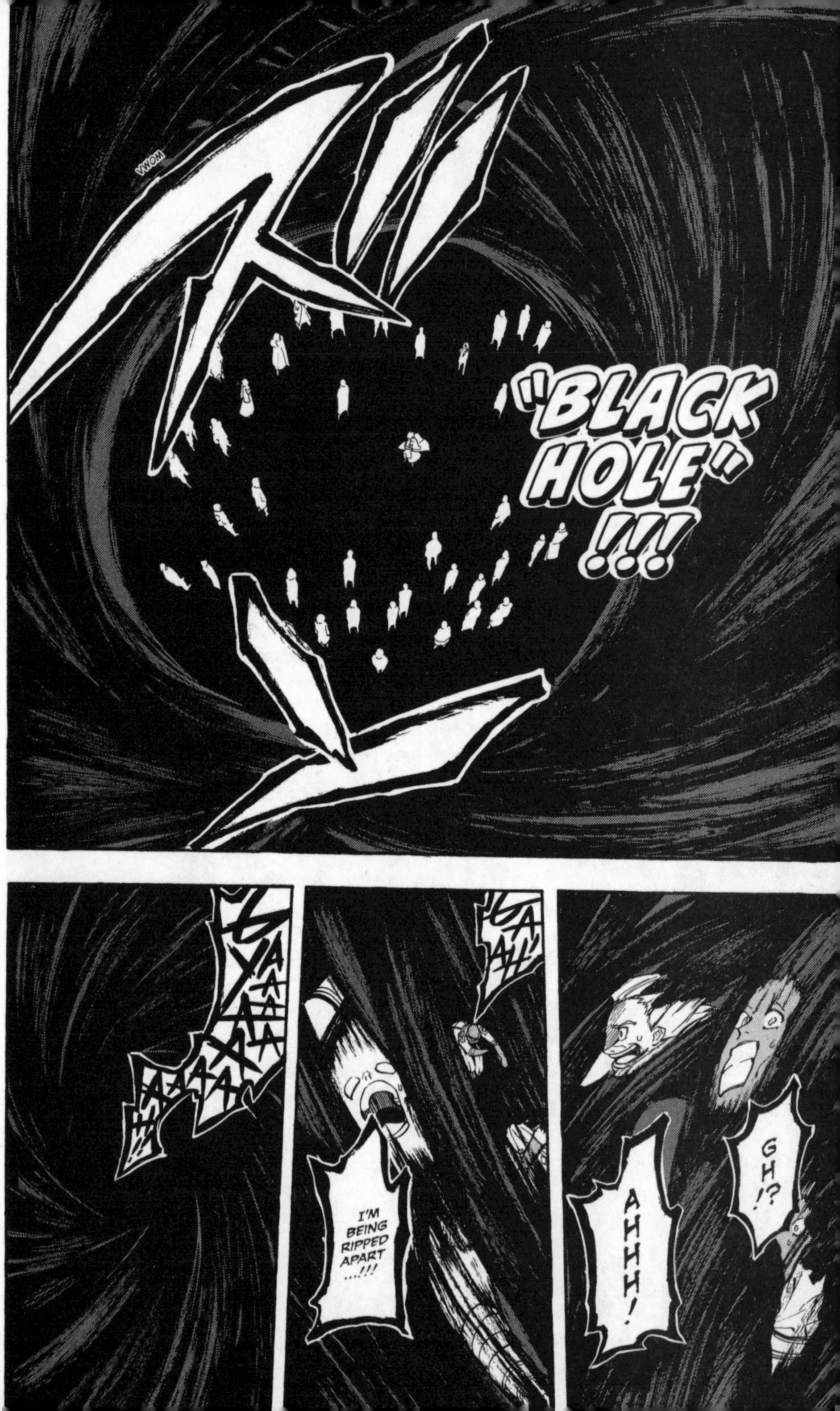
VWOM
"BLACK HOLE"!!!
GH!?
AHHH!
I'M BEING RIPPED APART ....!!!

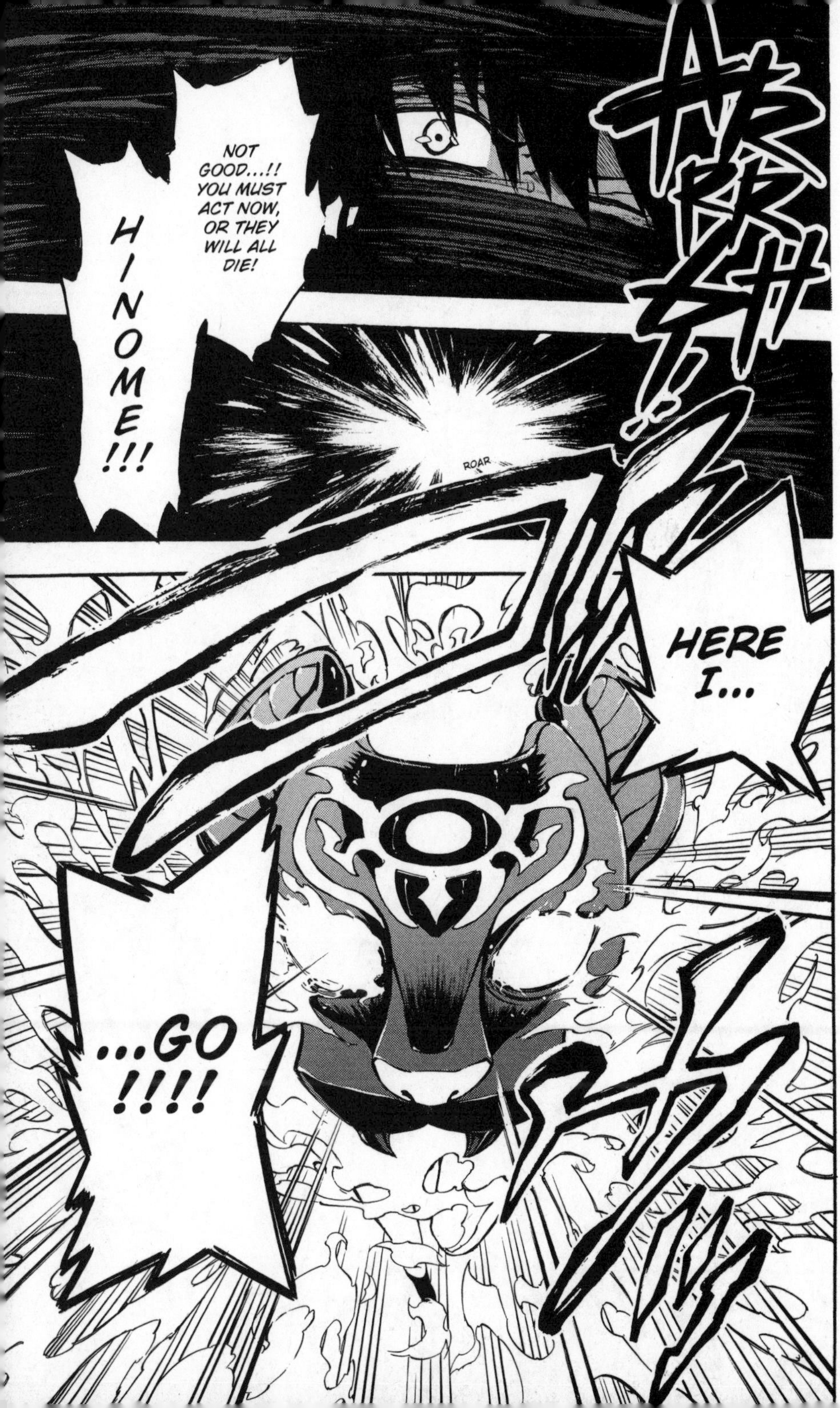
NOT GOOD...!! YOU MUST ACT NOW, OR THEY WILL ALL DIE!
HINOME!!!
ROAR
HERE I...
...GO!!!!

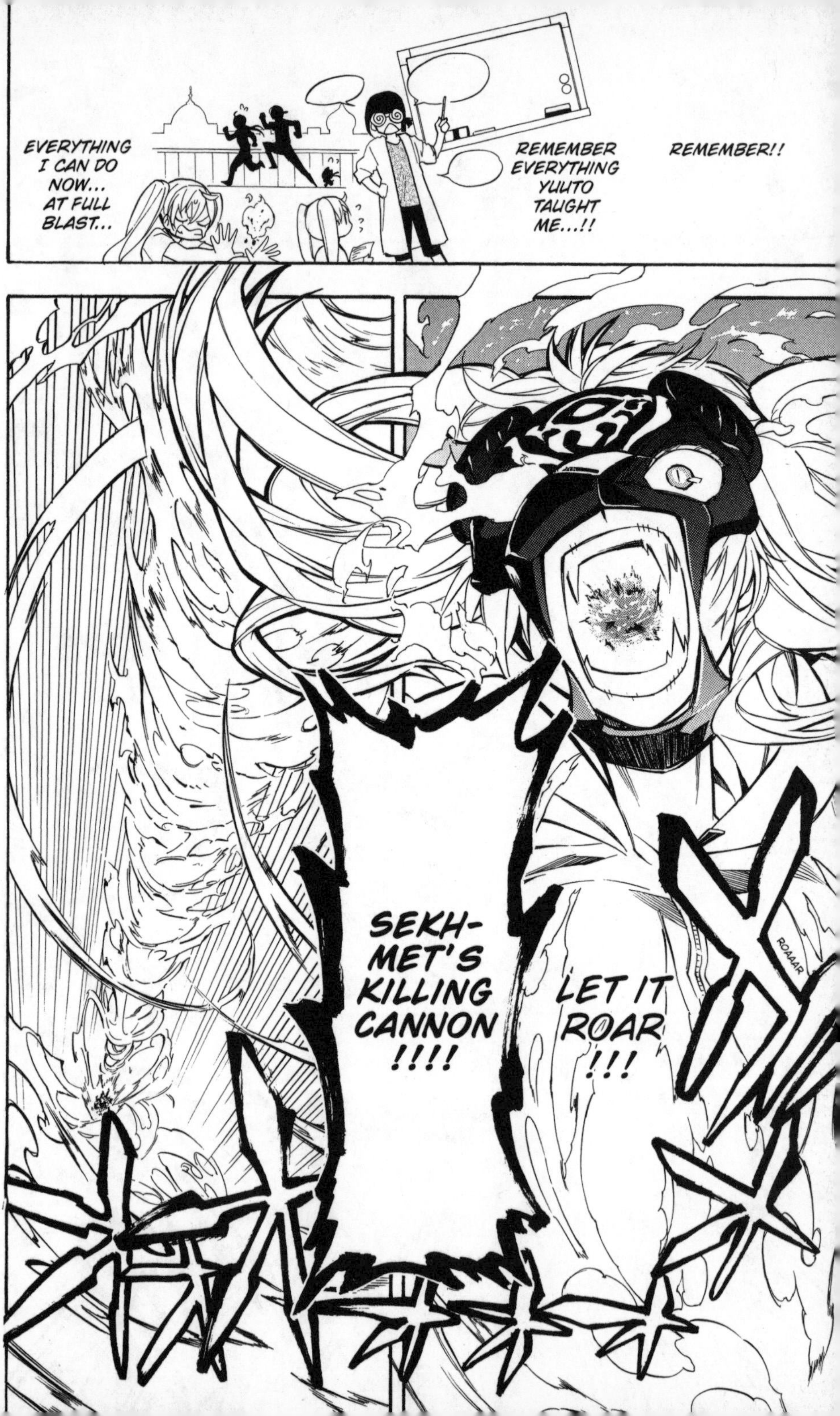
REMEMBER!!
REMEMBER EVERYTHING YUUTO TAUGHT ME...!!
EVERYTHING I CAN DO NOW... AT FULL BLAST...
ROAAAR
LET IT ROAR!!!
SEKH-MET'S KILLING CANNON!!!!

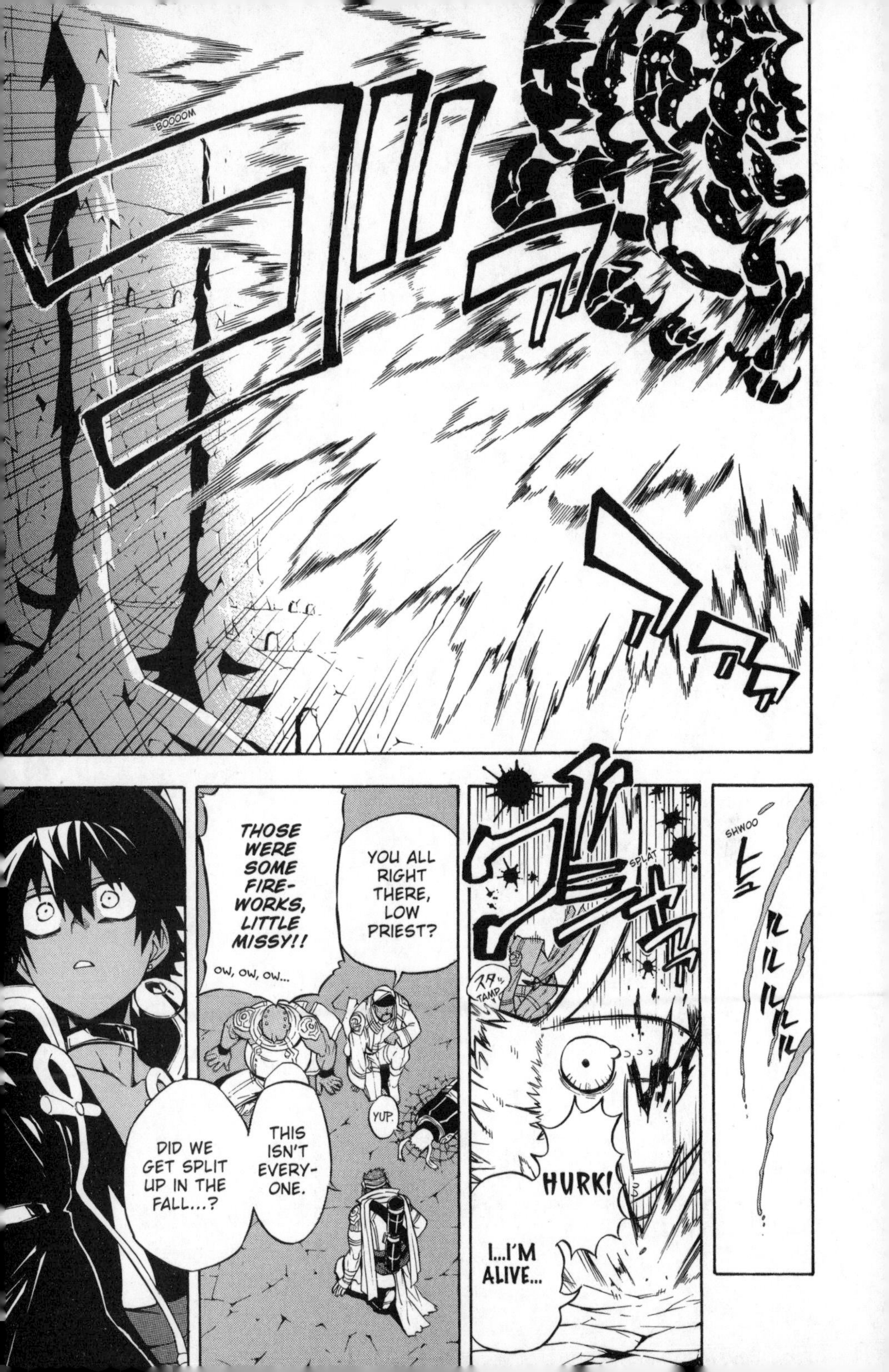
BOOOOM
SHWOO
SPLAT
TAMP
HURK!
I...I'M ALIVE...
YOU ALL RIGHT THERE, LOW PRIEST?
THOSE WERE SOME FIRE-WORKS, LITTLE MISSY!!
OW, OW, OW...
YUP.
THIS ISN'T EVERY-ONE.
DID WE GET SPLIT UP IN THE FALL...?

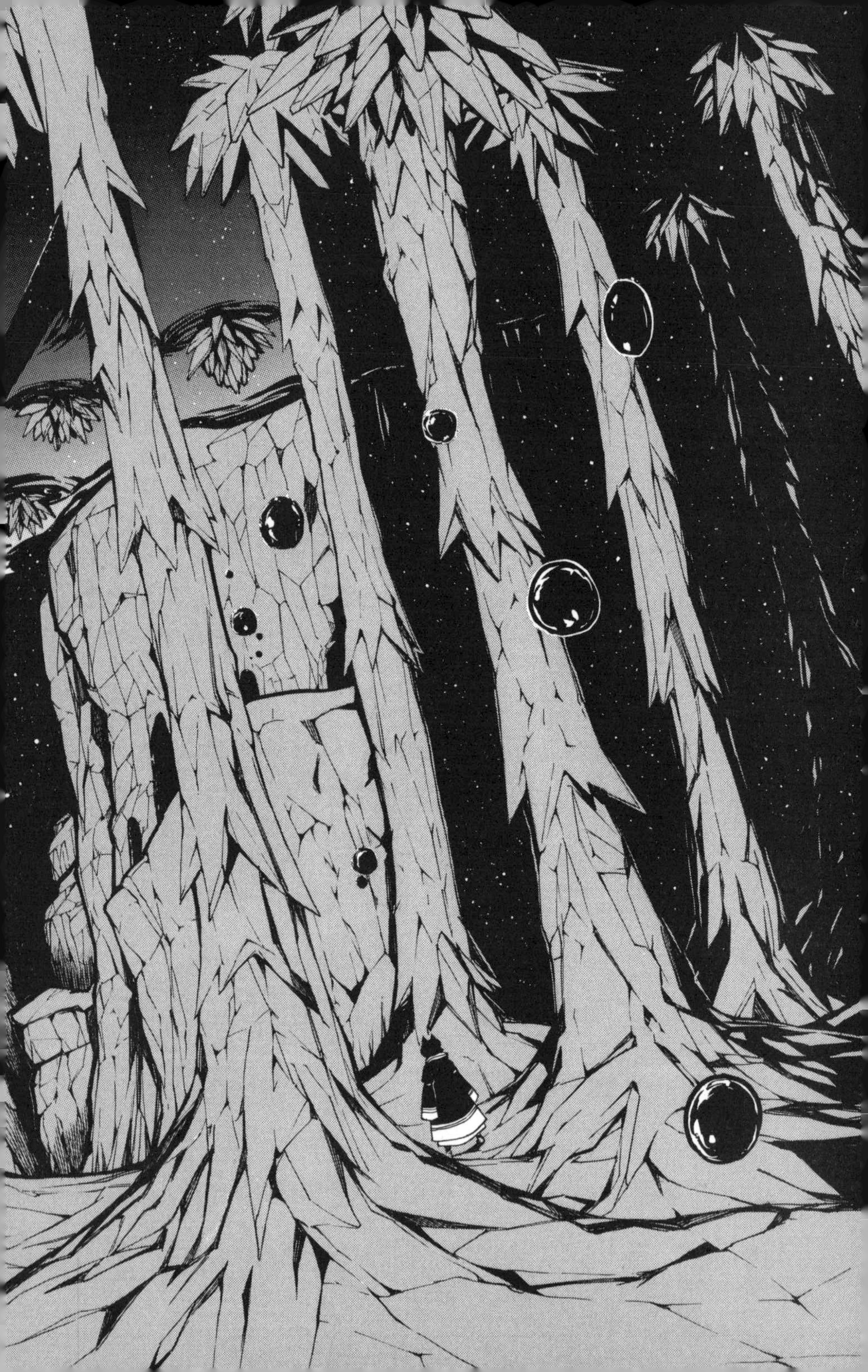

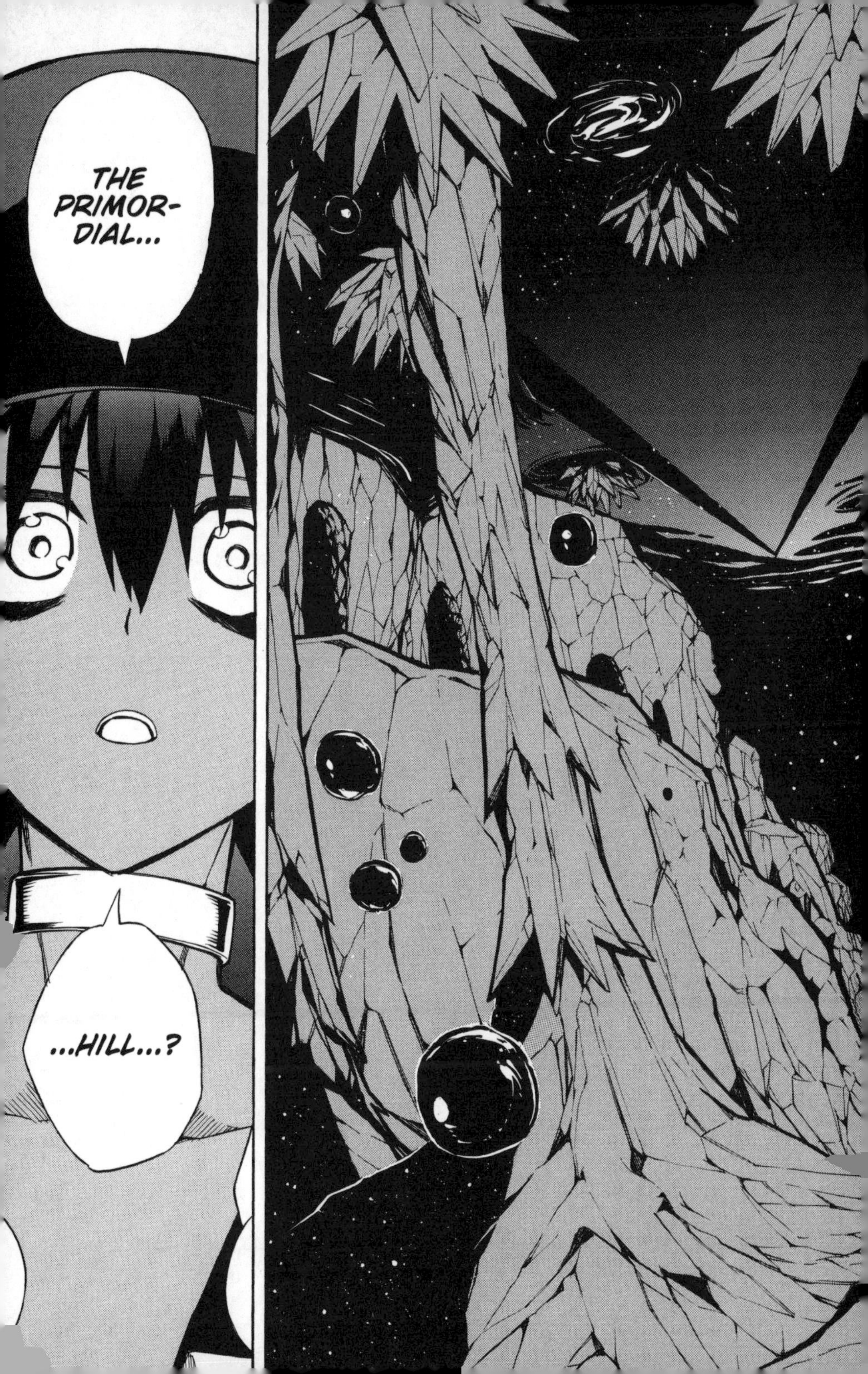
THE PRIMORDIAL...
...HILL...?

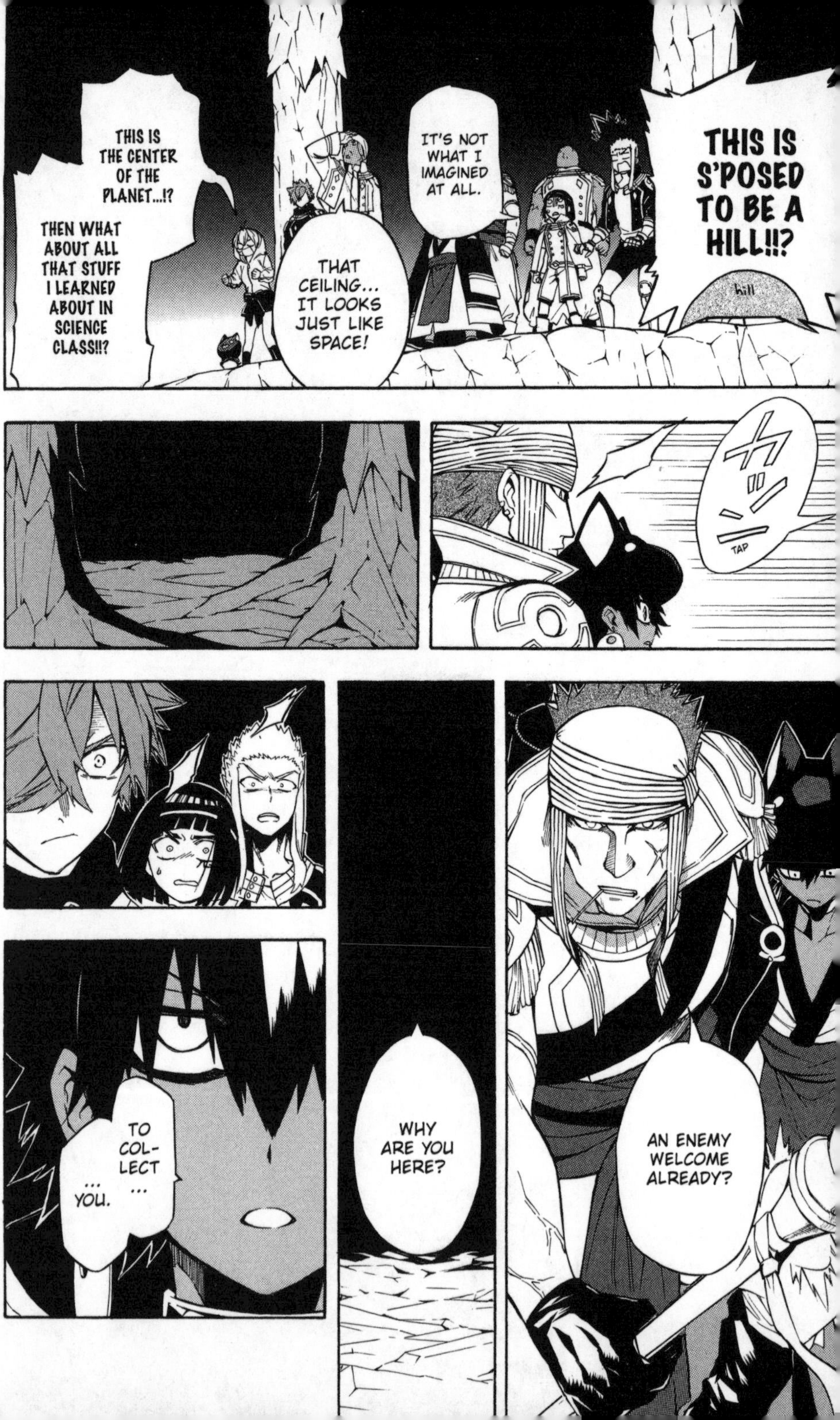
THIS IS S'POSED TO BE A HILL!!?
hill
IT'S NOT WHAT I IMAGINED AT ALL.
THAT CEILING... IT LOOKS JUST LIKE SPACE!
THIS IS THE CENTER OF THE PLANET...!?
THEN WHAT ABOUT ALL THAT STUFF I LEARNED ABOUT IN SCIENCE CLASS!!?
TAP
AN ENEMY WELCOME ALREADY?
WHY ARE YOU HERE?
TO COL-LECT ... ... YOU.

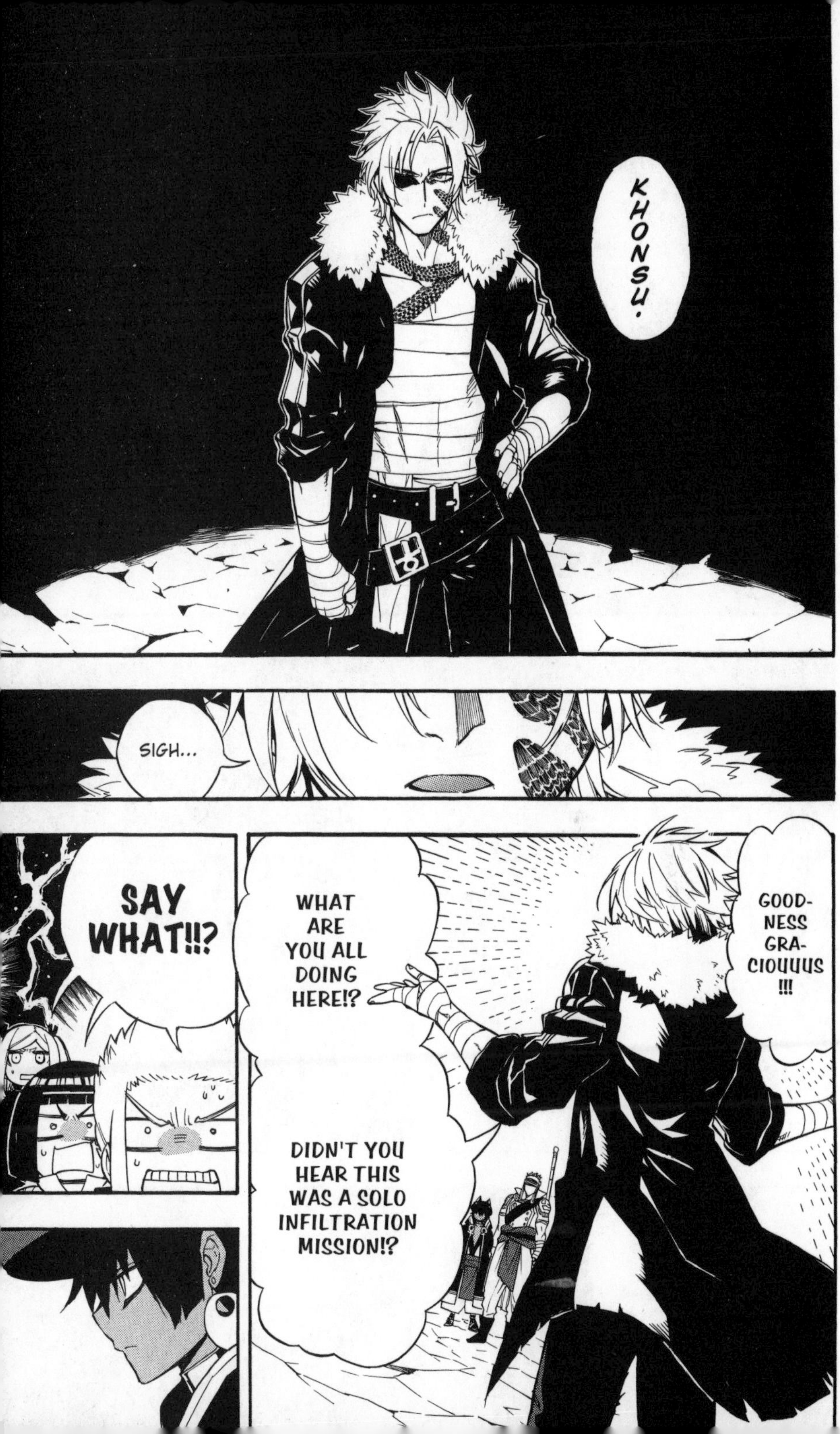
KHONSU.
SIGH...
GOODNESS GRACIOUUUS!!!
WHAT ARE YOU ALL DOING HERE!?
DIDN'T YOU HEAR THIS WAS A SOLO INFILTRATION MISSION!?
SAY WHAT!!?

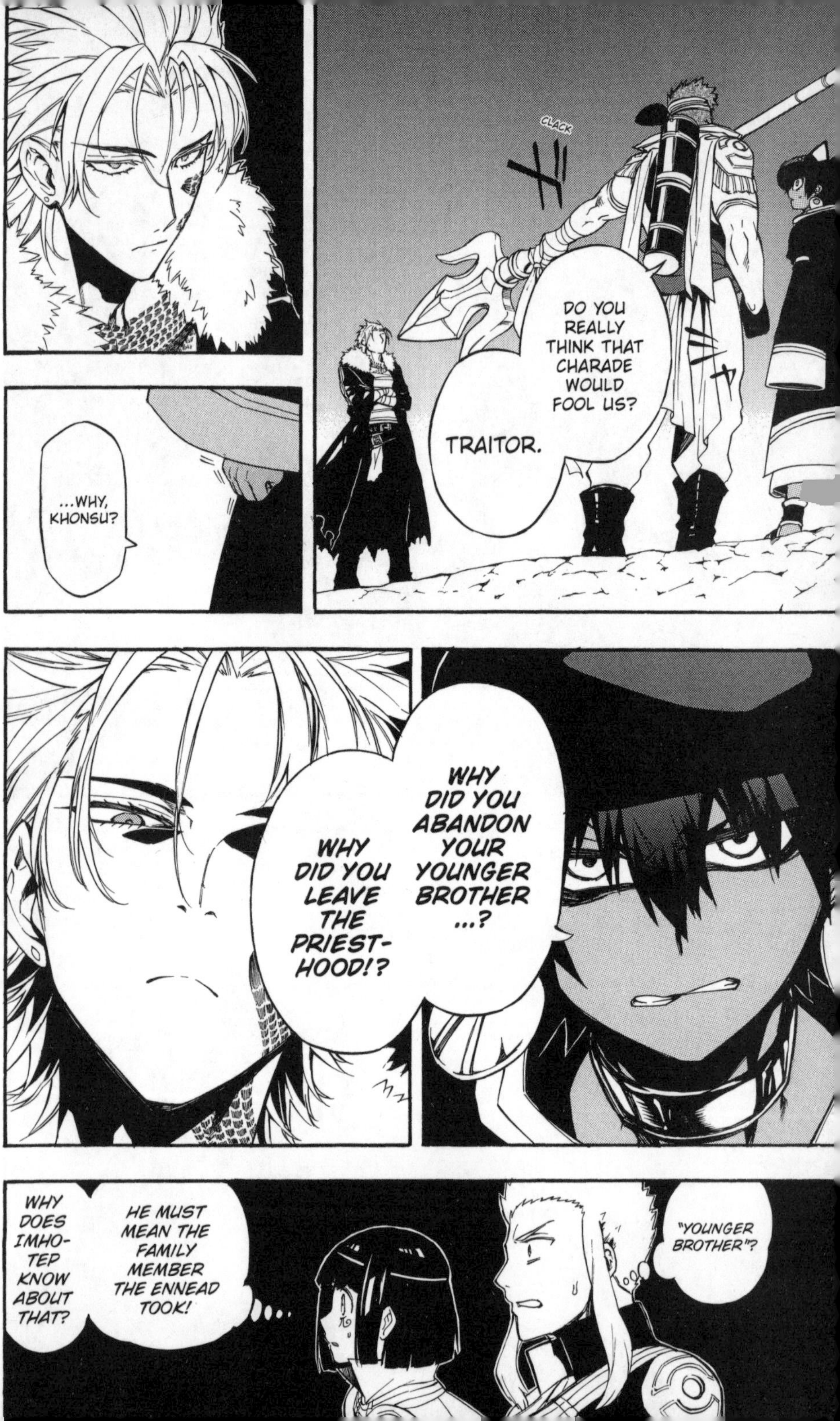
CLACK
DO YOU REALLY THINK THAT CHARADE WOULD FOOL US?
TRAITOR.
...WHY, KHONSU?
WHY DID YOU ABANDON YOUR YOUNGER BROTHER ...?
WHY DID YOU LEAVE THE PRIEST-HOOD!?
"YOUNGER BROTHER"?
HE MUST MEAN THE FAMILY MEMBER THE ENNEAD TOOK!
WHY DOES IMHO-TEP KNOW ABOUT THAT?

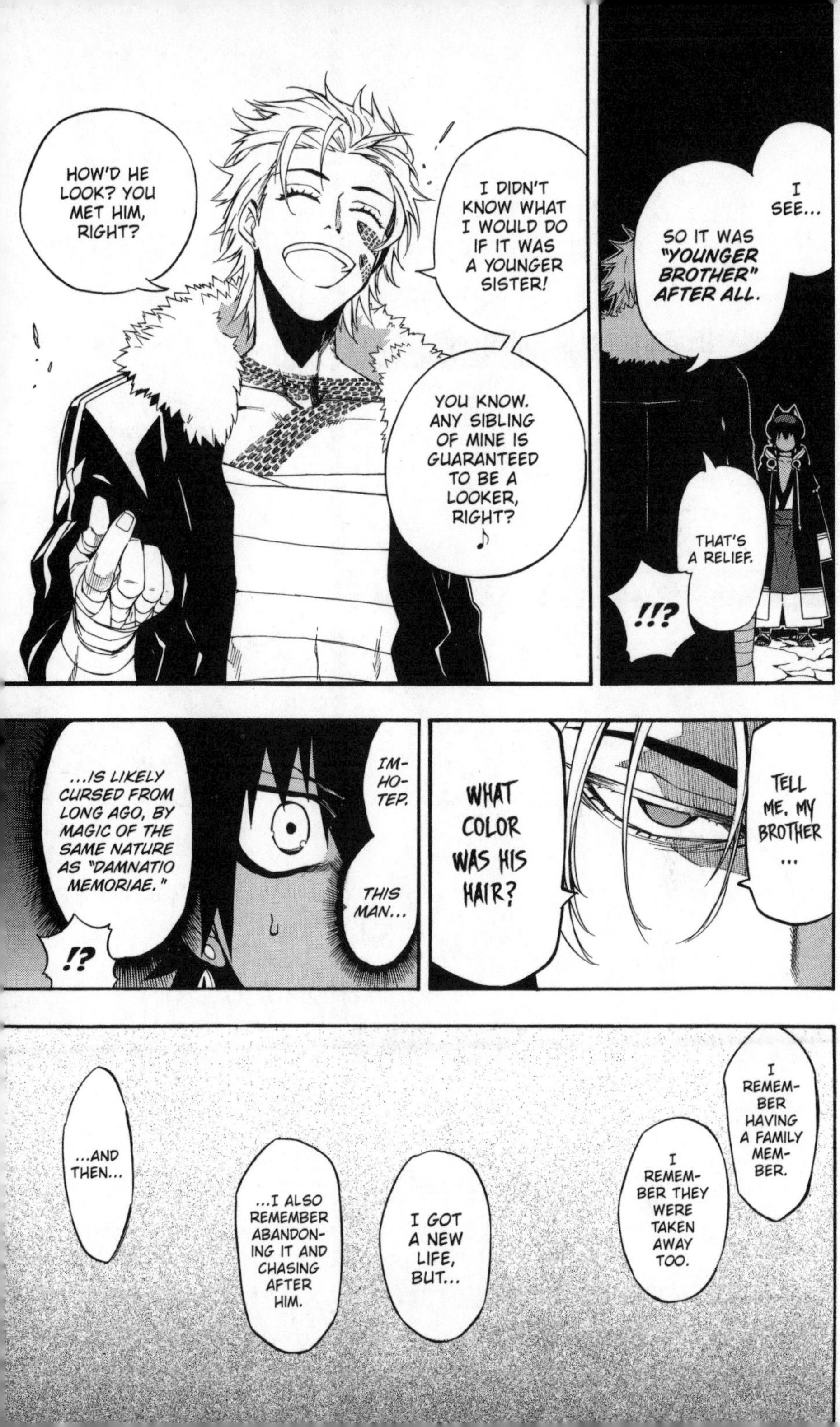
I SEE...
SO IT WAS "YOUNGER BROTHER" AFTER ALL.
THAT'S A RELIEF.
!!?
I DIDN'T KNOW WHAT I WOULD DO IF IT WAS A YOUNGER SISTER!
YOU KNOW. ANY SIBLING OF MINE IS GUARANTEED TO BE A LOOKER, RIGHT? ♪
HOW'D HE LOOK? YOU MET HIM, RIGHT?
TELL ME, MY BROTHER ...
WHAT COLOR WAS HIS HAIR?
IMHOTEP.
THIS MAN...
...IS LIKELY CURSED FROM LONG AGO, BY MAGIC OF THE SAME NATURE AS "DAMNATIO MEMORIAE."
!?
I REMEMBER HAVING A FAMILY MEMBER.
I REMEMBER THEY WERE TAKEN AWAY TOO.
I GOT A NEW LIFE, BUT...
...I ALSO REMEMBER ABANDONING IT AND CHASING AFTER HIM.
...AND THEN...

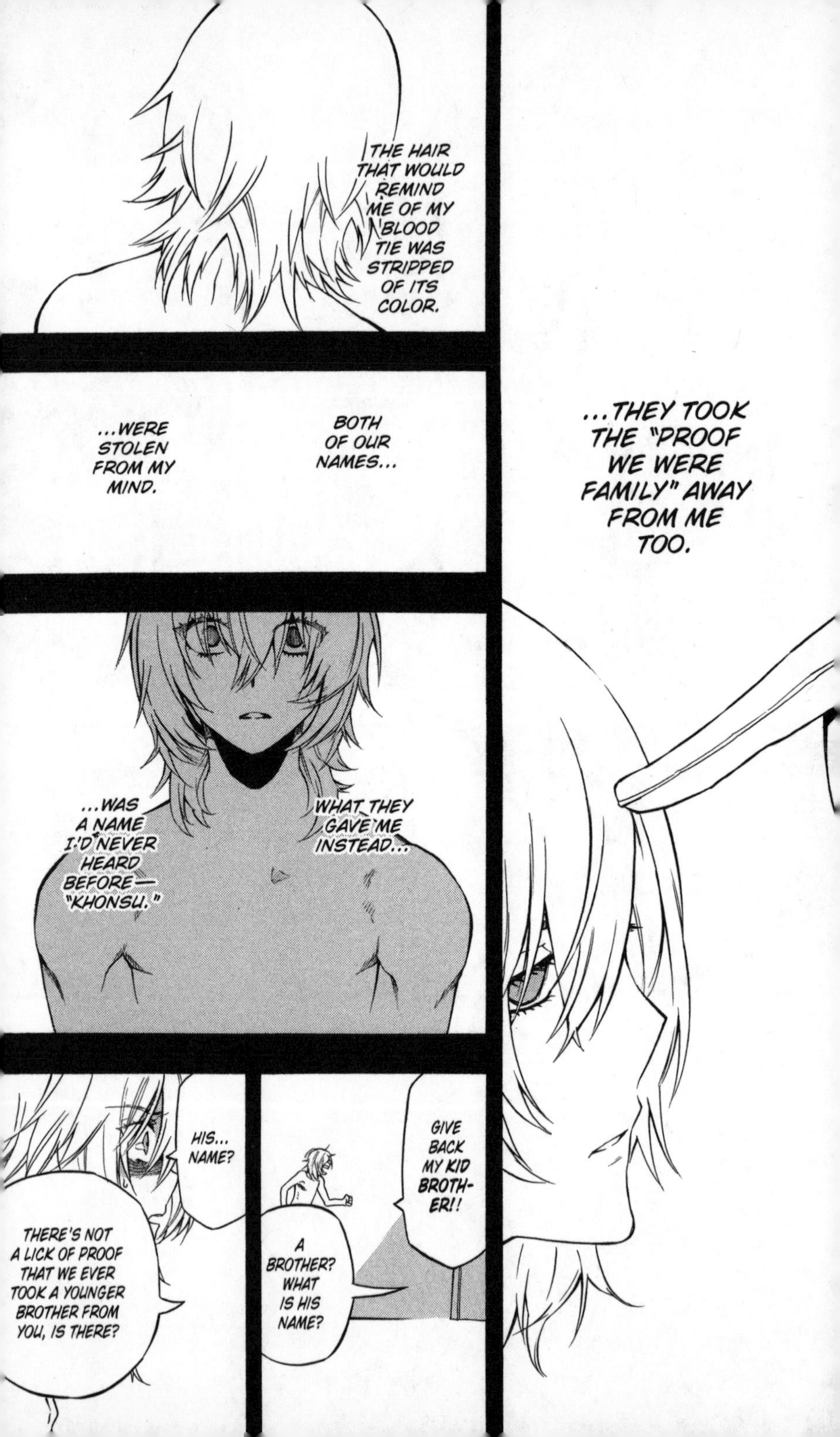
...THEY TOOK THE "PROOF WE WERE FAMILY" AWAY FROM ME TOO.
THE HAIR THAT WOULD REMIND ME OF MY BLOOD TIE WAS STRIPPED OF ITS COLOR.
BOTH OF OUR NAMES...
...WERE STOLEN FROM MY MIND.
WHAT THEY GAVE ME INSTEAD...
...WAS A NAME I'D NEVER HEARD BEFORE— "KHONSU."
GIVE BACK MY KID BROTHER!!
A BROTHER? WHAT IS HIS NAME?
HIS... NAME?
THERE'S NOT A LICK OF PROOF THAT WE EVER TOOK A YOUNGER BROTHER FROM YOU, IS THERE?

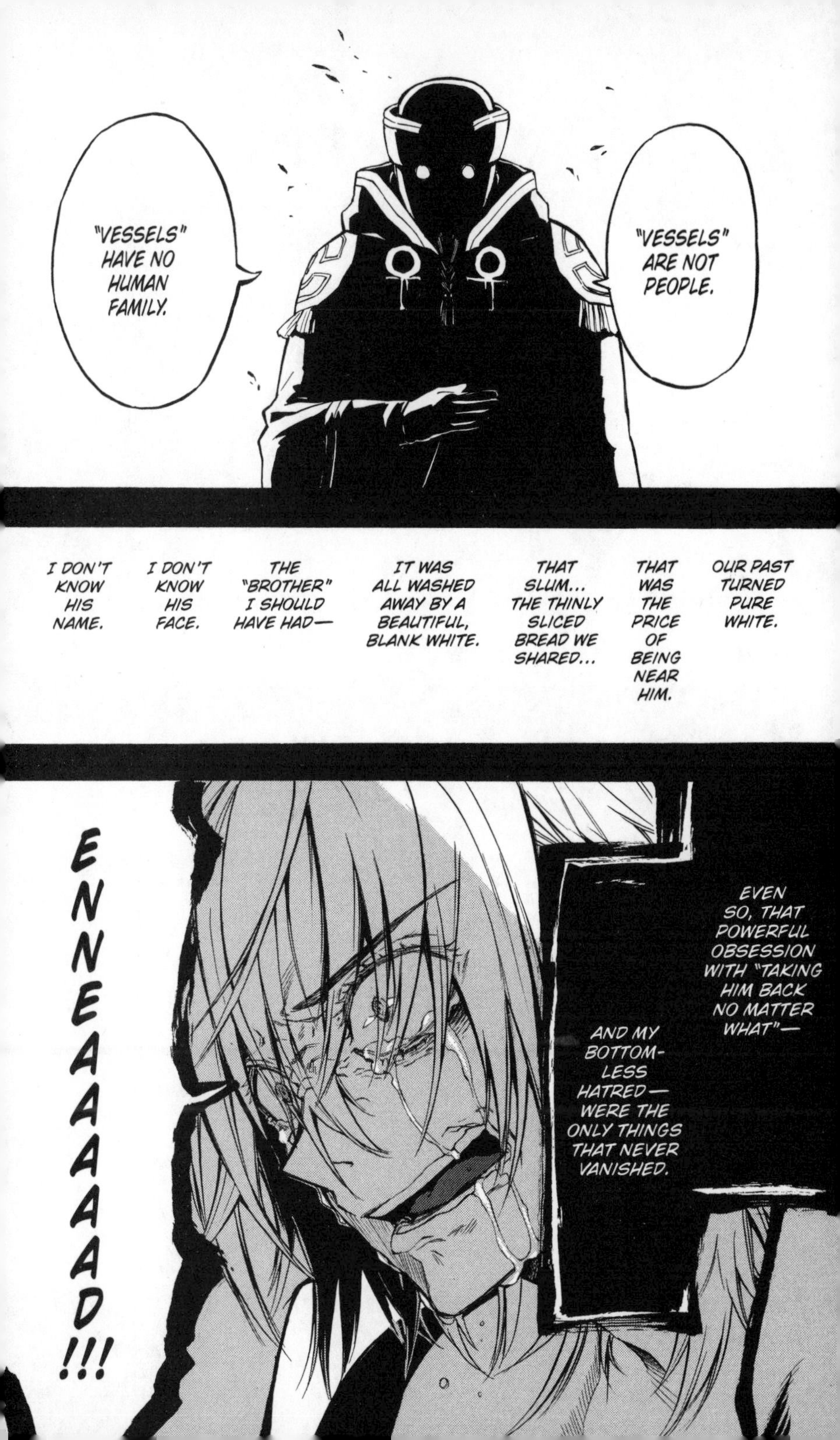
"VESSELS" ARE NOT PEOPLE.
"VESSELS" HAVE NO HUMAN FAMILY.
OUR PAST TURNED PURE WHITE.
THAT WAS THE PRICE OF BEING NEAR HIM.
THAT SLUM... THE THINLY SLICED BREAD WE SHARED...
IT WAS ALL WASHED AWAY BY A BEAUTIFUL, BLANK WHITE.
THE "BROTHER" I SHOULD HAVE HAD—
I DON'T KNOW HIS FACE.
I DON'T KNOW HIS NAME.
EVEN SO, THAT POWERFUL OBSESSION WITH "TAKING HIM BACK NO MATTER WHAT"—
AND MY BOTTOM-LESS HATRED—WERE THE ONLY THINGS THAT NEVER VANISHED.
ENNEAAAAAAAD!!!

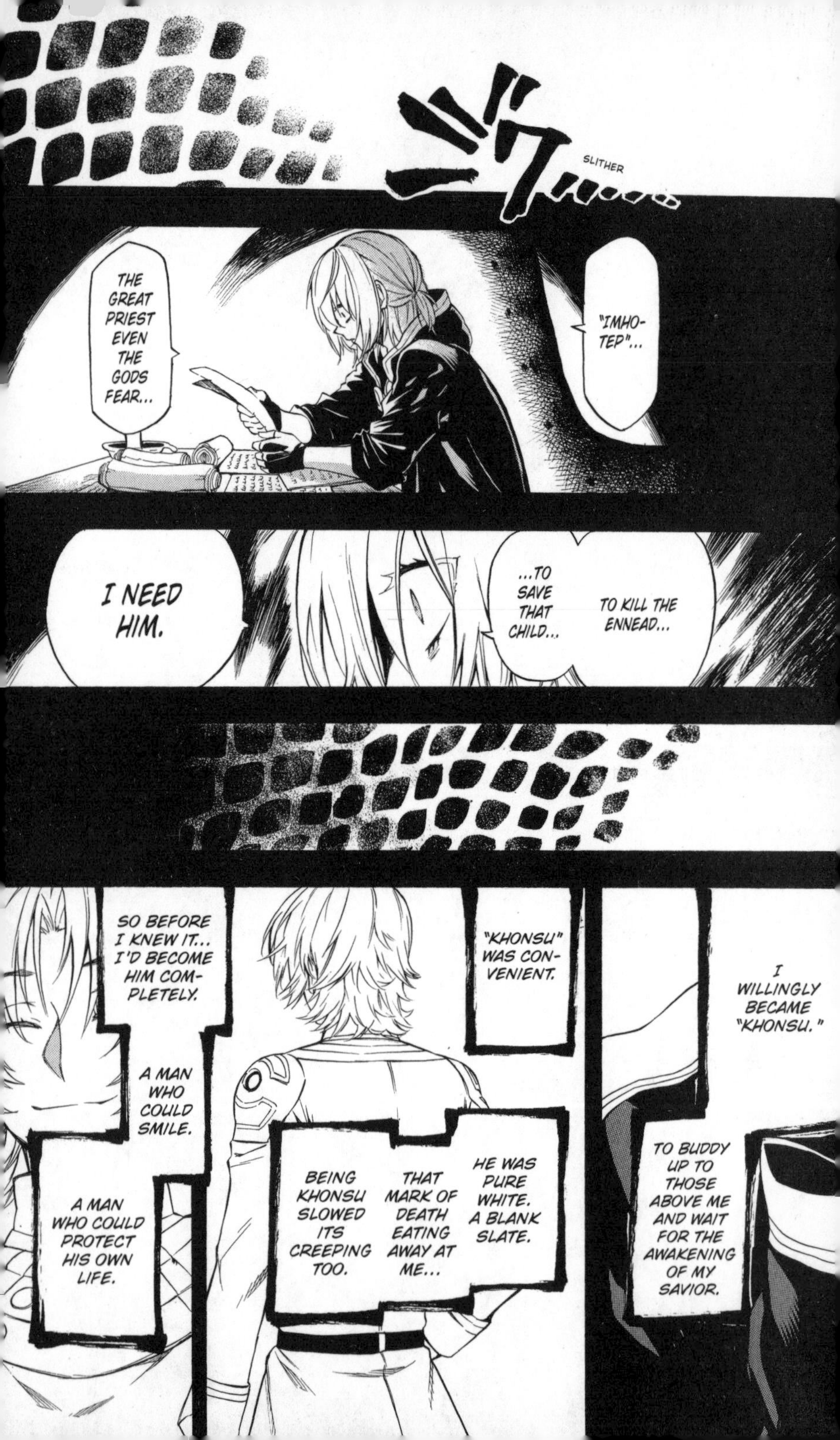
SLITHER
"IMHO-TEP"...
THE GREAT PRIEST EVEN THE GODS FEAR...
TO KILL THE ENNEAD...
...TO SAVE THAT CHILD...
I NEED HIM.
I WILLINGLY BECAME "KHONSU."
TO BUDDY UP TO THOSE ABOVE ME AND WAIT FOR THE AWAKENING OF MY SAVIOR.
"KHONSU" WAS CON-VENIENT.
HE WAS PURE WHITE. A BLANK SLATE.
THAT MARK OF DEATH EATING AWAY AT ME...
BEING KHONSU SLOWED ITS CREEPING TOO.
SO BEFORE I KNEW IT... I'D BECOME HIM COM-PLETELY.
A MAN WHO COULD SMILE.
A MAN WHO COULD PROTECT HIS OWN LIFE.

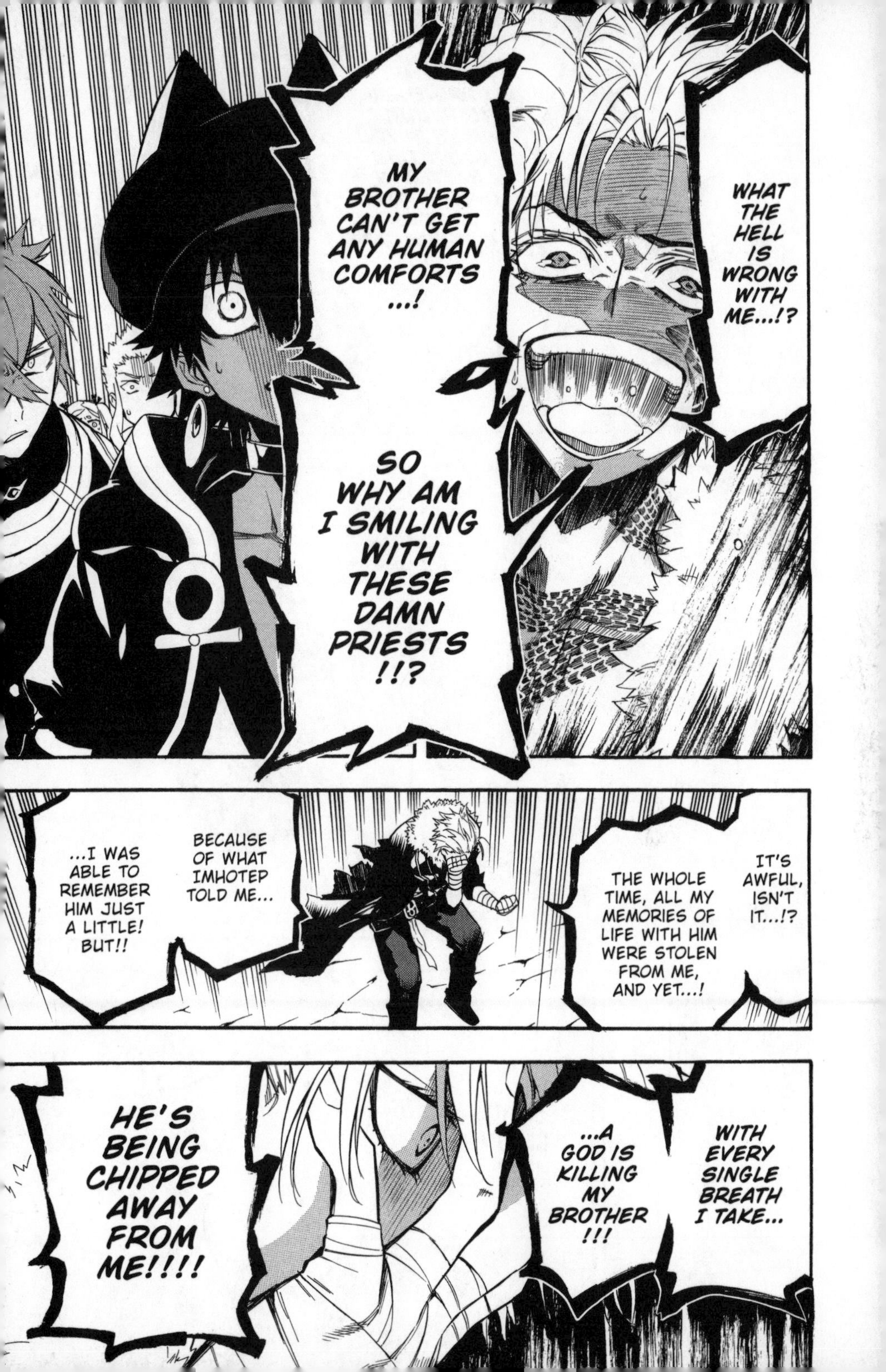
WHAT THE HELL IS WRONG WITH ME...!?
MY BROTHER CAN'T GET ANY HUMAN COMFORTS ...!
SO WHY AM I SMILING WITH THESE DAMN PRIESTS !!?
IT'S AWFUL, ISN'T IT...!?
THE WHOLE TIME, ALL MY MEMORIES OF LIFE WITH HIM WERE STOLEN FROM ME, AND YET...!
BECAUSE OF WHAT IMHOTEP TOLD ME...
...I WAS ABLE TO REMEMBER HIM JUST A LITTLE! BUT!!
WITH EVERY SINGLE BREATH I TAKE...
...A GOD IS KILLING MY BROTHER !!!
HE'S BEING CHIPPED AWAY FROM ME!!!!

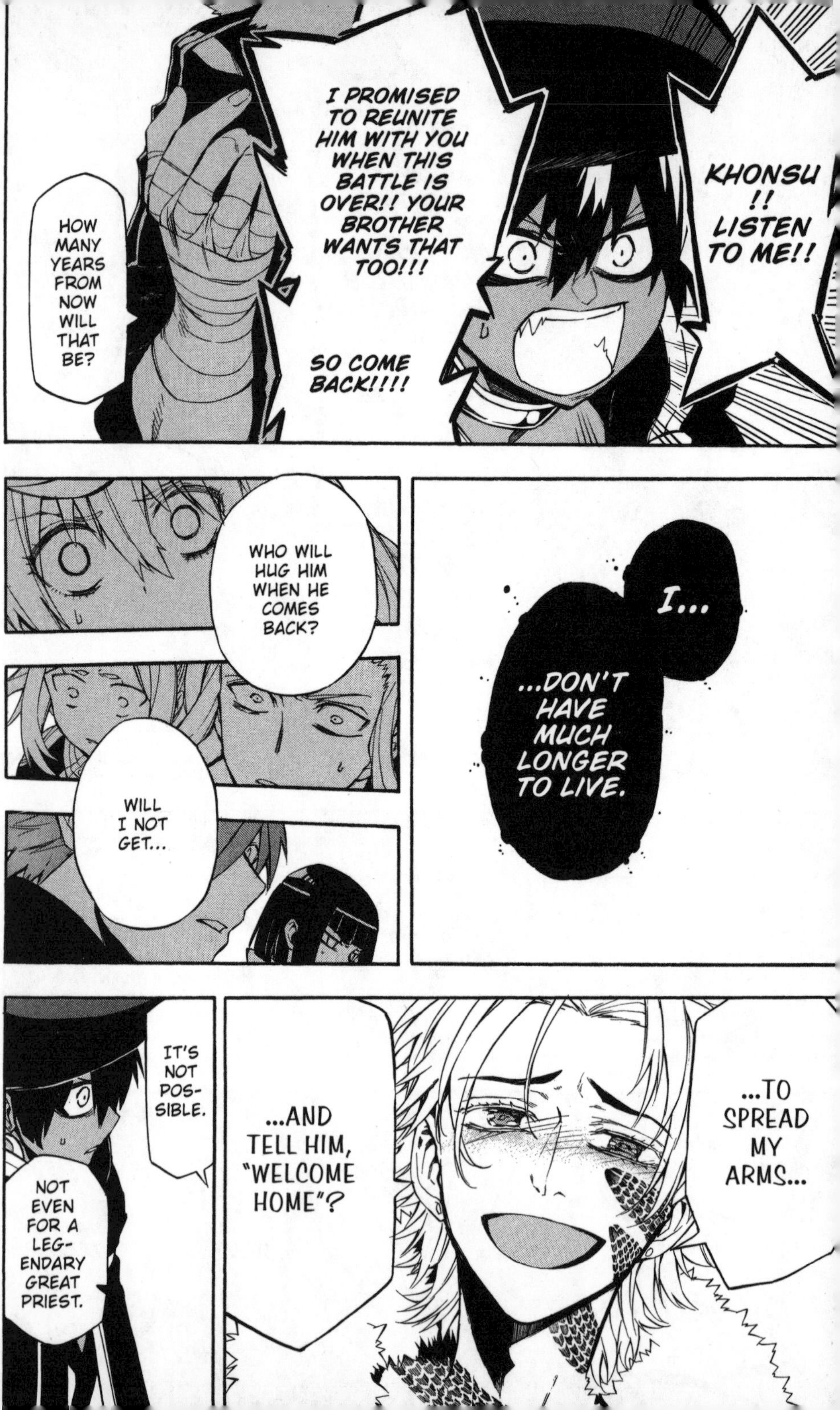
KHONSU!! LISTEN TO ME!!
I PROMISED TO REUNITE HIM WITH YOU WHEN THIS BATTLE IS OVER!! YOUR BROTHER WANTS THAT TOO!!!
SO COME BACK!!!!
HOW MANY YEARS FROM NOW WILL THAT BE?
I...
...DON'T HAVE MUCH LONGER TO LIVE.
WHO WILL HUG HIM WHEN HE COMES BACK?
WILL I NOT GET...
...TO SPREAD MY ARMS...
...AND TELL HIM, "WELCOME HOME"?
IT'S NOT POS-SIBLE.
NOT EVEN FOR A LEG-ENDARY GREAT PRIEST.

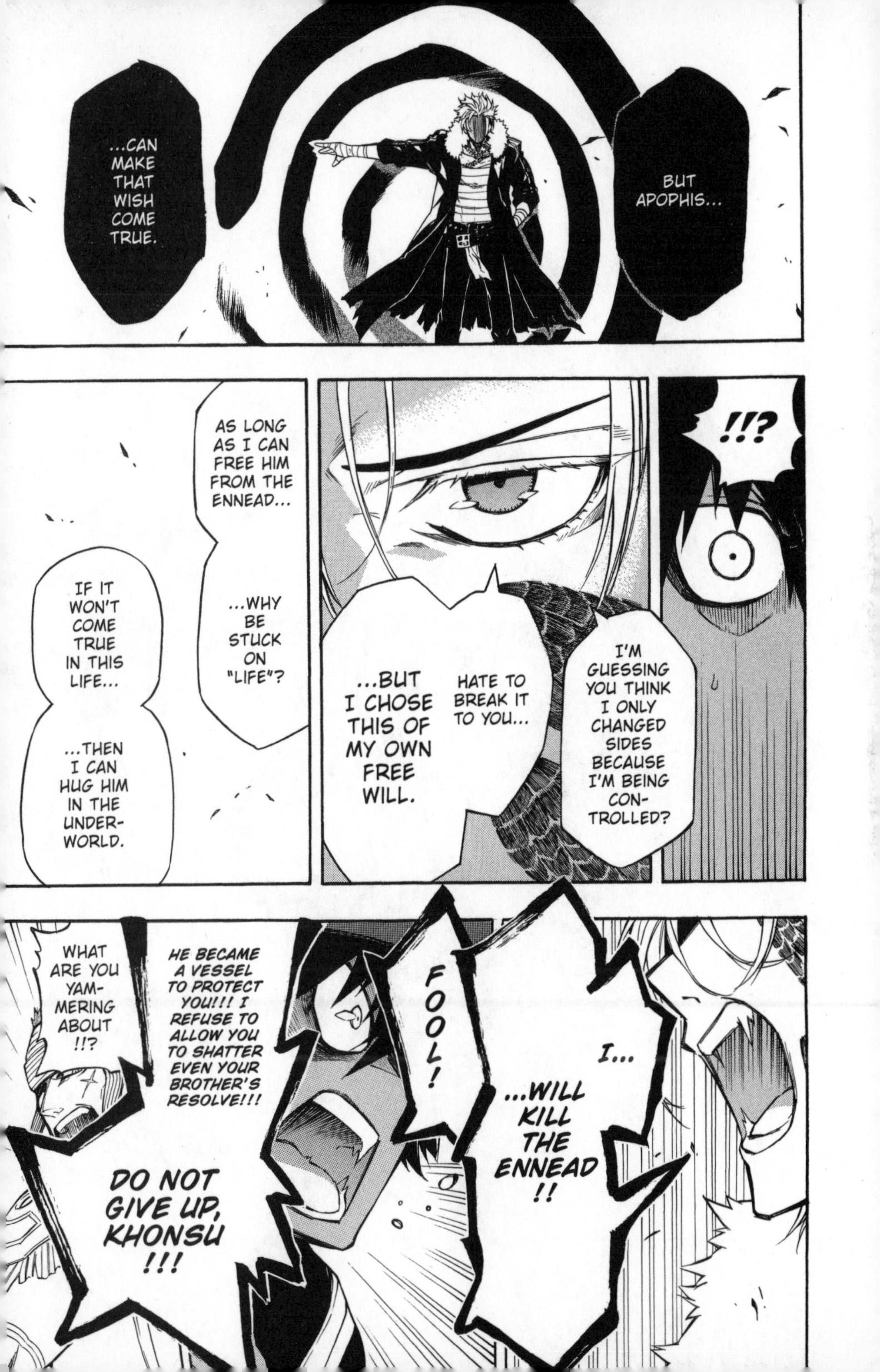
BUT APOPHIS...
...CAN MAKE THAT WISH COME TRUE.
!!?
I'M GUESSING YOU THINK I ONLY CHANGED SIDES BECAUSE I'M BEING CONTROLLED?
HATE TO BREAK IT TO YOU...
...BUT I CHOSE THIS OF MY OWN FREE WILL.
AS LONG AS I CAN FREE HIM FROM THE ENNEAD...
...WHY BE STUCK ON "LIFE"?
IF IT WON'T COME TRUE IN THIS LIFE...
...THEN I CAN HUG HIM IN THE UNDER-WORLD.
I...
...WILL KILL THE ENNEAD!!
FOOL!
HE BECAME A VESSEL TO PROTECT YOU!!! I REFUSE TO ALLOW YOU TO SHATTER EVEN YOUR BROTHER'S RESOLVE!!!
WHAT ARE YOU YAM-MERING ABOUT!!?
DO NOT GIVE UP, KHONSU!!!

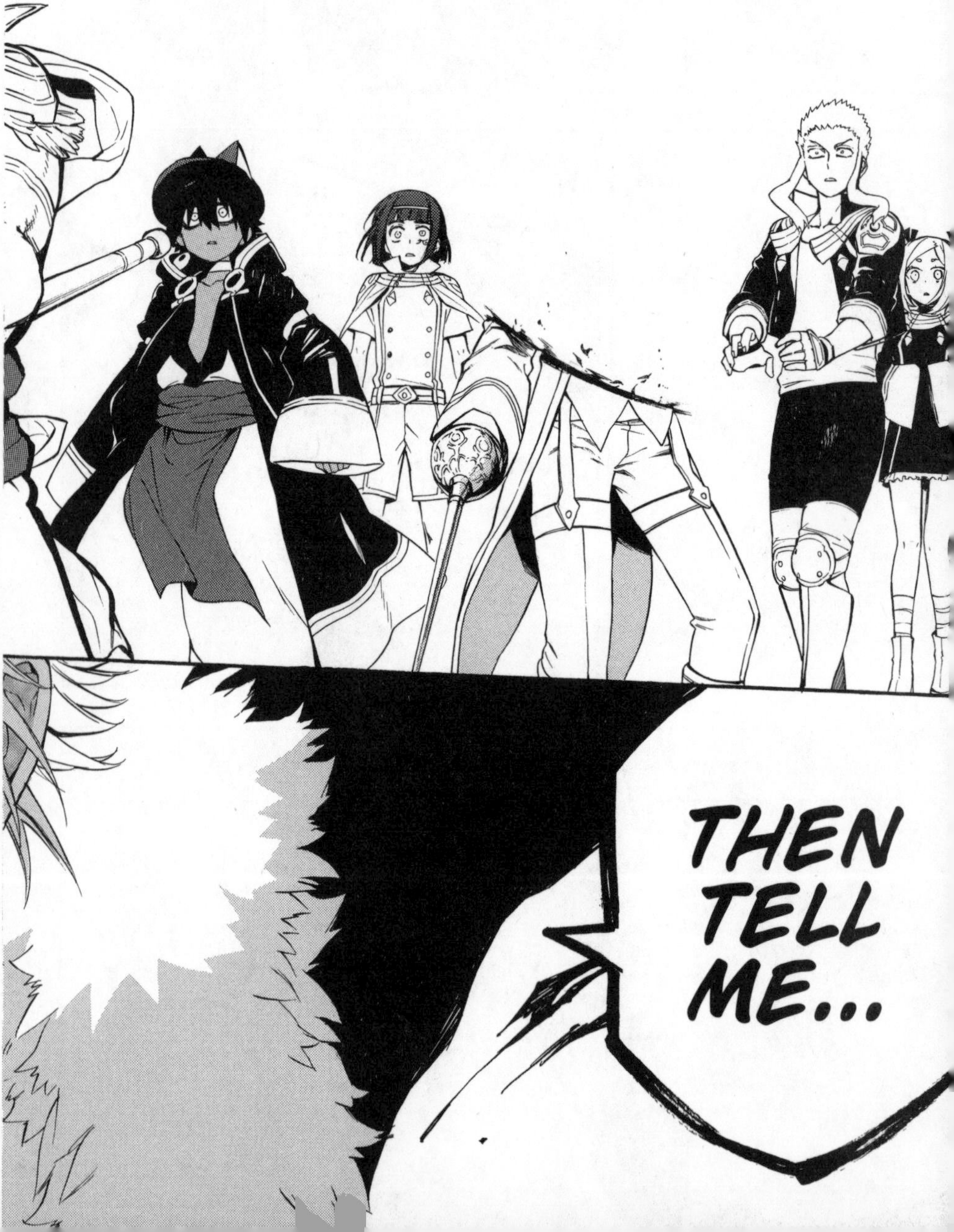
THEN TELL ME...

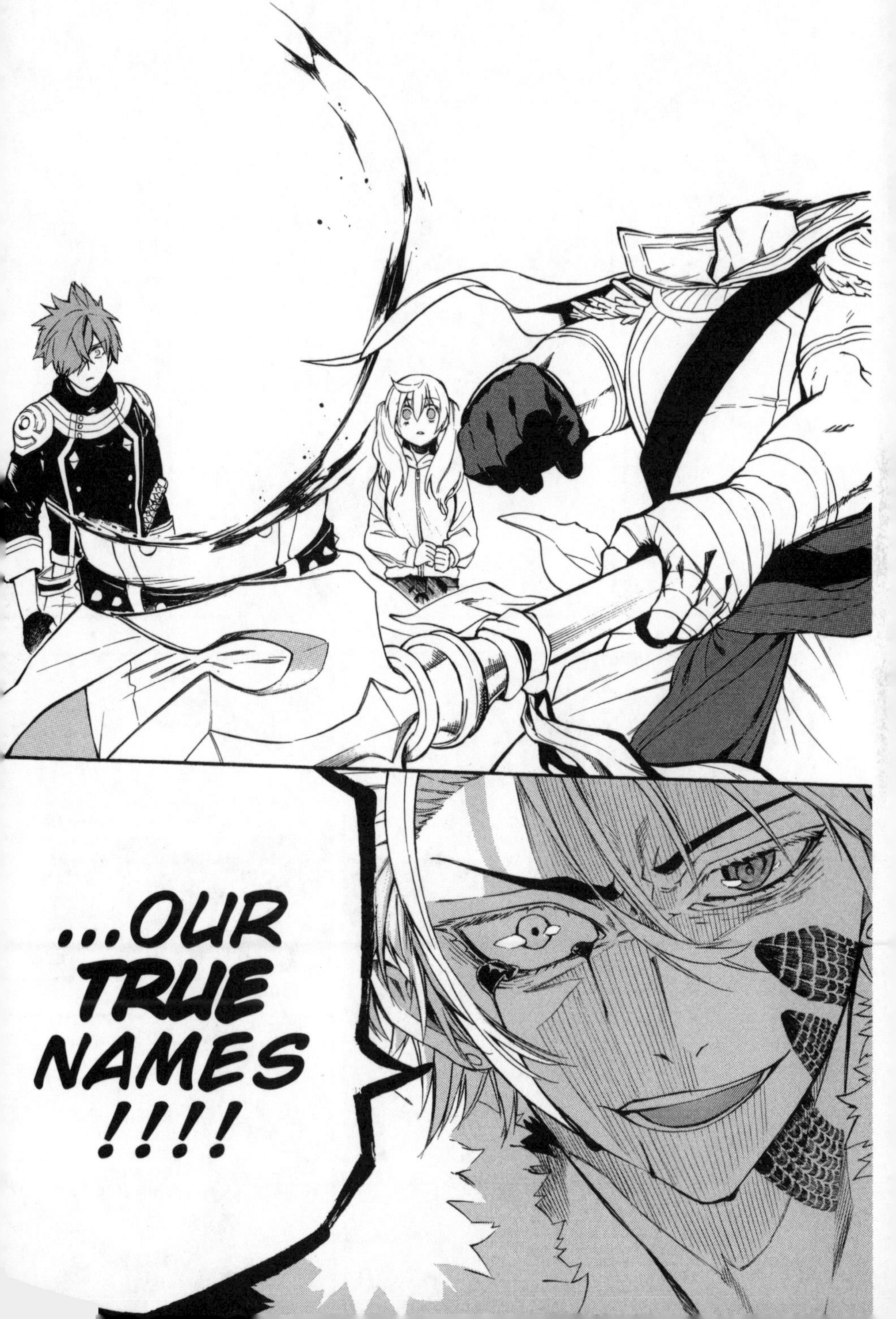
...OUR TRUE NAMES !!!!

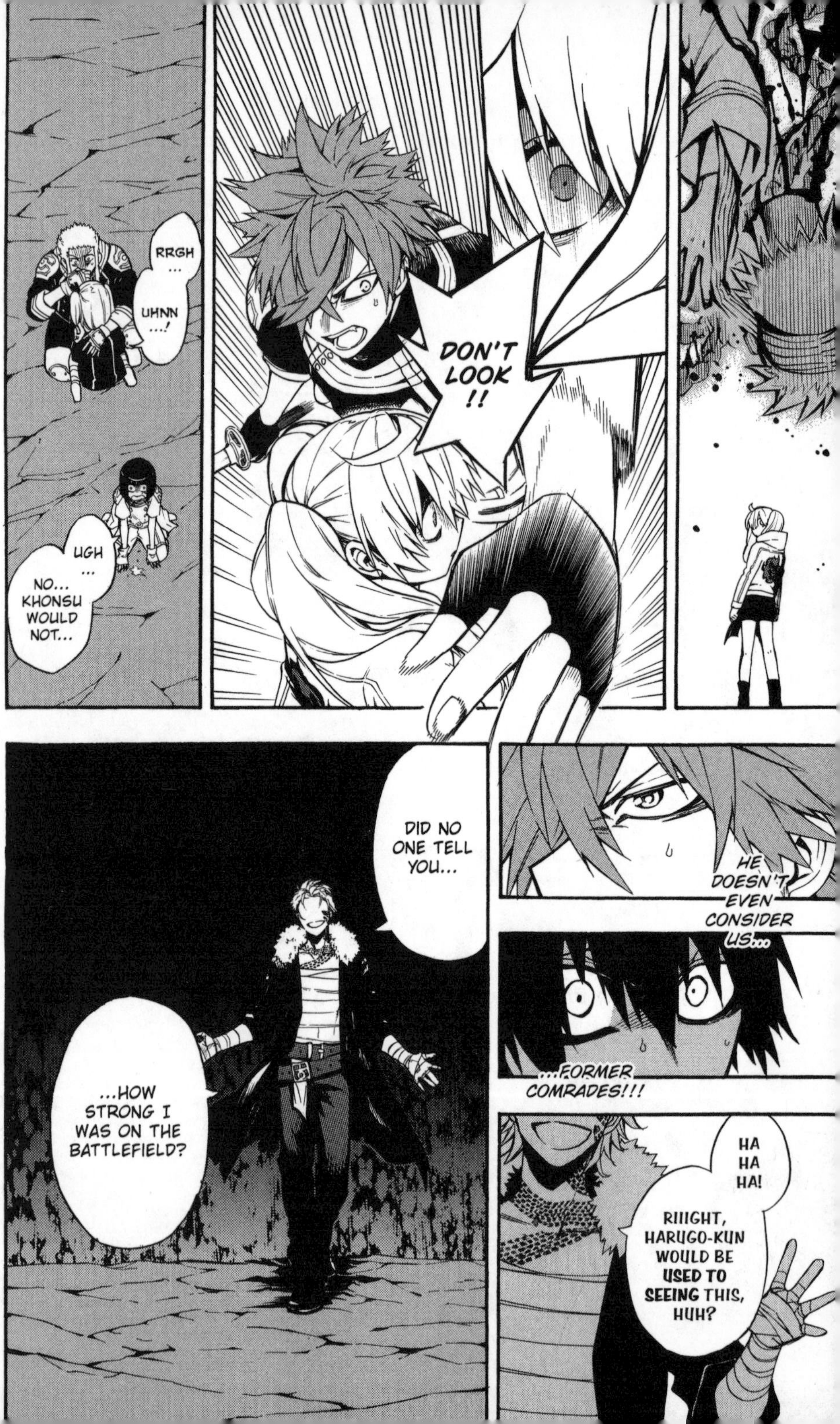
DON'T LOOK!!
RRGH...
UHNN...!
UGH...
NO... KHONSU WOULD NOT...
HE DOESN'T EVEN CONSIDER US...
...FORMER COMRADES!!!
HA HA HA!
RIIIGHT, HARUGO-KUN WOULD BE USED TO SEEING THIS, HUH?
DID NO ONE TELL YOU...
...HOW STRONG I WAS ON THE BATTLEFIELD?

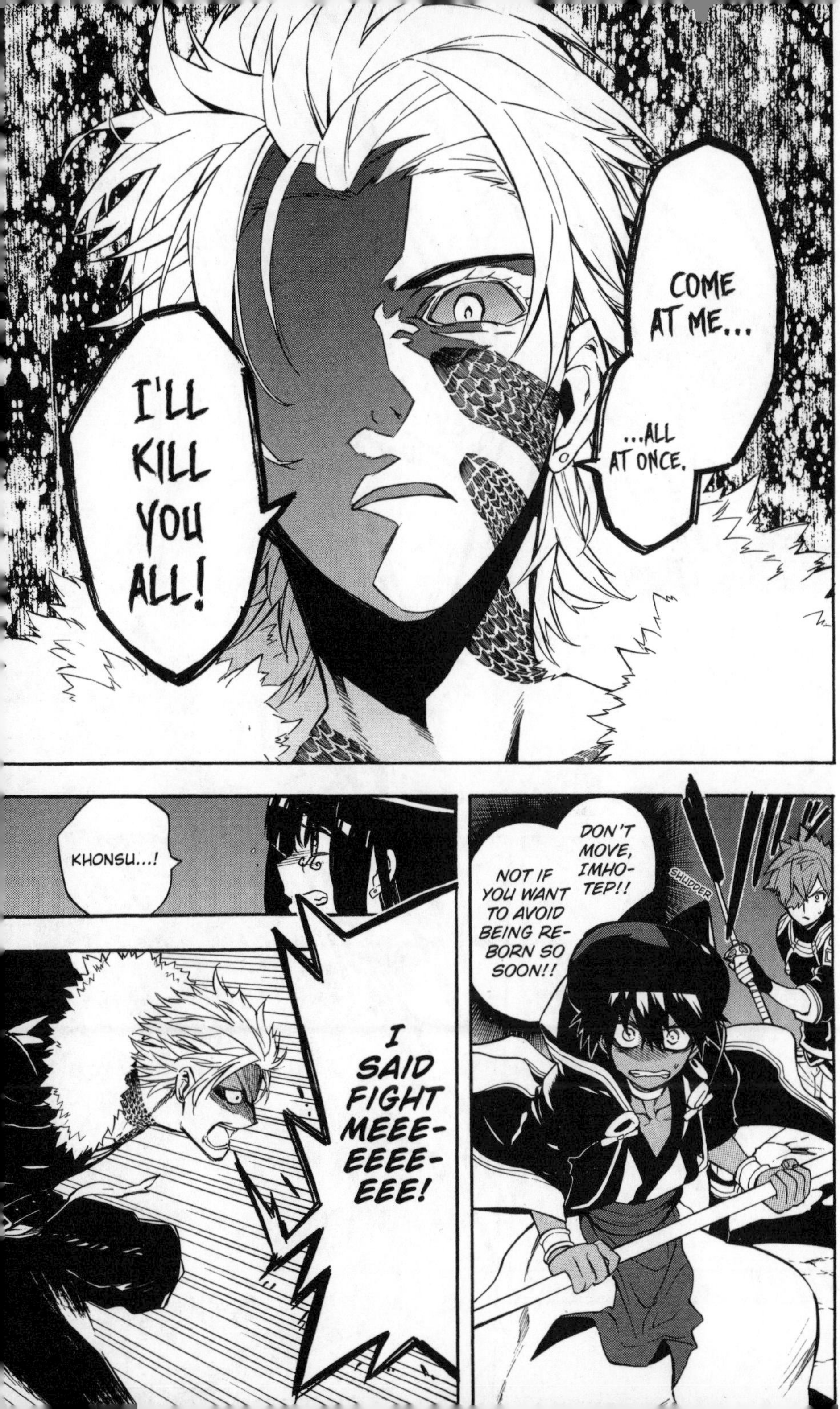
COME AT ME...
...ALL AT ONCE.
I'LL KILL YOU ALL!
DON'T MOVE, IMHOTEP!!
NOT IF YOU WANT TO AVOID BEING RE-BORN SO SOON!!
SHUDDER
KHONSU...!
I SAID FIGHT MEEEEEEEEEEE!

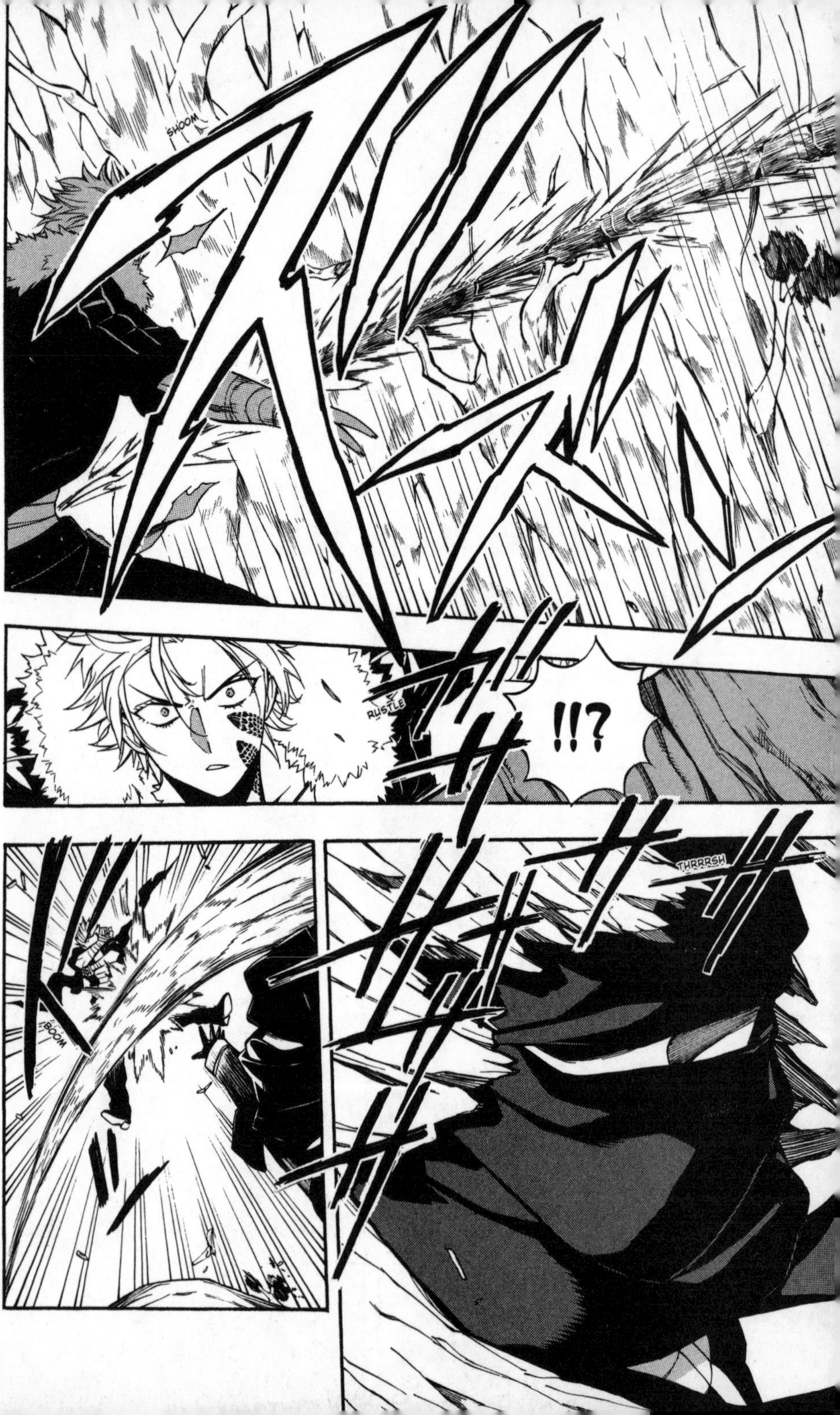
SHOOM
RUSTLE
!!?
THRRRSH
BOOM

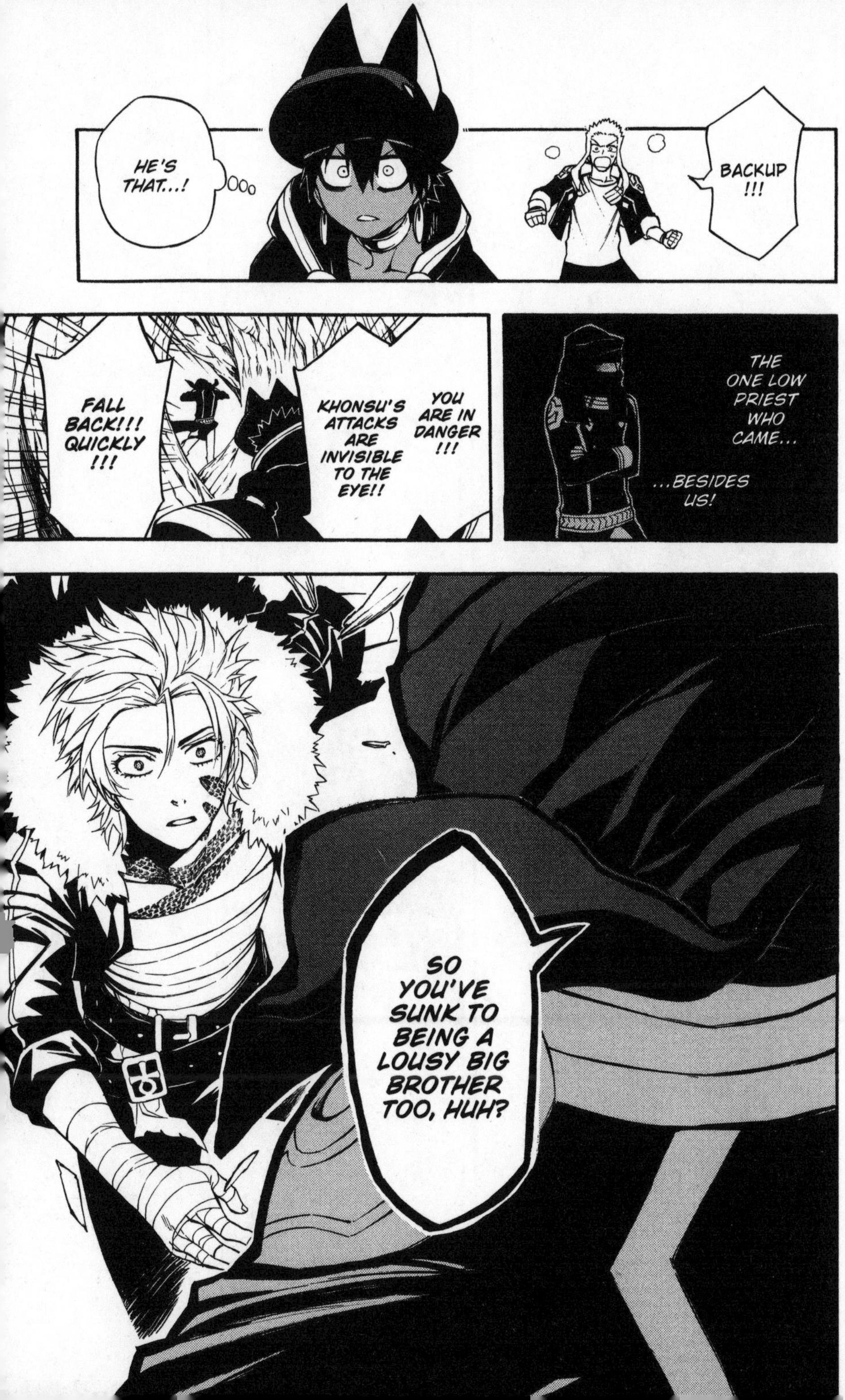
BACKUP!!!
HE'S THAT...!
THE ONE LOW PRIEST WHO CAME...
...BESIDES US!
YOU ARE IN DANGER!!!
KHONSU'S ATTACKS ARE INVISIBLE TO THE EYE!!
FALL BACK!!! QUICKLY!!!
SO YOU'VE SUNK TO BEING A LOUSY BIG BROTHER TOO, HUH?

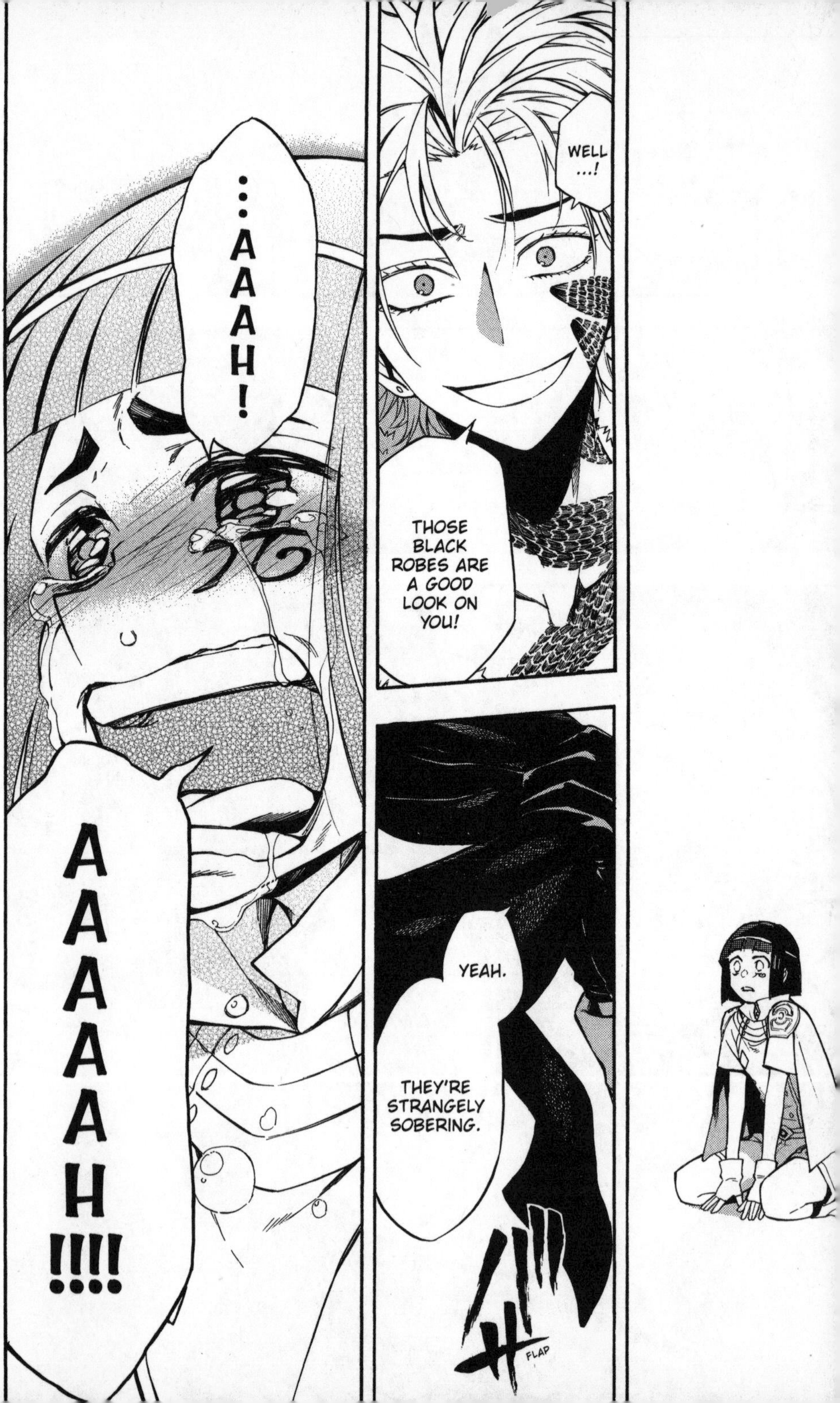
WELL ...!
THOSE BLACK ROBES ARE A GOOD LOOK ON YOU!
YEAH.
THEY'RE STRANGELY SOBERING.
FLAP
...AAAAH!
AAAAAH!!!!

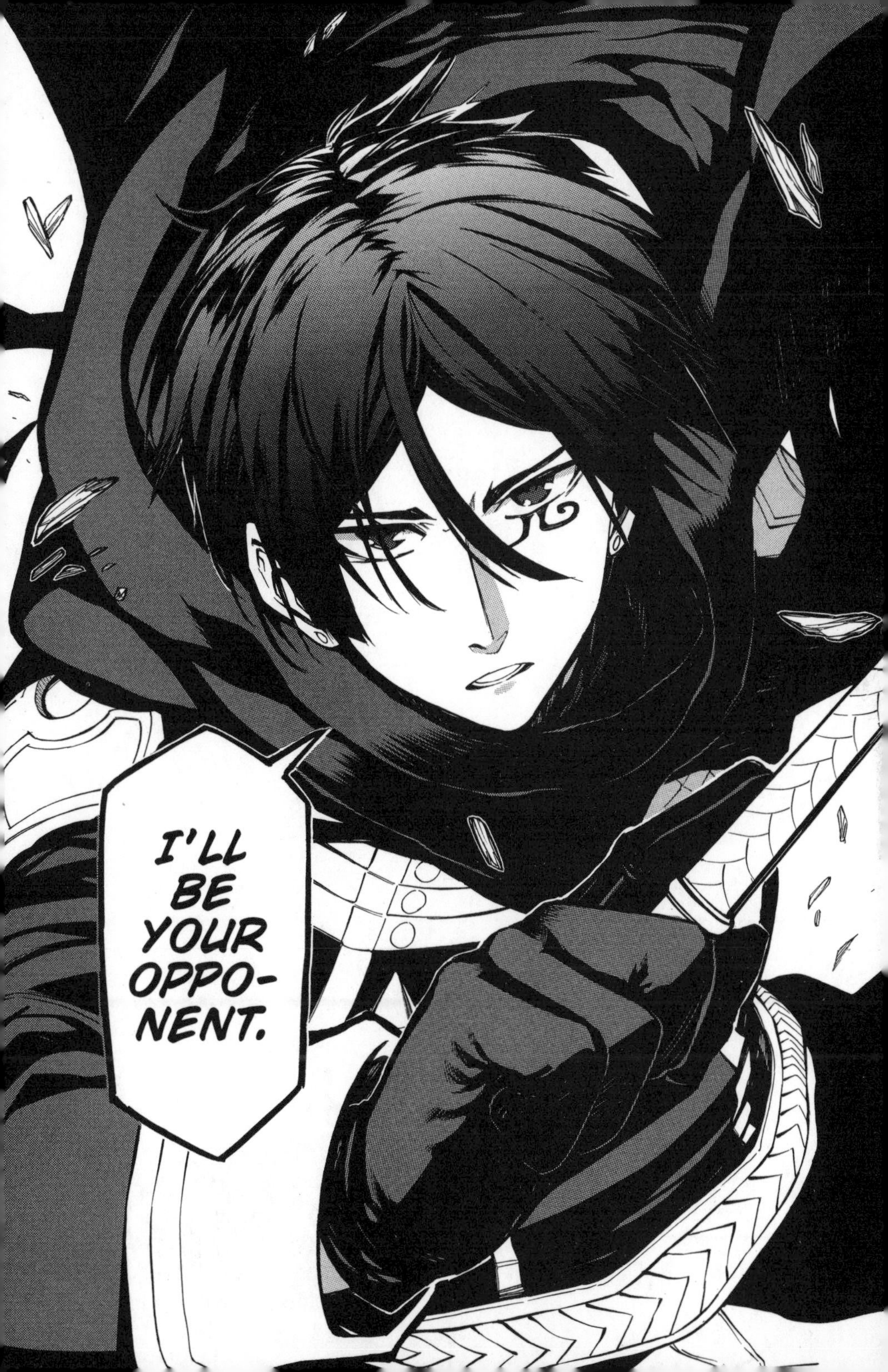
I'LL BE YOUR OPPO- NENT.

Im

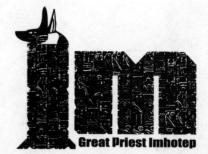

Great Priest Imhotep

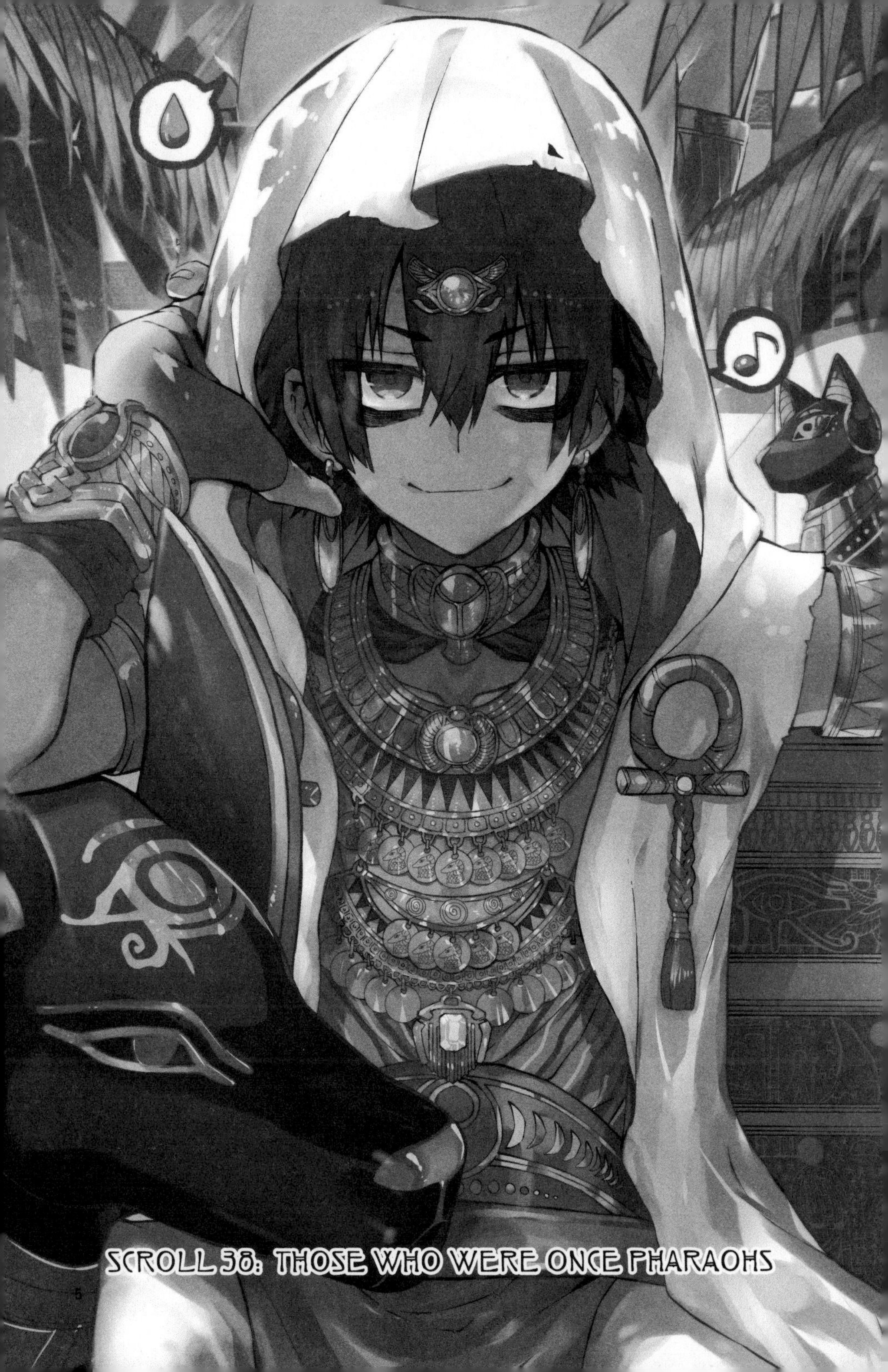

SCROLL 38: THOSE WHO WERE ONCE PHARAOHS

Great Priest Imhotep

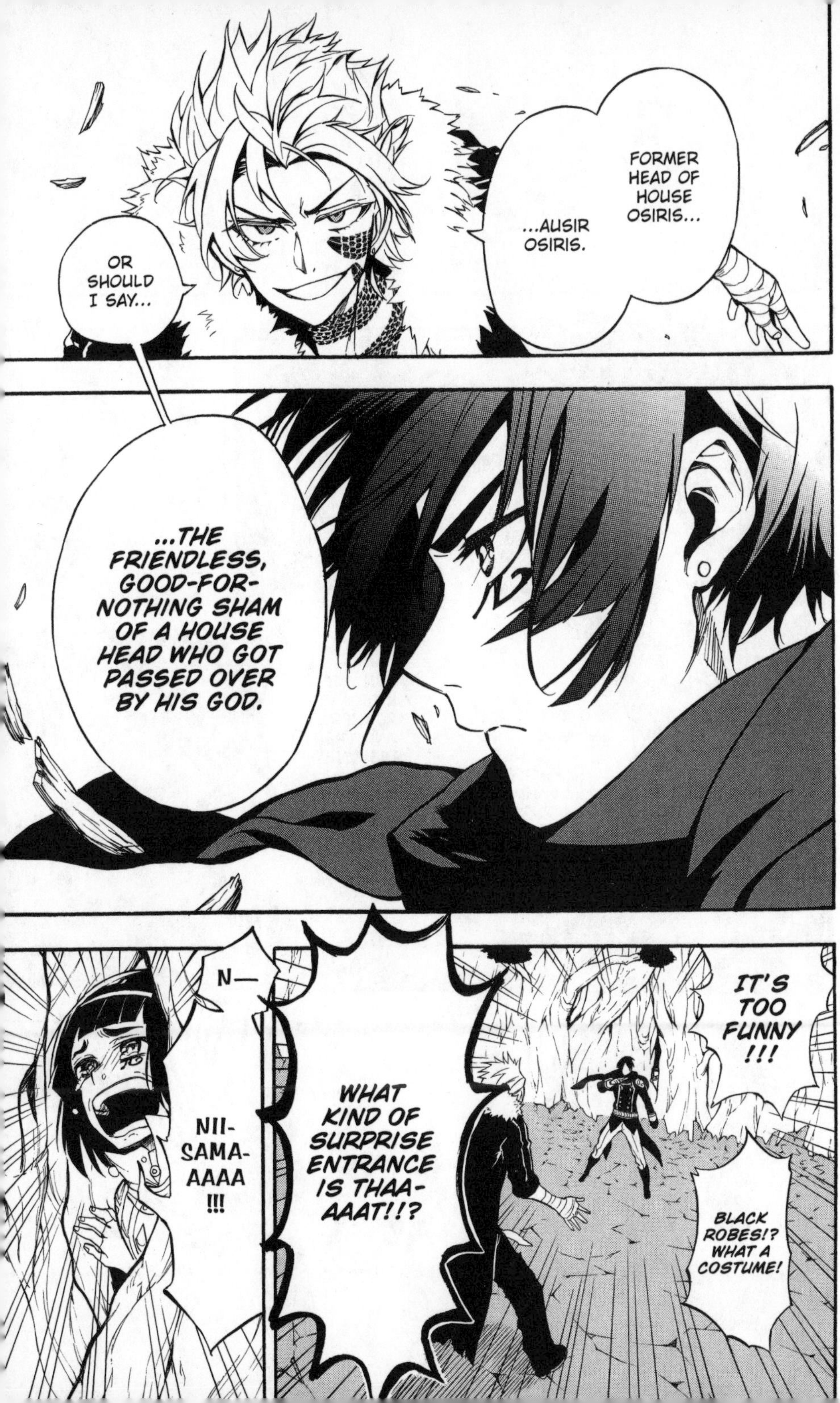
FORMER HEAD OF HOUSE OSIRIS...
...AUSIR OSIRIS.
OR SHOULD I SAY...
...THE FRIENDLESS, GOOD-FOR-NOTHING SHAM OF A HOUSE HEAD WHO GOT PASSED OVER BY HIS GOD.
IT'S TOO FUNNY!!!
BLACK ROBES!? WHAT A COSTUME!
WHAT KIND OF SURPRISE ENTRANCE IS THAA-AAAT!!?
N—
NII-SAMA-AAAA!!!

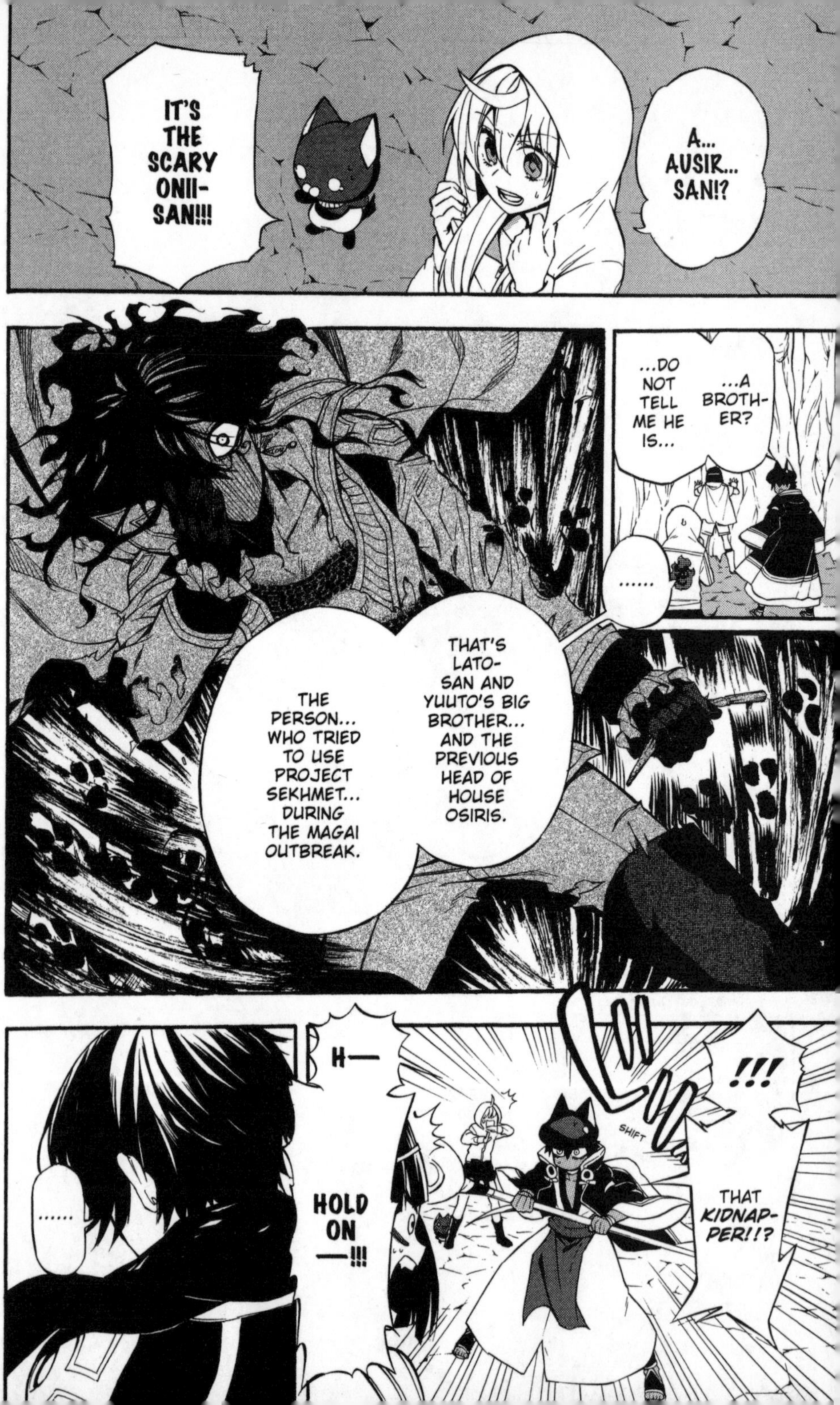
A... AUSIR... SAN!?
IT'S THE SCARY ONII-SAN!!!
...A BROTHER?
...DO NOT TELL ME HE IS...
......
THAT'S LATO-SAN AND YUUTO'S BIG BROTHER... AND THE PREVIOUS HEAD OF HOUSE OSIRIS.
THE PERSON... WHO TRIED TO USE PROJECT SEKHMET... DURING THE MAGAI OUTBREAK.
!!!
SHIFT
THAT KIDNAPPER!!?
H—
HOLD ON—!!!
......

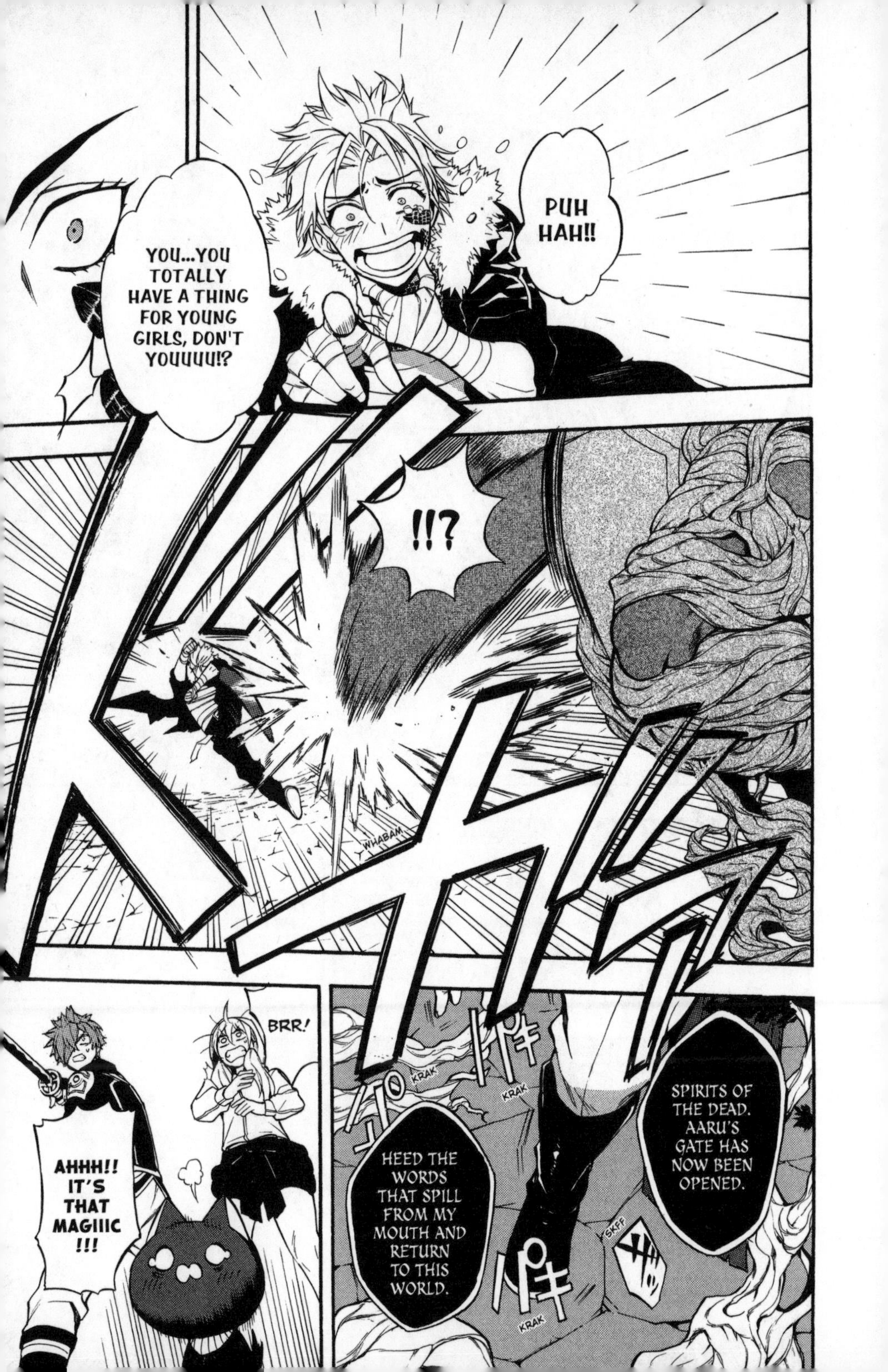
PUH HAH!!
YOU...YOU TOTALLY HAVE A THING FOR YOUNG GIRLS, DON'T YOUUUU!?
!!?
WHABAM
SPIRITS OF THE DEAD. AARU'S GATE HAS NOW BEEN OPENED.
HEED THE WORDS THAT SPILL FROM MY MOUTH AND RETURN TO THIS WORLD.
KRAK
KRAK
SKFF
KRAK
BRR!
AHHH!! IT'S THAT MAGIIIC!!!

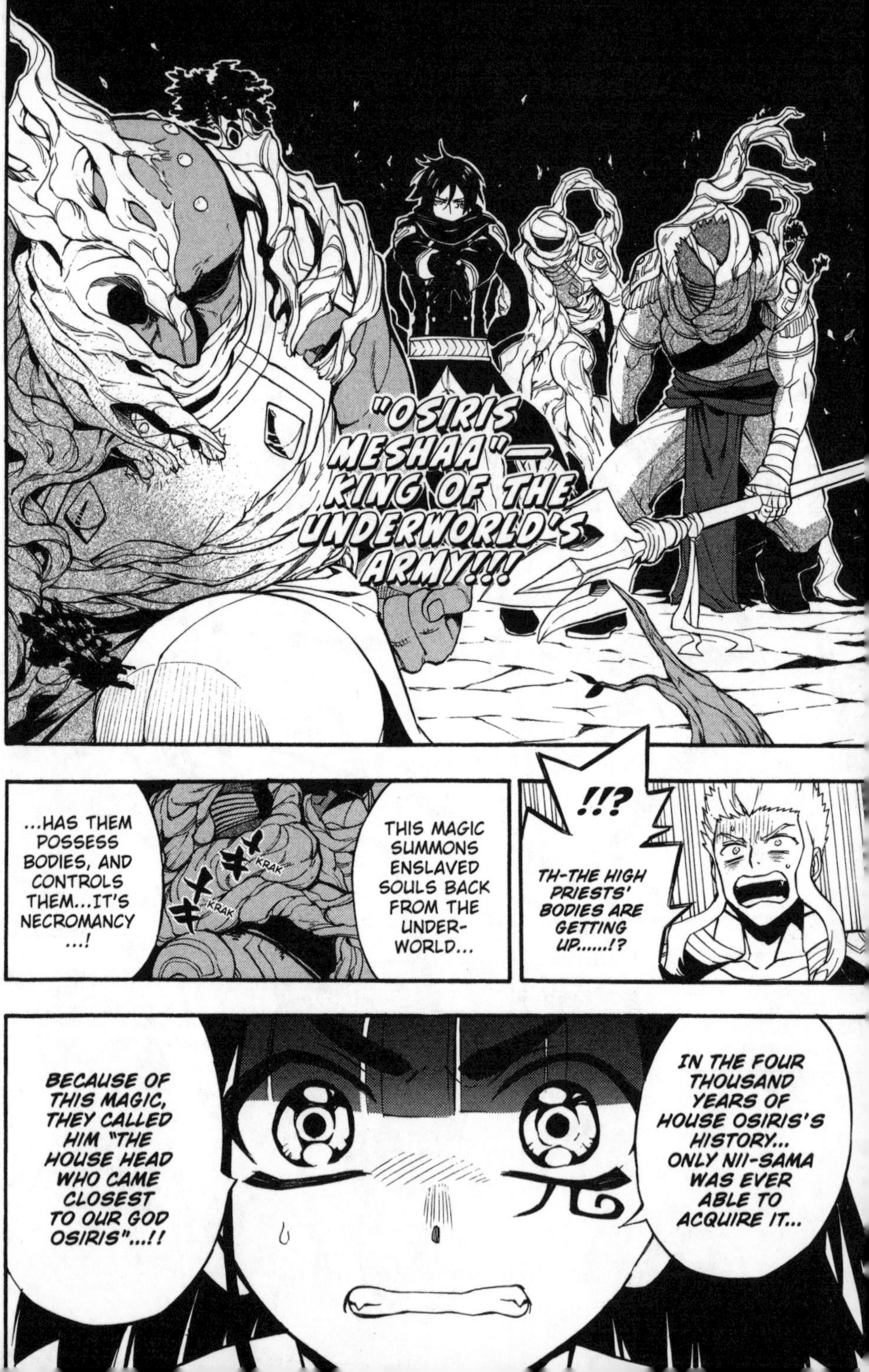
"OSIRIS MESHAA"— KING OF THE UNDERWORLD'S ARMY!!!
!!?
TH-THE HIGH PRIESTS' BODIES ARE GETTING UP......!?
THIS MAGIC SUMMONS ENSLAVED SOULS BACK FROM THE UNDER-WORLD...
KRAK
KRAK
...HAS THEM POSSESS BODIES, AND CONTROLS THEM...IT'S NECROMANCY ...!
IN THE FOUR THOUSAND YEARS OF HOUSE OSIRIS'S HISTORY... ONLY NII-SAMA WAS EVER ABLE TO ACQUIRE IT...
BECAUSE OF THIS MAGIC, THEY CALLED HIM "THE HOUSE HEAD WHO CAME CLOSEST TO OUR GOD OSIRIS"...!!

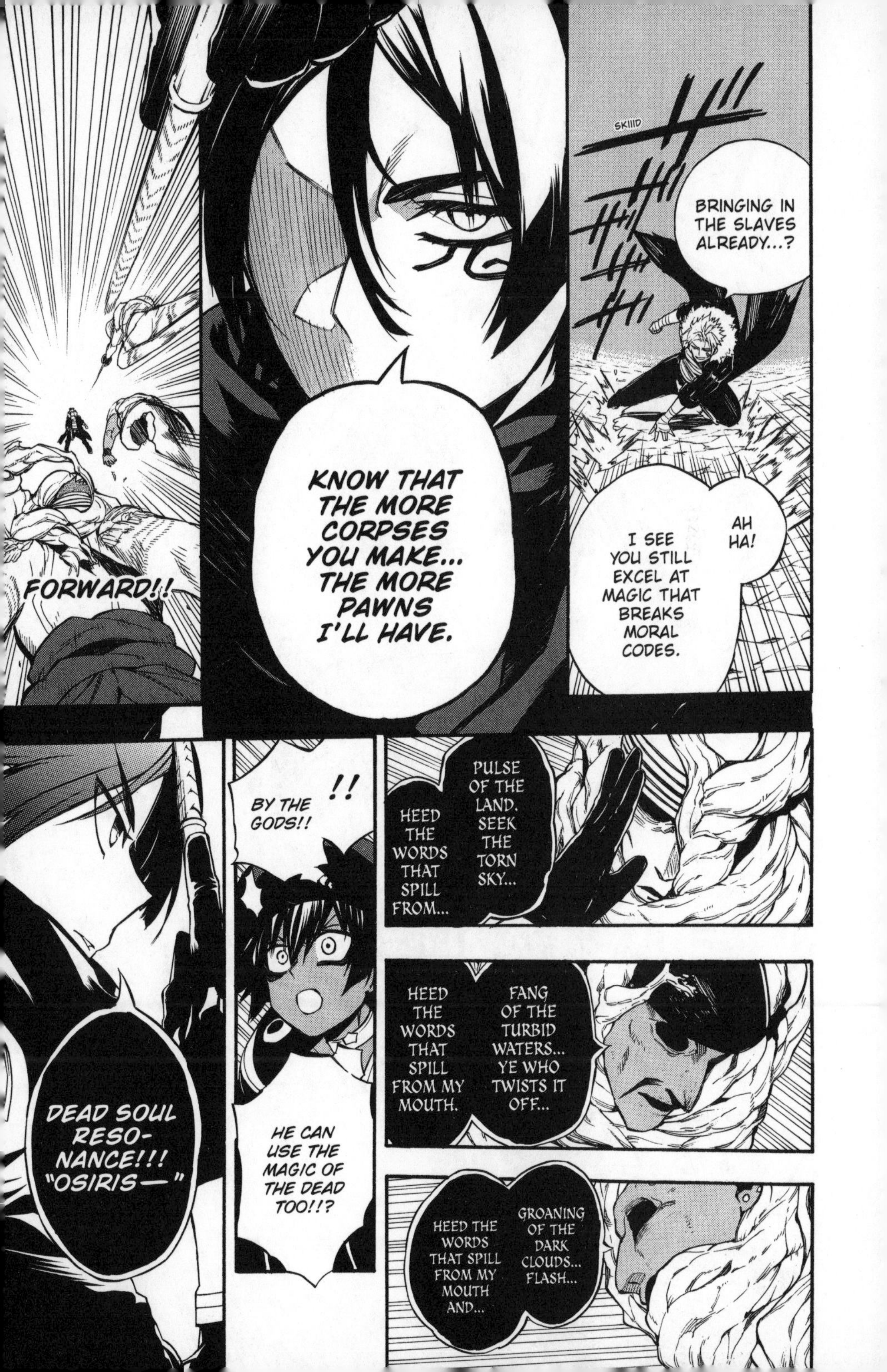
SKIIID
BRINGING IN THE SLAVES ALREADY...?
AH HA!
I SEE YOU STILL EXCEL AT MAGIC THAT BREAKS MORAL CODES.
KNOW THAT THE MORE CORPSES YOU MAKE... THE MORE PAWNS I'LL HAVE.
FORWARD!!
PULSE OF THE LAND. SEEK THE TORN SKY...
HEED THE WORDS THAT SPILL FROM...
FANG OF THE TURBID WATERS... YE WHO TWISTS IT OFF...
HEED THE WORDS THAT SPILL FROM MY MOUTH.
GROANING OF THE DARK CLOUDS... FLASH...
HEED THE WORDS THAT SPILL FROM MY MOUTH AND...
!!
BY THE GODS!!
HE CAN USE THE MAGIC OF THE DEAD TOO!!?
DEAD SOUL RESO-NANCE!!! "OSIRIS—"

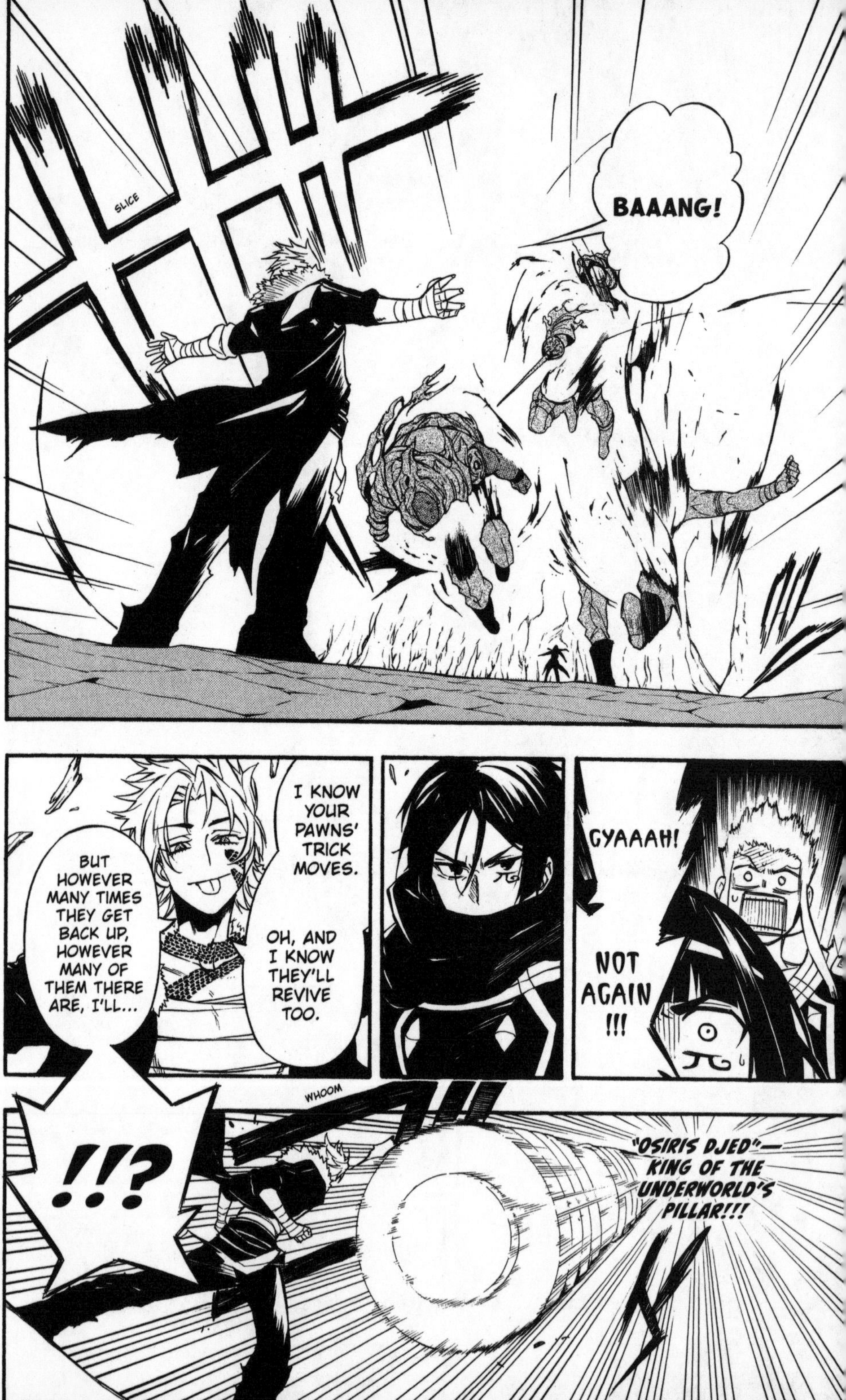
BAAANG!
SLICE
GYAAAH!
NOT AGAIN!!!
I KNOW YOUR PAWNS' TRICK MOVES.
OH, AND I KNOW THEY'LL REVIVE TOO.
BUT HOWEVER MANY TIMES THEY GET BACK UP, HOWEVER MANY OF THEM THERE ARE, I'LL...
"OSIRIS DJED"— KING OF THE UNDERWORLD'S PILLAR!!!
WHOOM
!!?

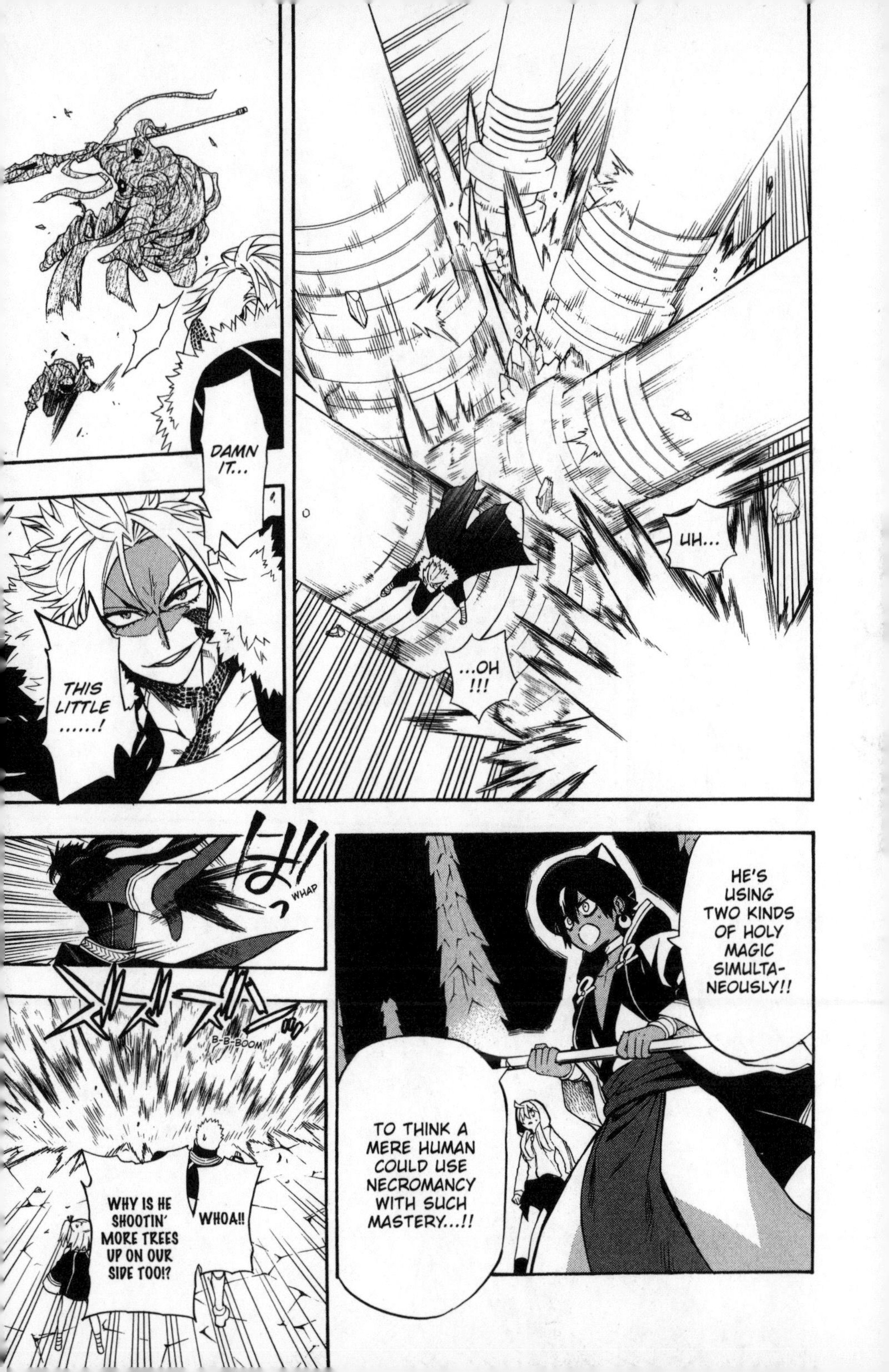
UH...
...OH !!!
DAMN IT...
THIS LITTLE ......!
HE'S USING TWO KINDS OF HOLY MAGIC SIMULTANEOUSLY!!
TO THINK A MERE HUMAN COULD USE NECROMANCY WITH SUCH MASTERY...!!
WHAP
B-B-BOOM
WHOA!!
WHY IS HE SHOOTIN' MORE TREES UP ON OUR SIDE TOO!?

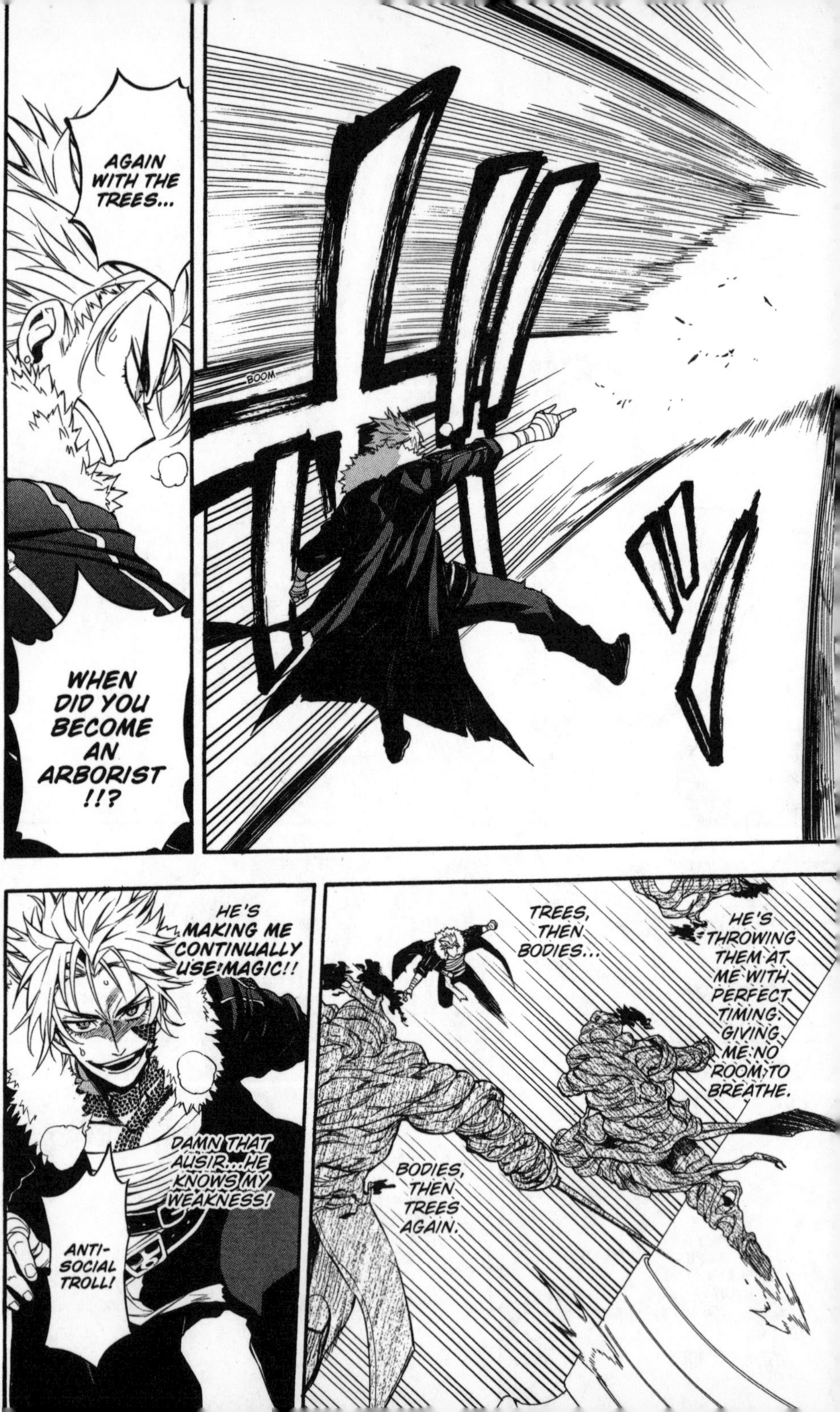
BOOM
AGAIN WITH THE TREES...
WHEN DID YOU BECOME AN ARBORIST!!?
TREES, THEN BODIES...
HE'S THROWING THEM AT ME WITH PERFECT TIMING, GIVING ME NO ROOM TO BREATHE.
BODIES, THEN TREES AGAIN.
HE'S MAKING ME CONTINUALLY USE MAGIC!!
DAMN THAT AUSIR...HE KNOWS MY WEAKNESS!
ANTI-SOCIAL TROLL!

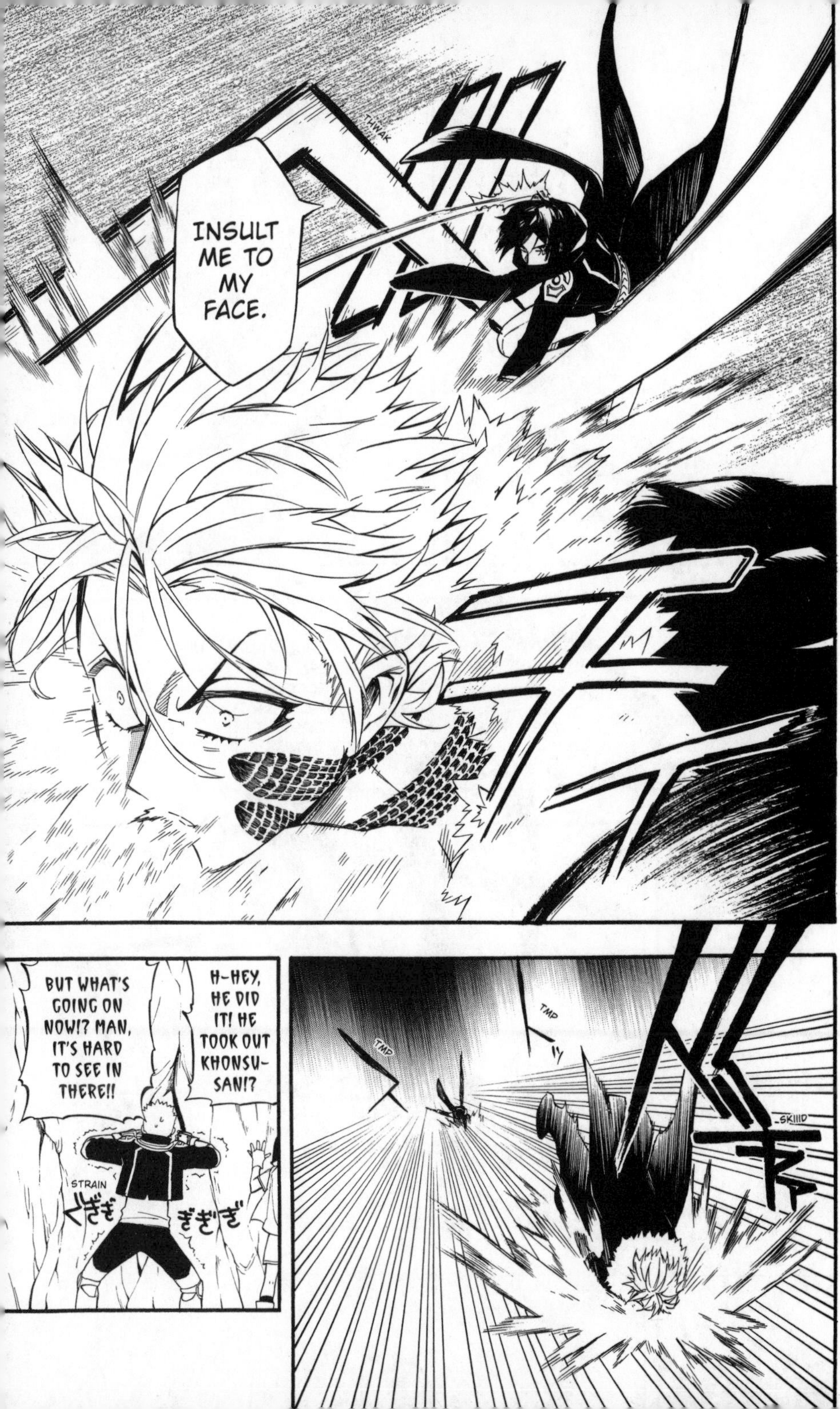
THWAK
INSULT ME TO MY FACE.
TMP
TMP
SKIIID
H-HEY, HE DID IT! HE TOOK OUT KHONSU-SAN!?
BUT WHAT'S GOING ON NOW!? MAN, IT'S HARD TO SEE IN THERE!!
STRAIN
ぐぎぎ
ぎぎぎ

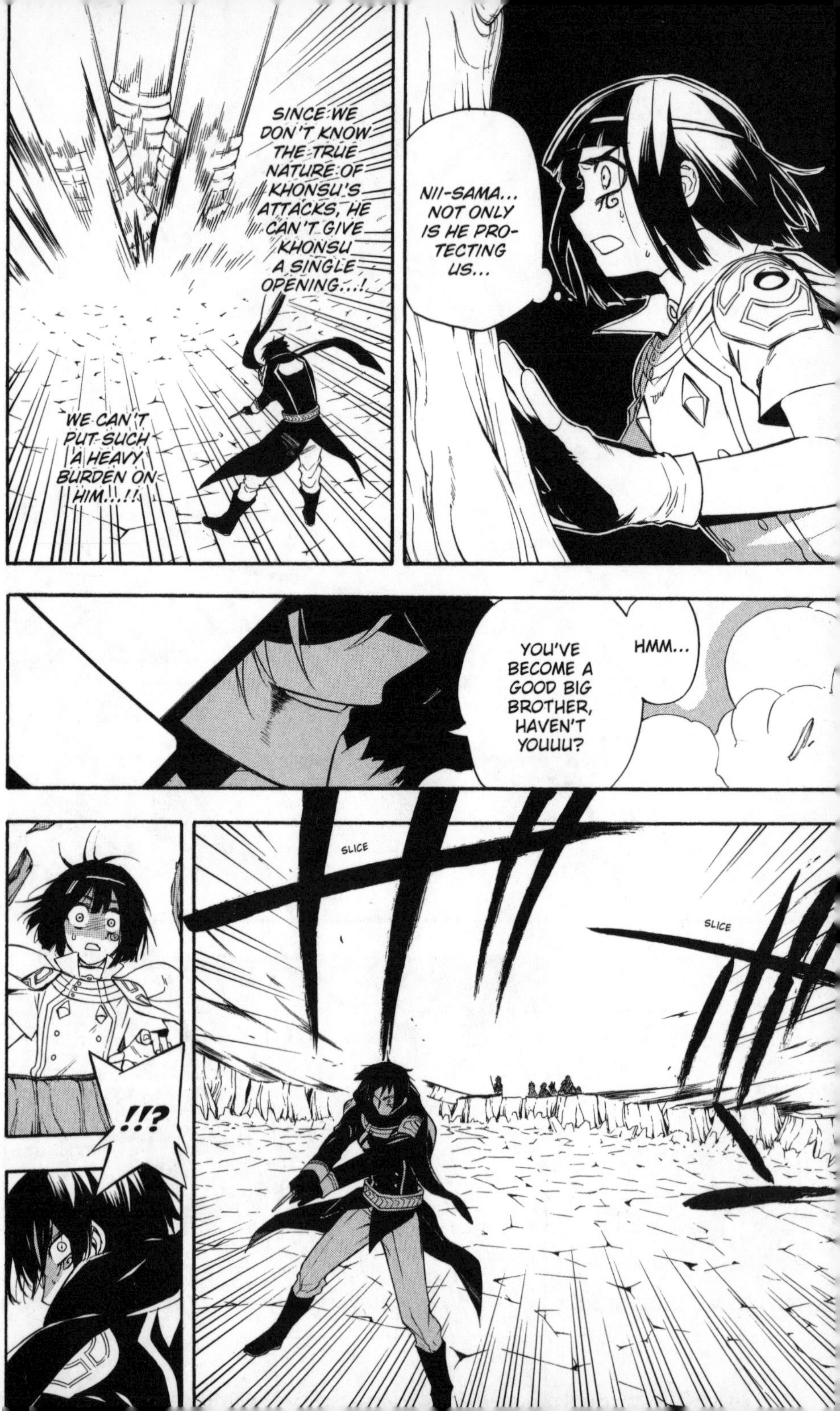
NII-SAMA... NOT ONLY IS HE PRO-TECTING US...
SINCE WE DON'T KNOW THE TRUE NATURE OF KHONSU'S ATTACKS, HE CAN'T GIVE KHONSU A SINGLE OPENING...!
WE CAN'T PUT SUCH A HEAVY BURDEN ON HIM...!!
HMM...
YOU'VE BECOME A GOOD BIG BROTHER, HAVEN'T YOUUU?
SLICE
SLICE
!!?

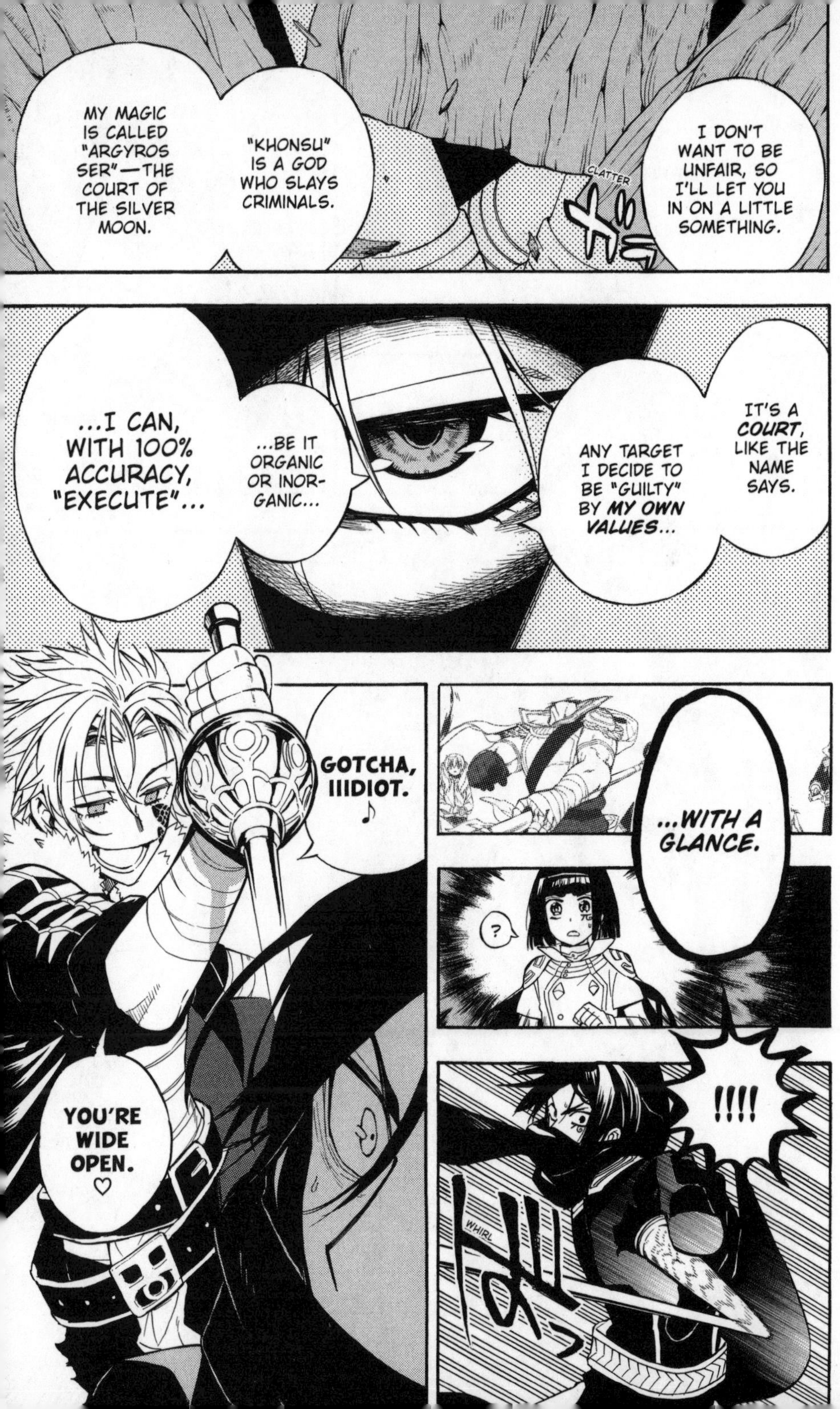
I DON'T WANT TO BE UNFAIR, SO I'LL LET YOU IN ON A LITTLE SOMETHING.
CLATTER
"KHONSU" IS A GOD WHO SLAYS CRIMINALS.
MY MAGIC IS CALLED "ARGYROS SER"—THE COURT OF THE SILVER MOON.
IT'S A COURT, LIKE THE NAME SAYS.
ANY TARGET I DECIDE TO BE "GUILTY" BY MY OWN VALUES...
...BE IT ORGANIC OR INORGANIC...
...I CAN, WITH 100% ACCURACY, "EXECUTE"...
...WITH A GLANCE.
?
!!!!
WHIRL
GOTCHA, IIIDIOT. ♪
YOU'RE WIDE OPEN. ♡

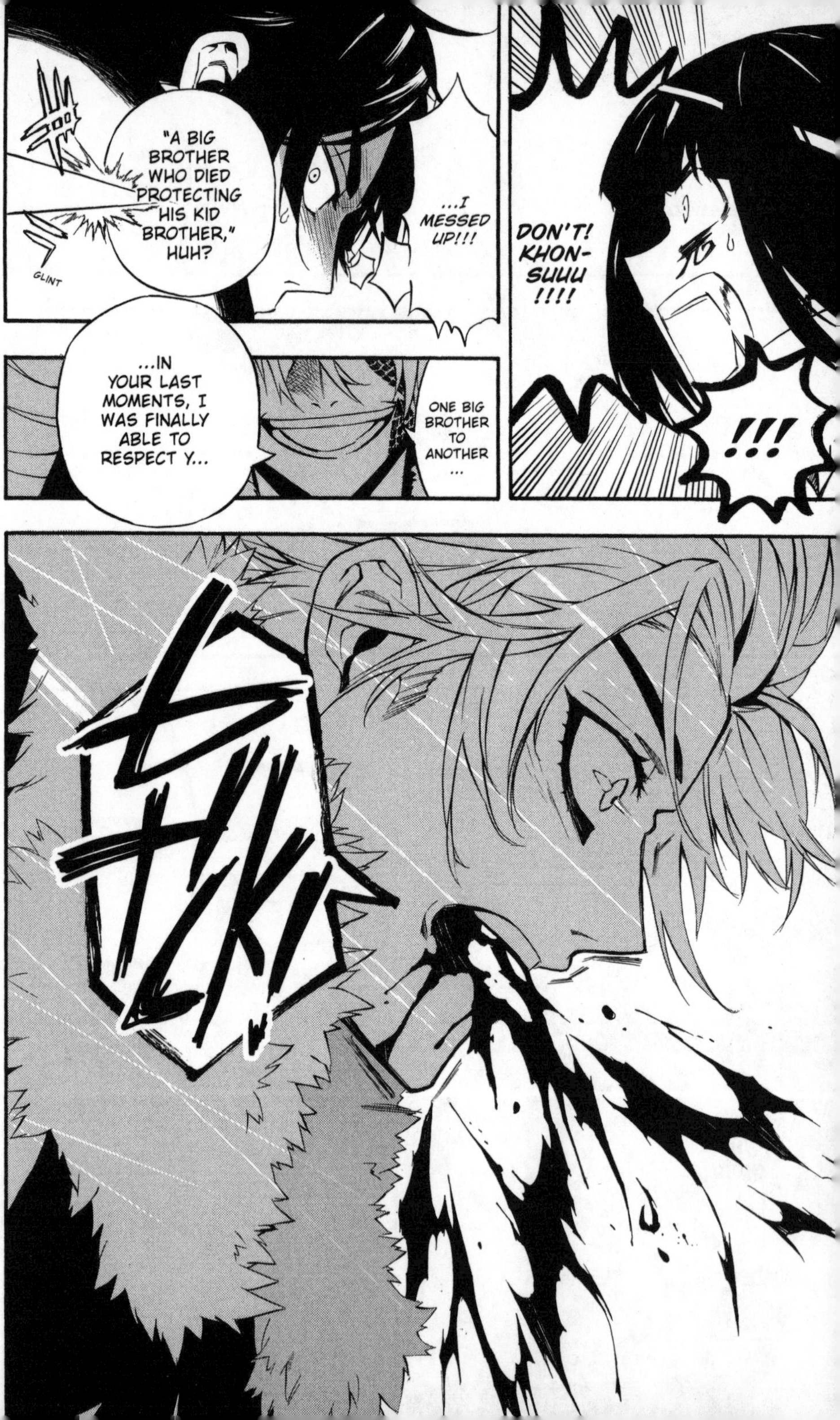
DON'T! KHON-SUUU!!!!
!!!
"A BIG BROTHER WHO DIED PROTECTING HIS KID BROTHER," HUH?
...I MESSED UP!!!
GLINT
...IN YOUR LAST MOMENTS, I WAS FINALLY ABLE TO RESPECT Y...
ONE BIG BROTHER TO ANOTHER...

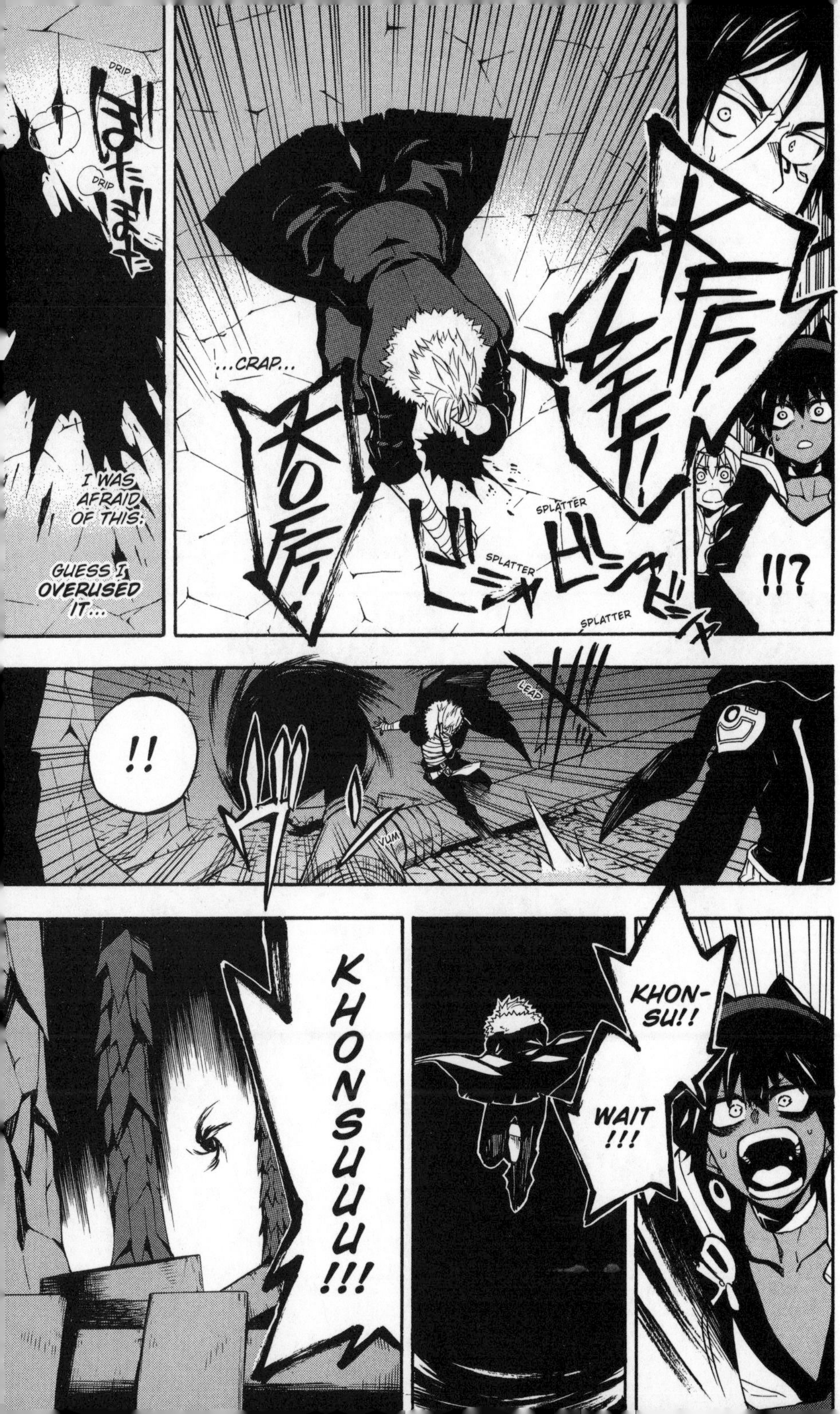

!!?
...CRAP...
SPLATTER
SPLATTER
SPLATTER
DRIP
DRIP
I WAS AFRAID OF THIS.
GUESS I OVERUSED IT...
LEAP
VUM
!!
KHON-SU!!
WAIT!!!
KHONSUUUU!!!

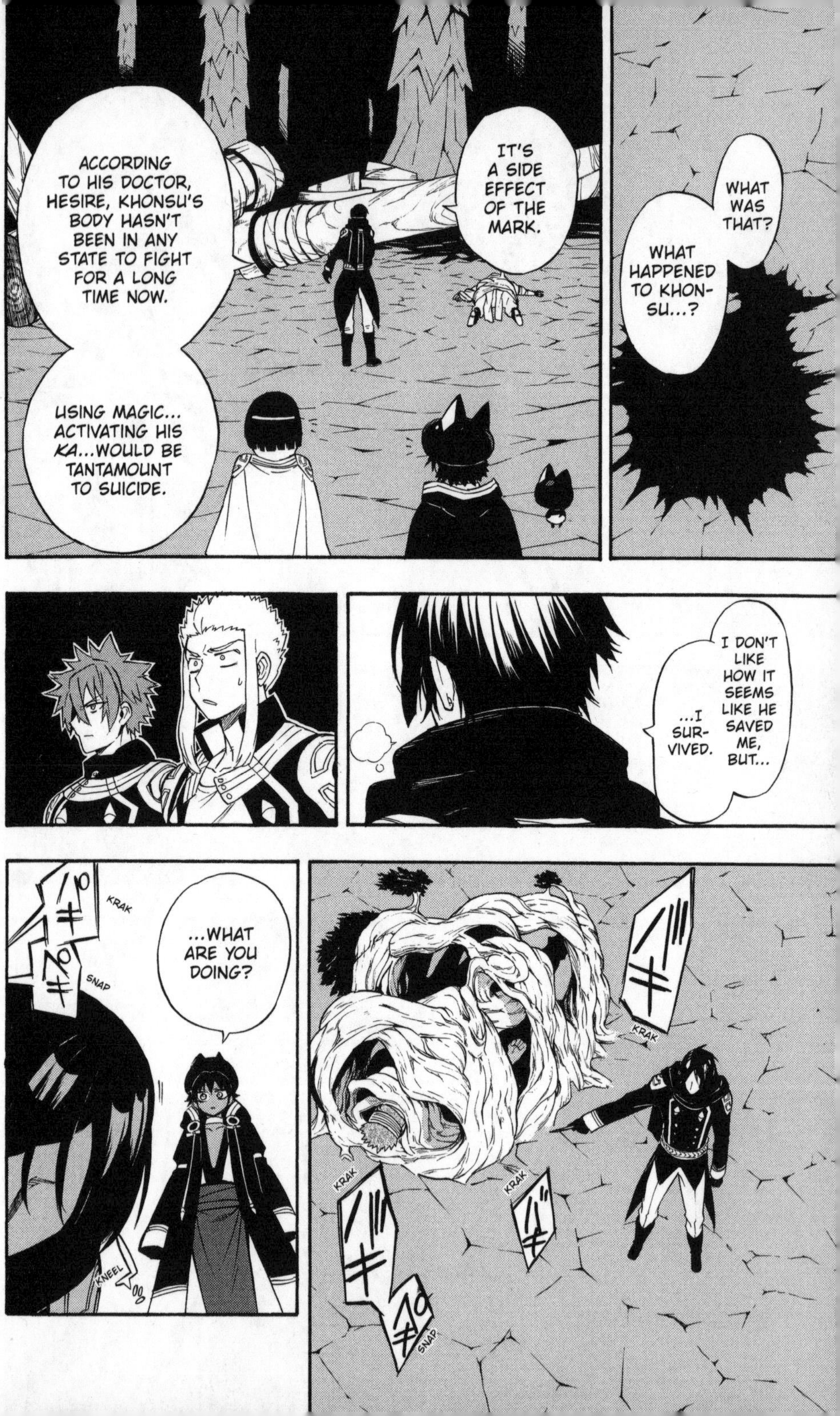
WHAT WAS THAT?
WHAT HAPPENED TO KHON-SU...?
IT'S A SIDE EFFECT OF THE MARK.
ACCORDING TO HIS DOCTOR, HESIRE, KHONSU'S BODY HASN'T BEEN IN ANY STATE TO FIGHT FOR A LONG TIME NOW.
USING MAGIC... ACTIVATING HIS *KA*...WOULD BE TANTAMOUNT TO SUICIDE.
I DON'T LIKE HOW IT SEEMS LIKE HE SAVED ME, BUT...
...I SUR-VIVED.
KRAK
KRAK
KRAK
SNAP
KRAK
SNAP
...WHAT ARE YOU DOING?
KNEEL

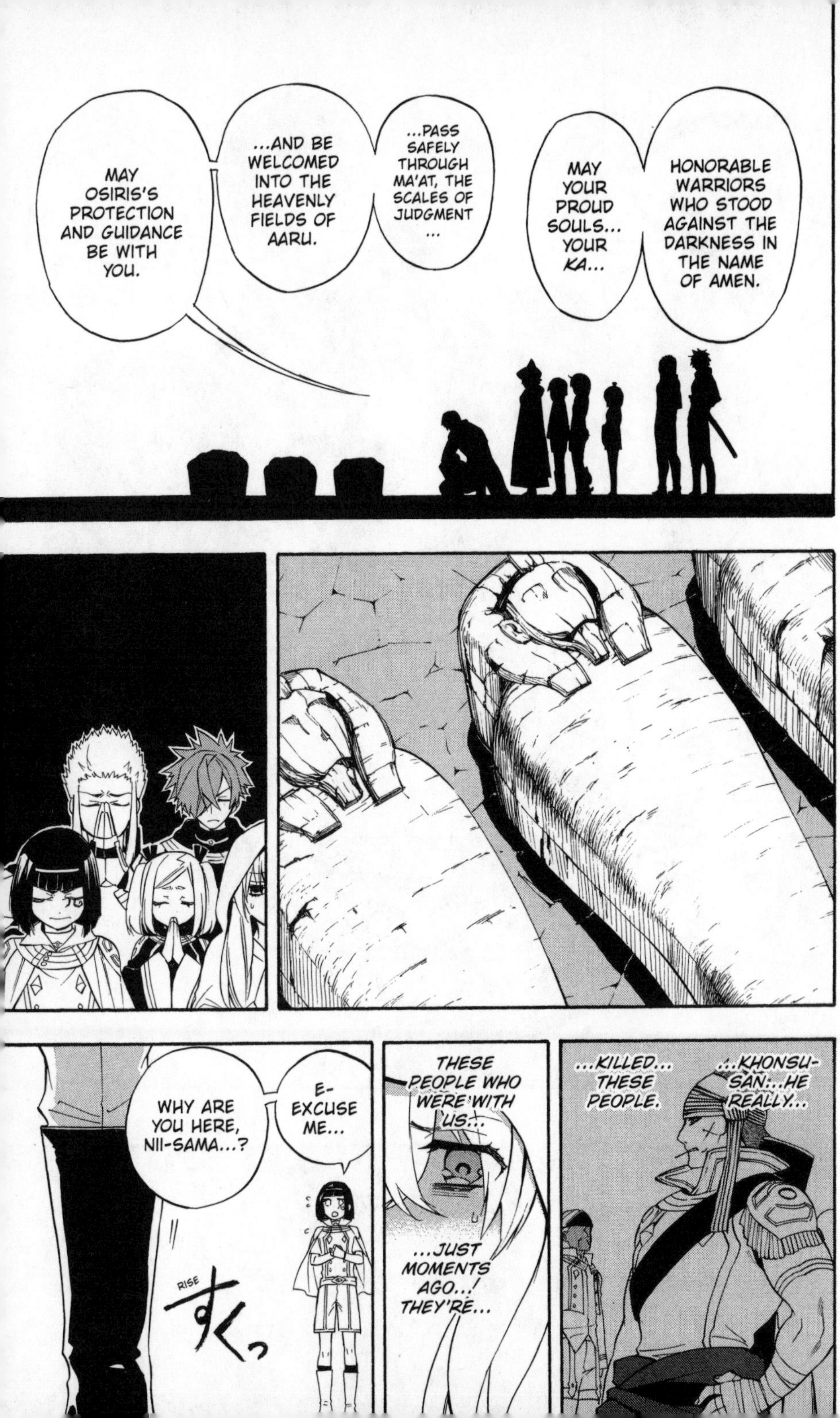
HONORABLE WARRIORS WHO STOOD AGAINST THE DARKNESS IN THE NAME OF AMEN.
MAY YOUR PROUD SOULS... YOUR KA...
...PASS SAFELY THROUGH MA'AT, THE SCALES OF JUDGMENT...
...AND BE WELCOMED INTO THE HEAVENLY FIELDS OF AARU.
MAY OSIRIS'S PROTECTION AND GUIDANCE BE WITH YOU.
...KHONSU-SAN... HE REALLY...
...KILLED... THESE PEOPLE.
THESE PEOPLE WHO WERE WITH US...
...JUST MOMENTS AGO...! THEY'RE...
E-EXCUSE ME...
WHY ARE YOU HERE, NII-SAMA...?
RISE
すくっ

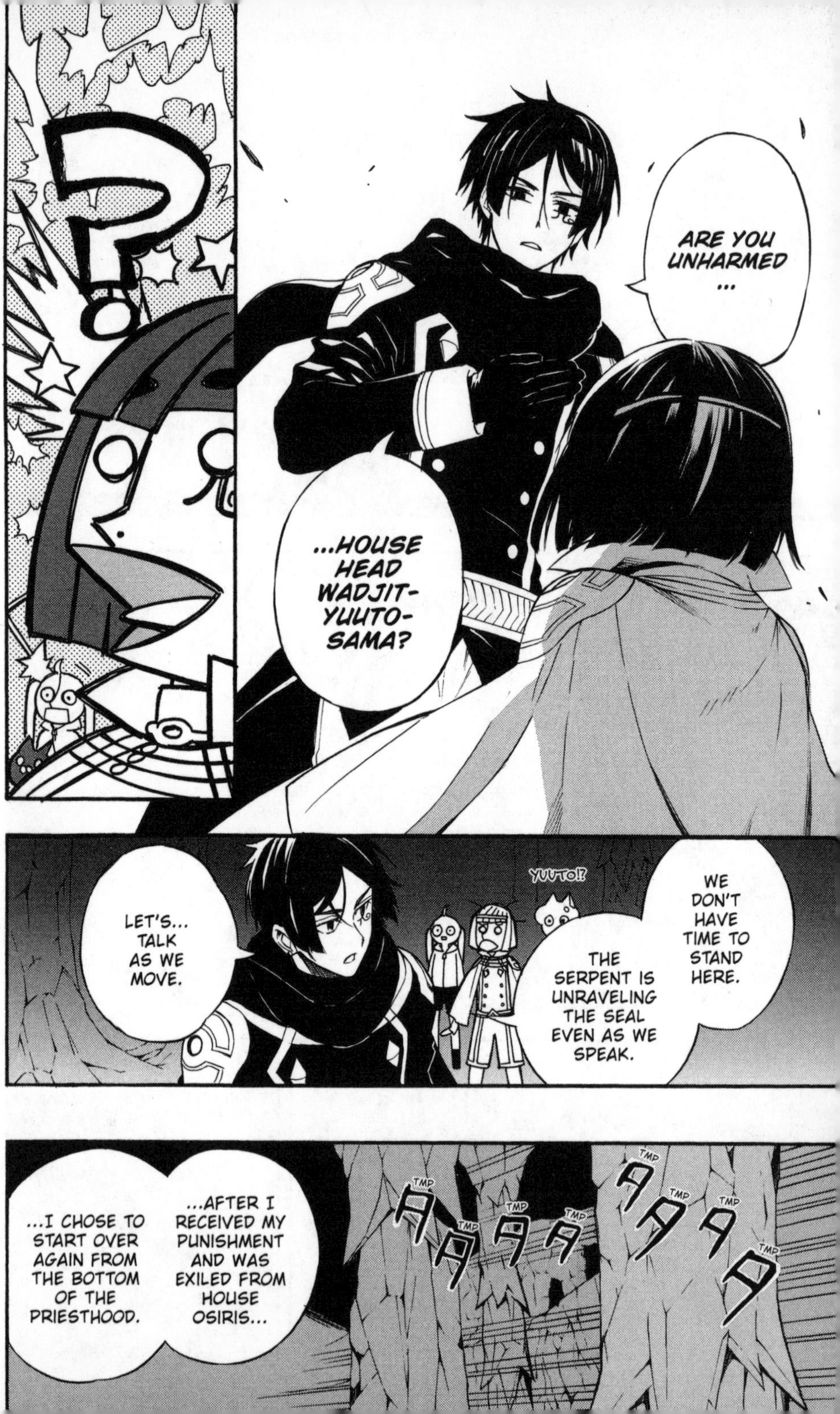
ARE YOU UNHARMED...
...HOUSE HEAD WADJIT-YUUTO-SAMA?
WE DON'T HAVE TIME TO STAND HERE.
YUUTO!?
THE SERPENT IS UNRAVELING THE SEAL EVEN AS WE SPEAK.
LET'S... TALK AS WE MOVE.
TMP TMP TMP TMP TMP TMP TMP
...AFTER I RECEIVED MY PUNISHMENT AND WAS EXILED FROM HOUSE OSIRIS...
...I CHOSE TO START OVER AGAIN FROM THE BOTTOM OF THE PRIESTHOOD.

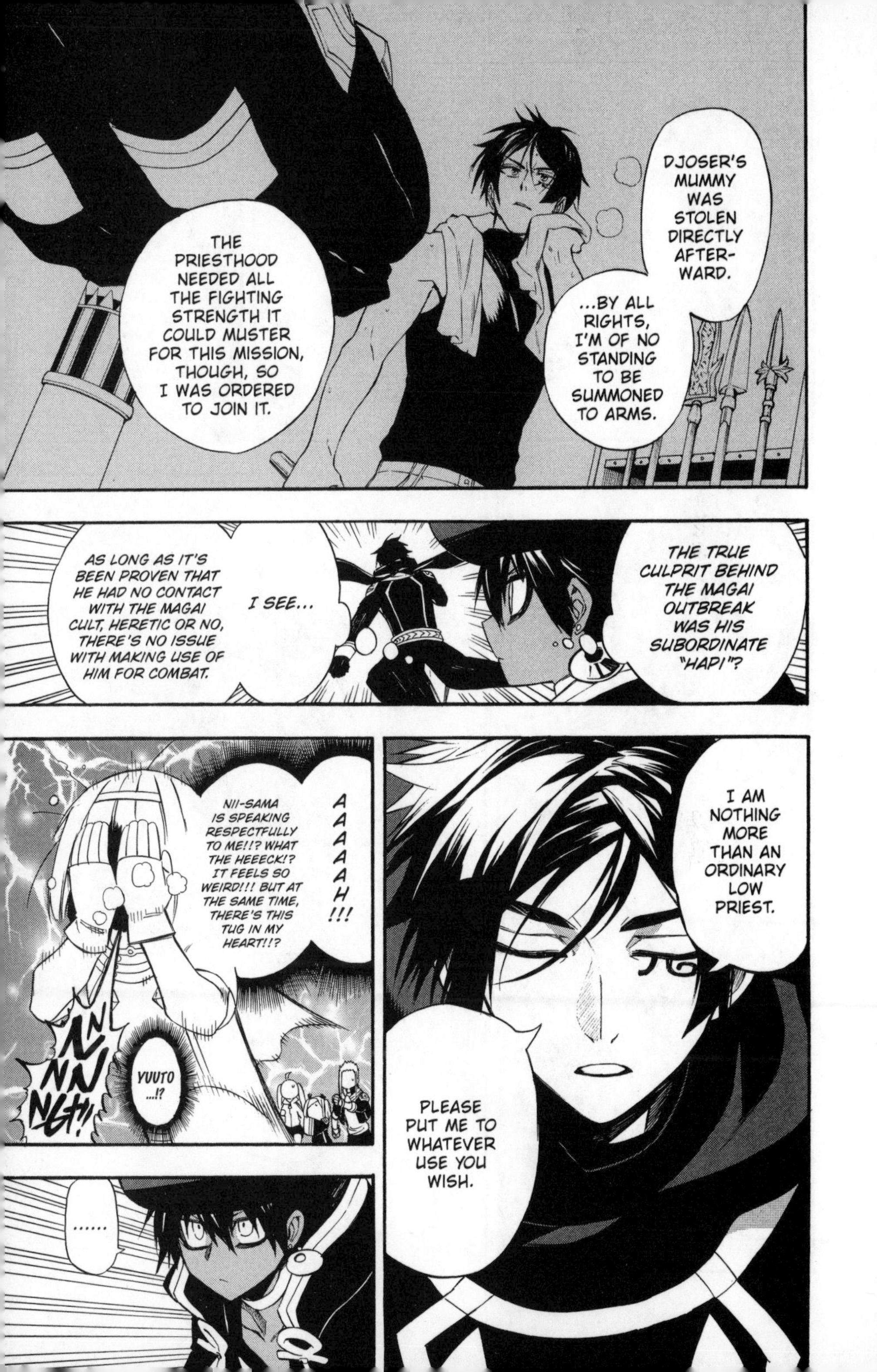
DJOSER'S MUMMY WAS STOLEN DIRECTLY AFTER-WARD.
...BY ALL RIGHTS, I'M OF NO STANDING TO BE SUMMONED TO ARMS.
THE PRIESTHOOD NEEDED ALL THE FIGHTING STRENGTH IT COULD MUSTER FOR THIS MISSION, THOUGH, SO I WAS ORDERED TO JOIN IT.
THE TRUE CULPRIT BEHIND THE MAGAI OUTBREAK WAS HIS SUBORDINATE "HAPI"?
I SEE...
AS LONG AS IT'S BEEN PROVEN THAT HE HAD NO CONTACT WITH THE MAGAI CULT, HERETIC OR NO, THERE'S NO ISSUE WITH MAKING USE OF HIM FOR COMBAT.
I AM NOTHING MORE THAN AN ORDINARY LOW PRIEST.
PLEASE PUT ME TO WHATEVER USE YOU WISH.
AAAAAAH!!!
NII-SAMA IS SPEAKING RESPECTFULLY TO ME!!? WHAT THE HEEECK!? IT FEELS SO WEIRD!!! BUT AT THE SAME TIME, THERE'S THIS TUG IN MY HEART!!?
YUUTO ...!?
NNNNNG!!
......

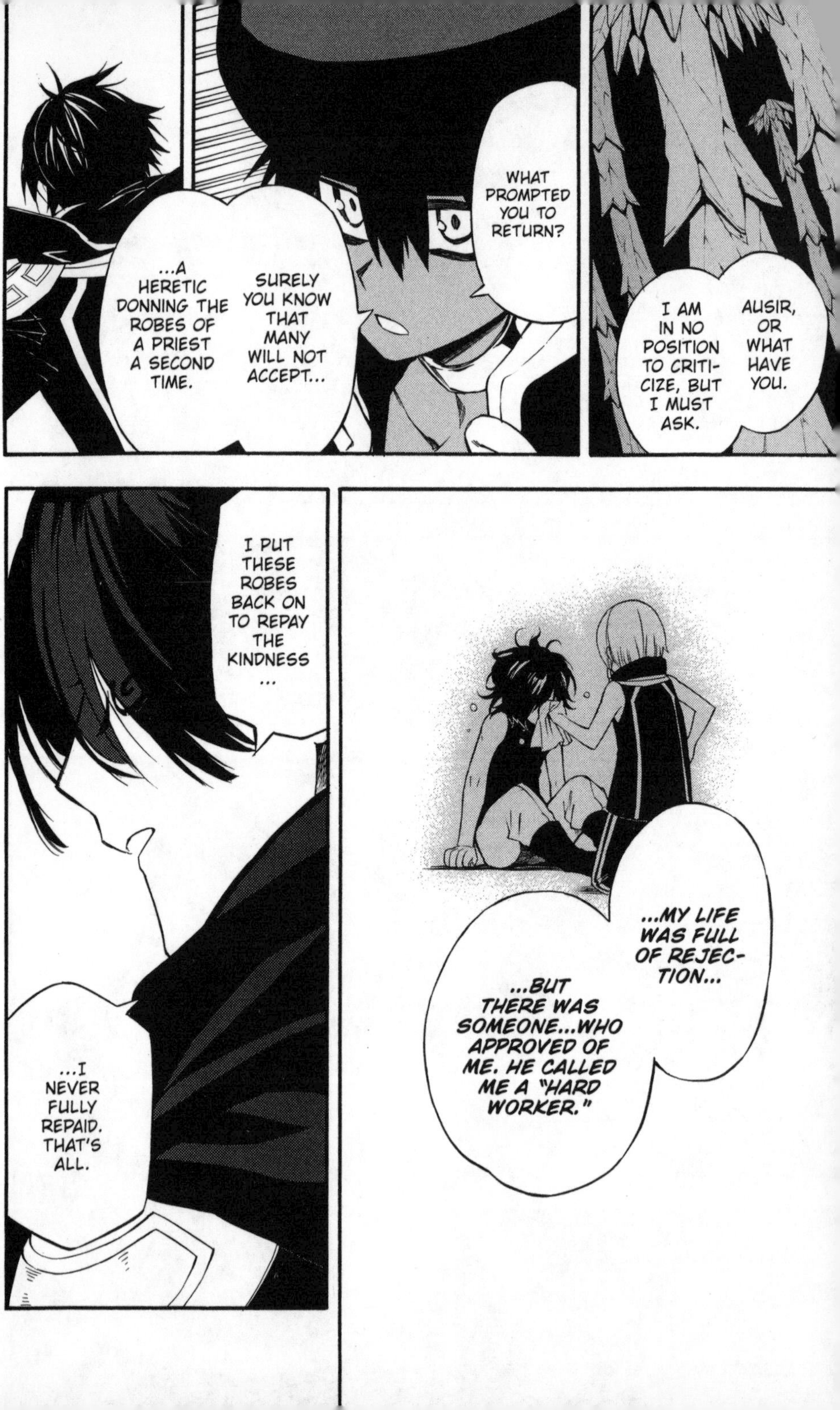
AUSIR, OR WHAT HAVE YOU.
I AM IN NO POSITION TO CRITI-CIZE, BUT I MUST ASK.
WHAT PROMPTED YOU TO RETURN?
SURELY YOU KNOW THAT MANY WILL NOT ACCEPT...
...A HERETIC DONNING THE ROBES OF A PRIEST A SECOND TIME.
...MY LIFE WAS FULL OF REJEC-TION...
...BUT THERE WAS SOMEONE...WHO APPROVED OF ME. HE CALLED ME A "HARD WORKER."
I PUT THESE ROBES BACK ON TO REPAY THE KINDNESS ...
...I NEVER FULLY REPAID. THAT'S ALL.

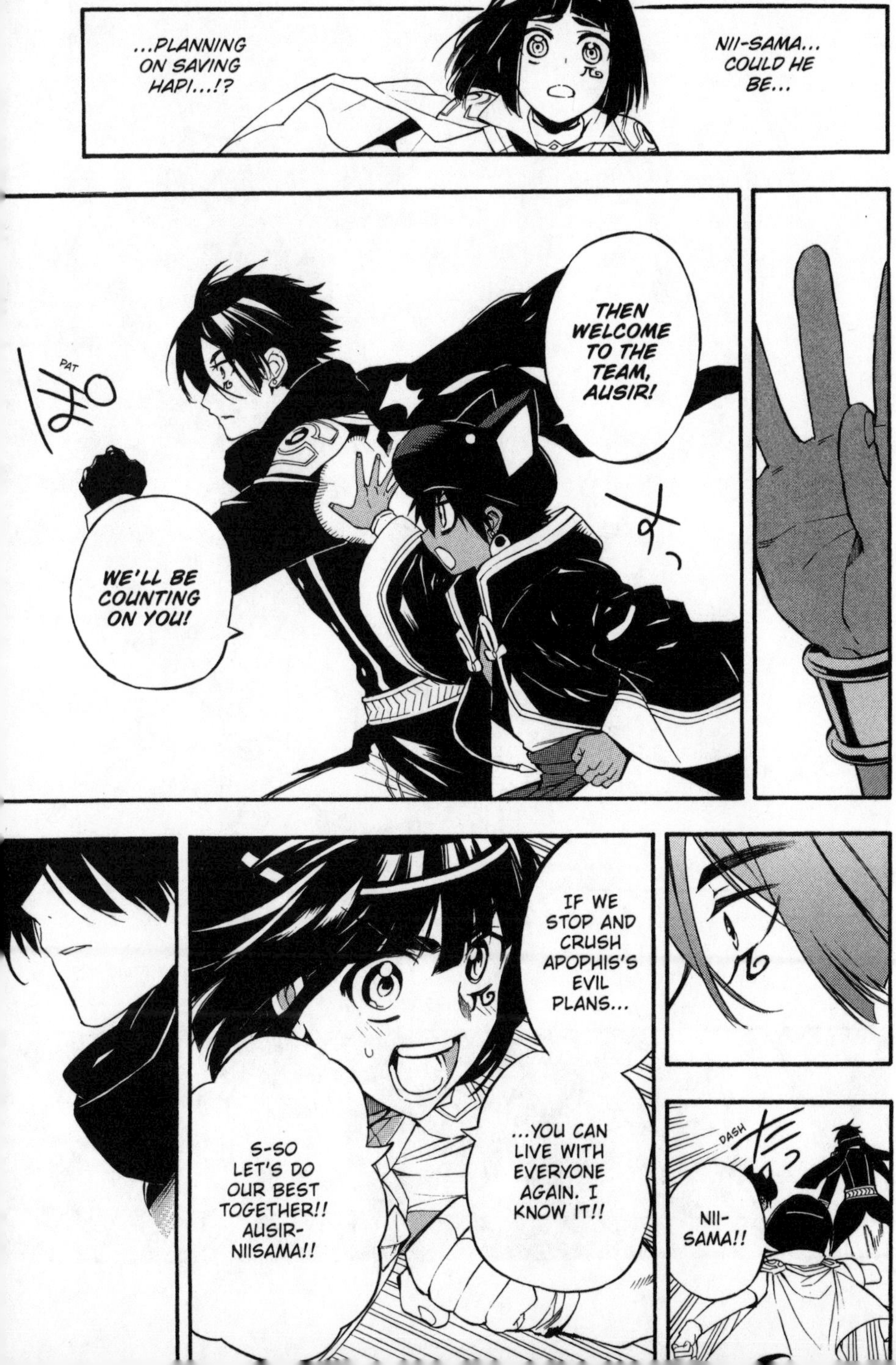
NII-SAMA... COULD HE BE...
...PLANNING ON SAVING HAPI...!?
THEN WELCOME TO THE TEAM, AUSIR!
PAT
WE'LL BE COUNTING ON YOU!
DASH
NII-SAMA!!
IF WE STOP AND CRUSH APOPHIS'S EVIL PLANS...
...YOU CAN LIVE WITH EVERYONE AGAIN. I KNOW IT!!
S-SO LET'S DO OUR BEST TOGETHER!! AUSIR-NIISAMA!!

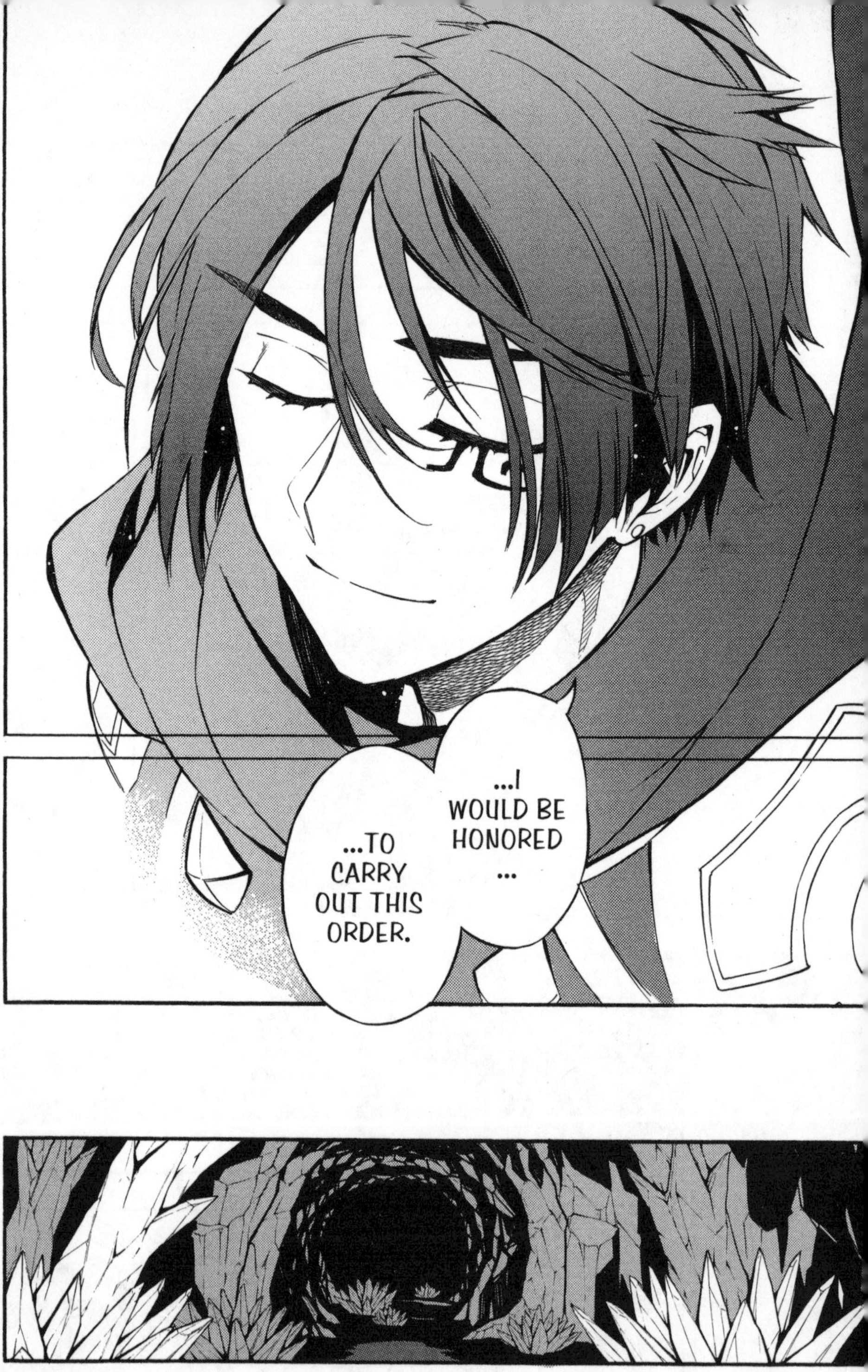
...I WOULD BE HONORED ...
...TO CARRY OUT THIS ORDER.

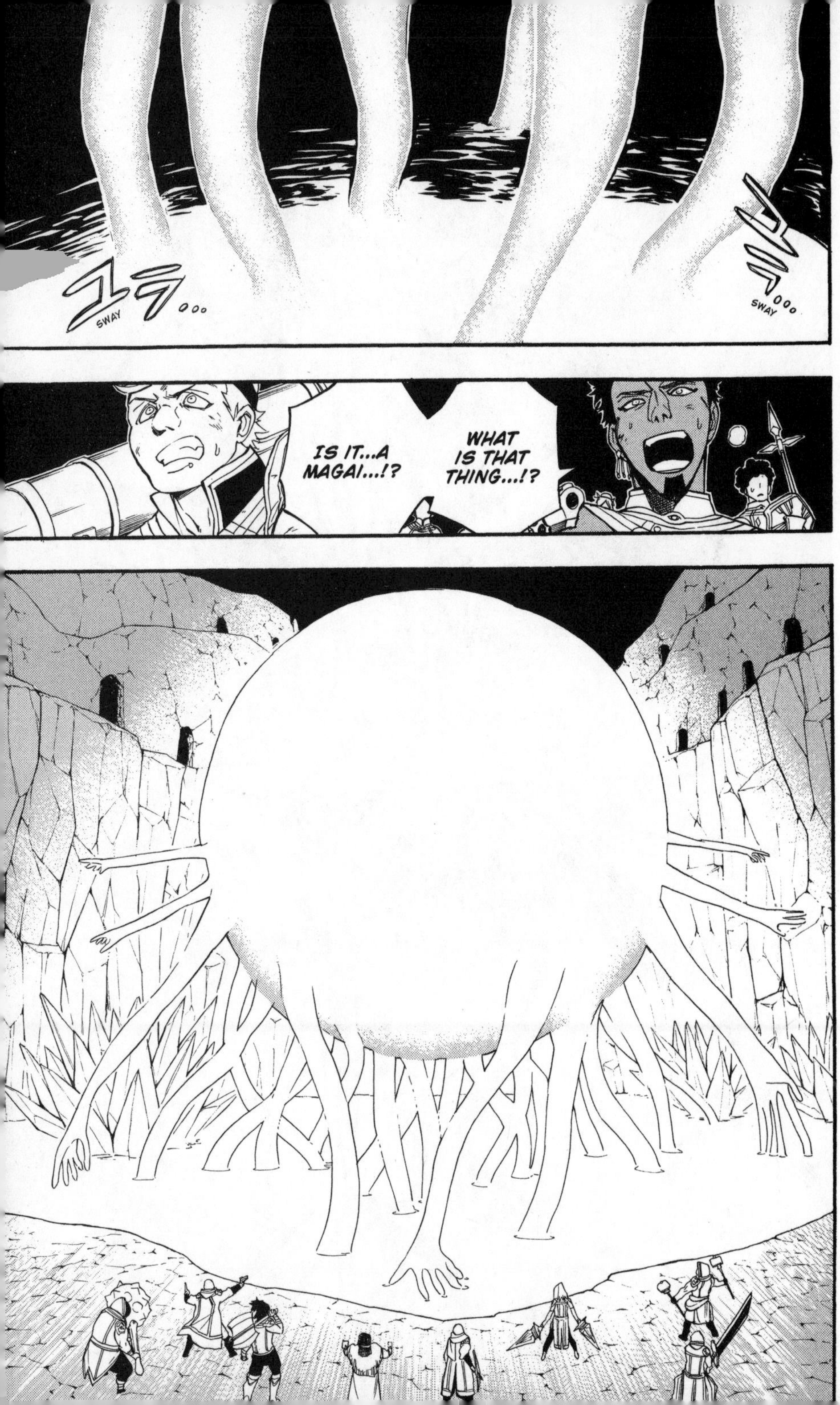
ユラ...
SWAY
ユラ...
SWAY
WHAT IS THAT THING...!?
IS IT...A MAGAI...!?

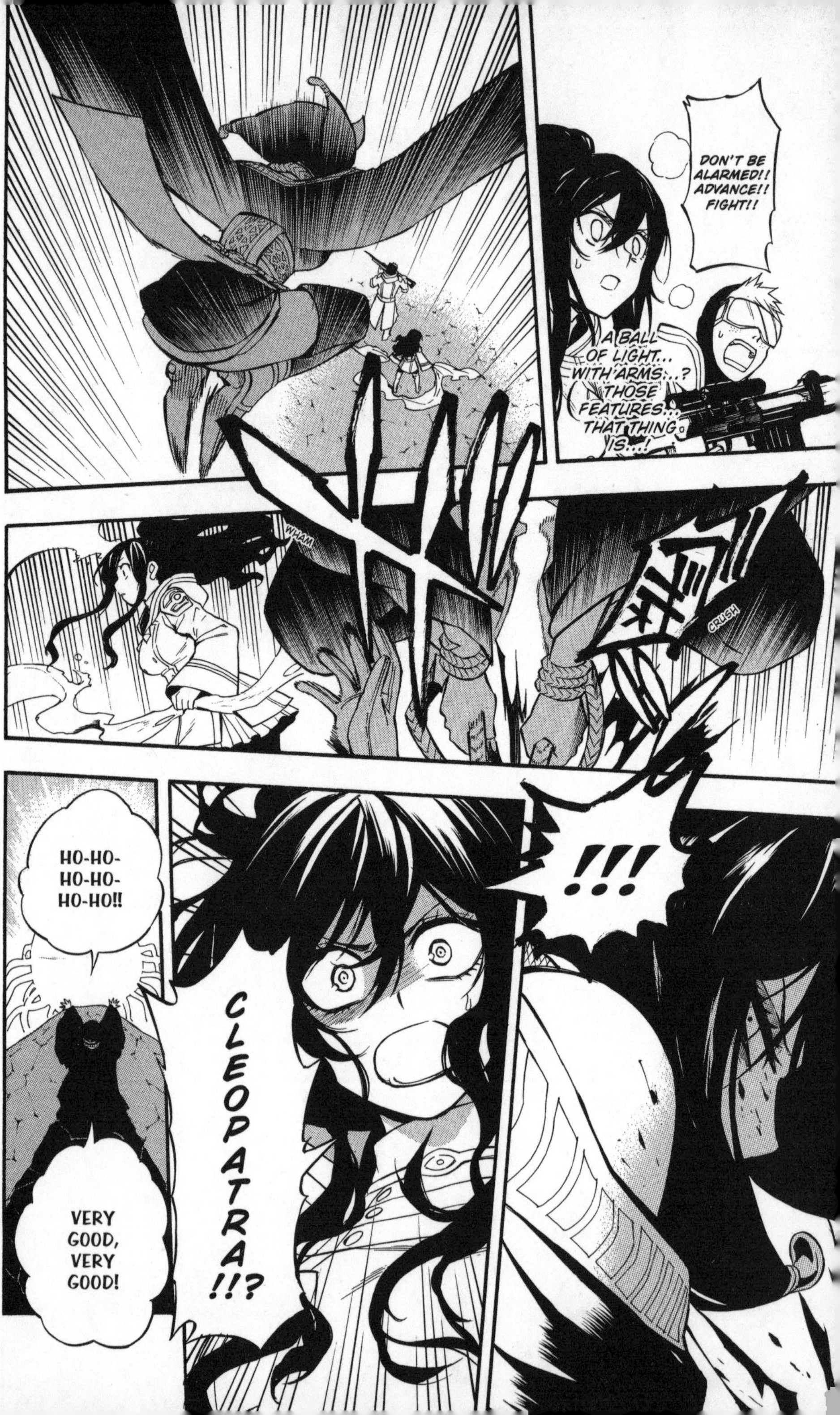

DON'T BE ALARMED!! ADVANCE!! FIGHT!!
A BALL OF LIGHT... WITH ARMS...? THOSE FEATURES... THAT THING IS...!
CRUSH
WHAM
!!!
CLEOPATRA!!?
HO-HO-HO-HO-HO-HO!!
VERY GOOD, VERY GOOD!

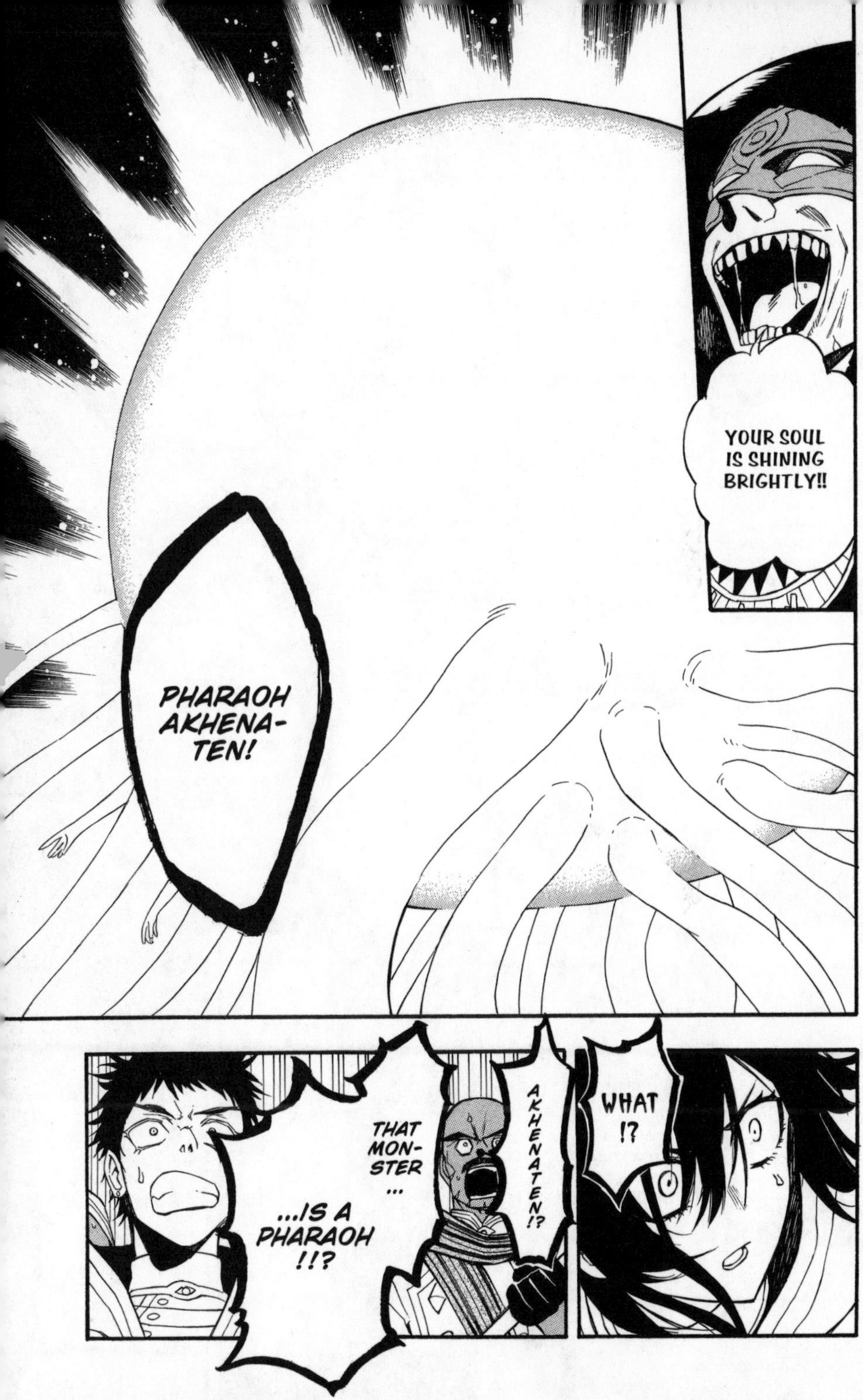

YOUR SOUL IS SHINING BRIGHTLY!!
PHARAOH AKHENA-TEN!
WHAT!?
AKHENATEN!?
THAT MON-STER...
...IS A PHARAOH!!?

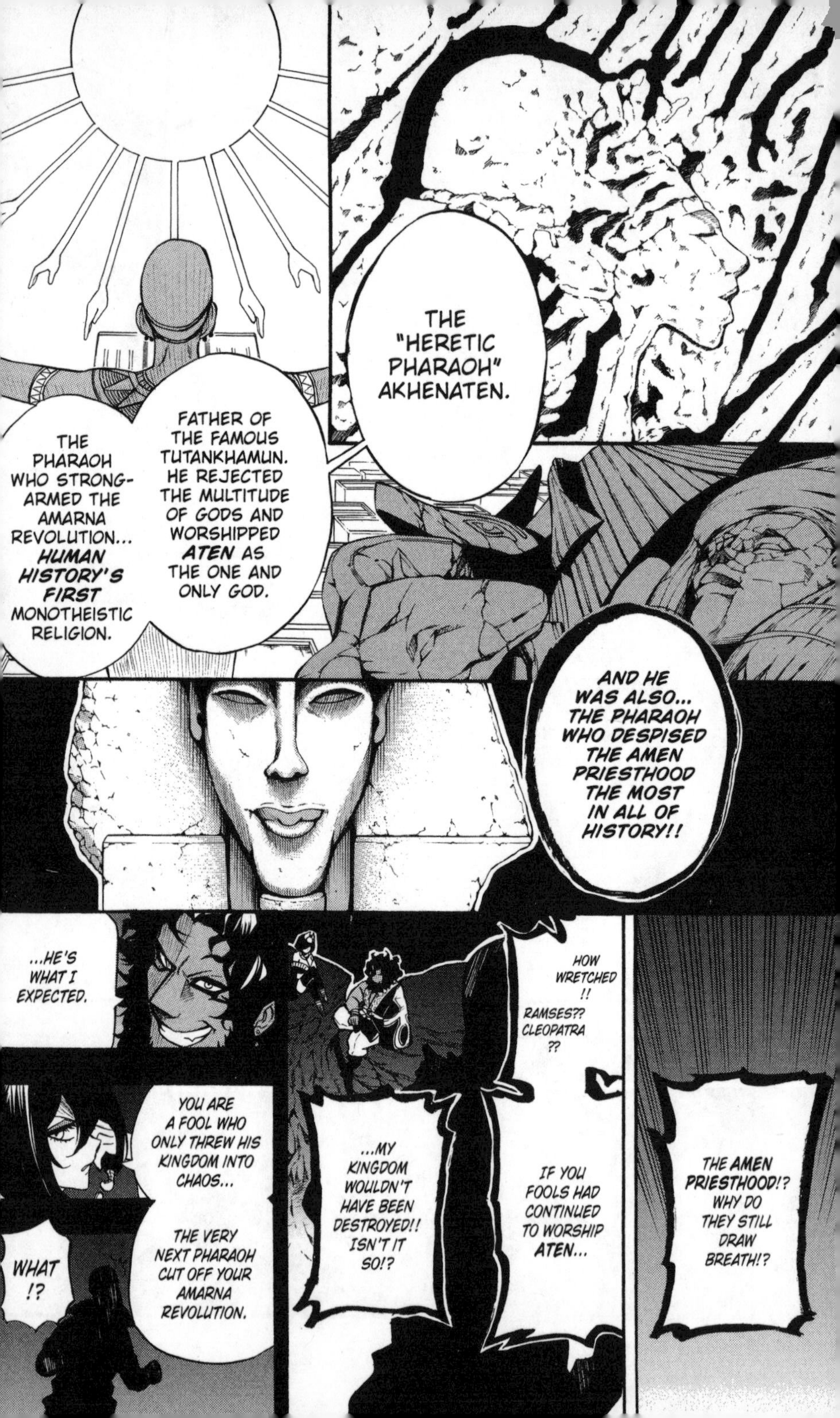
THE "HERETIC PHARAOH" AKHENATEN.
FATHER OF THE FAMOUS TUTANKHAMUN. HE REJECTED THE MULTITUDE OF GODS AND WORSHIPPED ATEN AS THE ONE AND ONLY GOD.
THE PHARAOH WHO STRONG-ARMED THE AMARNA REVOLUTION... HUMAN HISTORY'S FIRST MONOTHEISTIC RELIGION.
AND HE WAS ALSO... THE PHARAOH WHO DESPISED THE AMEN PRIESTHOOD THE MOST IN ALL OF HISTORY!!
THE AMEN PRIESTHOOD!? WHY DO THEY STILL DRAW BREATH!?
HOW WRETCHED !!
RAMSES?? CLEOPATRA ??
IF YOU FOOLS HAD CONTINUED TO WORSHIP ATEN...
...MY KINGDOM WOULDN'T HAVE BEEN DESTROYED!! ISN'T IT SO!?
...HE'S WHAT I EXPECTED.
YOU ARE A FOOL WHO ONLY THREW HIS KINGDOM INTO CHAOS...
THE VERY NEXT PHARAOH CUT OFF YOUR AMARNA REVOLUTION.
WHAT !?

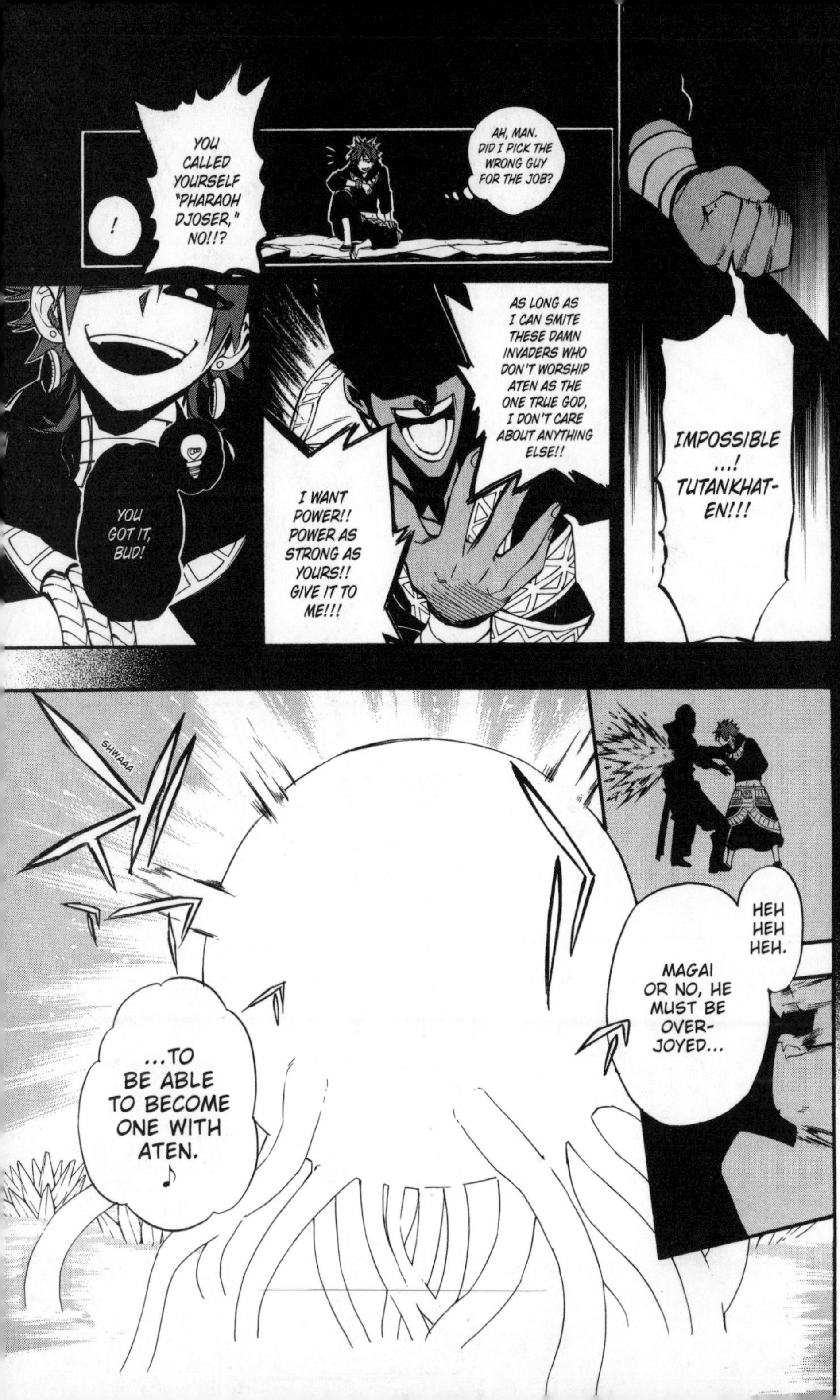
IMPOSSIBLE...! TUTANKHATEN!!!
YOU CALLED YOURSELF "PHARAOH DJOSER," NO!!?
AH, MAN. DID I PICK THE WRONG GUY FOR THE JOB?
!
AS LONG AS I CAN SMITE THESE DAMN INVADERS WHO DON'T WORSHIP ATEN AS THE ONE TRUE GOD, I DON'T CARE ABOUT ANYTHING ELSE!!
I WANT POWER!! POWER AS STRONG AS YOURS!! GIVE IT TO ME!!!
YOU GOT IT, BUD!
HEH HEH HEH.
MAGAI OR NO, HE MUST BE OVERJOYED...
...TO BE ABLE TO BECOME ONE WITH ATEN. ♪
SHWAAA

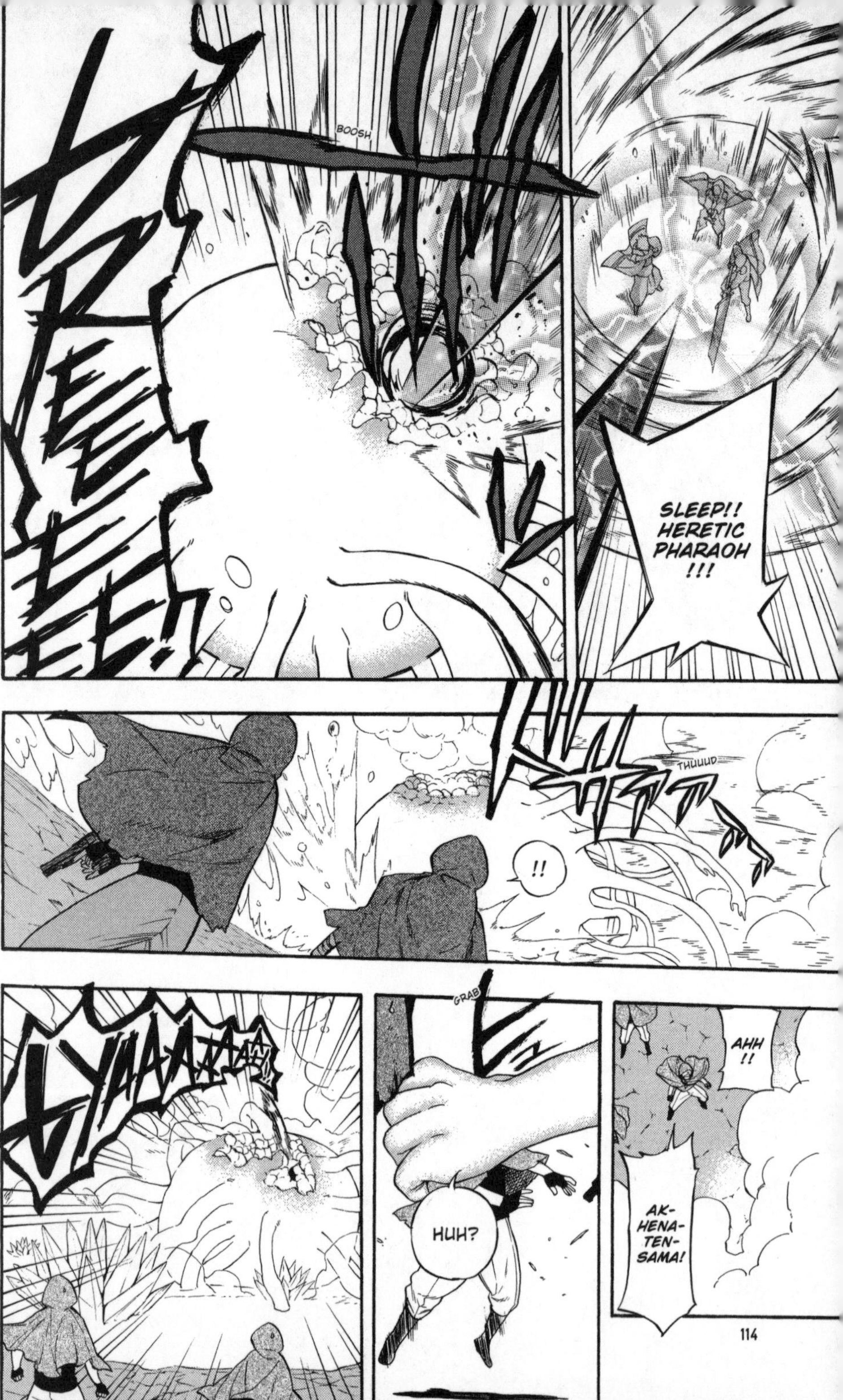
BOOSH
SLEEP!! HERETIC PHARAOH!!!
THUUUD
!!
AHH!!
AK-HENA-TEN-SAMA!
GRAB
HUH?

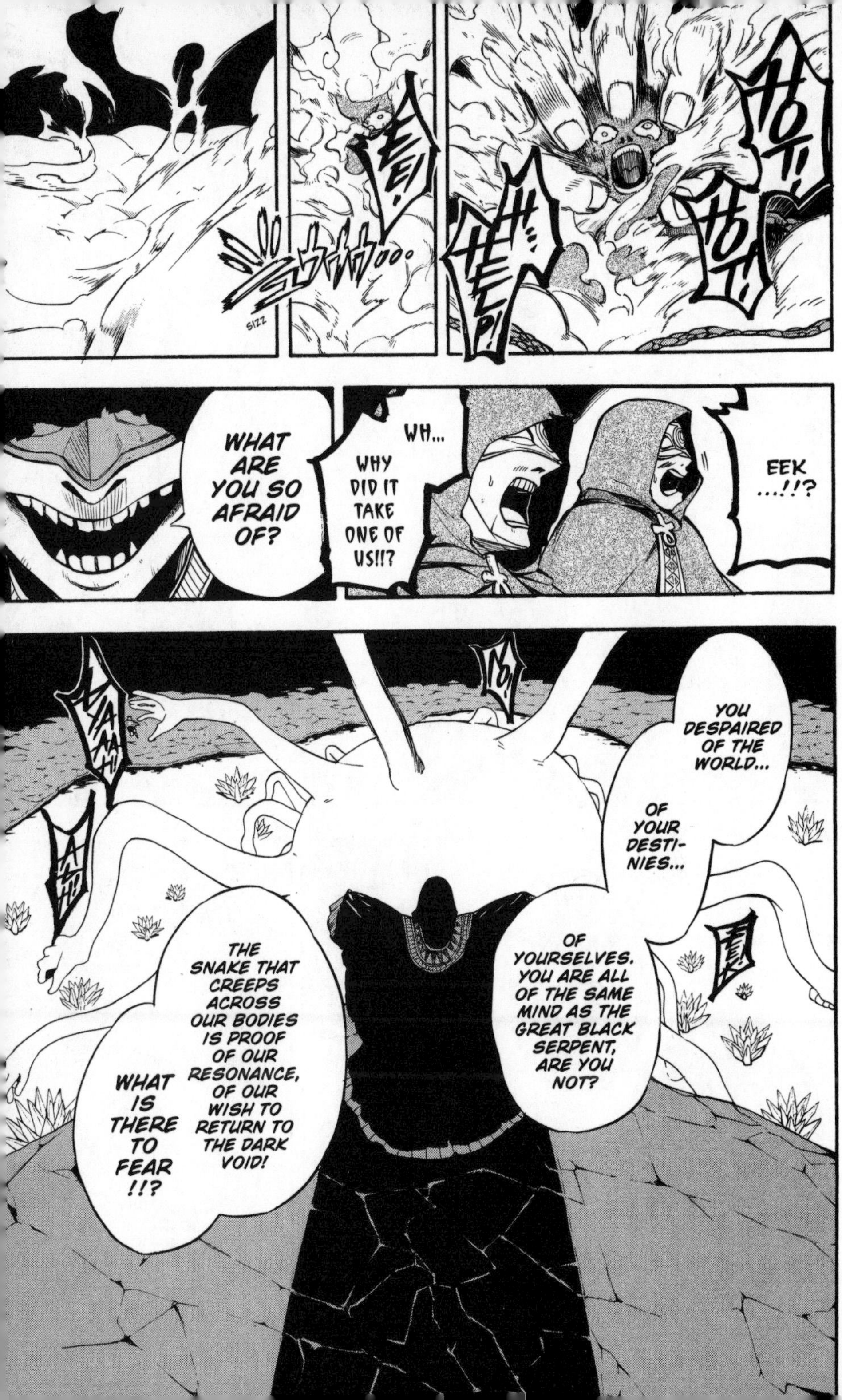
HOT!! HOT!!
H...
HELP!
EE!
SIZZ
EEK ...!!?
WH...
WHY DID IT TAKE ONE OF US!!?
WHAT ARE YOU SO AFRAID OF?
NO!
YOU DESPAIRED OF THE WORLD...
OF YOUR DESTINIES...
OF YOURSELVES. YOU ARE ALL OF THE SAME MIND AS THE GREAT BLACK SERPENT, ARE YOU NOT?
THE SNAKE THAT CREEPS ACROSS OUR BODIES IS PROOF OF OUR RESONANCE, OF OUR WISH TO RETURN TO THE DARK VOID!
WHAT IS THERE TO FEAR!!?
AAAAH!
AAH!!

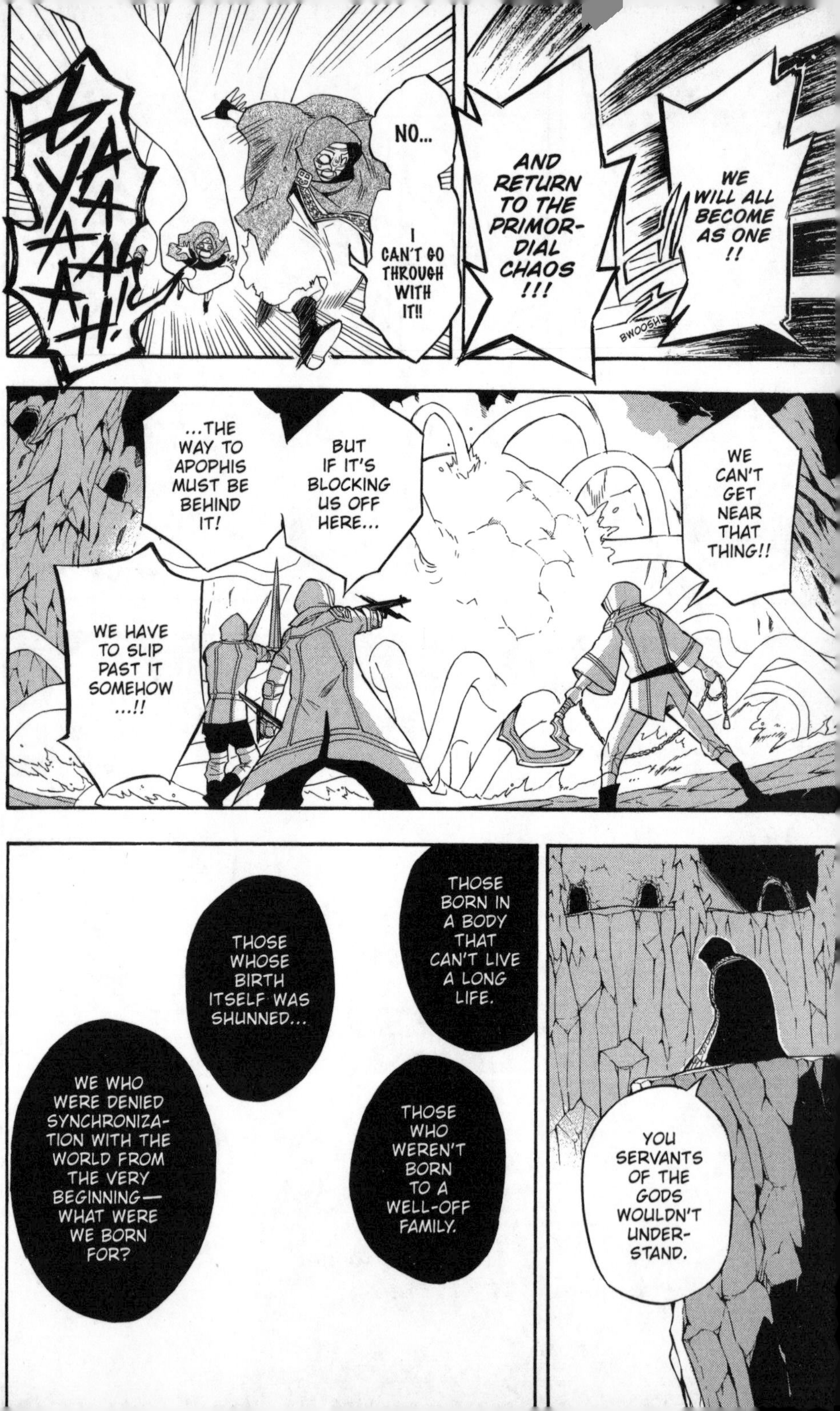
WE WILL ALL BECOME AS ONE!!
AND RETURN TO THE PRIMORDIAL CHAOS!!!
BWOOSH
NO...
I CAN'T GO THROUGH WITH IT!!
MYAAAAAH!!
WE CAN'T GET NEAR THAT THING!!
BUT IF IT'S BLOCKING US OFF HERE...
...THE WAY TO APOPHIS MUST BE BEHIND IT!
WE HAVE TO SLIP PAST IT SOMEHOW...!!
YOU SERVANTS OF THE GODS WOULDN'T UNDERSTAND.
THOSE BORN IN A BODY THAT CAN'T LIVE A LONG LIFE.
THOSE WHOSE BIRTH ITSELF WAS SHUNNED...
THOSE WHO WEREN'T BORN TO A WELL-OFF FAMILY.
WE WHO WERE DENIED SYNCHRONIZATION WITH THE WORLD FROM THE VERY BEGINNING—WHAT WERE WE BORN FOR?

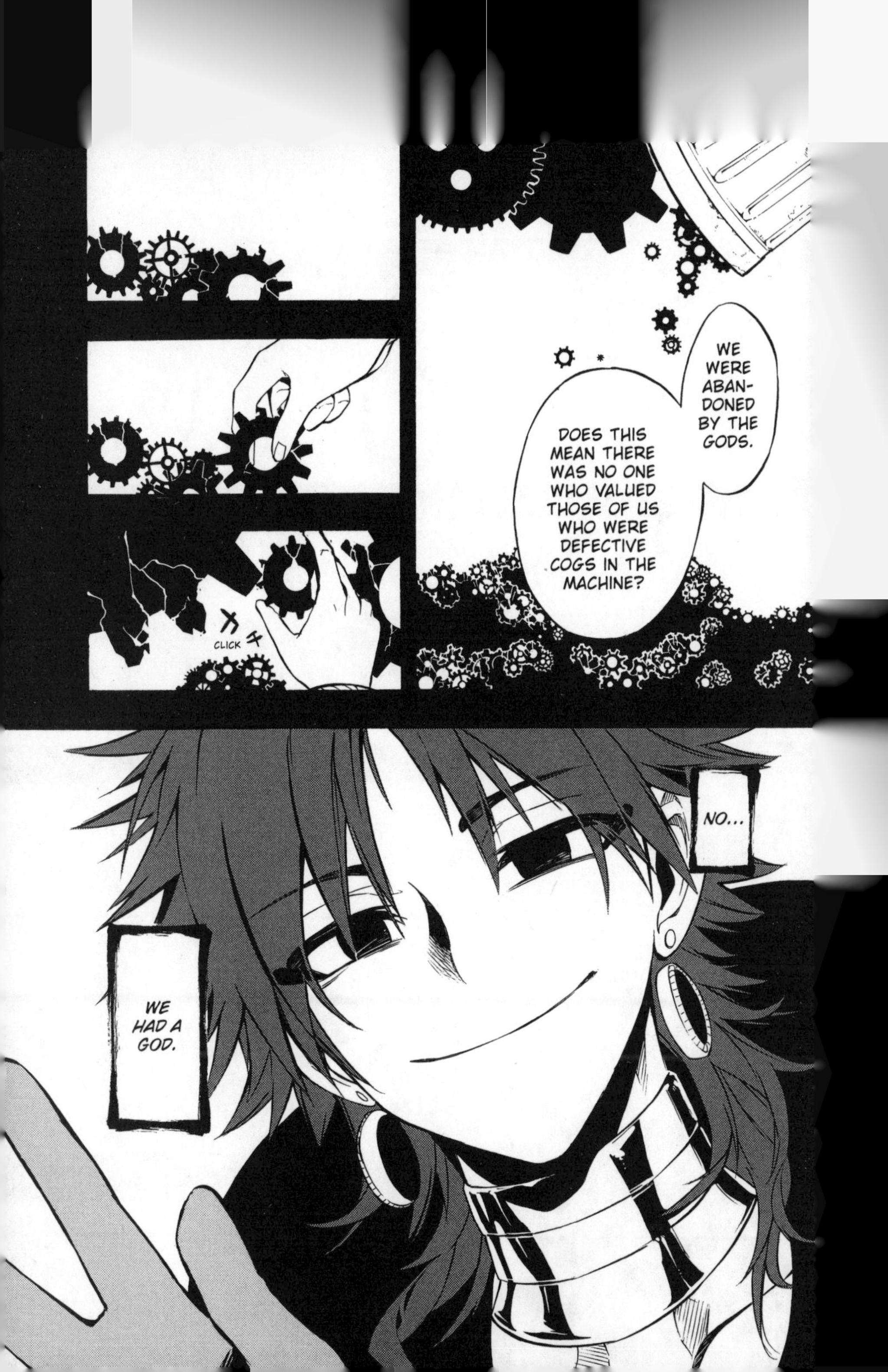
WE WERE ABAN-DONED BY THE GODS.
DOES THIS MEAN THERE WAS NO ONE WHO VALUED THOSE OF US WHO WERE DEFECTIVE COGS IN THE MACHINE?
カチ
CLICK
NO...
WE HAD A GOD.

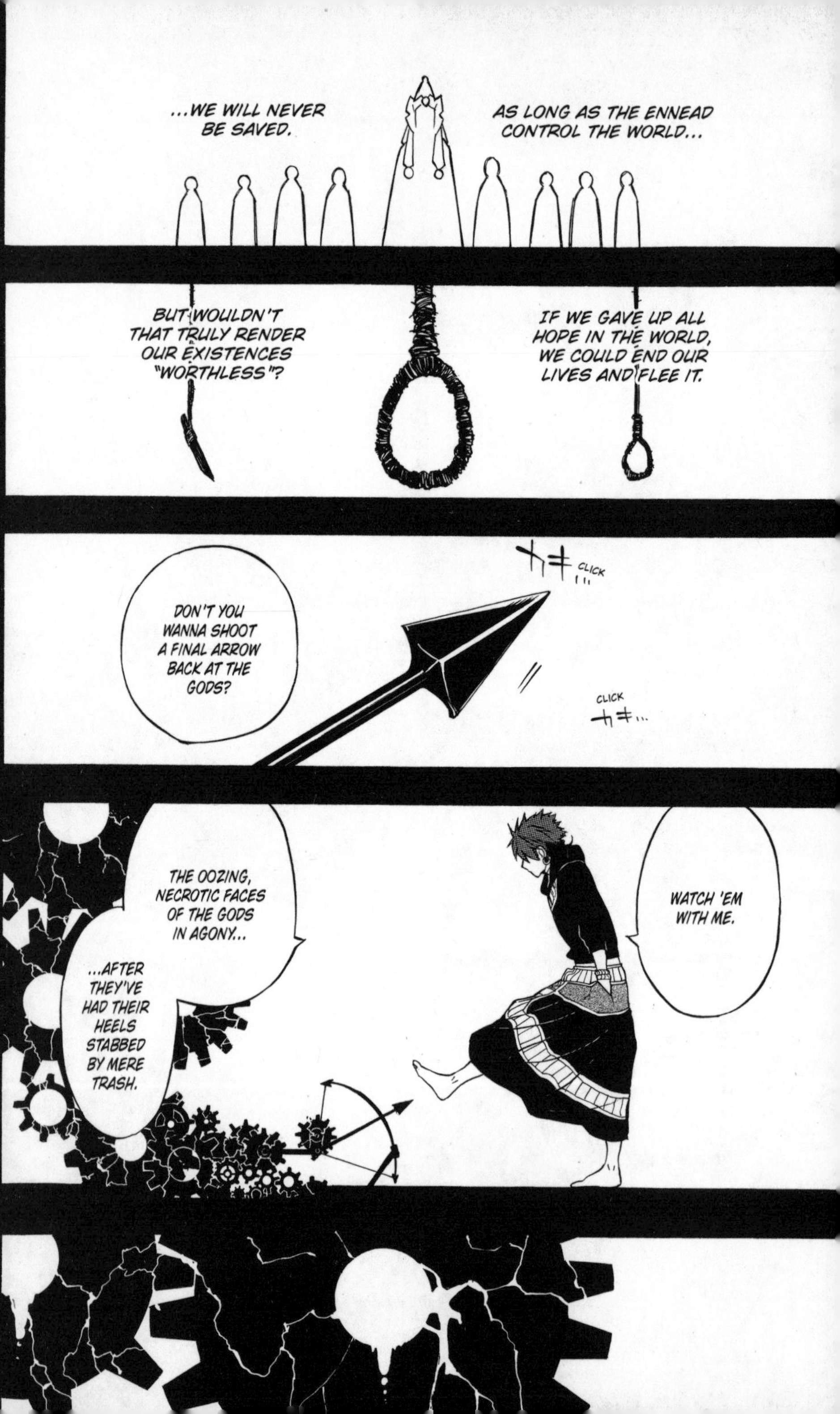
AS LONG AS THE ENNEAD CONTROL THE WORLD...
...WE WILL NEVER BE SAVED.
IF WE GAVE UP ALL HOPE IN THE WORLD, WE COULD END OUR LIVES AND FLEE IT.
BUT WOULDN'T THAT TRULY RENDER OUR EXISTENCES "WORTHLESS"?
カキ CLICK
CLICK カキ...
DON'T YOU WANNA SHOOT A FINAL ARROW BACK AT THE GODS?
WATCH 'EM WITH ME.
THE OOZING, NECROTIC FACES OF THE GODS IN AGONY...
...AFTER THEY'VE HAD THEIR HEELS STABBED BY MERE TRASH.

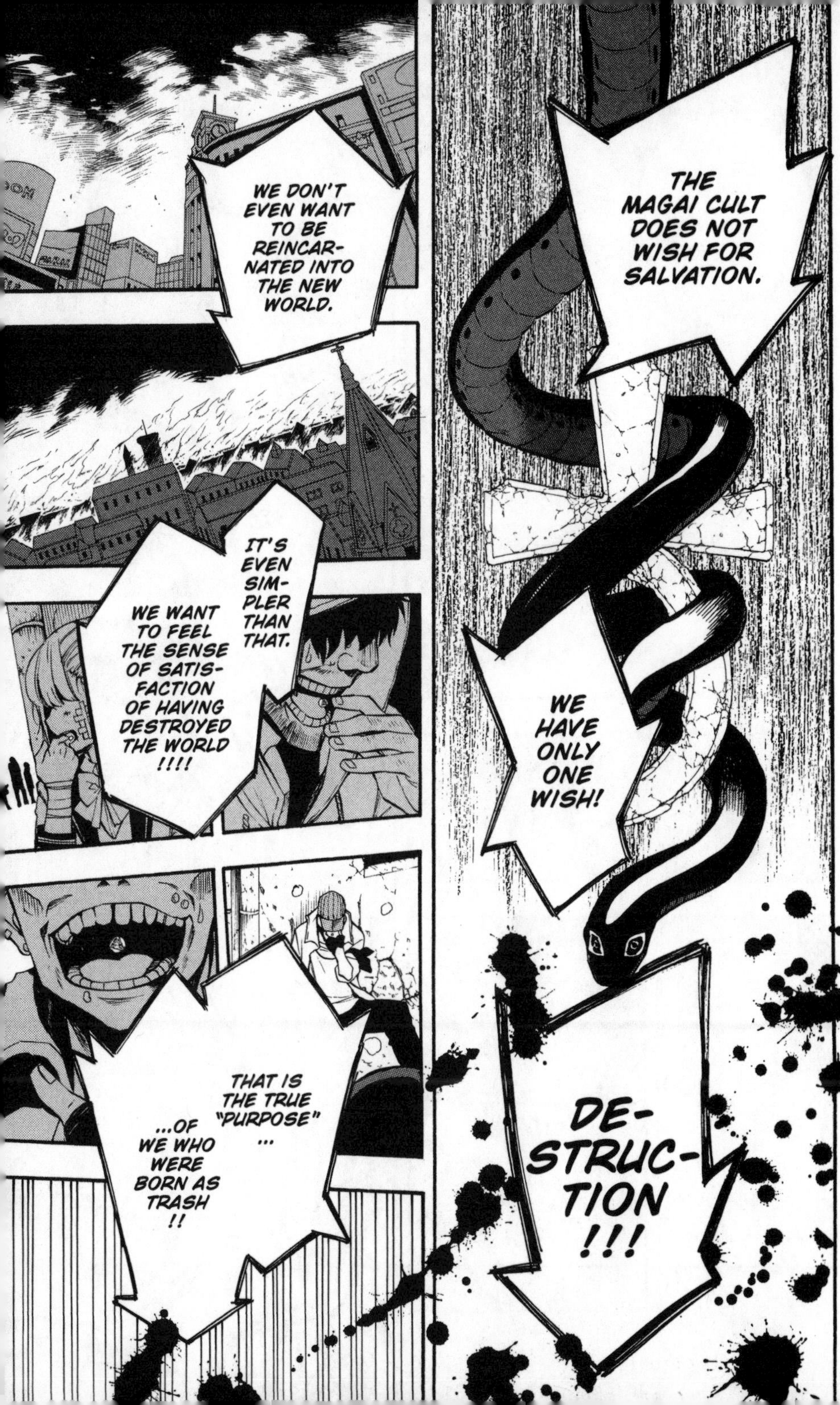
THE MAGAI CULT DOES NOT WISH FOR SALVATION.
WE HAVE ONLY ONE WISH!
DE-STRUC-TION!!!
WE DON'T EVEN WANT TO BE REINCAR-NATED INTO THE NEW WORLD.
IT'S EVEN SIM-PLER THAN THAT.
WE WANT TO FEEL THE SENSE OF SATIS-FACTION OF HAVING DESTROYED THE WORLD!!!!
THAT IS THE TRUE "PURPOSE"...
...OF WE WHO WERE BORN AS TRASH!!

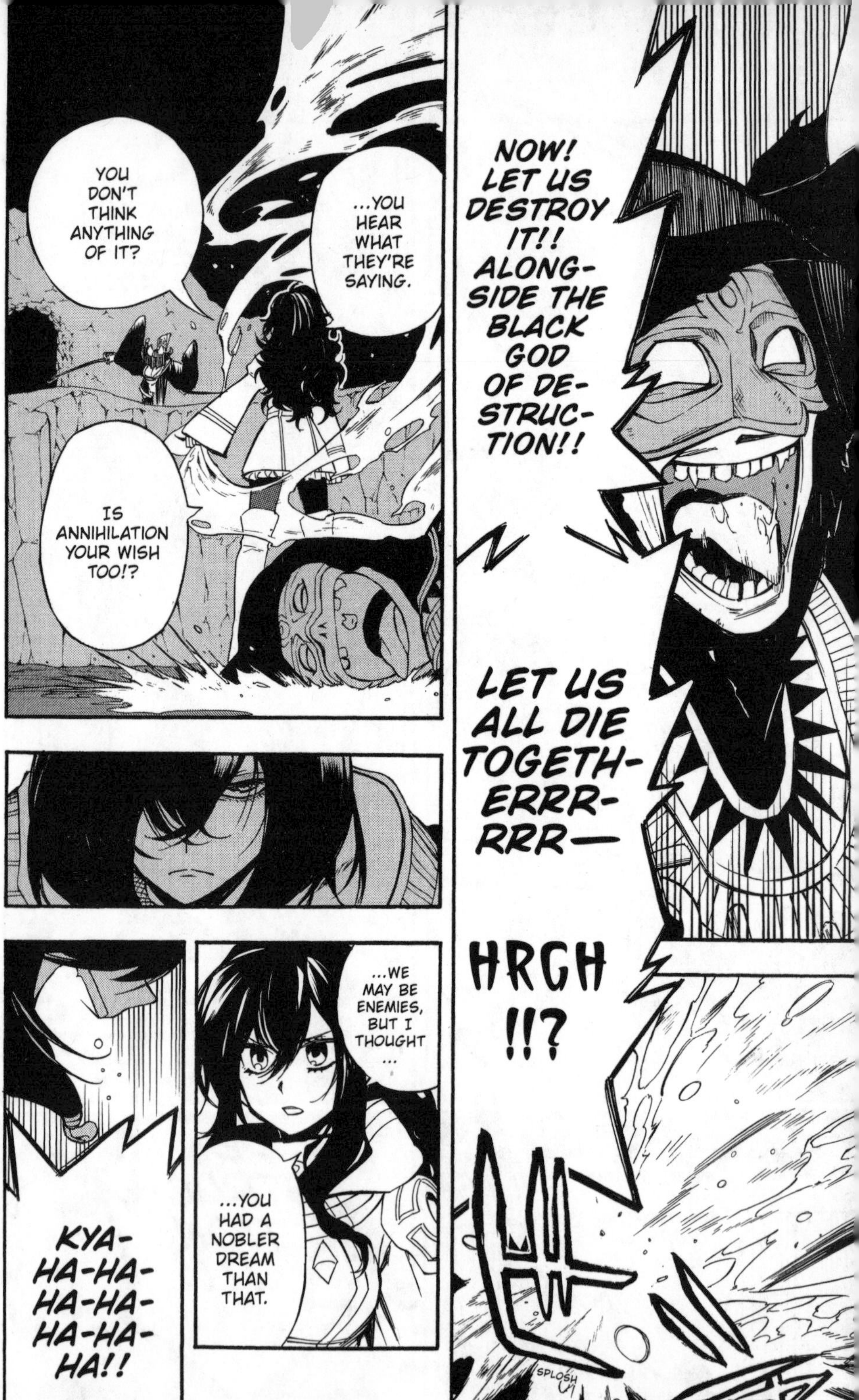

NOW! LET US DESTROY IT!! ALONG-SIDE THE BLACK GOD OF DE-STRUC-TION!!
LET US ALL DIE TOGETH-ERRRR-RRR—
HRGH !!?
SPLOSH
...YOU HEAR WHAT THEY'RE SAYING.
YOU DON'T THINK ANYTHING OF IT?
IS ANNIHILATION YOUR WISH TOO!?
...WE MAY BE ENEMIES, BUT I THOUGHT ...
...YOU HAD A NOBLER DREAM THAN THAT.
KYA-HA-HA-HA-HA-HA-HA-HA!!

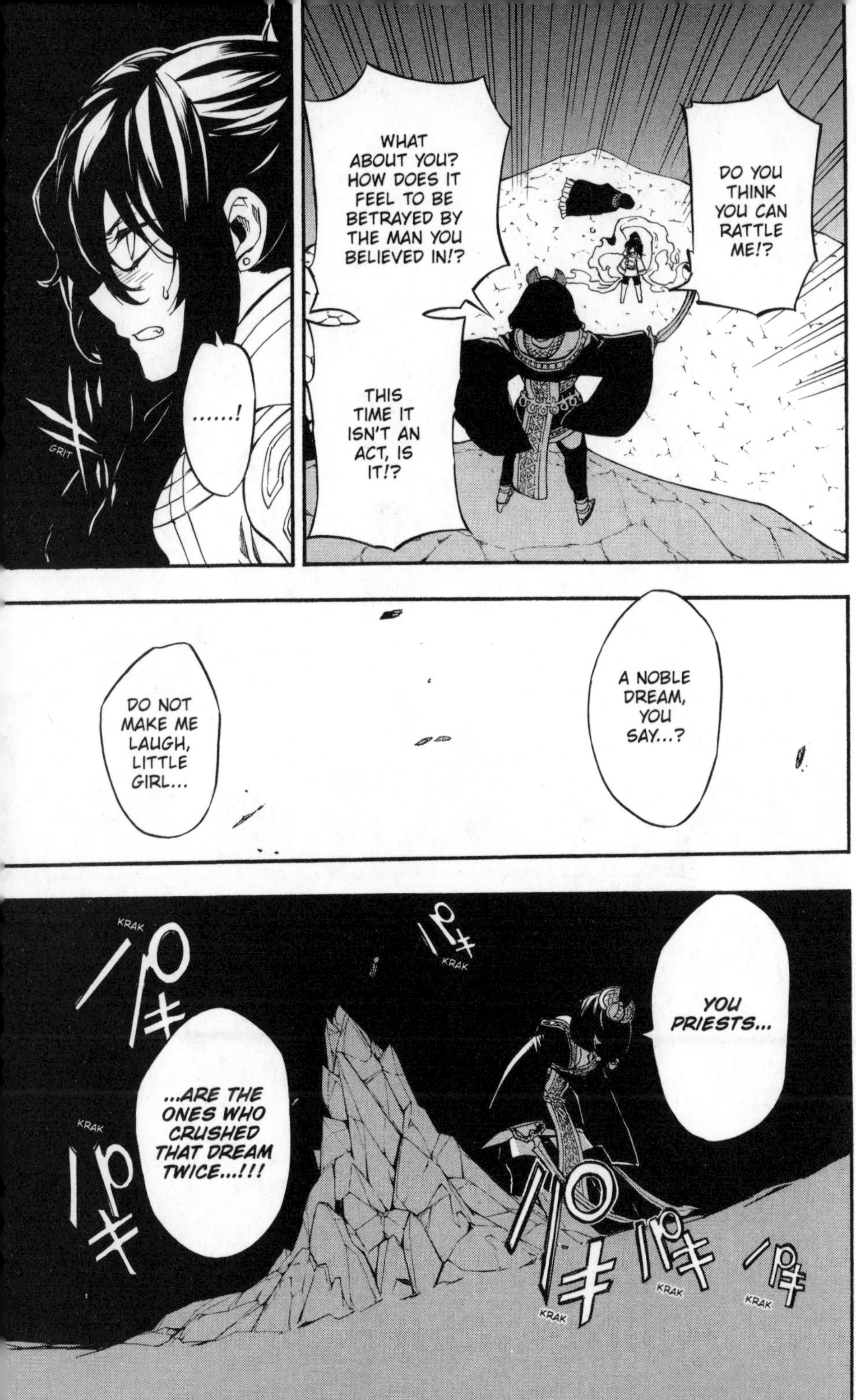
DO YOU THINK YOU CAN RATTLE ME!?
WHAT ABOUT YOU? HOW DOES IT FEEL TO BE BETRAYED BY THE MAN YOU BELIEVED IN!?
THIS TIME IT ISN'T AN ACT, IS IT!?
GRIT
......!
A NOBLE DREAM, YOU SAY...?
DO NOT MAKE ME LAUGH, LITTLE GIRL...
KRAK
KRAK
YOU PRIESTS...
...ARE THE ONES WHO CRUSHED THAT DREAM TWICE...!!!
KRAK
KRAK
KRAK
KRAK

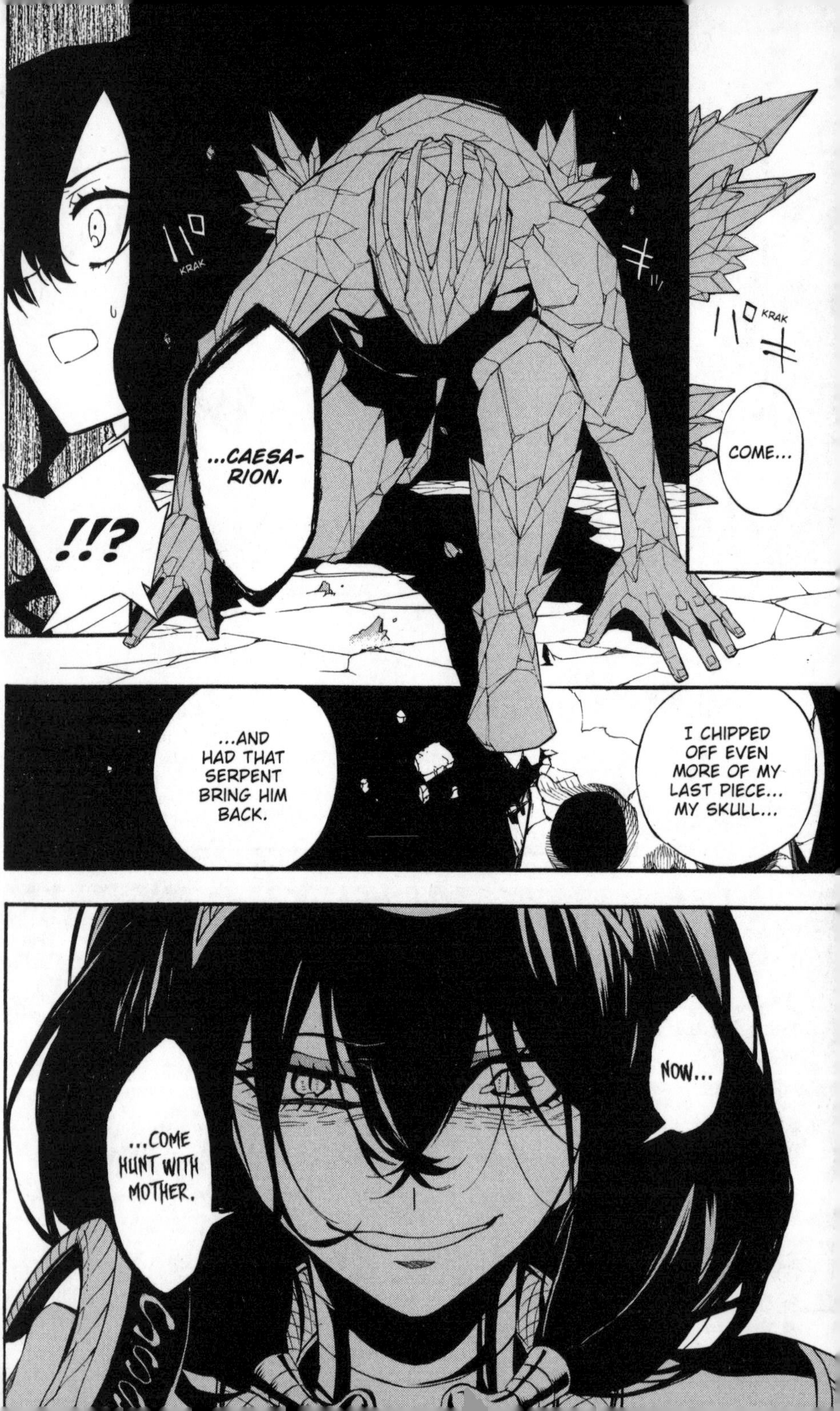
KRAK
COME...
KRAK
...CAESARION.
!!?
I CHIPPED OFF EVEN MORE OF MY LAST PIECE... MY SKULL...
...AND HAD THAT SERPENT BRING HIM BACK.
NOW...
...COME HUNT WITH MOTHER.

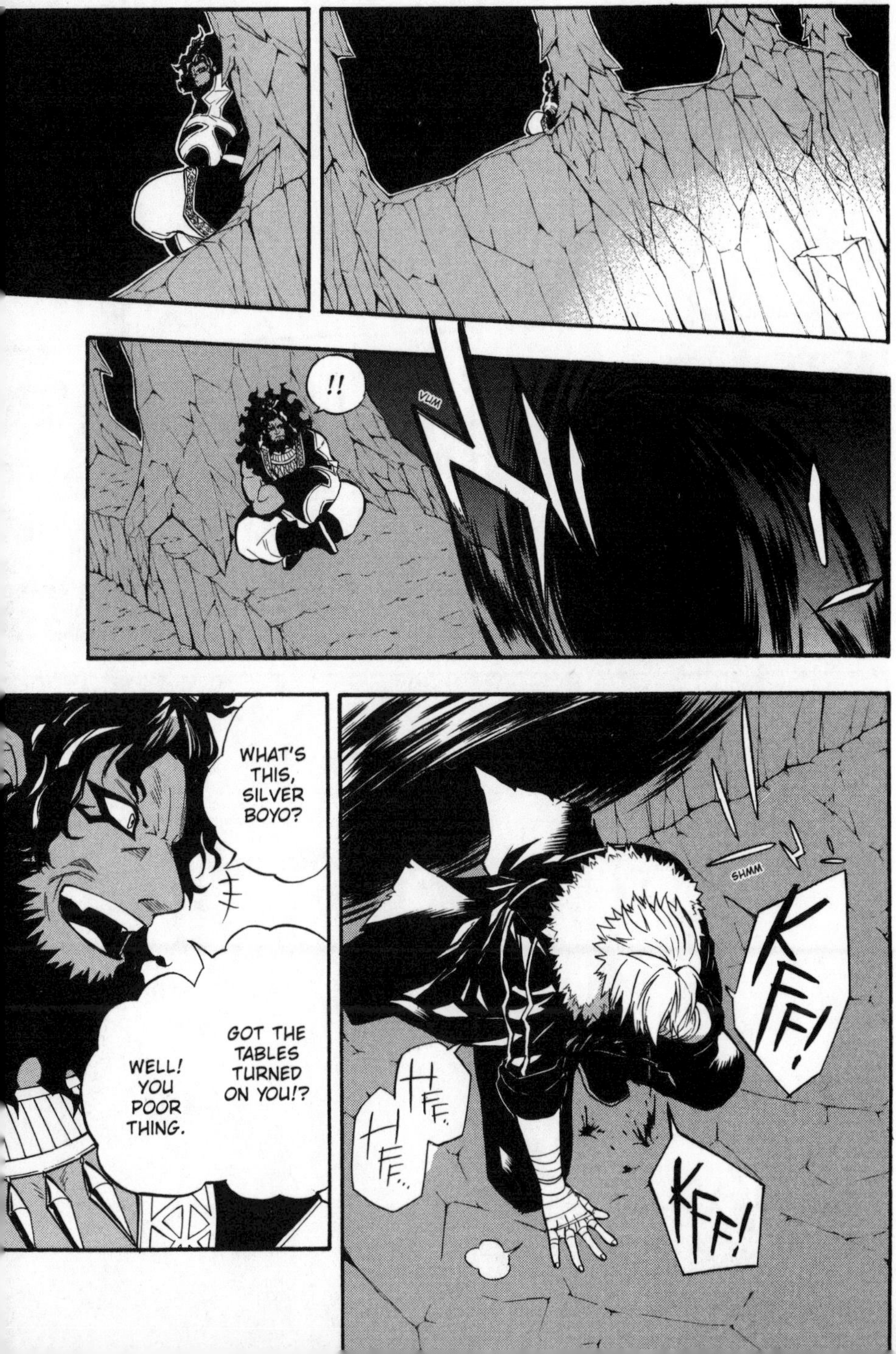
!!
VUM
SHMM
KFF!
HFF.. HFF...
KFF!
WHAT'S THIS, SILVER BOYO?
GOT THE TABLES TURNED ON YOU!?
WELL! YOU POOR THING.

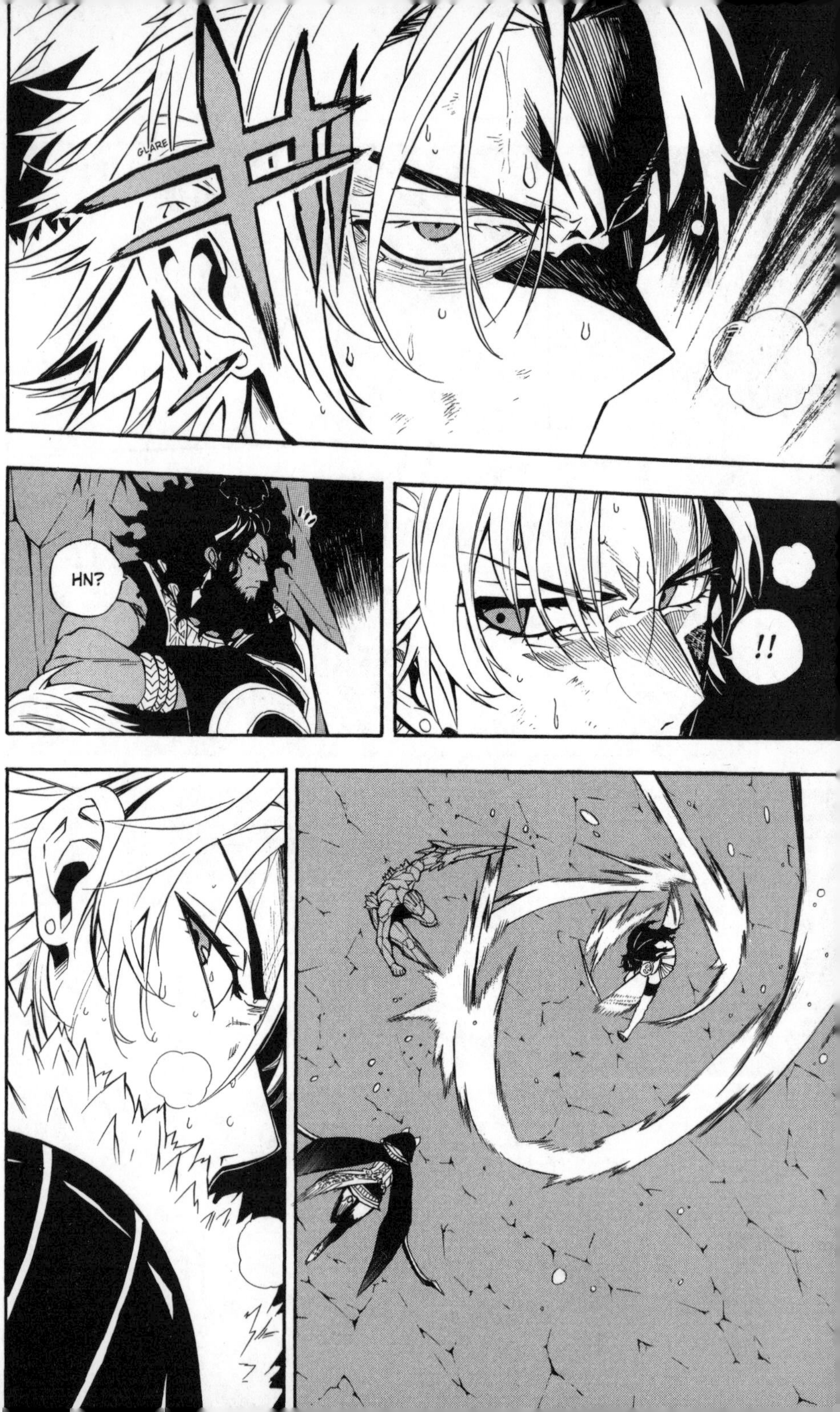
GLARE
!!
HN?

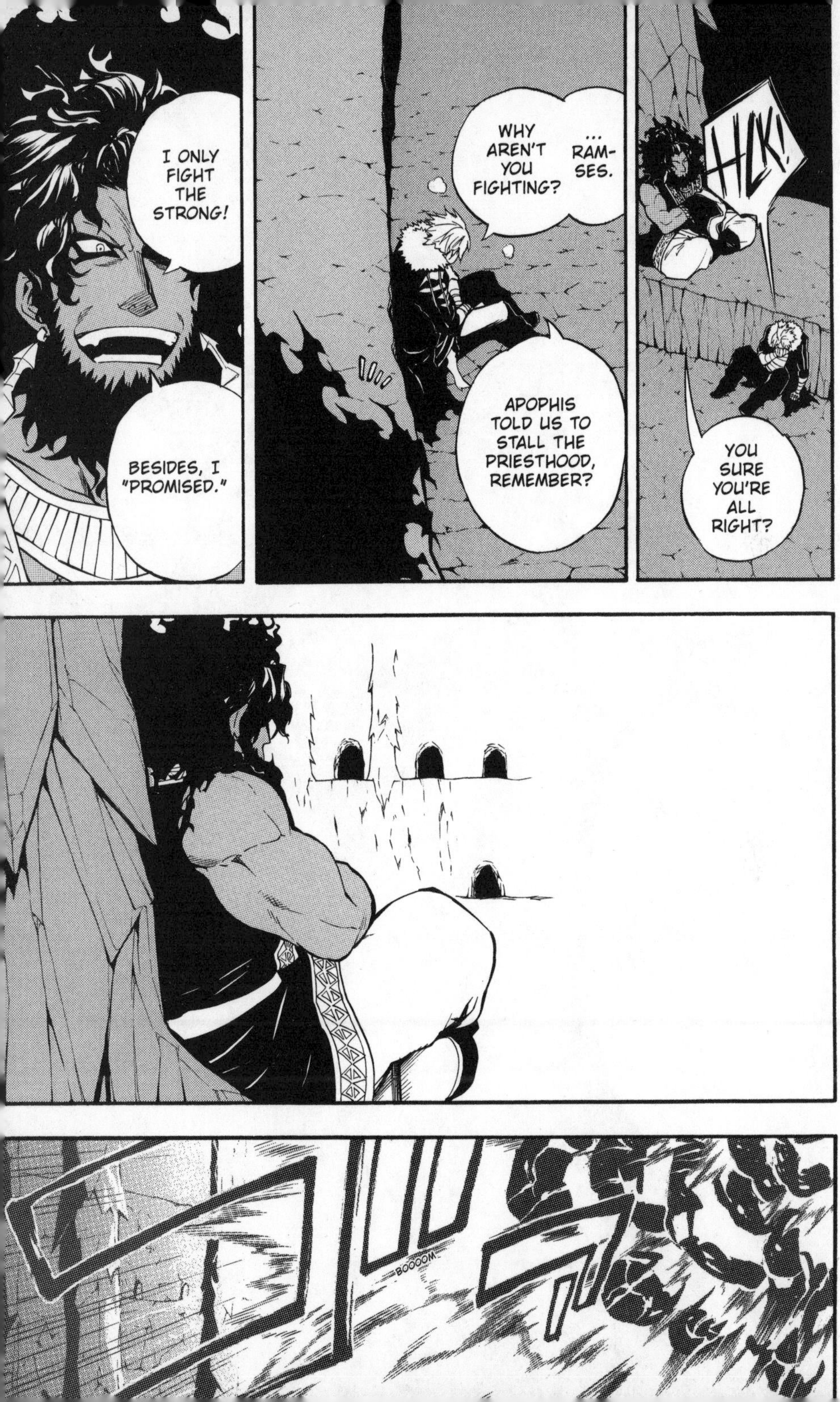
HCK!
YOU SURE YOU'RE ALL RIGHT?
... RAMSES.
WHY AREN'T YOU FIGHTING?
APOPHIS TOLD US TO STALL THE PRIESTHOOD, REMEMBER?
I ONLY FIGHT THE STRONG!
BESIDES, I "PROMISED."
BOOOOM

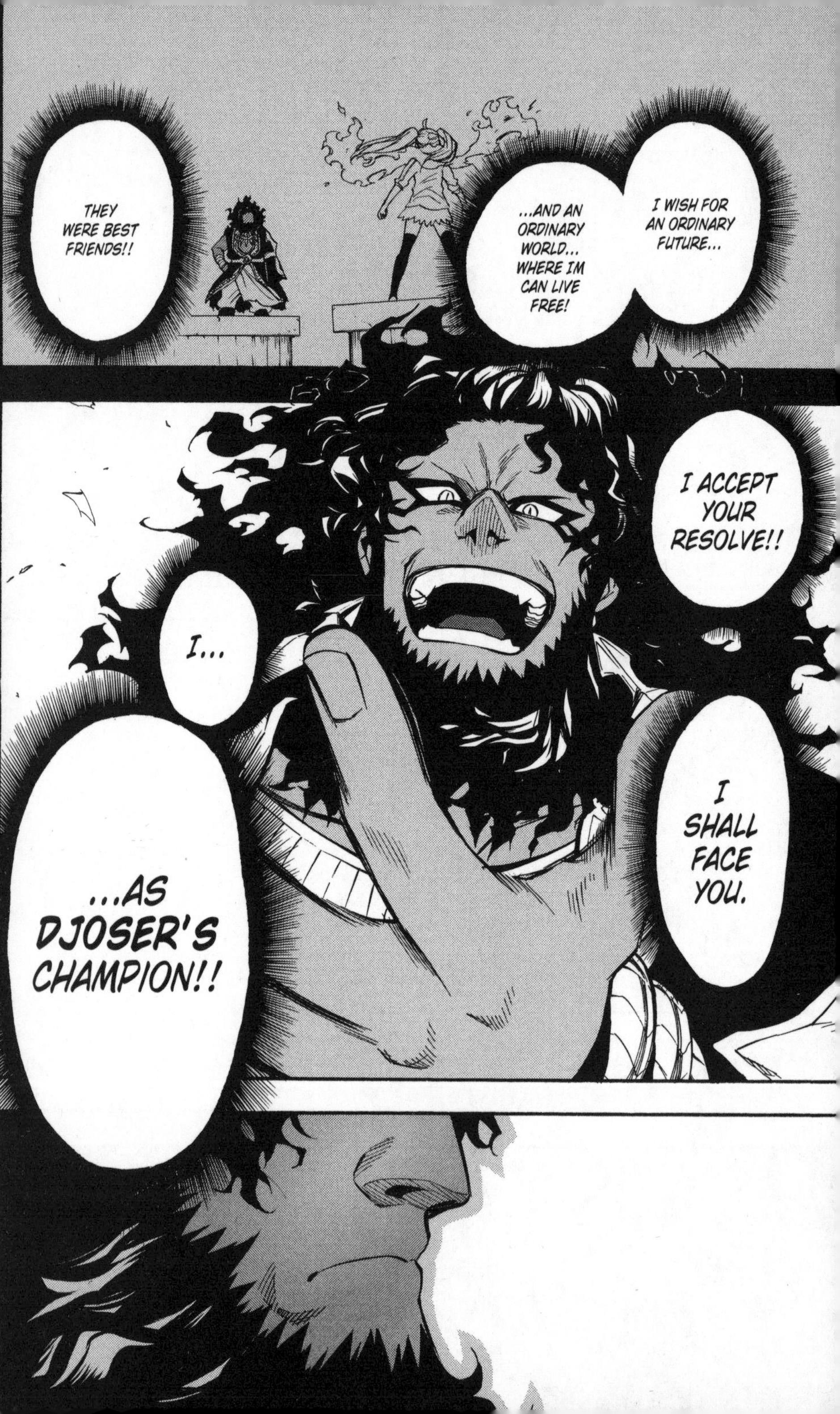
I WISH FOR AN ORDINARY FUTURE...
...AND AN ORDINARY WORLD... WHERE IM CAN LIVE FREE!
THEY WERE BEST FRIENDS!!
I ACCEPT YOUR RESOLVE!!
I...
I SHALL FACE YOU.
...AS DJOSER'S CHAMPION!!

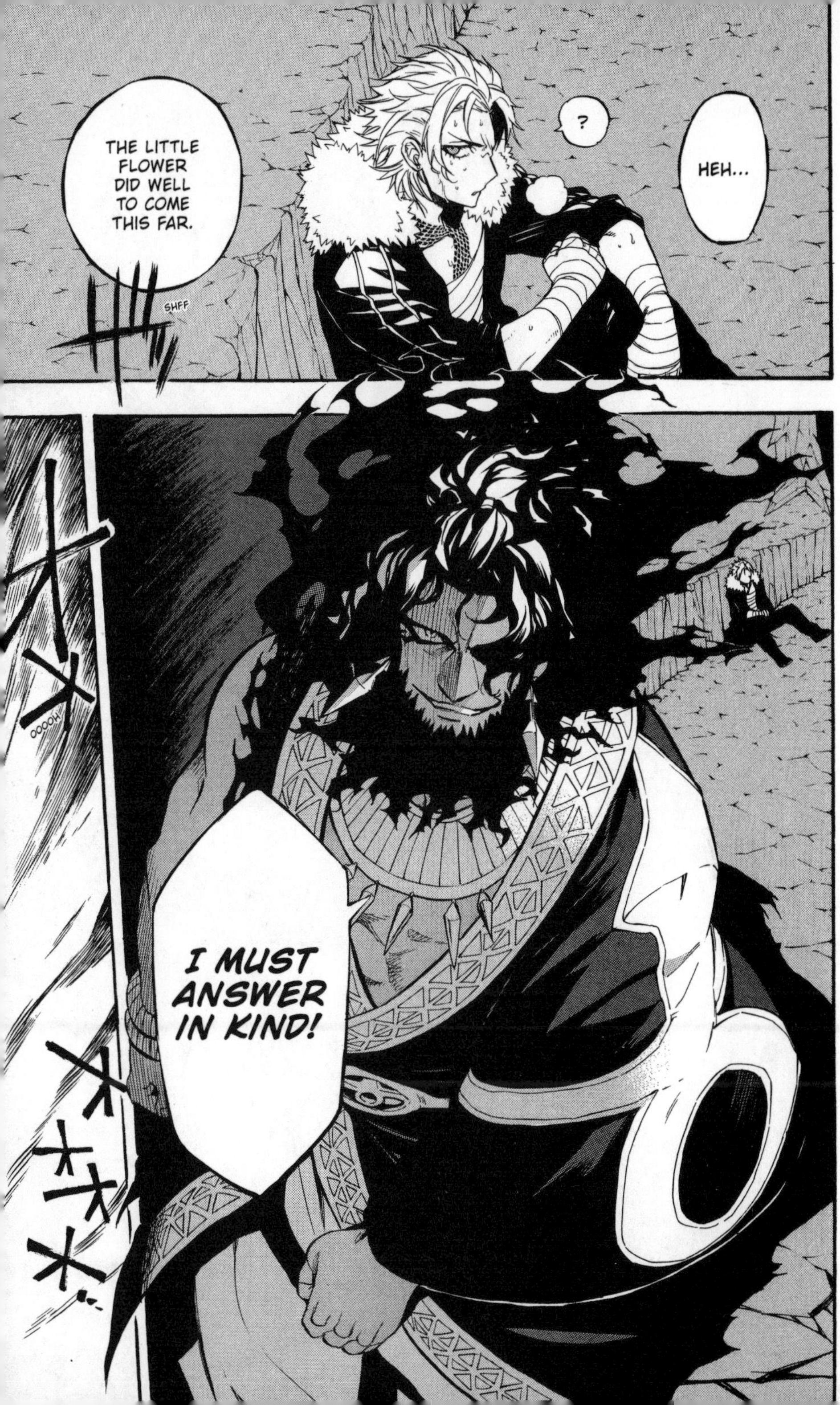
HEH...
?
THE LITTLE FLOWER DID WELL TO COME THIS FAR.
SHFF
I MUST ANSWER IN KIND!
HOOOOO

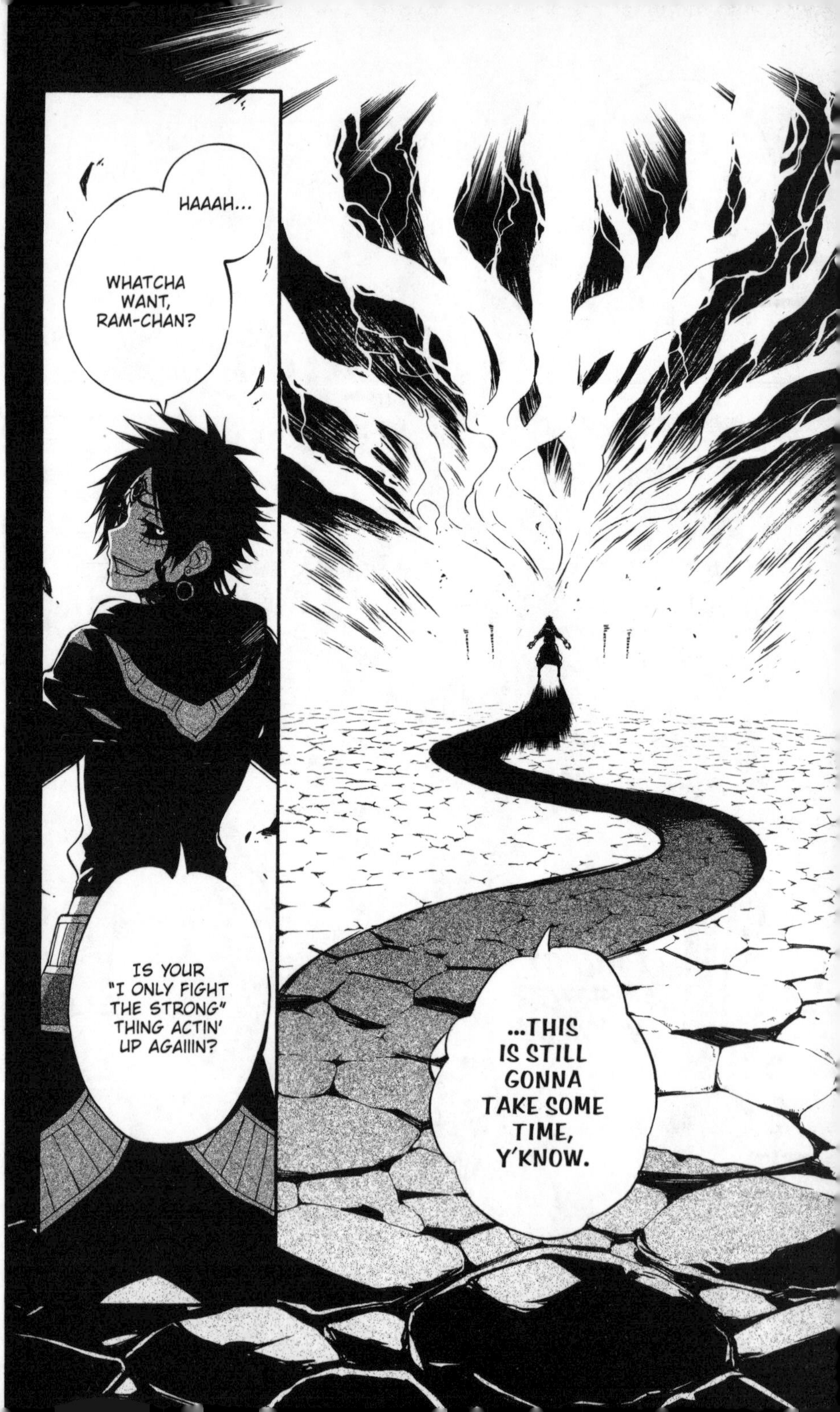
...THIS IS STILL GONNA TAKE SOME TIME, Y'KNOW.
HAAAH...
WHATCHA WANT, RAM-CHAN?
IS YOUR "I ONLY FIGHT THE STRONG" THING ACTIN' UP AGAIIIN?

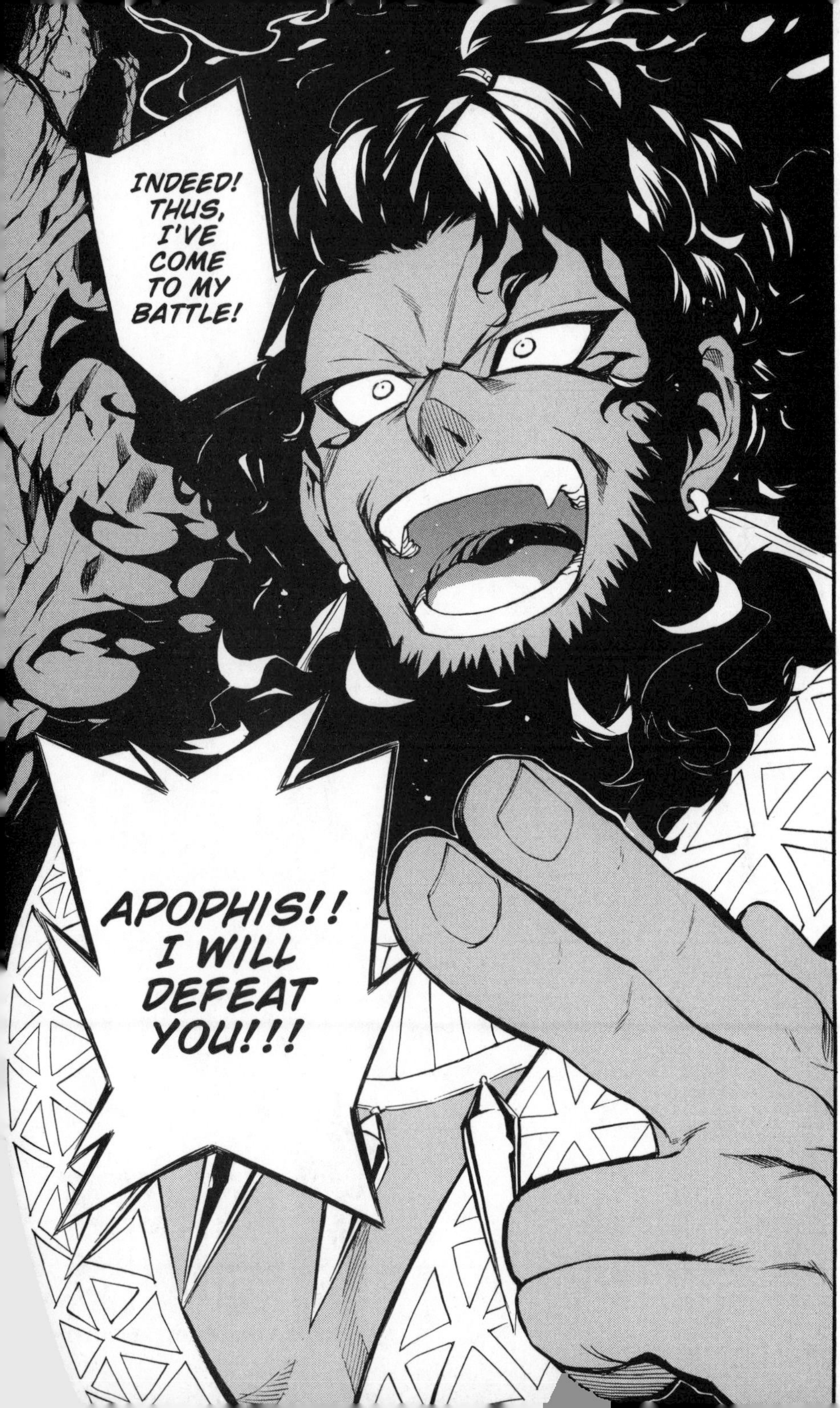
INDEED! THUS, I'VE COME TO MY BATTLE!
APOPHIS!! I WILL DEFEAT YOU!!!

Great Priest Imhotep

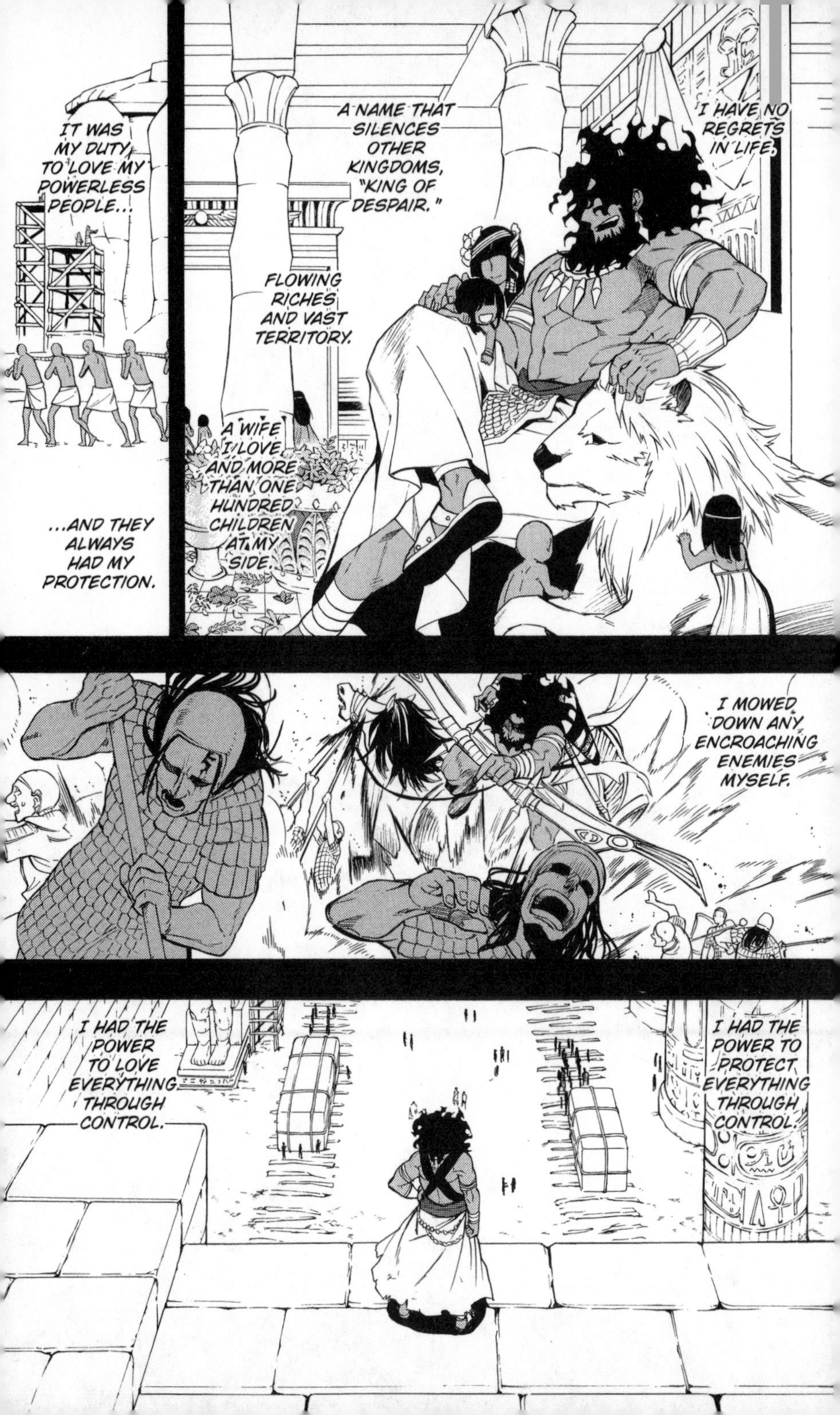
I HAVE NO REGRETS IN LIFE.
A NAME THAT SILENCES OTHER KINGDOMS, "KING OF DESPAIR."
FLOWING RICHES AND VAST TERRITORY.
A WIFE I LOVE AND MORE THAN ONE HUNDRED CHILDREN AT MY SIDE.
IT WAS MY DUTY TO LOVE MY POWERLESS PEOPLE...
...AND THEY ALWAYS HAD MY PROTECTION.
I MOWED DOWN ANY ENCROACHING ENEMIES MYSELF.
I HAD THE POWER TO PROTECT EVERYTHING THROUGH CONTROL.
I HAD THE POWER TO LOVE EVERYTHING THROUGH CONTROL.

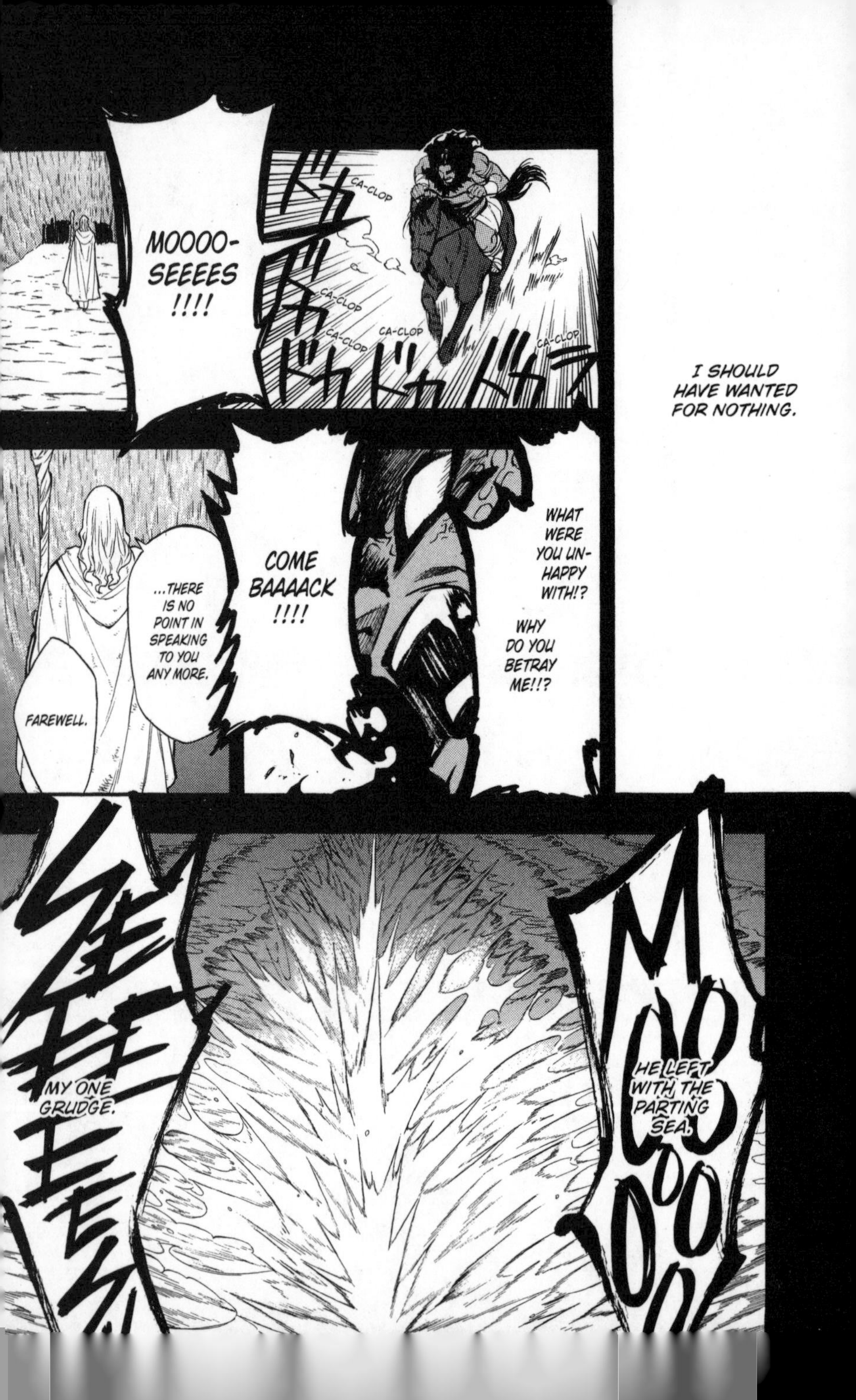
I SHOULD HAVE WANTED FOR NOTHING.
CA-CLOP
CA-CLOP
CA-CLOP
CA-CLOP
CA-CLOP
MOOOO-SEEEES!!!!
WHAT WERE YOU UN-HAPPY WITH!?
WHY DO YOU BETRAY ME!!?
COME BAAAACK!!!!
...THERE IS NO POINT IN SPEAKING TO YOU ANY MORE.
FAREWELL.
HE LEFT WITH THE PARTING SEA.
MY ONE GRUDGE.

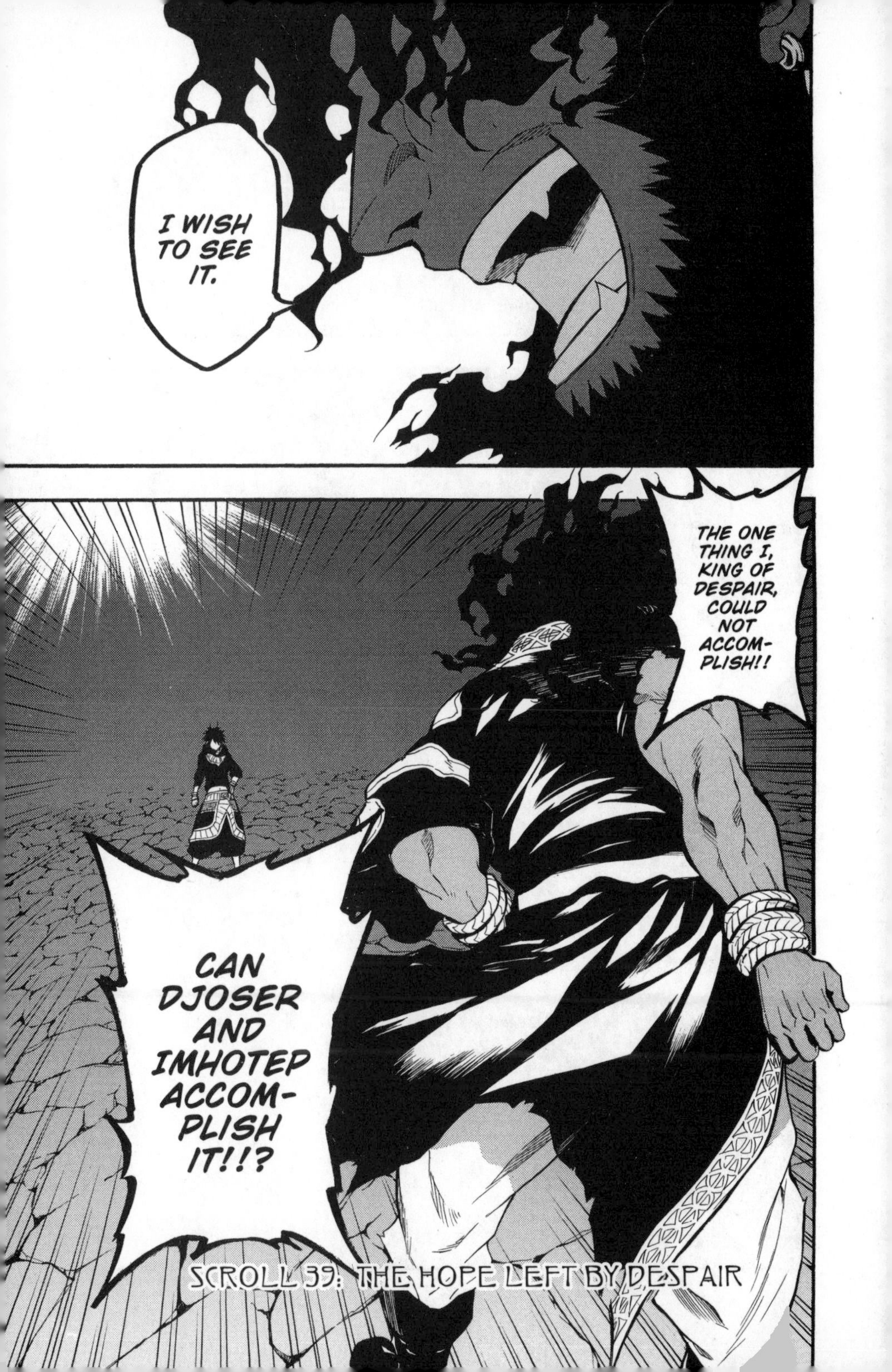
I WISH TO SEE IT.
THE ONE THING I, KING OF DESPAIR, COULD NOT ACCOMPLISH!!
CAN DJOSER AND IMHOTEP ACCOMPLISH IT!!?
SCROLL 39: THE HOPE LEFT BY DESPAIR

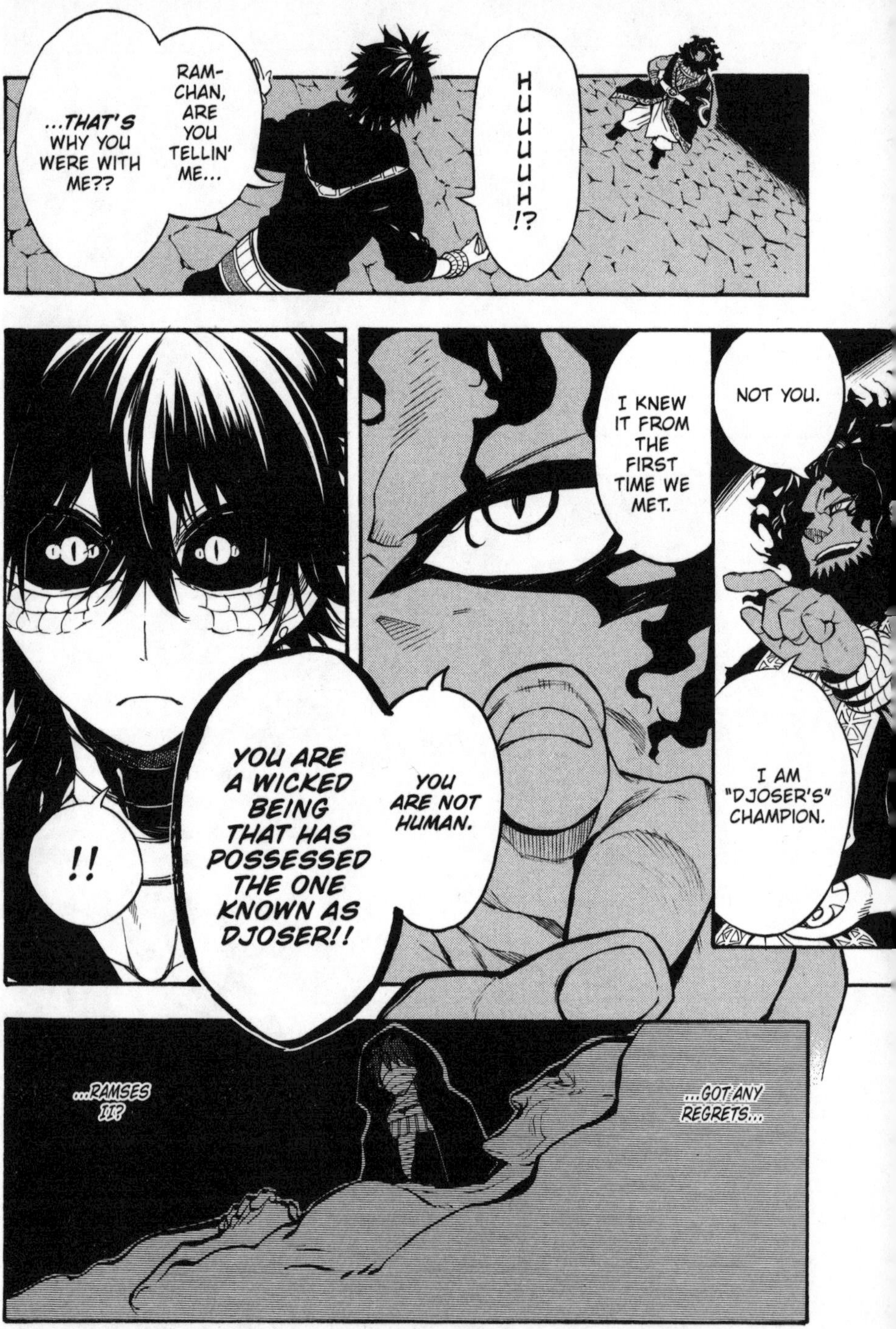
HUUUUH!?
RAM-CHAN, ARE YOU TELLIN' ME...
...THAT'S WHY YOU WERE WITH ME??
NOT YOU.
I AM "DJOSER'S" CHAMPION.
I KNEW IT FROM THE FIRST TIME WE MET.
YOU ARE NOT HUMAN.
YOU ARE A WICKED BEING THAT HAS POSSESSED THE ONE KNOWN AS DJOSER!!
!!
...GOT ANY REGRETS...
...RAMSES II?

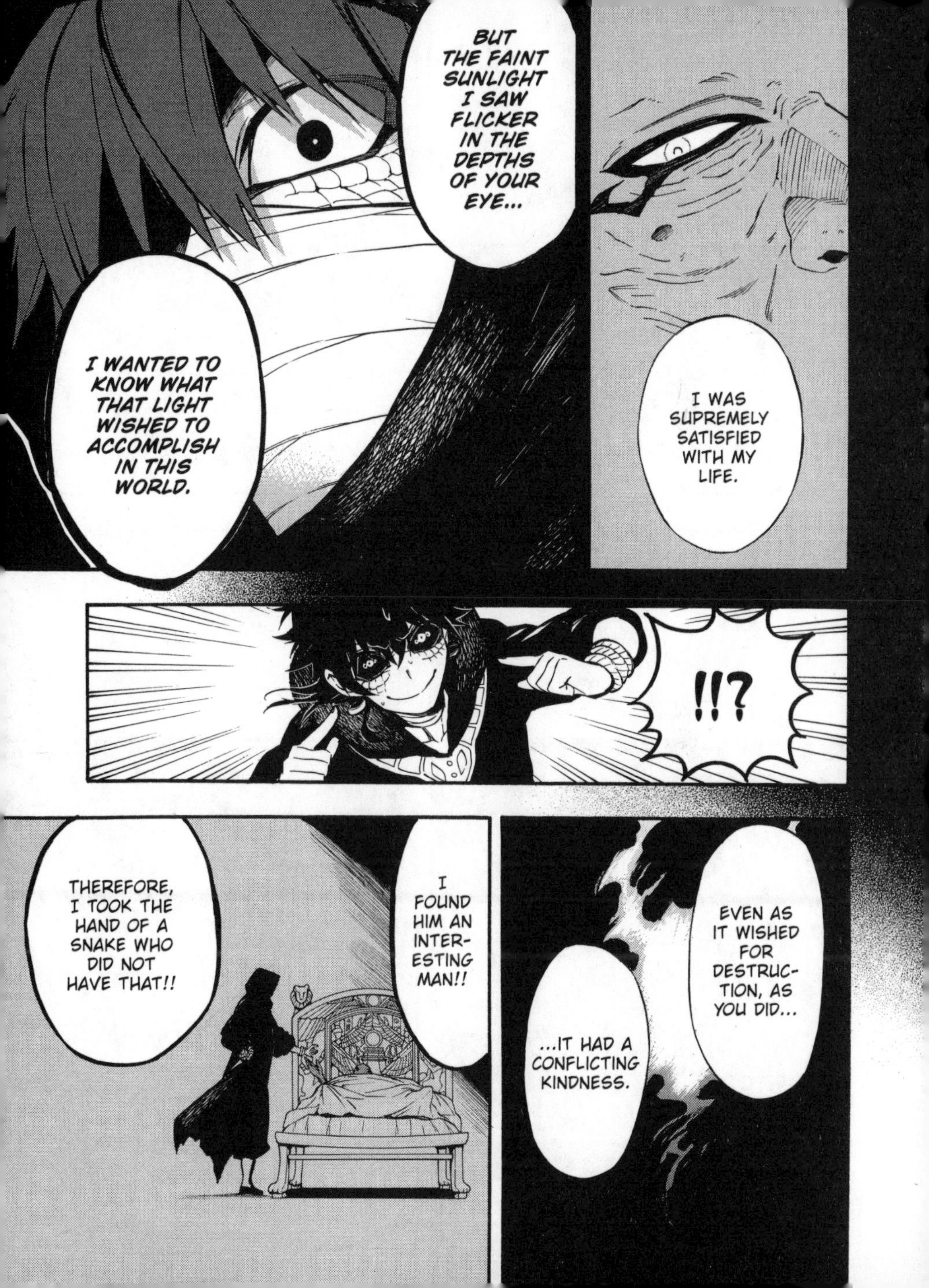
I WAS SUPREMELY SATISFIED WITH MY LIFE.
BUT THE FAINT SUNLIGHT I SAW FLICKER IN THE DEPTHS OF YOUR EYE...
I WANTED TO KNOW WHAT THAT LIGHT WISHED TO ACCOMPLISH IN THIS WORLD.
!!?
EVEN AS IT WISHED FOR DESTRUC-TION, AS YOU DID...
...IT HAD A CONFLICTING KINDNESS.
I FOUND HIM AN INTER-ESTING MAN!!
THEREFORE, I TOOK THE HAND OF A SNAKE WHO DID NOT HAVE THAT!!

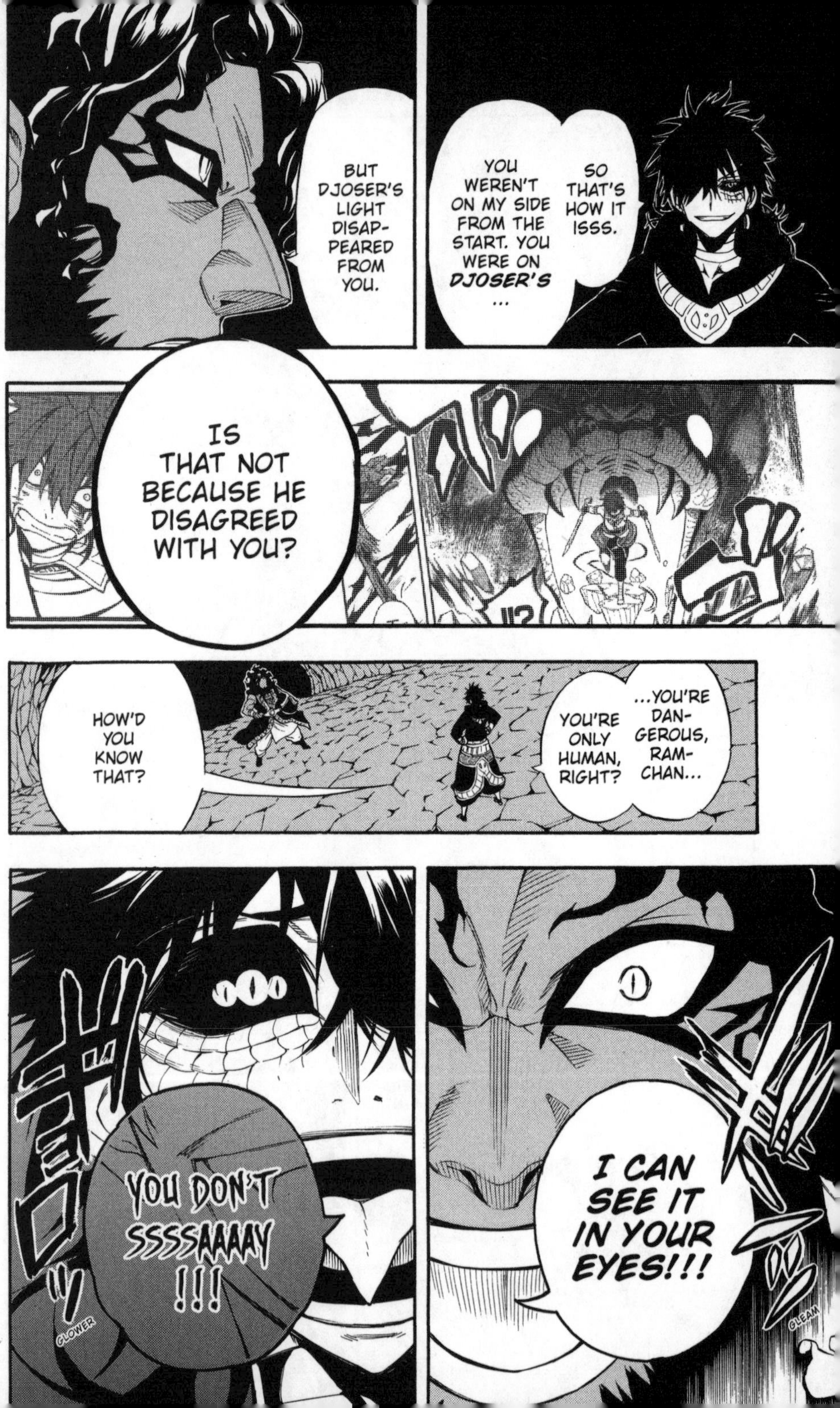
SO THAT'S HOW IT ISSS.
YOU WEREN'T ON MY SIDE FROM THE START. YOU WERE ON DJOSER'S ...
BUT DJOSER'S LIGHT DISAP-PEARED FROM YOU.
IS THAT NOT BECAUSE HE DISAGREED WITH YOU?
!?
...YOU'RE DAN-GEROUS, RAM-CHAN...
YOU'RE ONLY HUMAN, RIGHT?
HOW'D YOU KNOW THAT?
I CAN SEE IT IN YOUR EYES!!!
GLEAM
YOU DON'T SSSSAAAAY !!!
GLOWER

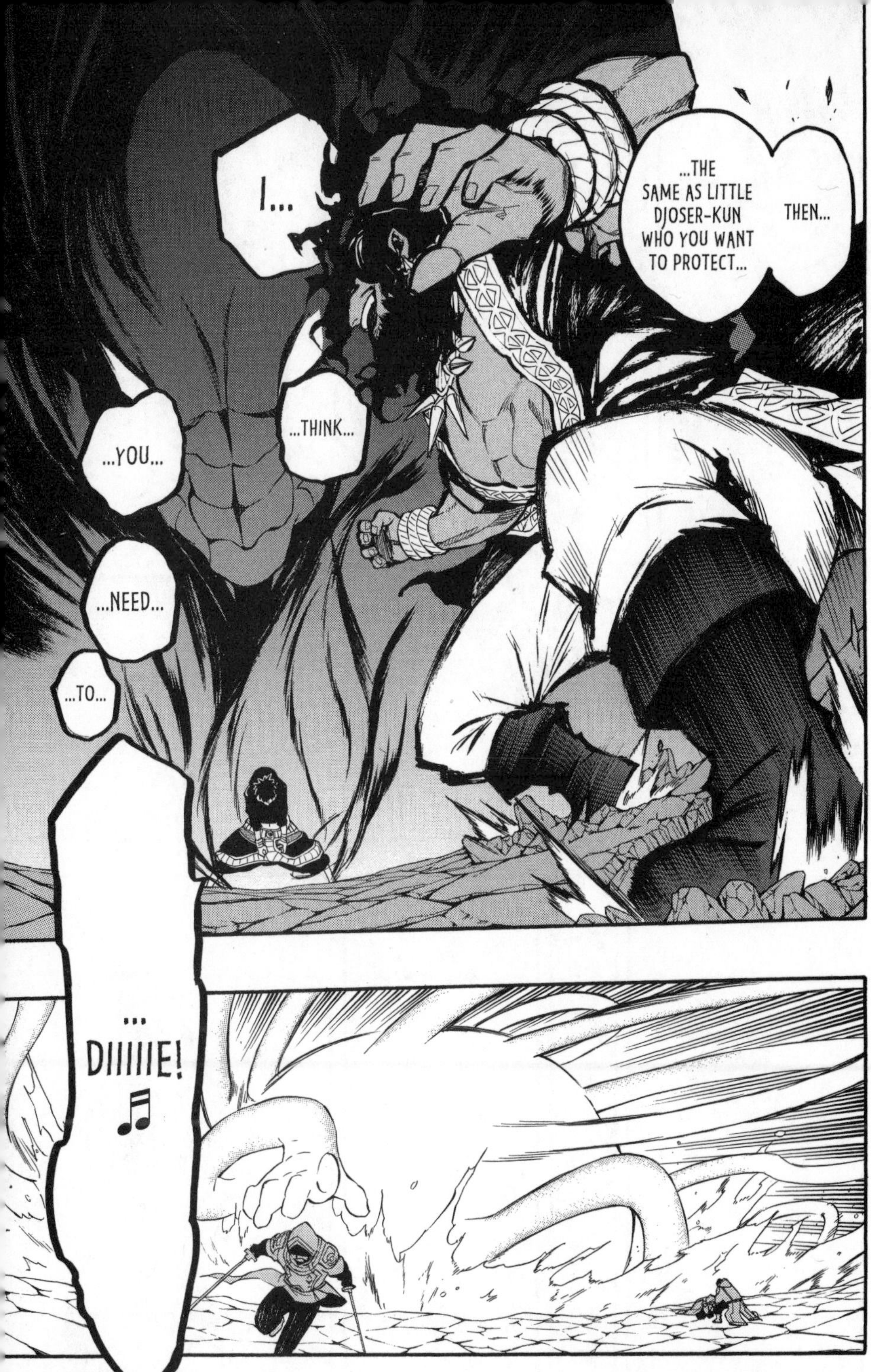
THEN...
...THE SAME AS LITTLE DJOSER-KUN WHO YOU WANT TO PROTECT...
I...
...THINK...
...YOU...
...NEED...
...TO...
... DIIIIIE! ♬

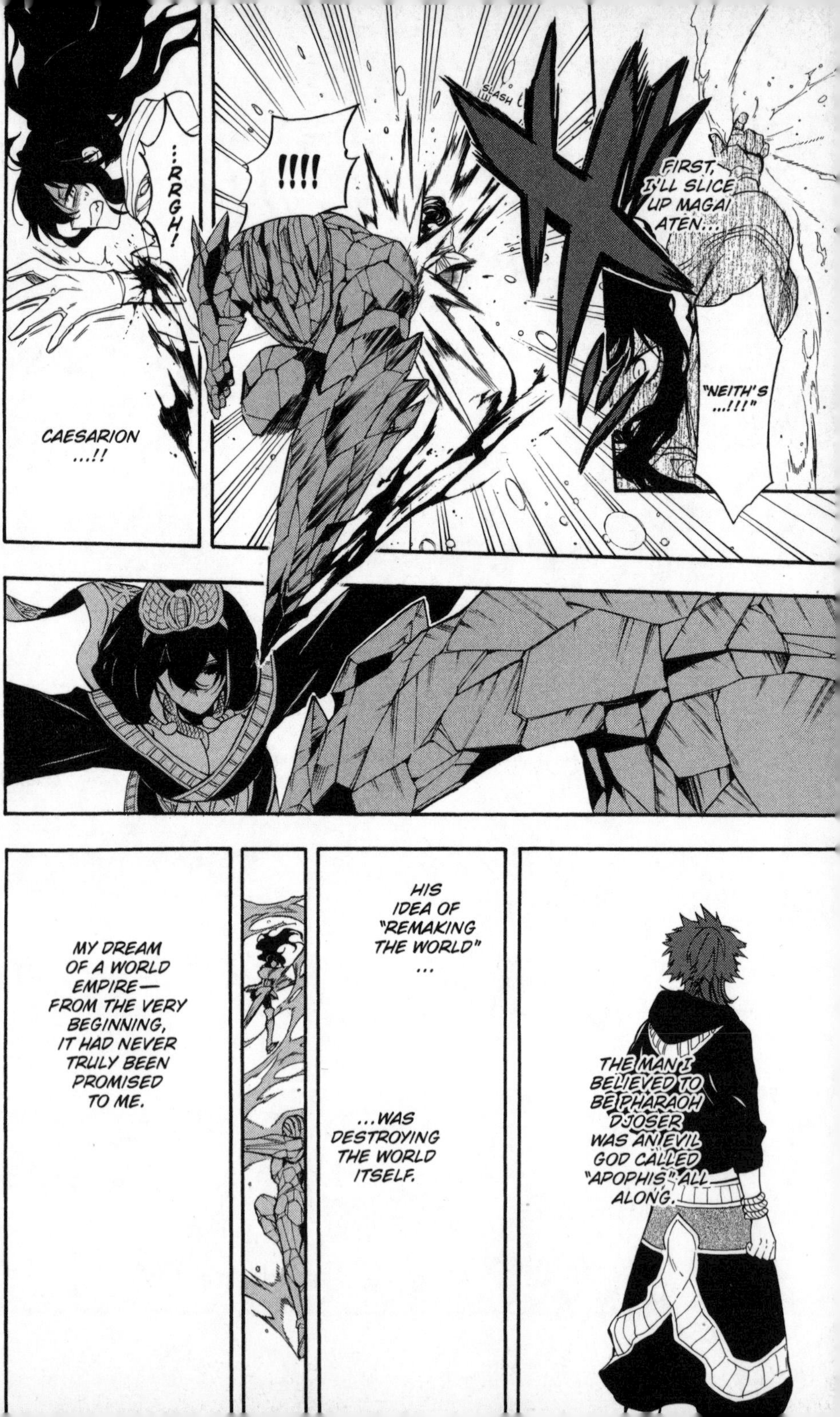
SLASH
FIRST, I'LL SLICE UP MAGAI ATEN...
"NEITH'S ...!!!"
!!!!
...RRGH!
CAESARION ...!!
THE MAN I BELIEVED TO BE PHARAOH DJOSER WAS AN EVIL GOD CALLED "APOPHIS" ALL ALONG.
HIS IDEA OF "REMAKING THE WORLD" ...
...WAS DESTROYING THE WORLD ITSELF.
MY DREAM OF A WORLD EMPIRE— FROM THE VERY BEGINNING, IT HAD NEVER TRULY BEEN PROMISED TO ME.

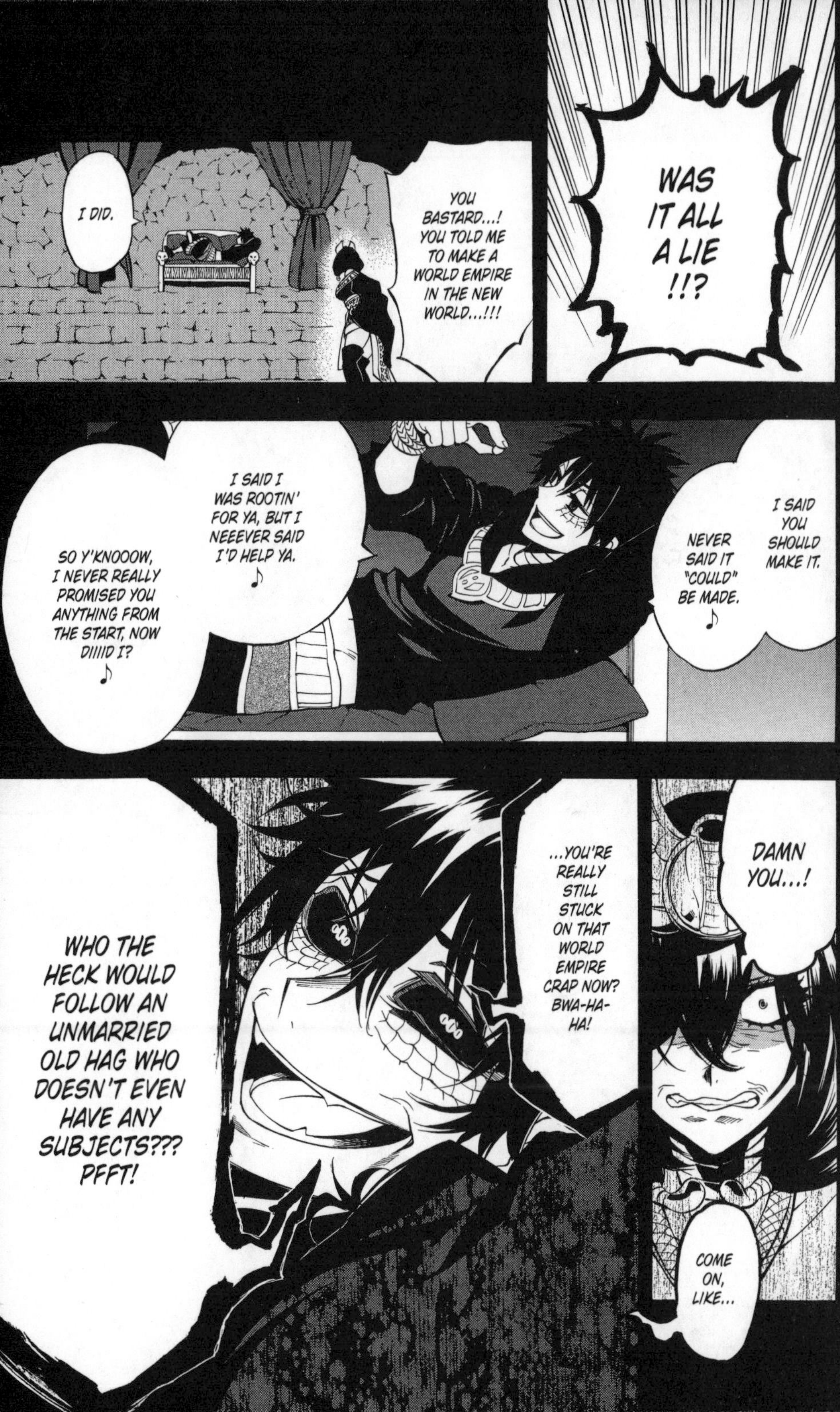
WAS IT ALL A LIE !!?
YOU BASTARD...! YOU TOLD ME TO MAKE A WORLD EMPIRE IN THE NEW WORLD...!!!
I DID.
I SAID YOU SHOULD MAKE IT.
NEVER SAID IT "COULD" BE MADE. ♪
I SAID I WAS ROOTIN' FOR YA, BUT I NEEEVER SAID I'D HELP YA. ♪
SO Y'KNOOOW, I NEVER REALLY PROMISED YOU ANYTHING FROM THE START, NOW DIIIID I? ♪
DAMN YOU...!
COME ON, LIKE...
...YOU'RE REALLY STILL STUCK ON THAT WORLD EMPIRE CRAP NOW? BWA-HA-HA!
WHO THE HECK WOULD FOLLOW AN UNMARRIED OLD HAG WHO DOESN'T EVEN HAVE ANY SUBJECTS??? PFFT!

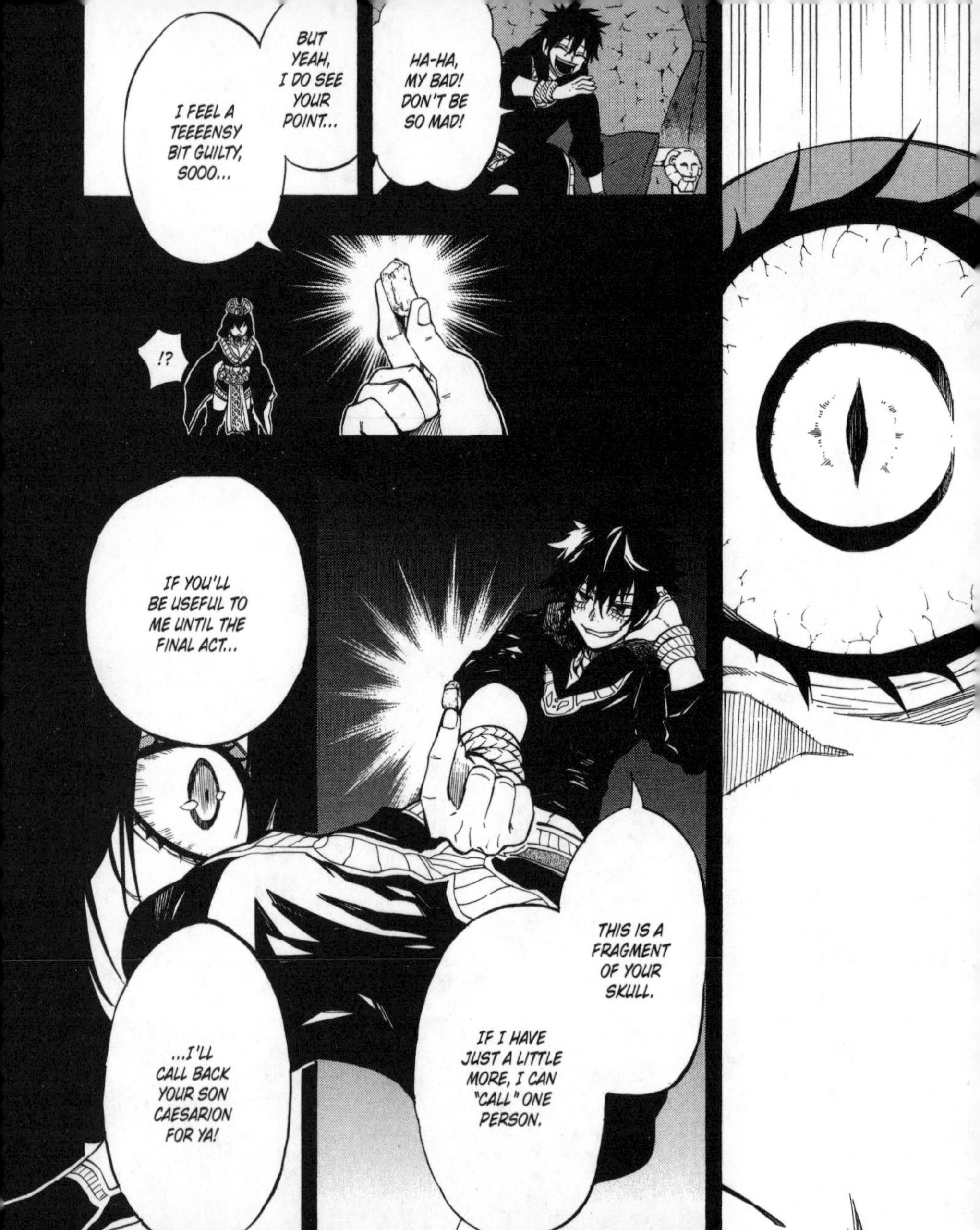
HA-HA, MY BAD! DON'T BE SO MAD!
BUT YEAH, I DO SEE YOUR POINT...
I FEEL A TEEEENSY BIT GUILTY, SOOO...
!?
THIS IS A FRAGMENT OF YOUR SKULL.
IF I HAVE JUST A LITTLE MORE, I CAN "CALL" ONE PERSON.
IF YOU'LL BE USEFUL TO ME UNTIL THE FINAL ACT...
...I'LL CALL BACK YOUR SON CAESARION FOR YA!

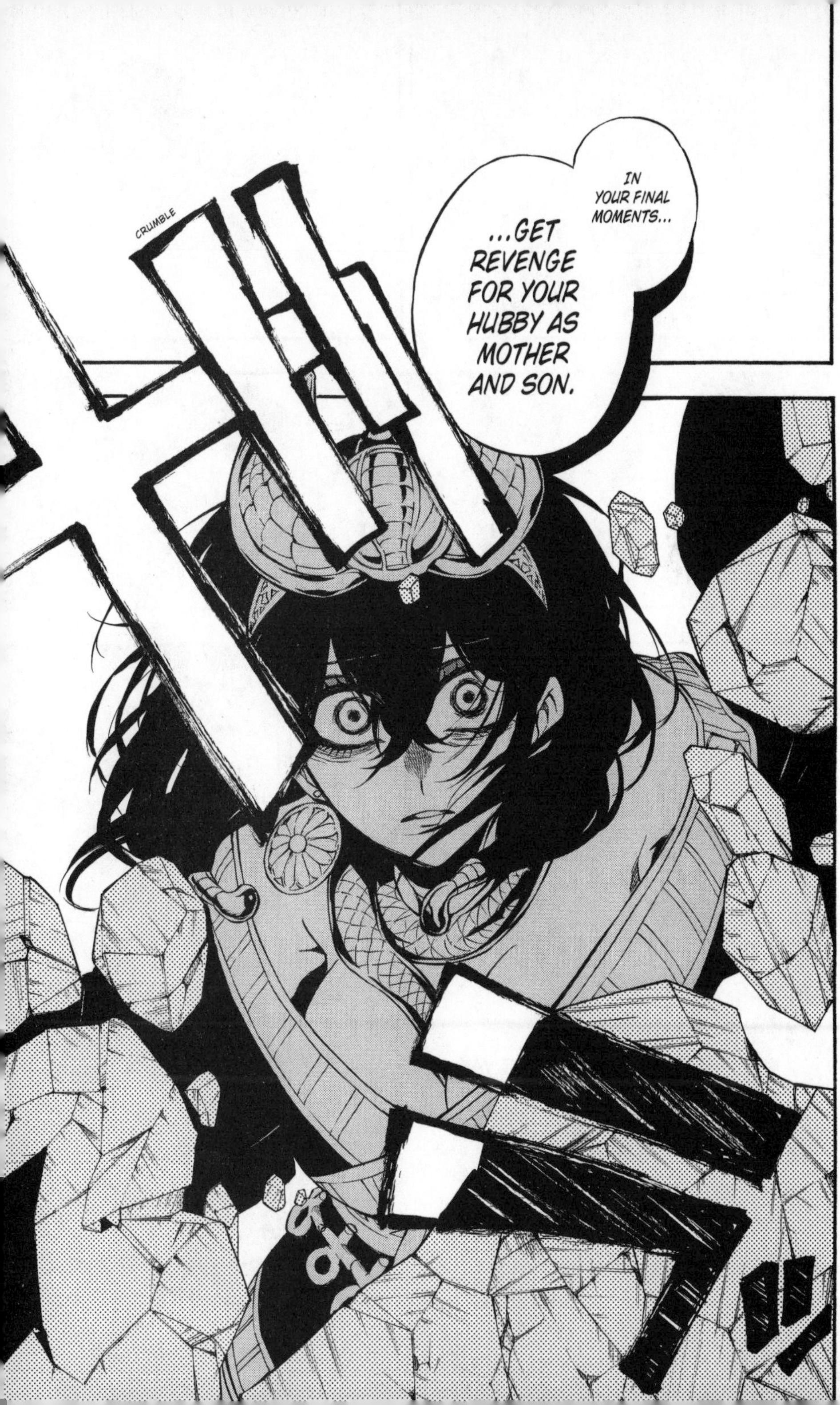
IN YOUR FINAL MOMENTS...
...GET REVENGE FOR YOUR HUBBY AS MOTHER AND SON.
CRUMBLE

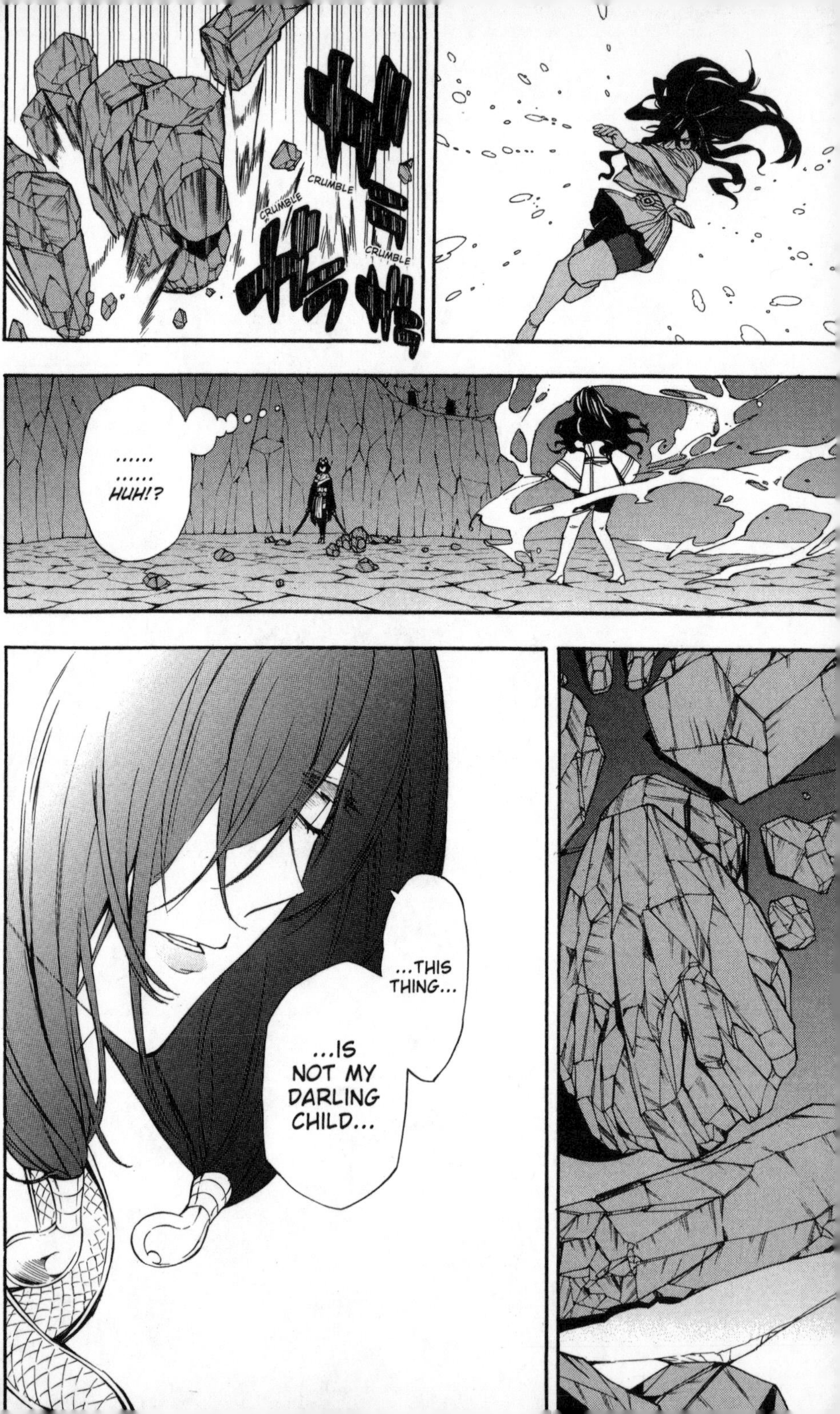
CRUMBLE
CRUMBLE
CRUMBLE
.... HUH!?
...THIS THING...
...IS NOT MY DARLING CHILD...

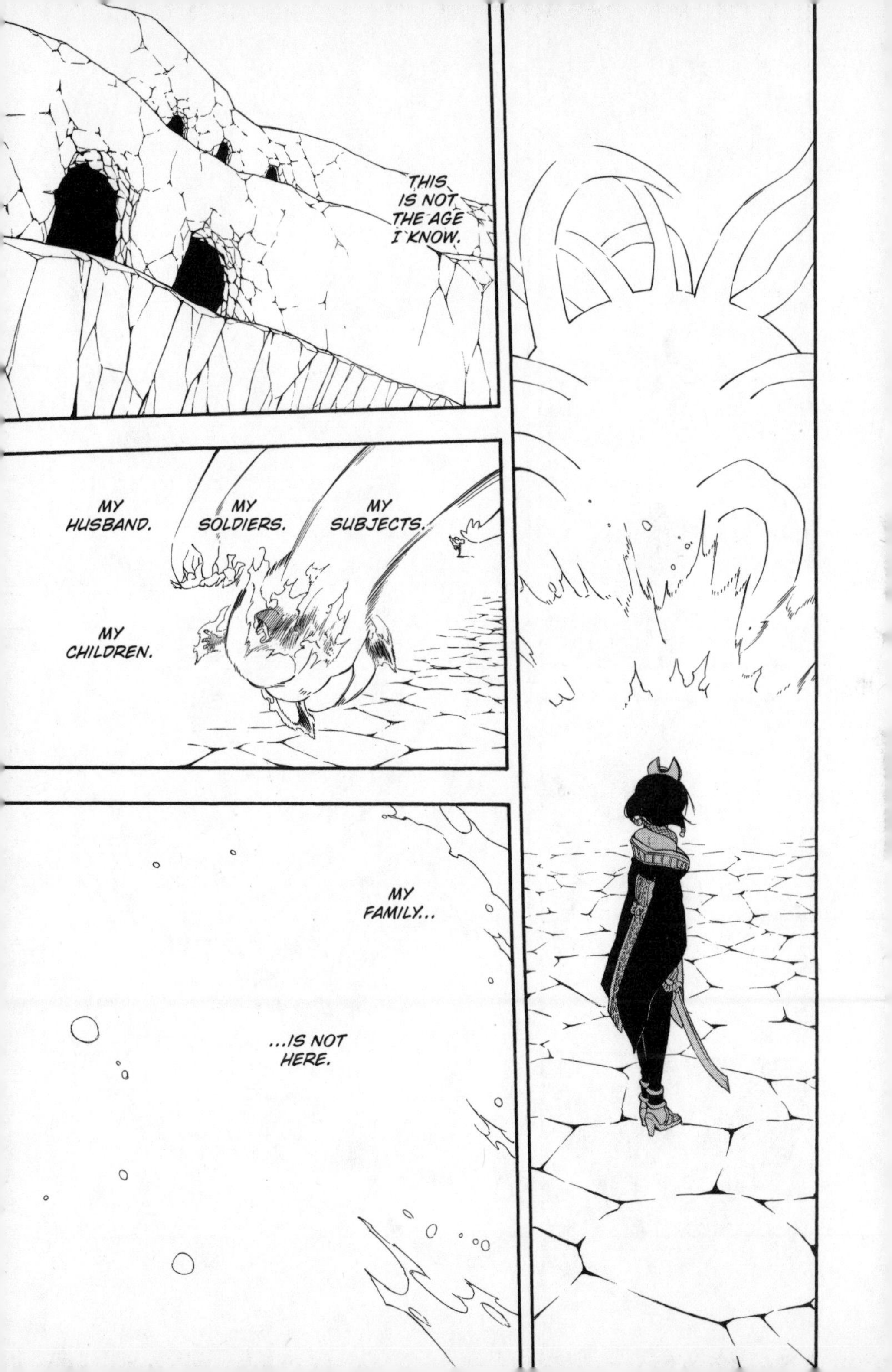
THIS IS NOT THE AGE I KNOW.
MY SUBJECTS.
MY SOLDIERS.
MY HUSBAND.
MY CHILDREN.
MY FAMILY...
...IS NOT HERE.

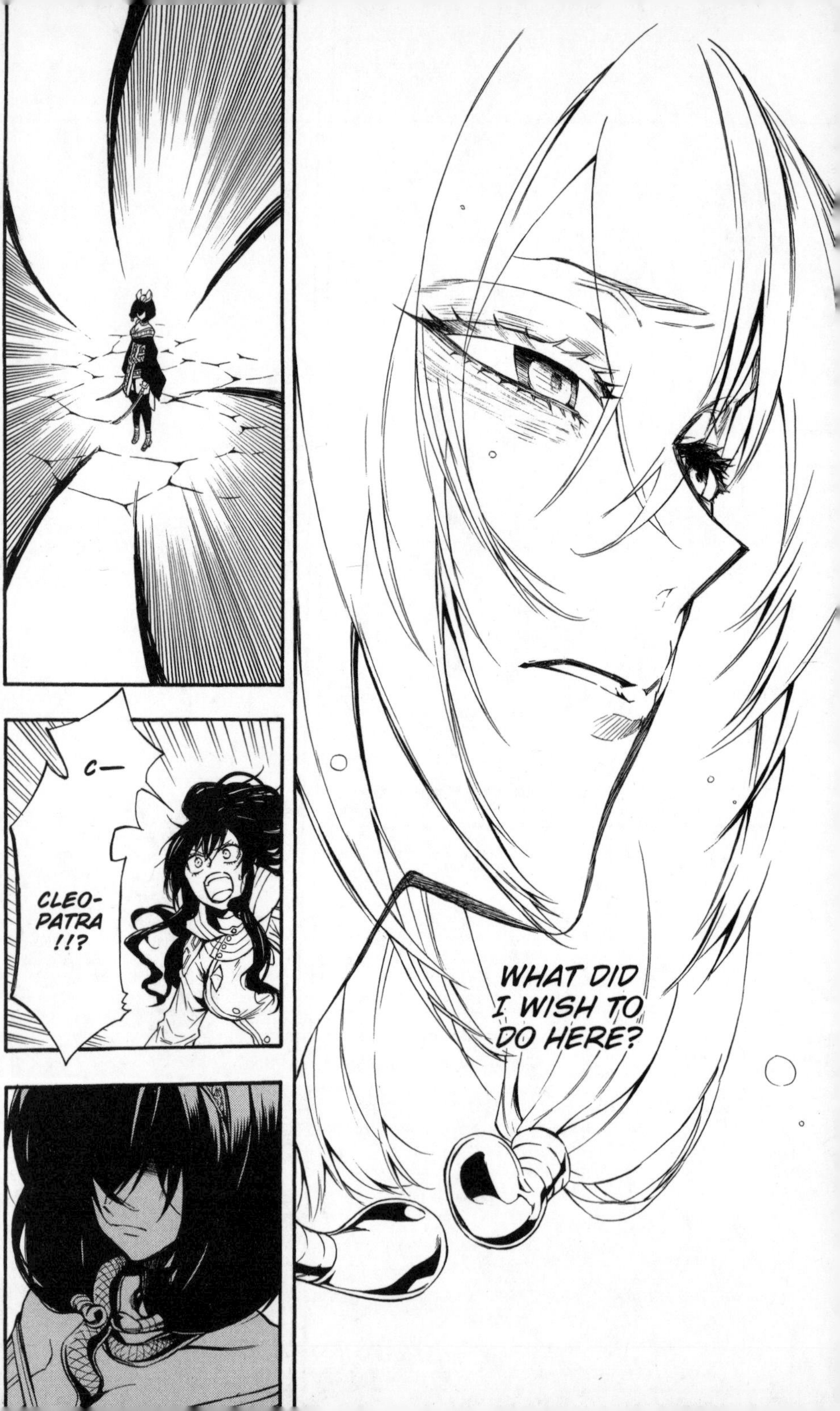
WHAT DID I WISH TO DO HERE?
C—
CLEO-PATRA!!?

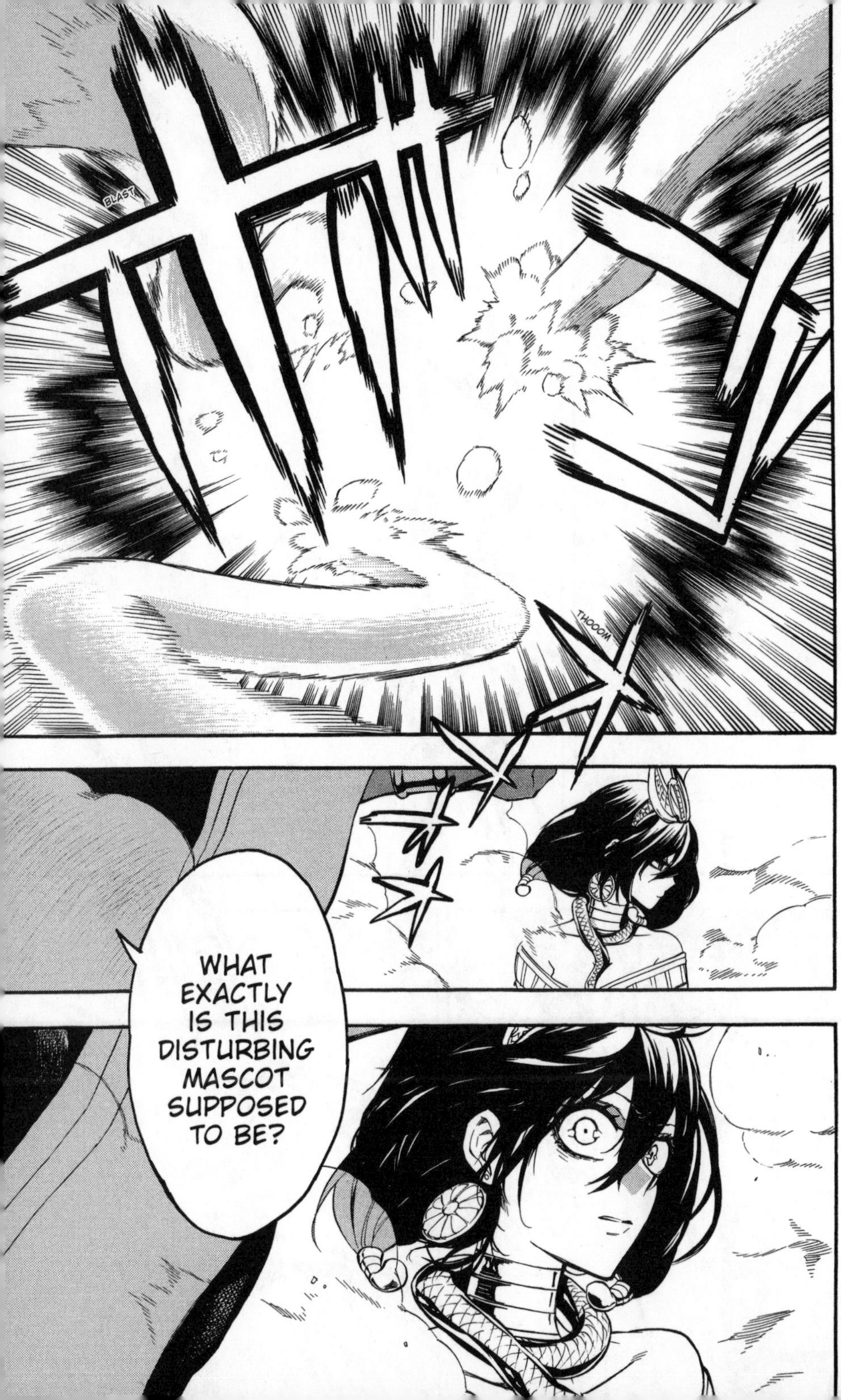
BLAST
THOOOM
WHAT EXACTLY IS THIS DISTURBING MASCOT SUPPOSED TO BE?

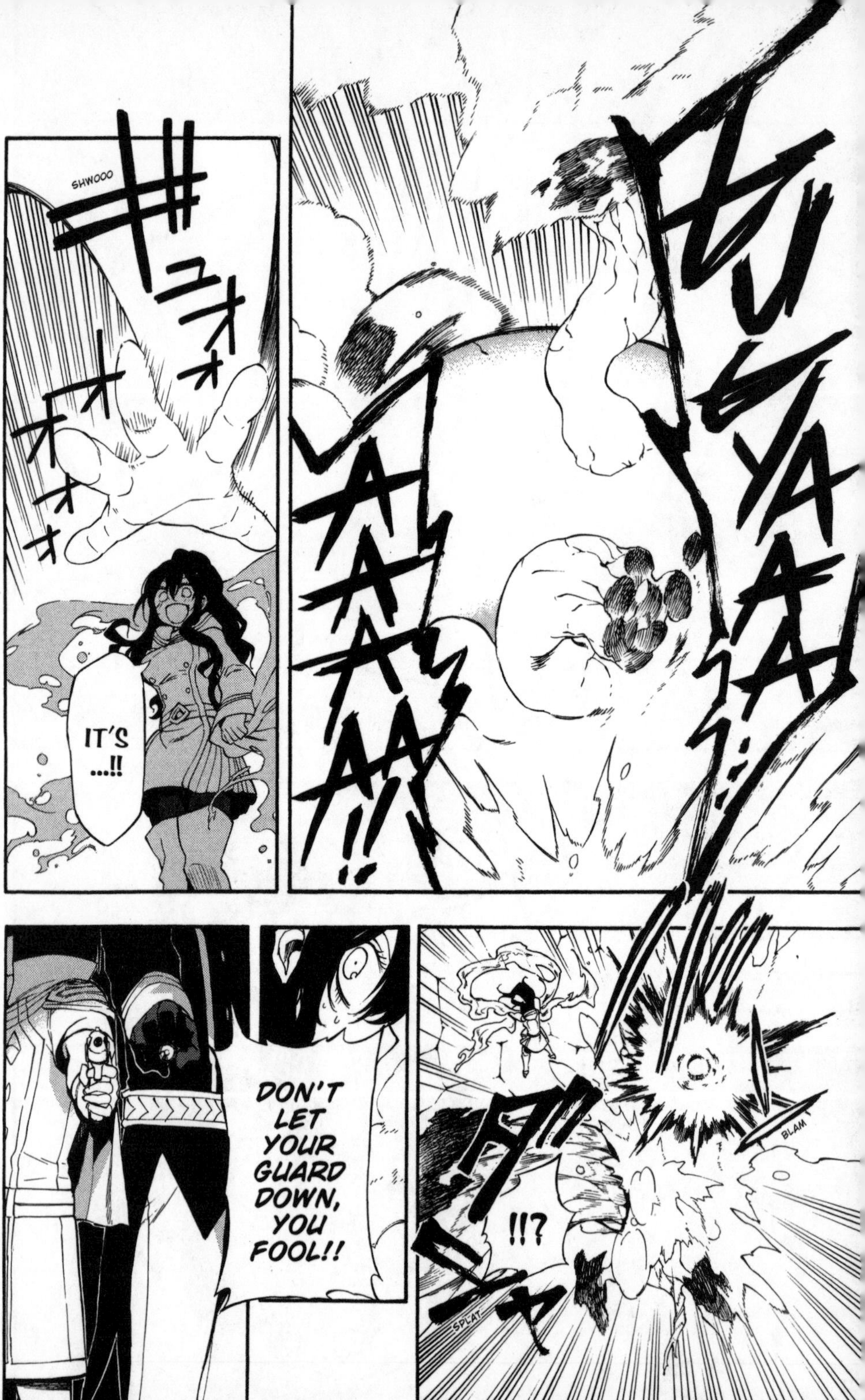
SHWOOO
IT'S ...!!
BLAM
!!?
SPLAT
DON'T LET YOUR GUARD DOWN, YOU FOOL!!

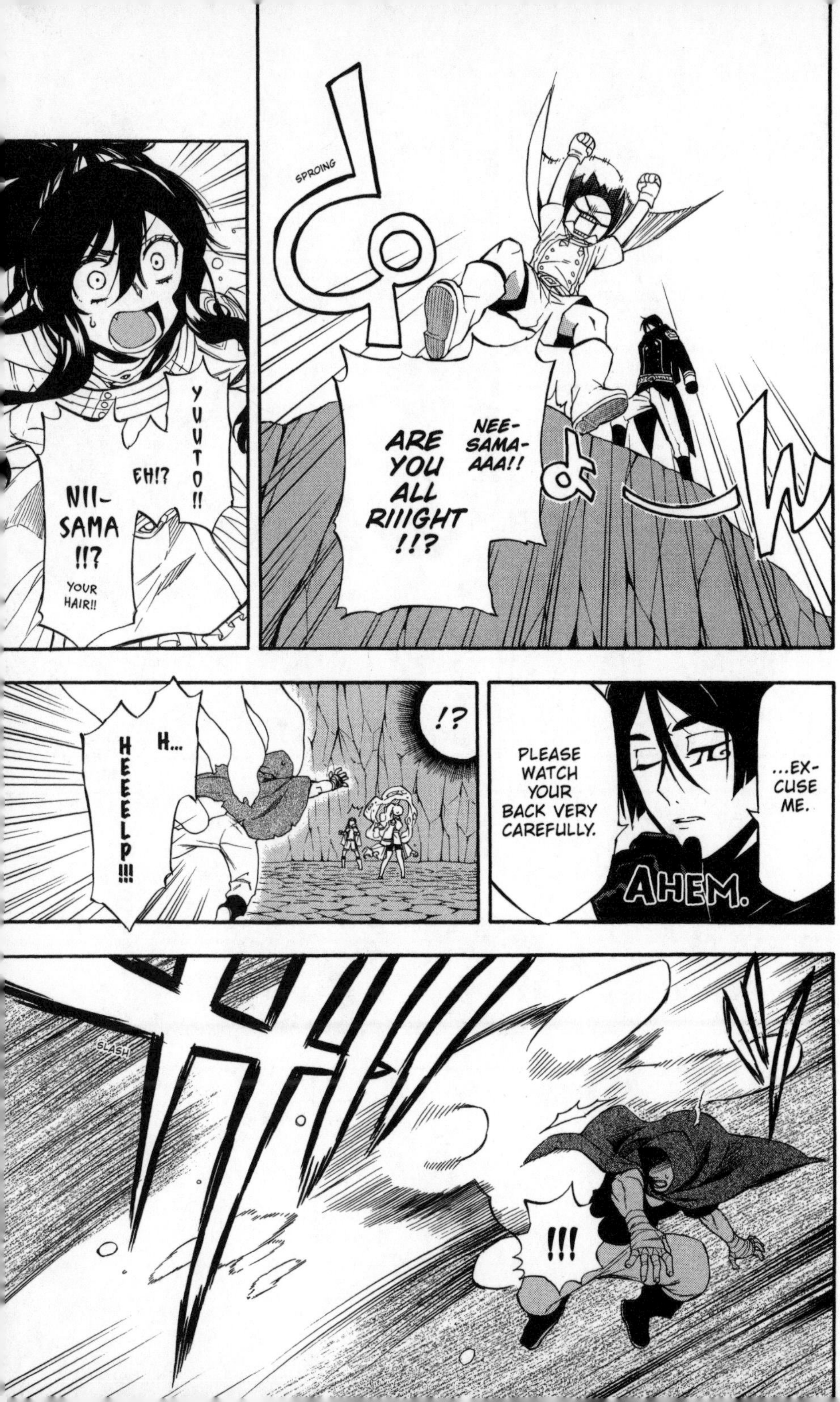

SPROING
NEE-SAMA-AAA!!
ARE YOU ALL RIIIGHT!!?
YUUTO!!
EH!?
NII-SAMA!!?
YOUR HAIR!!
...EX-CUSE ME.
AHEM.
PLEASE WATCH YOUR BACK VERY CAREFULLY.
!?
H...
HEEEELP!!!
SLASH
!!!

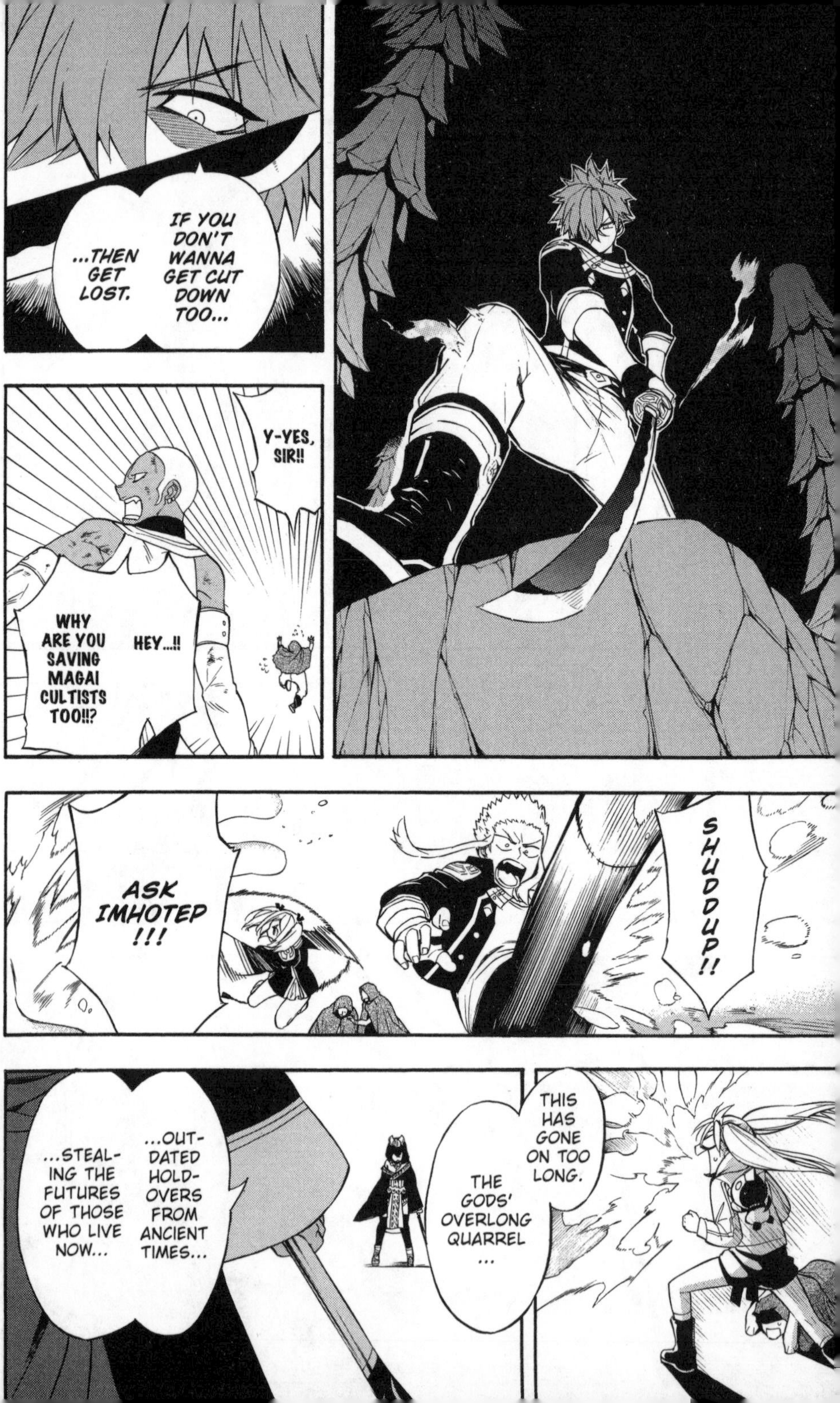

IF YOU DON'T WANNA GET CUT DOWN TOO...
...THEN GET LOST.
Y-YES, SIR!!
HEY...!!
WHY ARE YOU SAVING MAGAI CULTISTS TOO!!?
SHUDDUP!!
ASK IMHOTEP!!!
THIS HAS GONE ON TOO LONG.
THE GODS' OVERLONG QUARREL...
...OUT-DATED HOLD-OVERS FROM ANCIENT TIMES...
...STEAL-ING THE FUTURES OF THOSE WHO LIVE NOW...

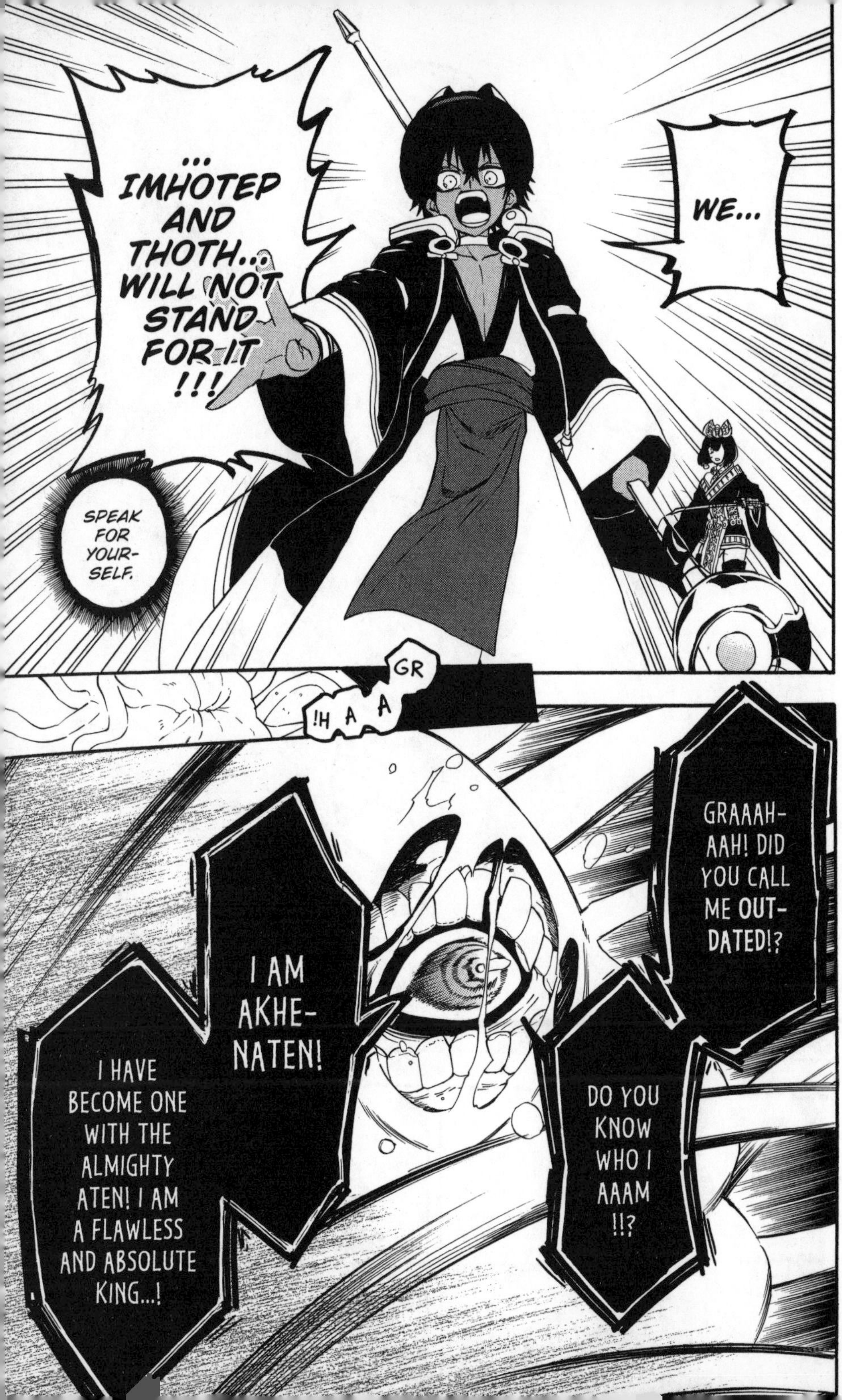
WE...
...IMHÖTEP AND THOTH... WILL NOT STAND FOR IT!!!
SPEAK FOR YOURSELF.
GRAAH!
GRAAAH-AAH! DID YOU CALL ME OUTDATED!?
I AM AKHENATEN!
DO YOU KNOW WHO I AAAM!!?
I HAVE BECOME ONE WITH THE ALMIGHTY ATEN! I AM A FLAWLESS AND ABSOLUTE KING...!

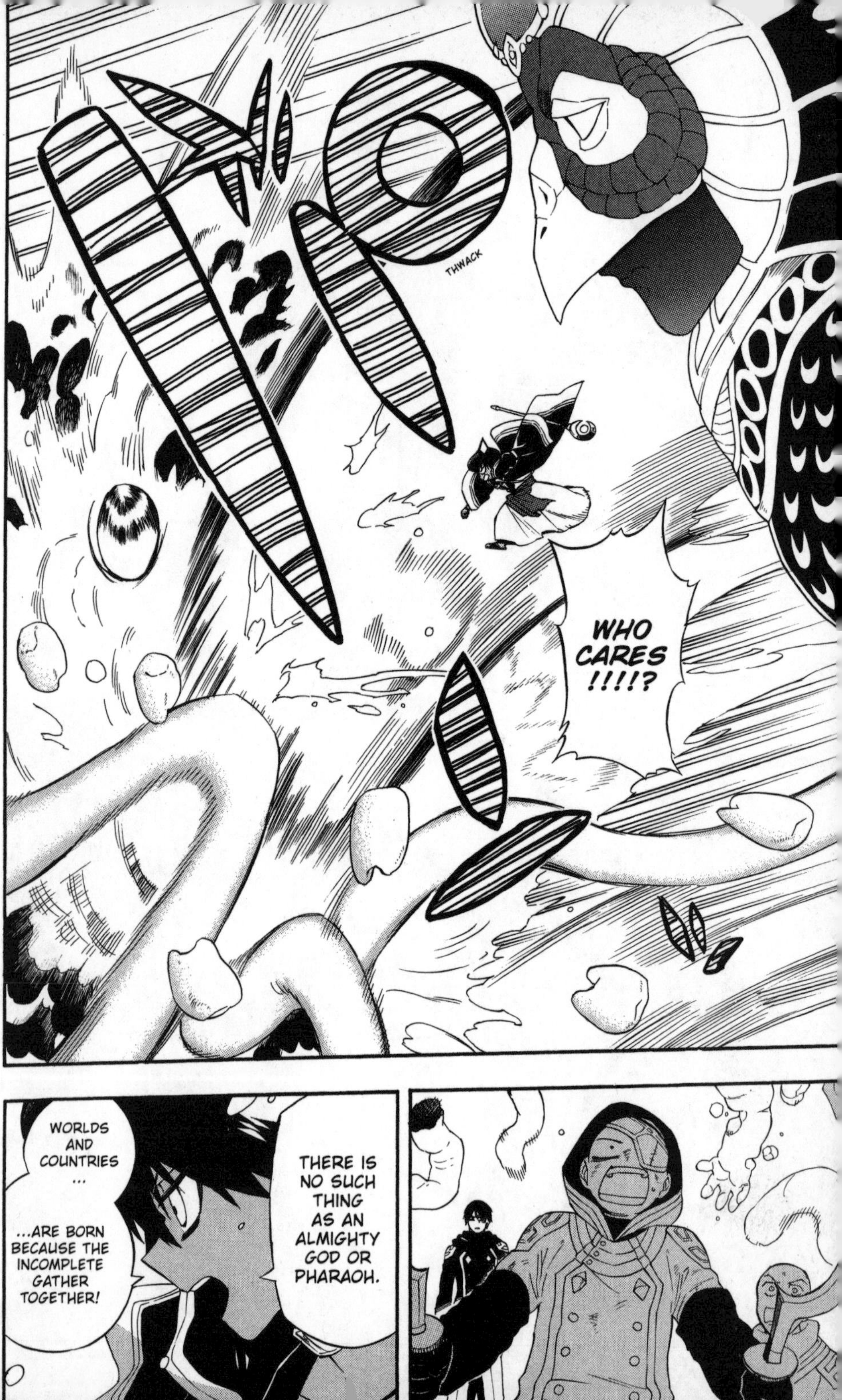
THWACK
WHO CARES !!!!?
THERE IS NO SUCH THING AS AN ALMIGHTY GOD OR PHARAOH.
WORLDS AND COUNTRIES ...
...ARE BORN BECAUSE THE INCOMPLETE GATHER TOGETHER!

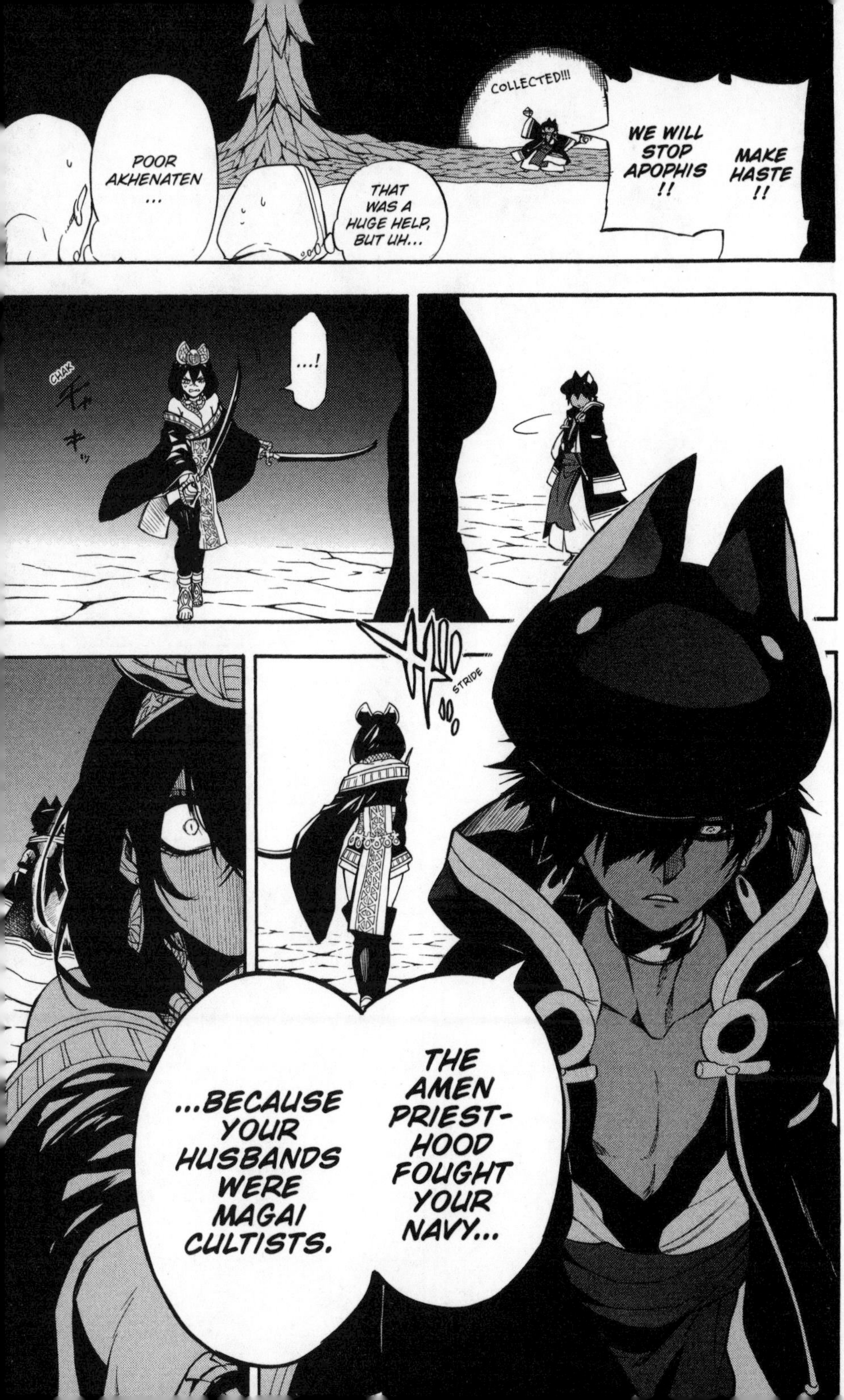
MAKE HASTE !!
WE WILL STOP APOPHIS !!
COLLECTED!!!
THAT WAS A HUGE HELP, BUT UH...
POOR AKHENATEN ...
...!
CHAK
STRIDE
THE AMEN PRIEST-HOOD FOUGHT YOUR NAVY...
...BECAUSE YOUR HUSBANDS WERE MAGAI CULTISTS.

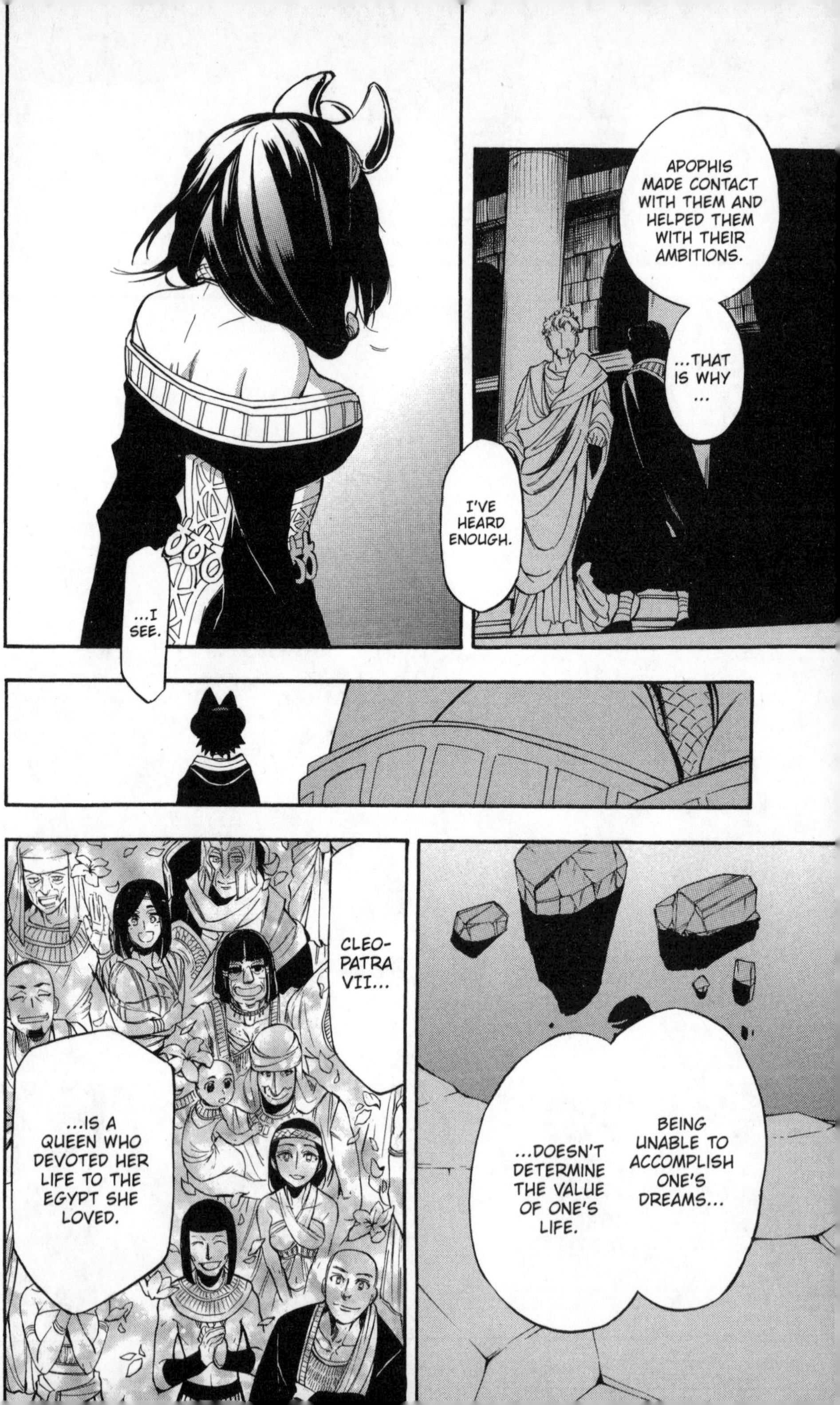
APOPHIS MADE CONTACT WITH THEM AND HELPED THEM WITH THEIR AMBITIONS.
...THAT IS WHY ...
I'VE HEARD ENOUGH.
...I SEE.
BEING UNABLE TO ACCOMPLISH ONE'S DREAMS...
...DOESN'T DETERMINE THE VALUE OF ONE'S LIFE.
CLEO-PATRA VII...
...IS A QUEEN WHO DEVOTED HER LIFE TO THE EGYPT SHE LOVED.

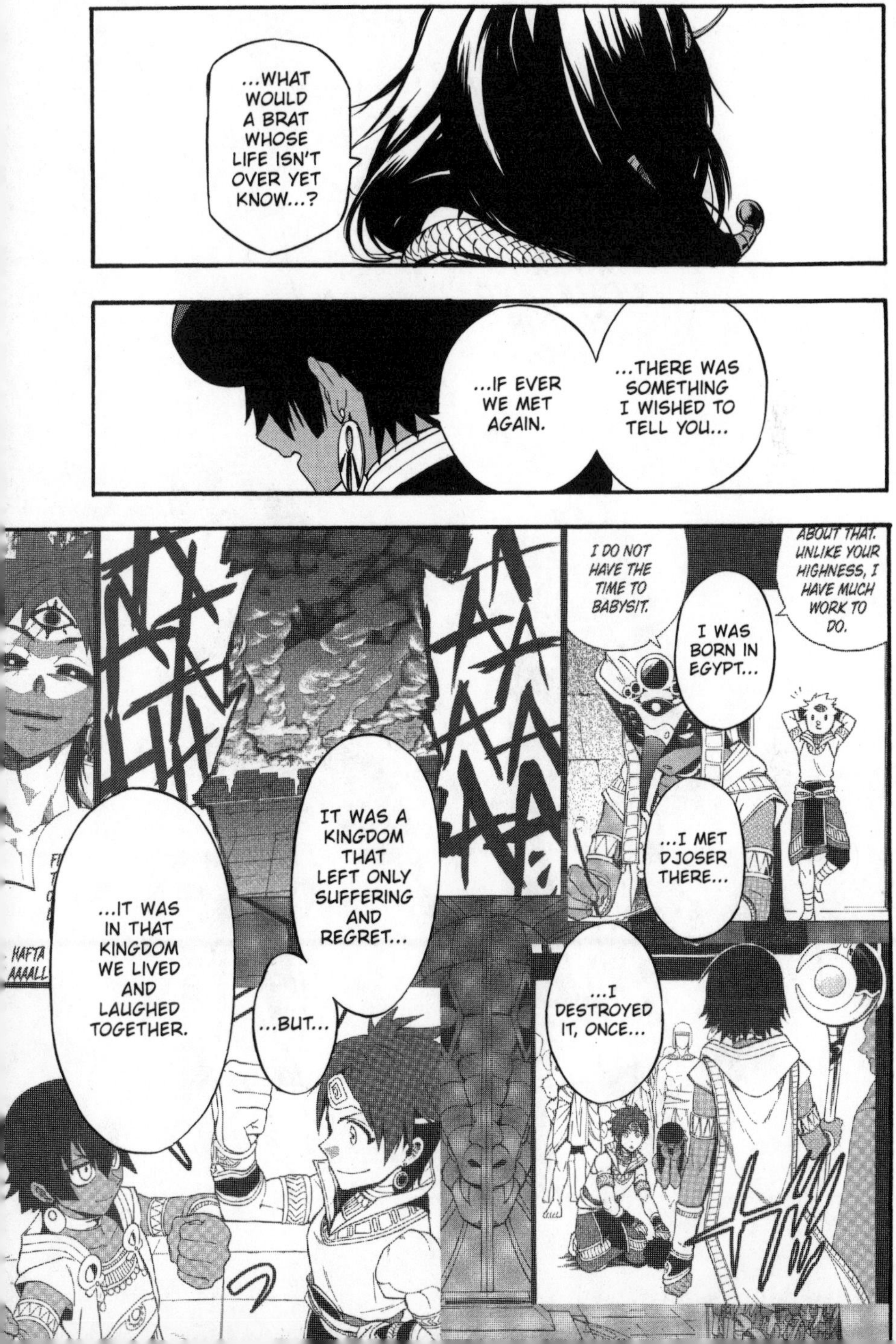
...WHAT WOULD A BRAT WHOSE LIFE ISN'T OVER YET KNOW...?
...THERE WAS SOMETHING I WISHED TO TELL YOU...
...IF EVER WE MET AGAIN.
ABOUT THAT. UNLIKE YOUR HIGHNESS, I HAVE MUCH WORK TO DO.
I DO NOT HAVE THE TIME TO BABYSIT.
I WAS BORN IN EGYPT...
...I MET DJOSER THERE...
...I DESTROYED IT, ONCE...
IT WAS A KINGDOM THAT LEFT ONLY SUFFERING AND REGRET...
...BUT...
...IT WAS IN THAT KINGDOM WE LIVED AND LAUGHED TOGETHER.

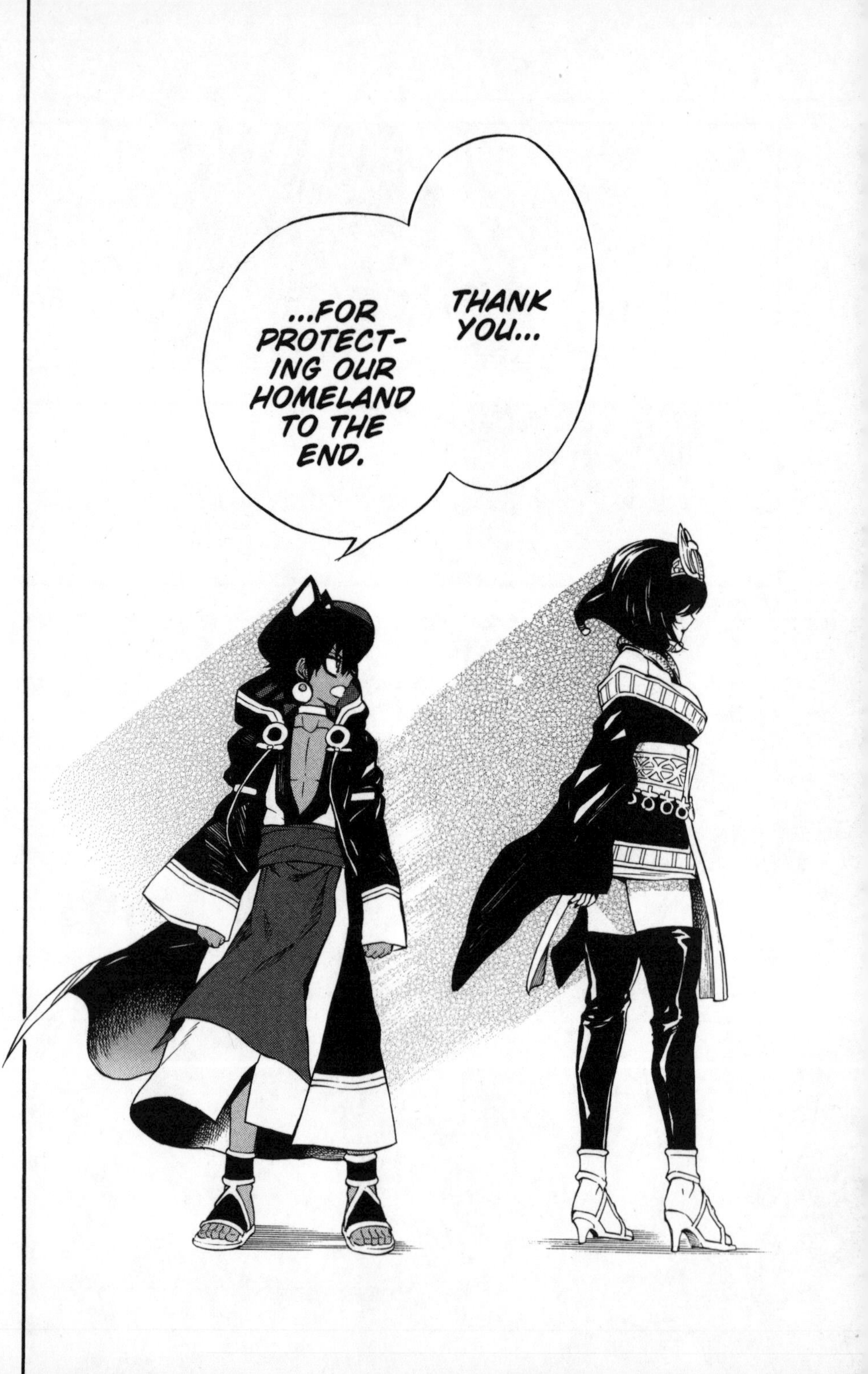
THANK YOU...
...FOR PROTECTING OUR HOMELAND TO THE END.

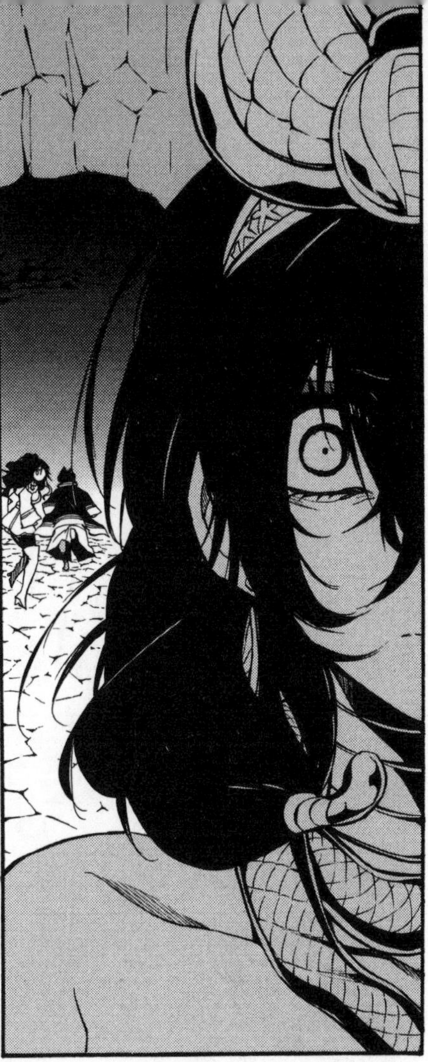

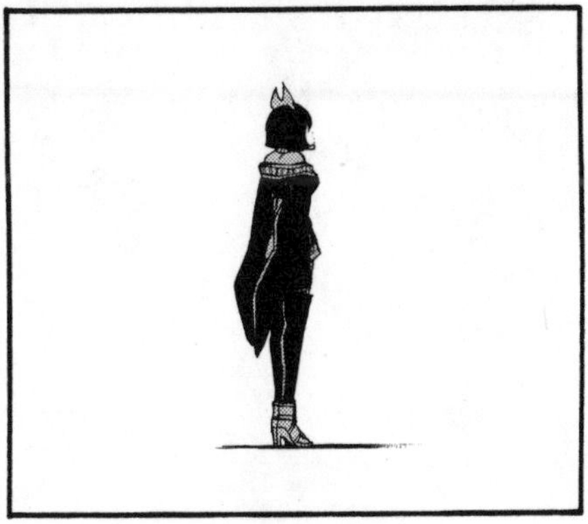

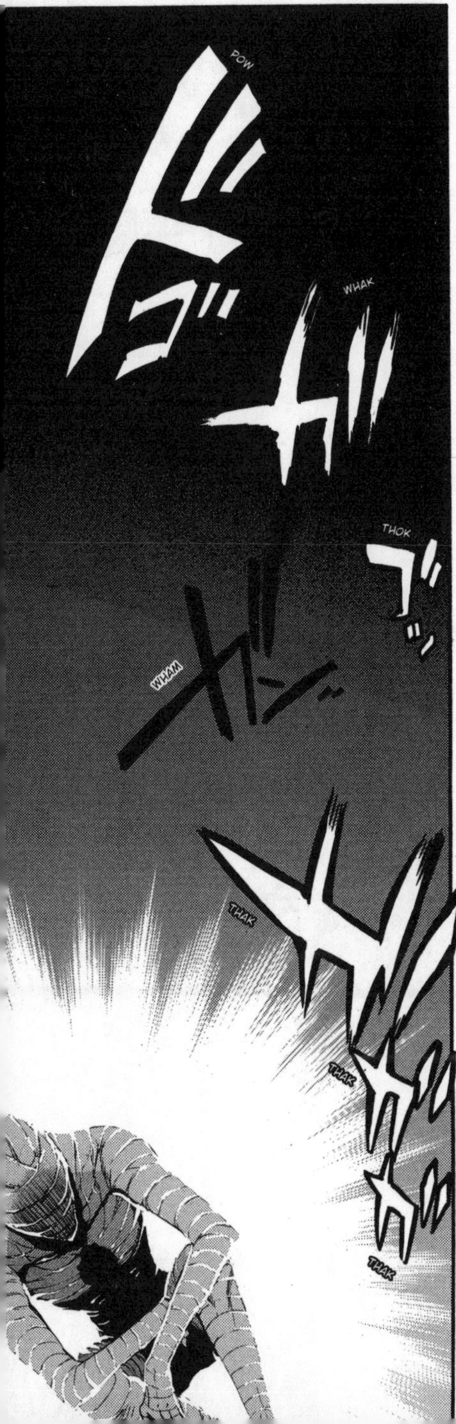
POW
WHAK
THOK
WHAM
THAK
THAK
THAK

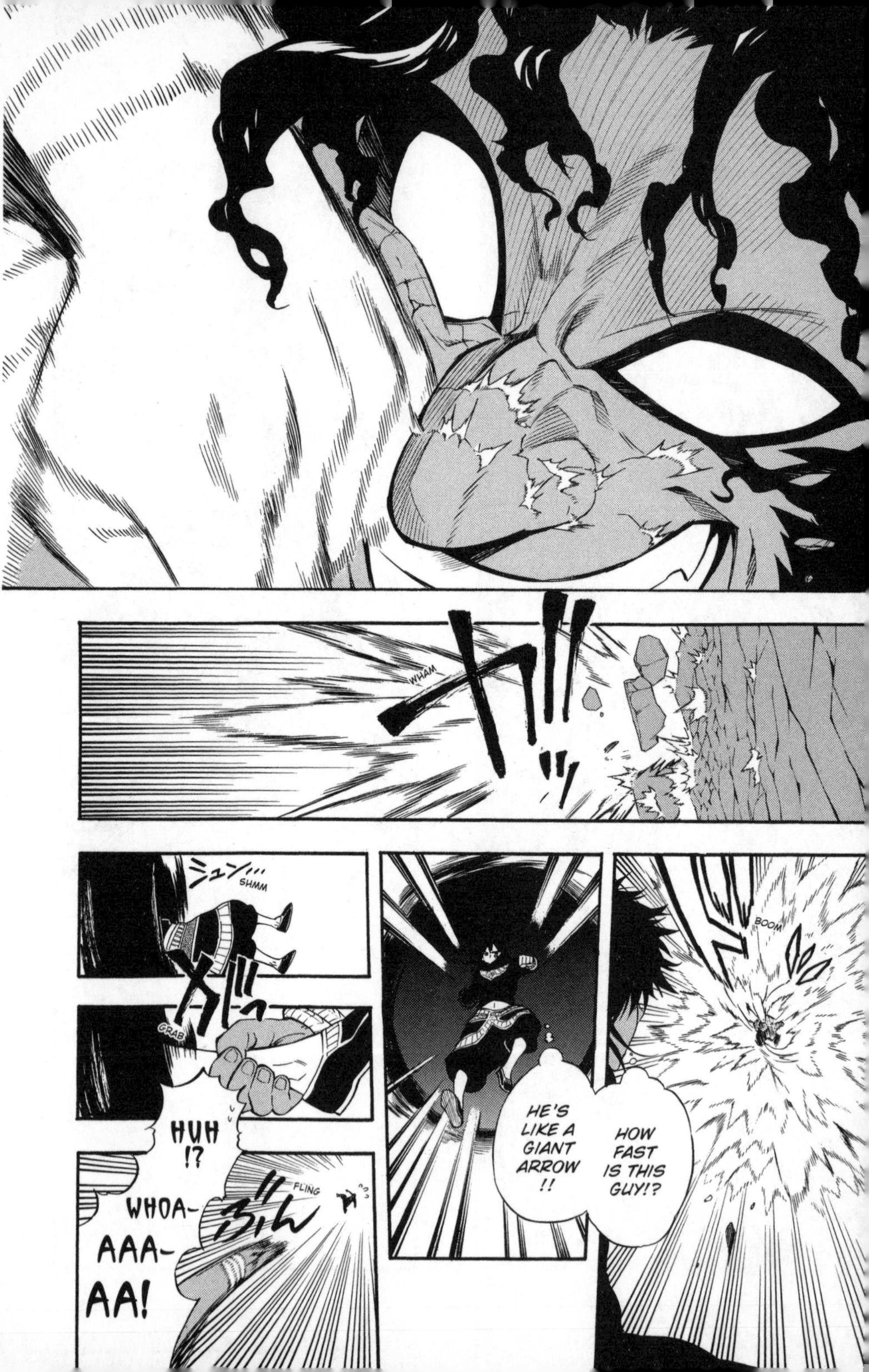
WHAM
BOOM
HOW FAST IS THIS GUY!?
HE'S LIKE A GIANT ARROW!!
SHMM
GRAB
HUH!?
FLING
WHOA-AAA-AA!

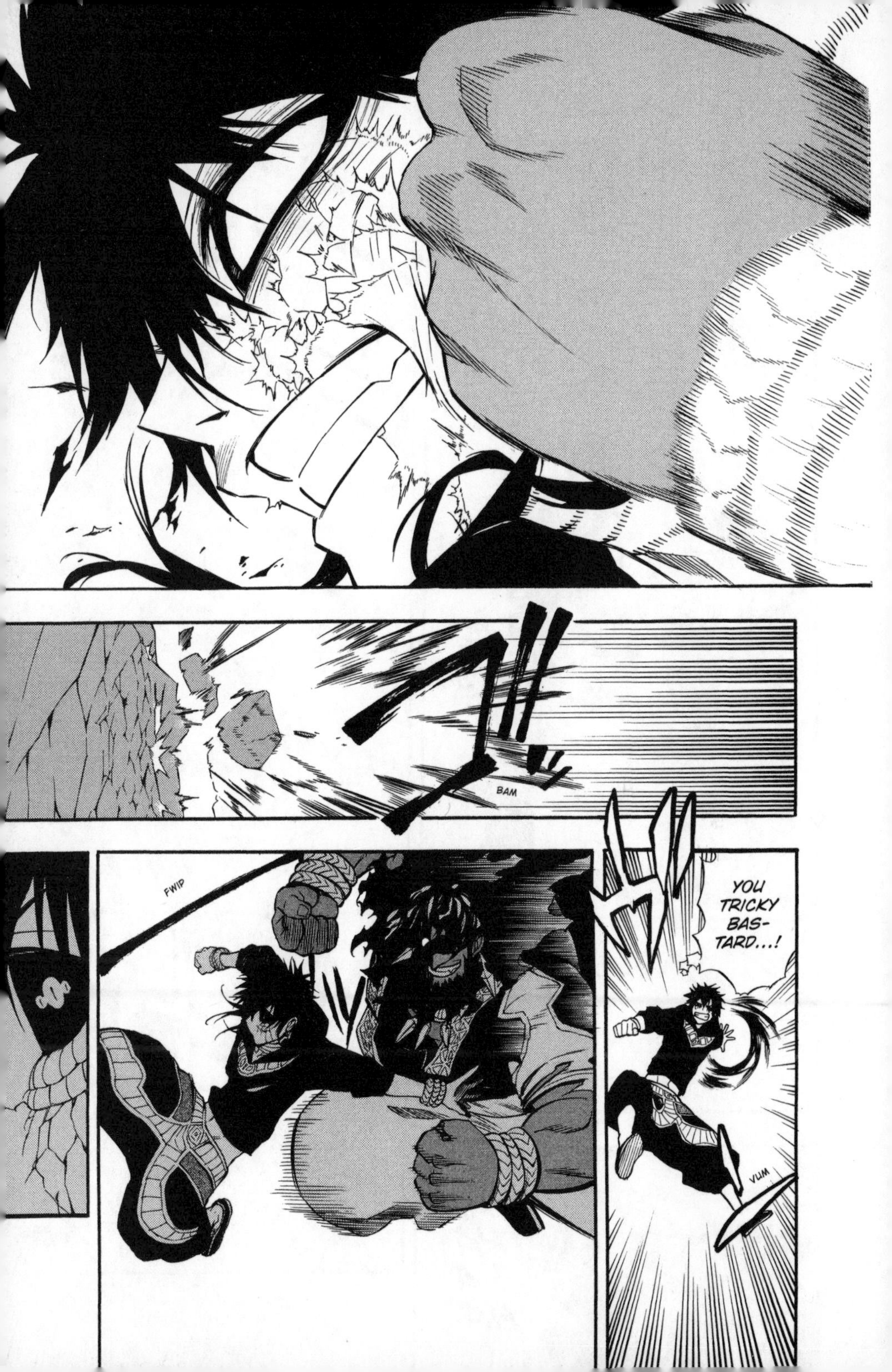
BAM
YOU TRICKY BAS-TARD...!
VUM
FWIP

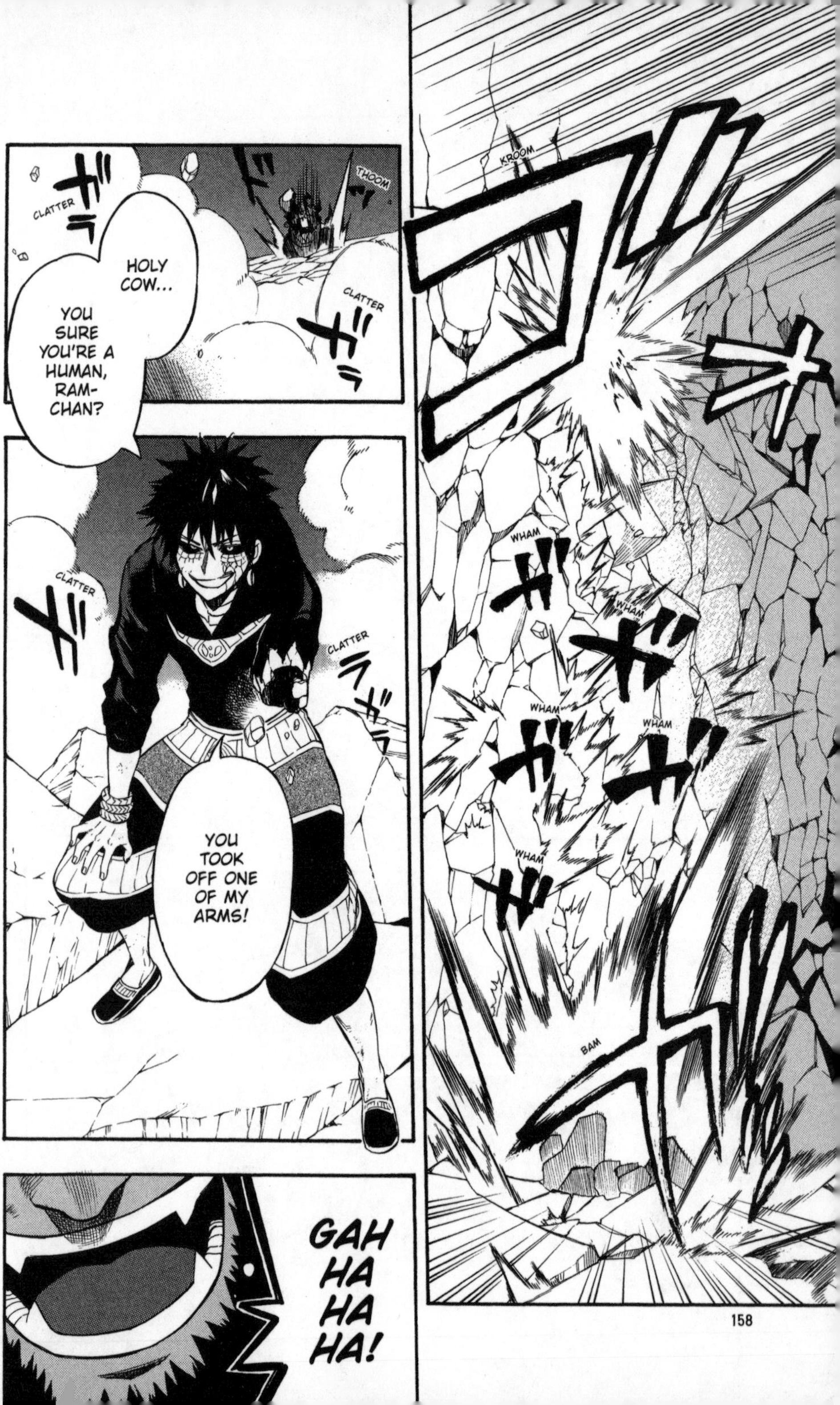
KROOM
WHAM
WHAM
WHAM
WHAM
WHAM
BAM
THOOM
CLATTER
HOLY COW... YOU SURE YOU'RE A HUMAN, RAM-CHAN?
CLATTER
CLATTER
CLATTER
YOU TOOK OFF ONE OF MY ARMS!
GAH HA HA HA!

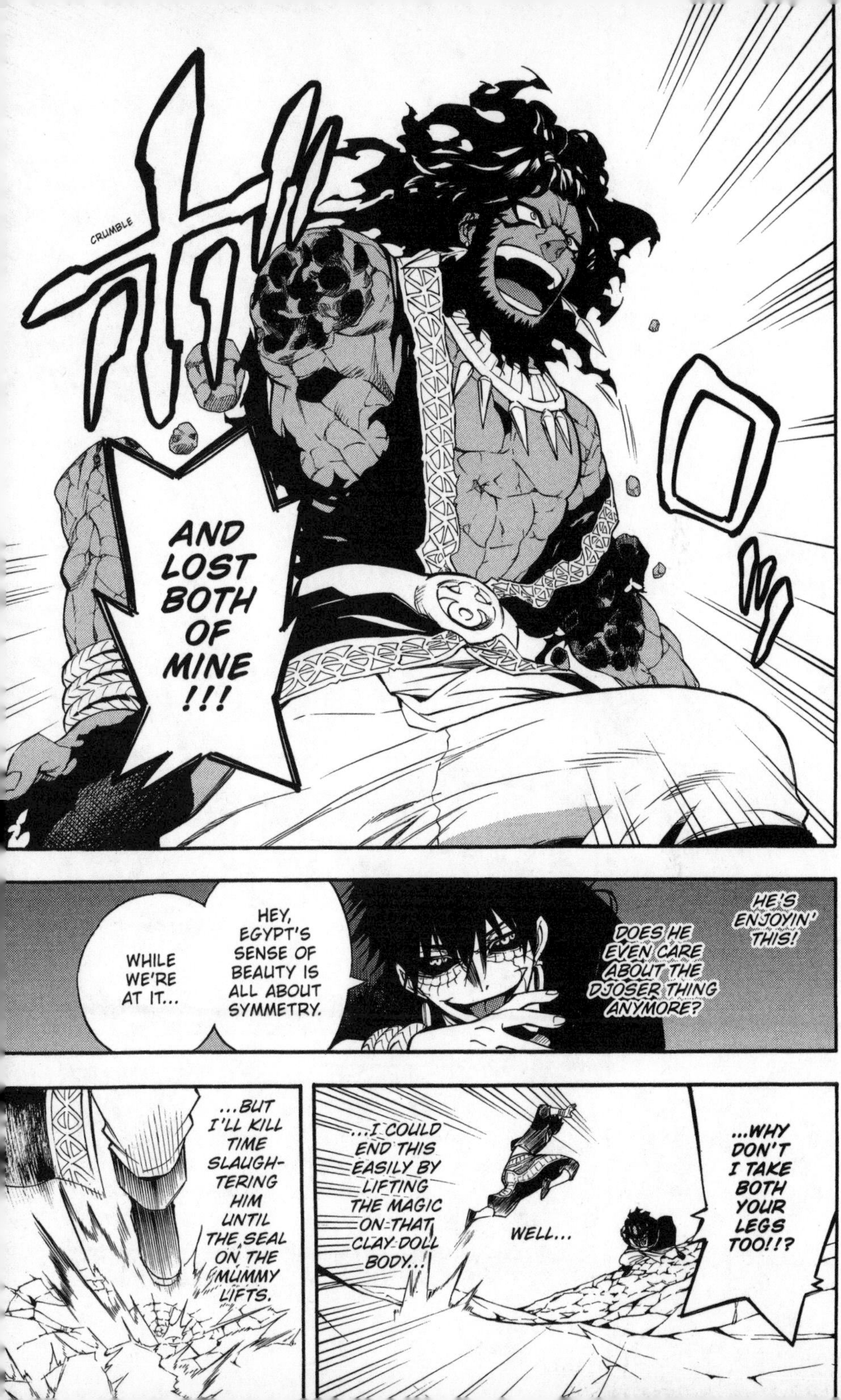
CRUMBLE
AND LOST BOTH OF MINE!!!
HE'S ENJOYIN' THIS!
DOES HE EVEN CARE ABOUT THE DJOSER THING ANYMORE?
HEY, EGYPT'S SENSE OF BEAUTY IS ALL ABOUT SYMMETRY.
WHILE WE'RE AT IT...
...WHY DON'T I TAKE BOTH YOUR LEGS TOO!!?
WELL...
...I COULD END THIS EASILY BY LIFTING THE MAGIC ON THAT CLAY DOLL BODY...
...BUT I'LL KILL TIME SLAUGHTERING HIM UNTIL THE SEAL ON THE MUMMY LIFTS.

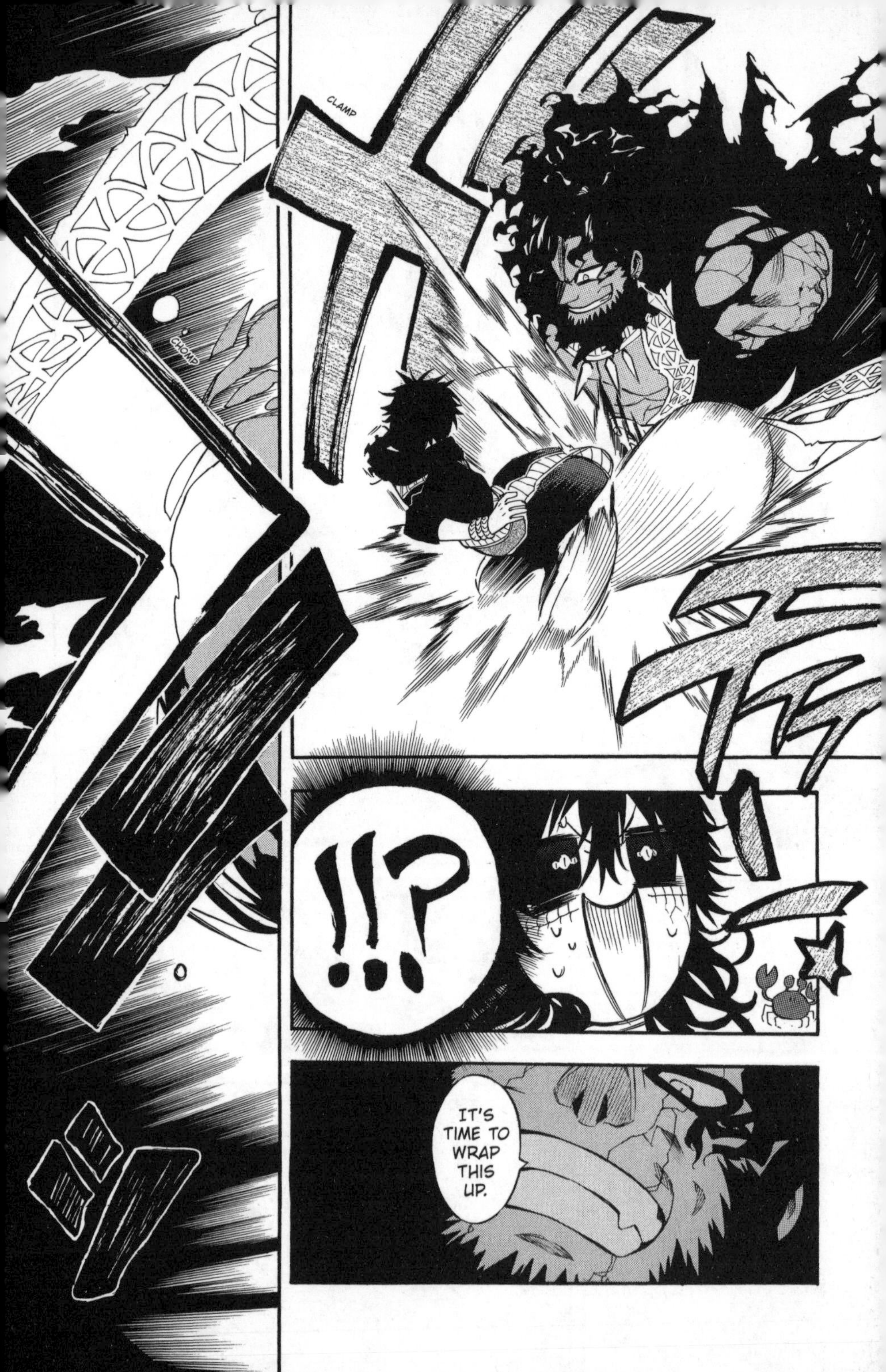
CLAMP
!!?
IT'S TIME TO WRAP THIS UP.
CHOMP

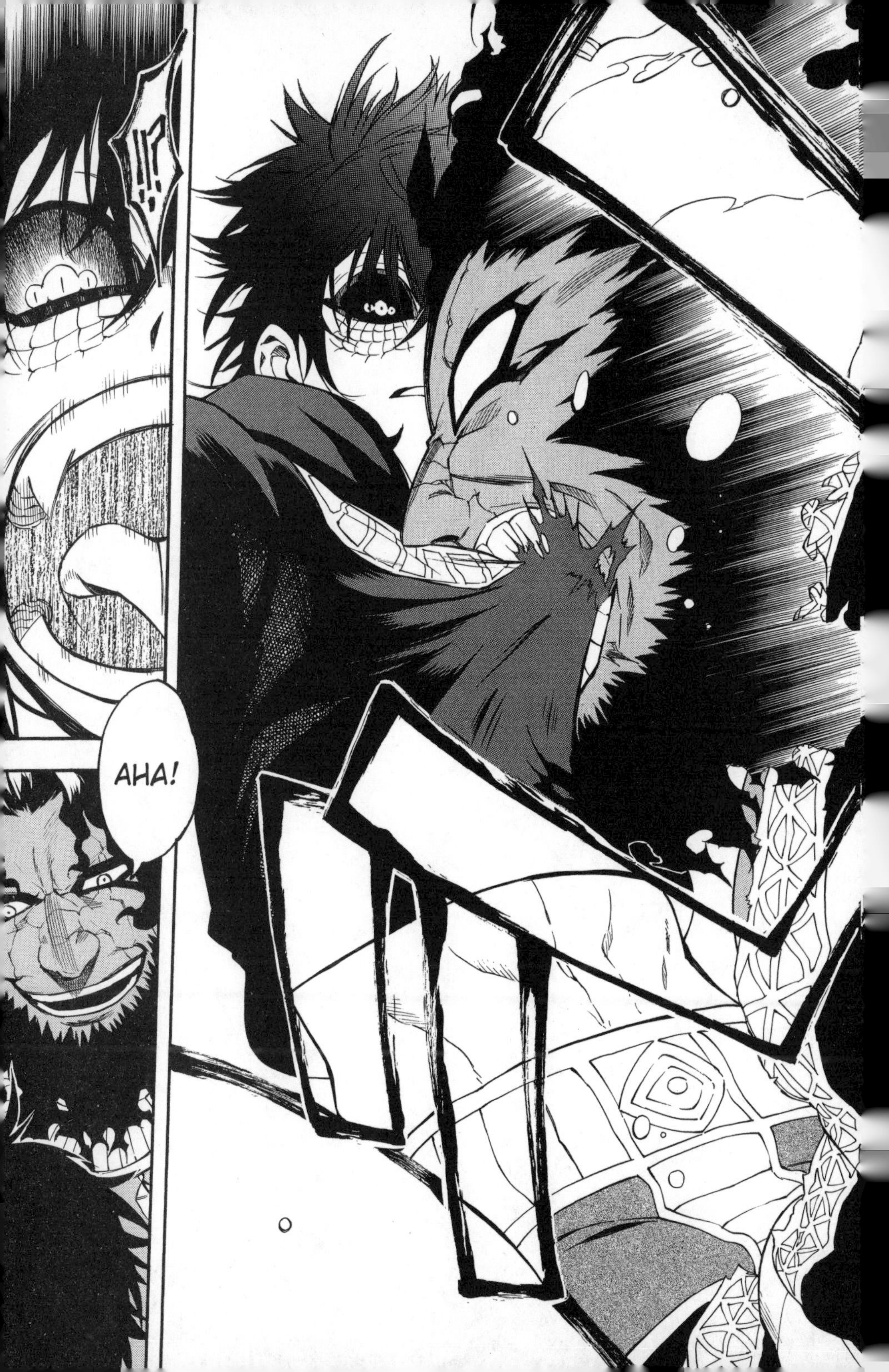
!!?
AHA!

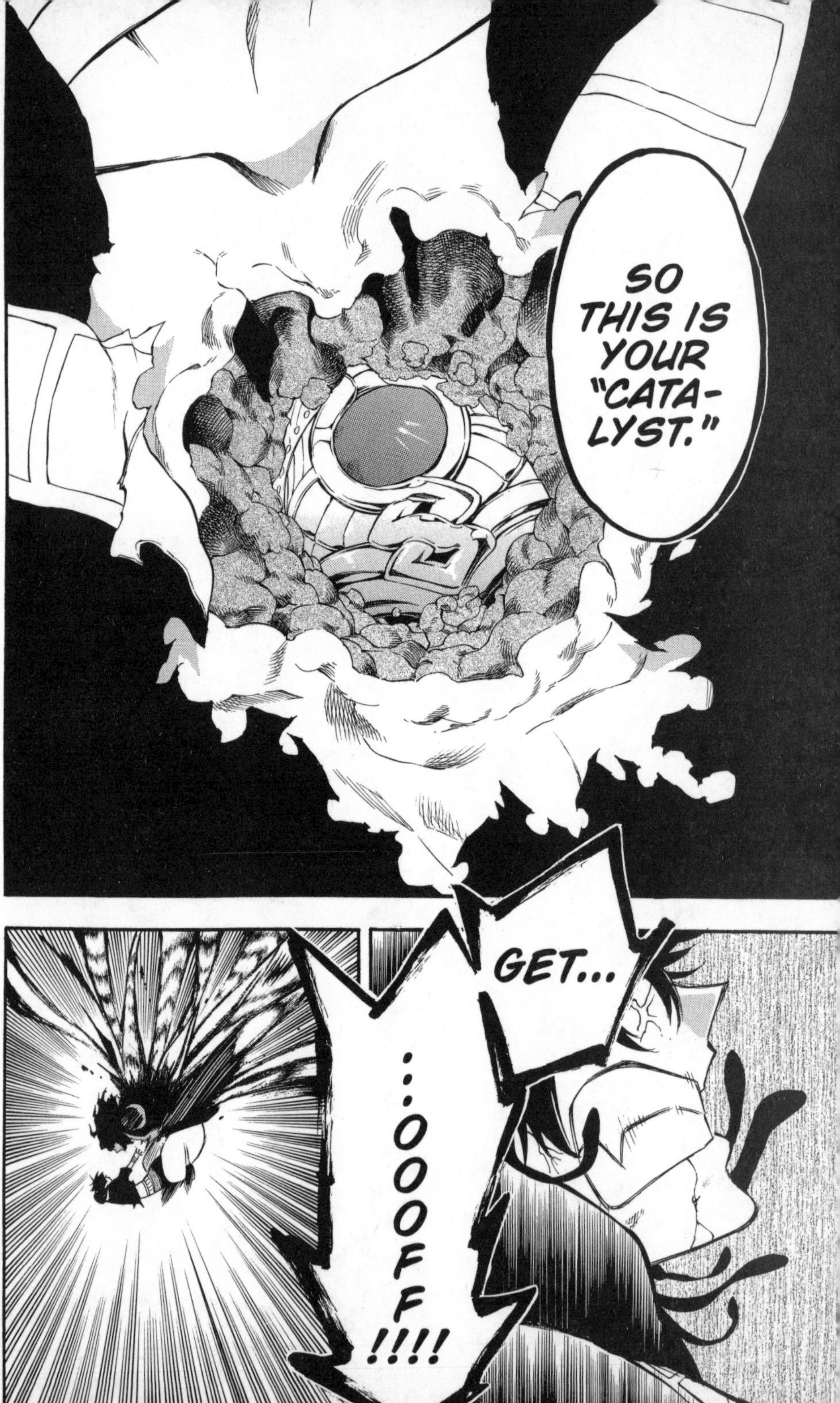
SO THIS IS YOUR "CATA-LYST."
GET...
...OOOOFF!!!!

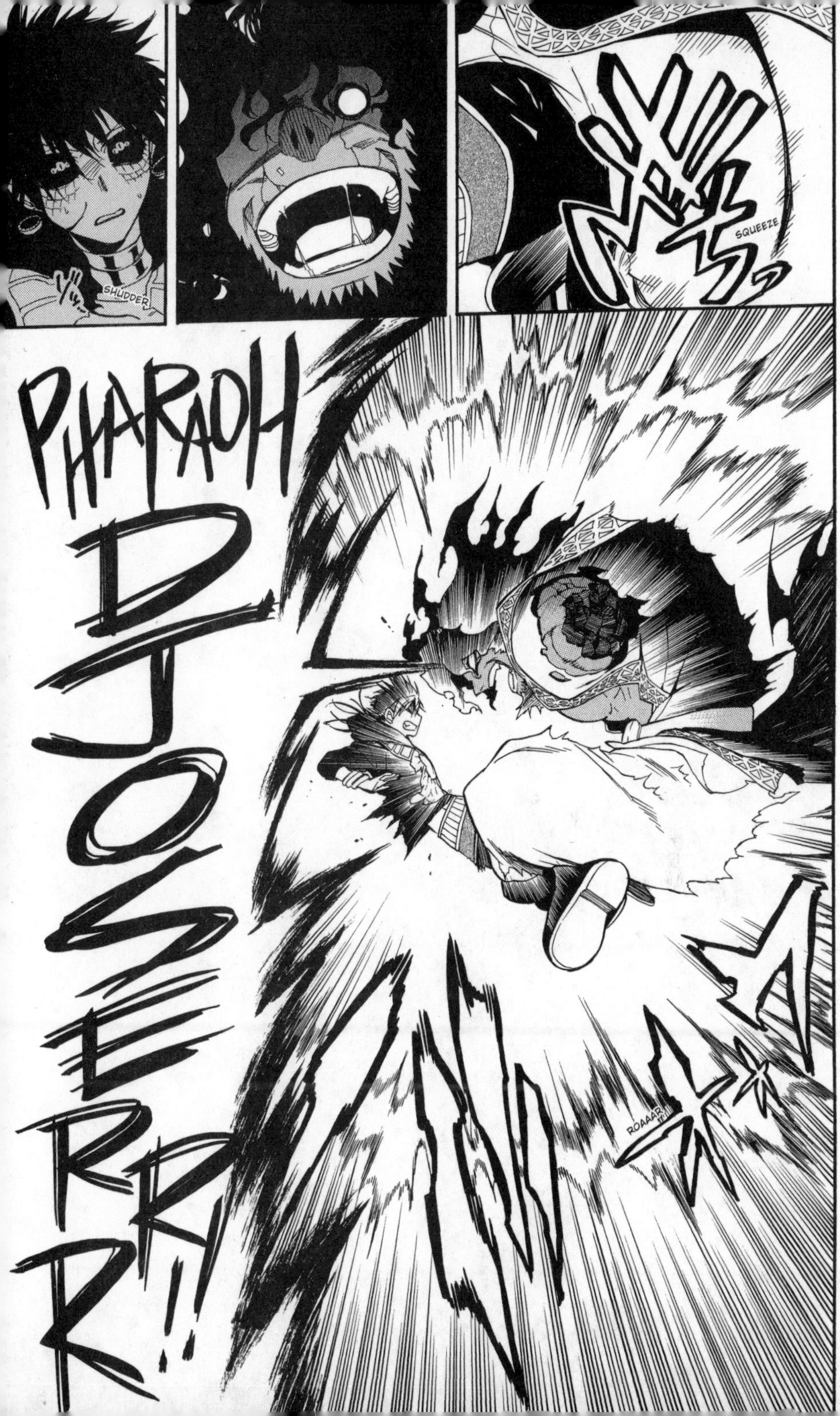
SQUEEZE
SHUDDER
PHARAOH DJOSERRR!!
ROAAAR

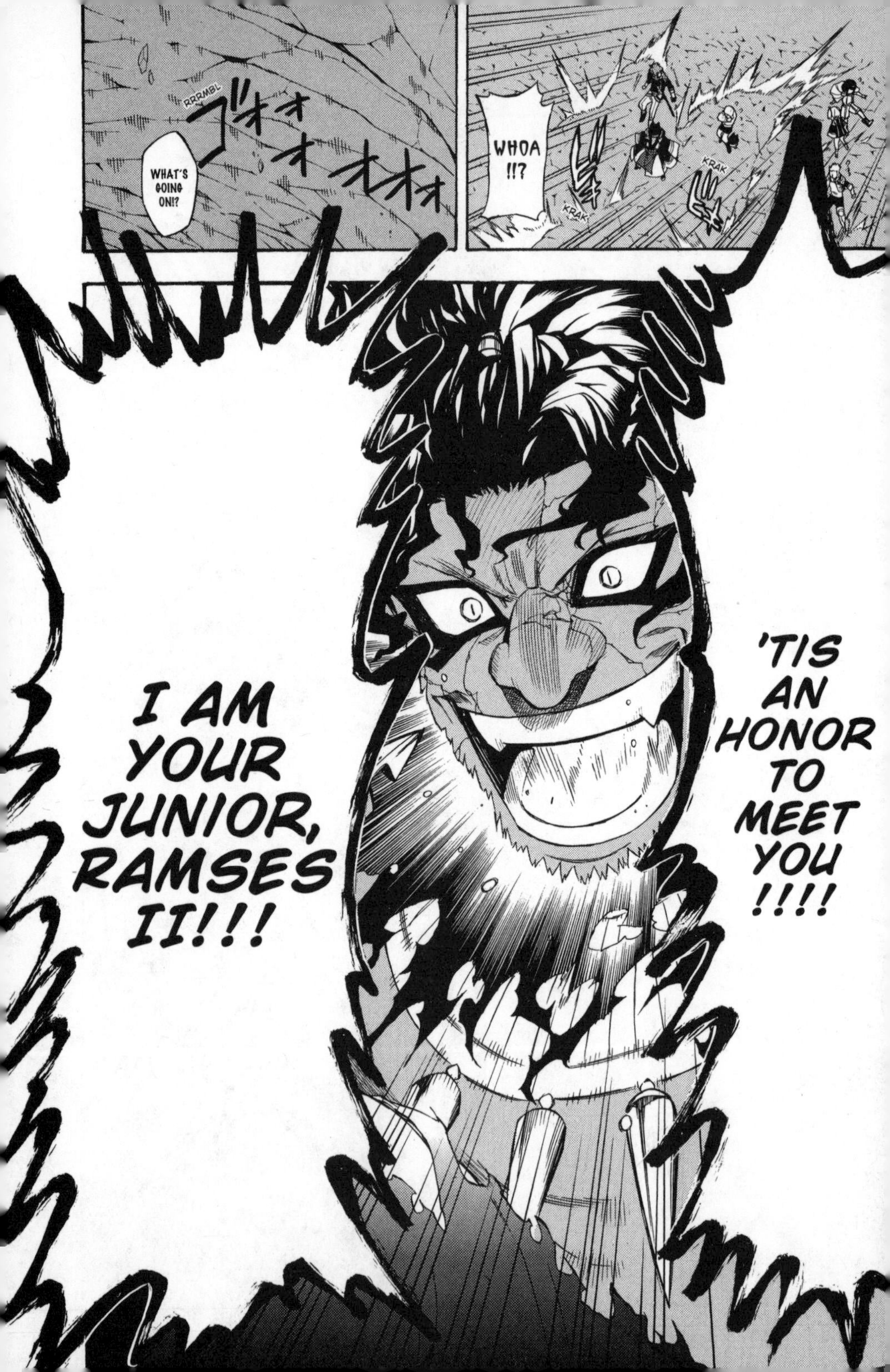

WHOA!!?
KRAK
KRAK
RRRMBL
WHAT'S GOING ON!?
'TIS AN HONOR TO MEET YOU!!!!
I AM YOUR JUNIOR, RAMSES II!!!

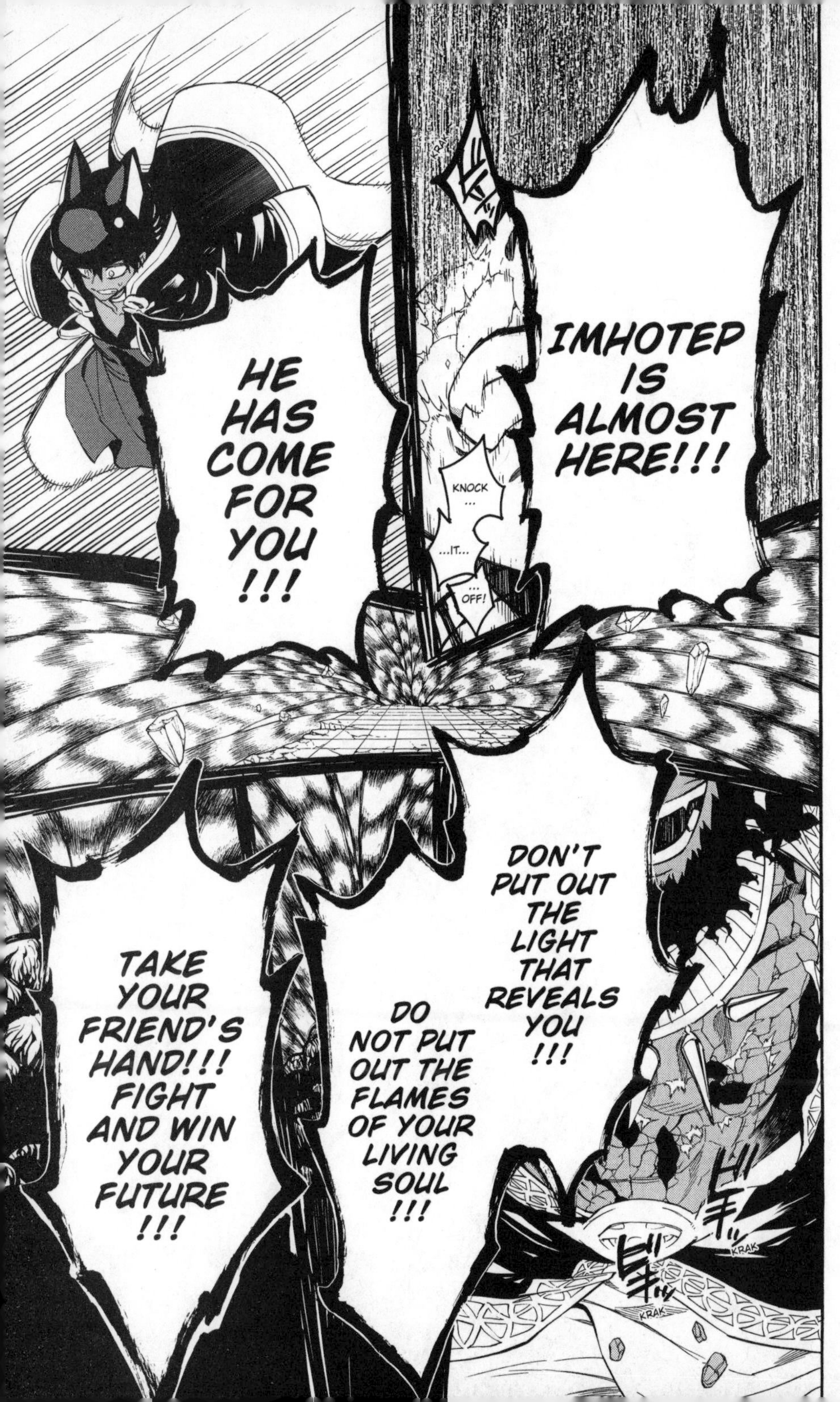
IMHOTEP IS ALMOST HERE!!!
KRAK
KNOCK ... ...IT... ...OFF!
HE HAS COME FOR YOU!!!
DON'T PUT OUT THE LIGHT THAT REVEALS YOU!!!
KRAK
KRAK
DO NOT PUT OUT THE FLAMES OF YOUR LIVING SOUL!!!
TAKE YOUR FRIEND'S HAND!!! FIGHT AND WIN YOUR FUTURE!!!

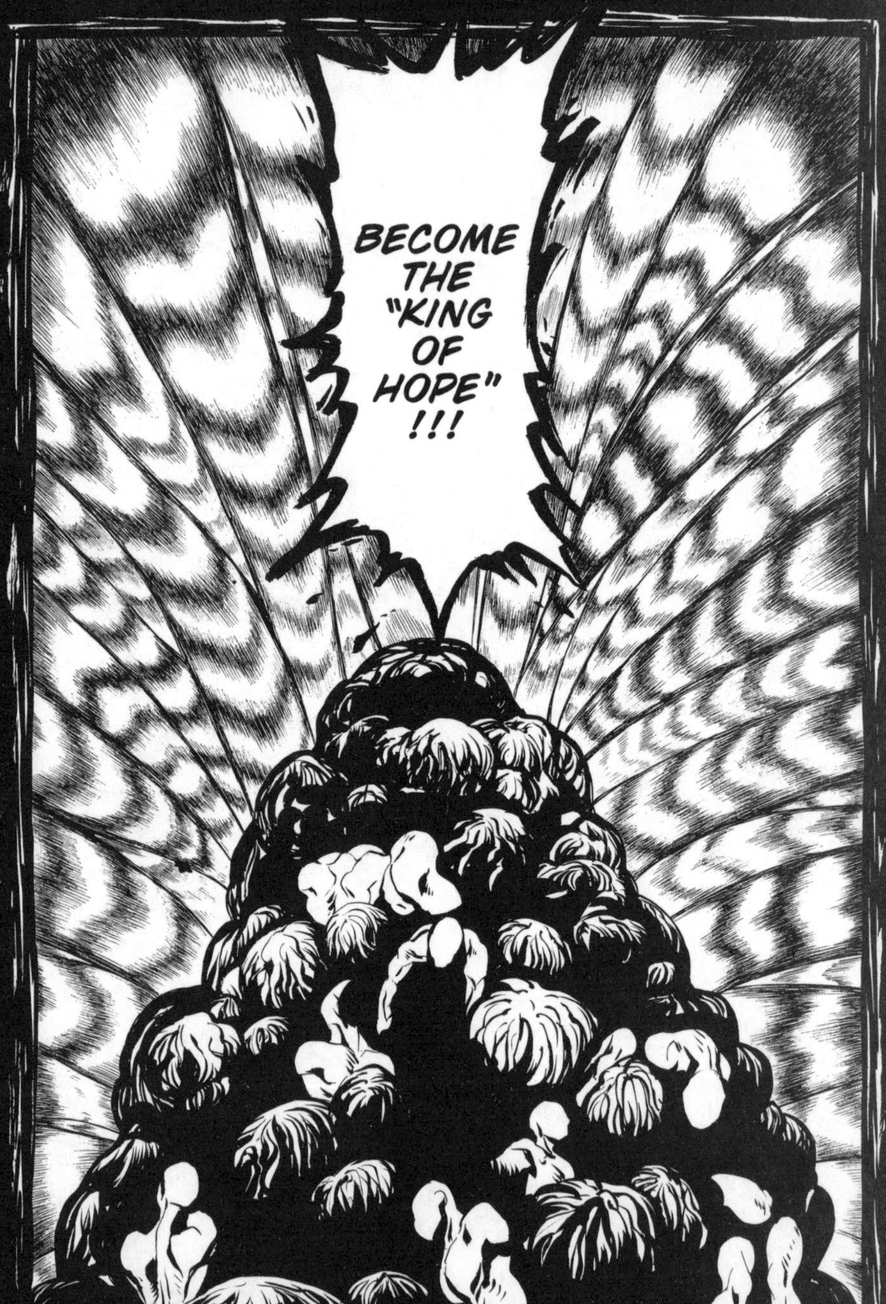
BECOME THE "KING OF HOPE" !!!

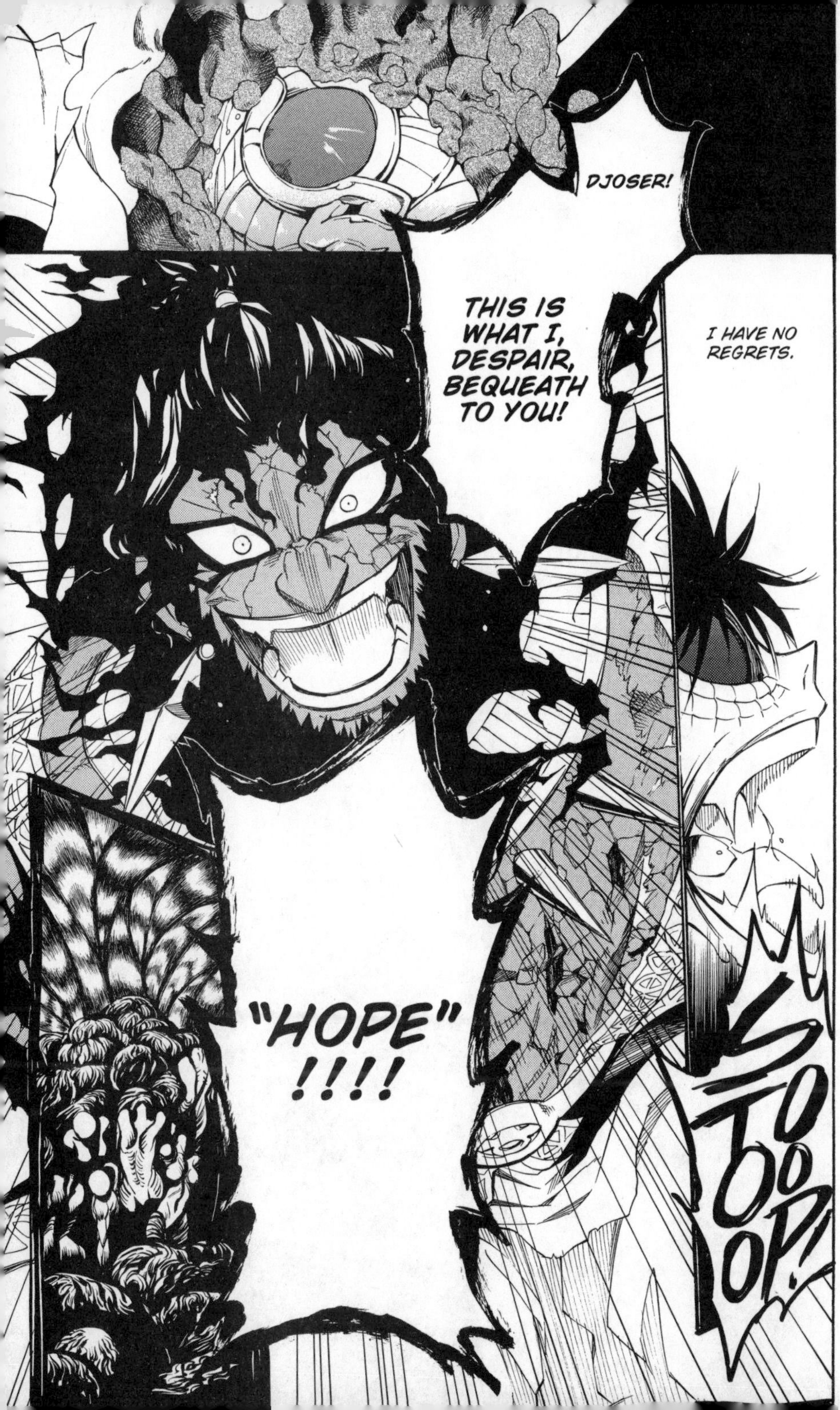
DJOSER!
I HAVE NO REGRETS.
THIS IS WHAT I, DESPAIR, BEQUEATH TO YOU!
"HOPE" !!!!
STOOOOP!

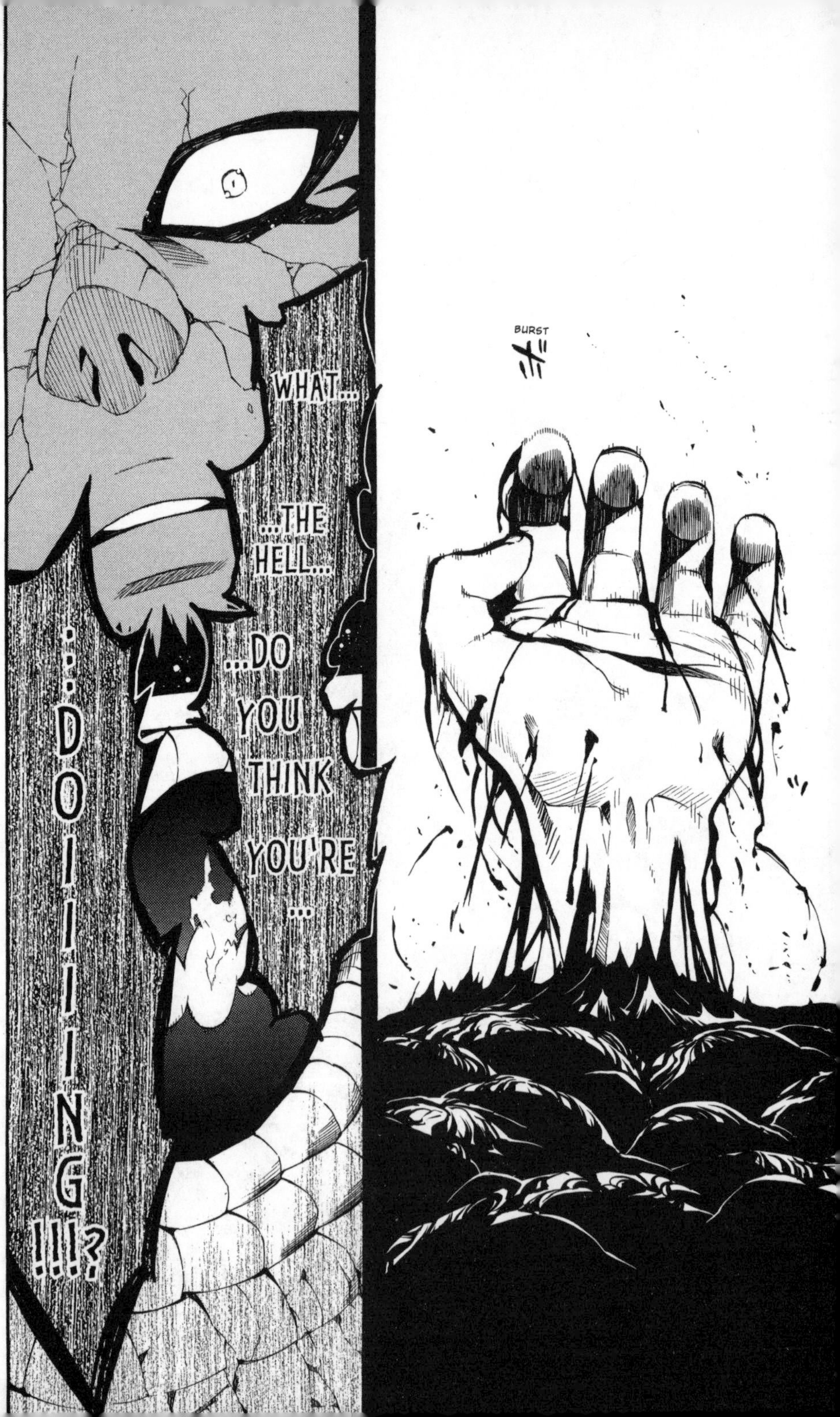
BURST
WHAT...
...THE HELL...
...DO YOU THINK YOU'RE ...
...DOIIING!!!?

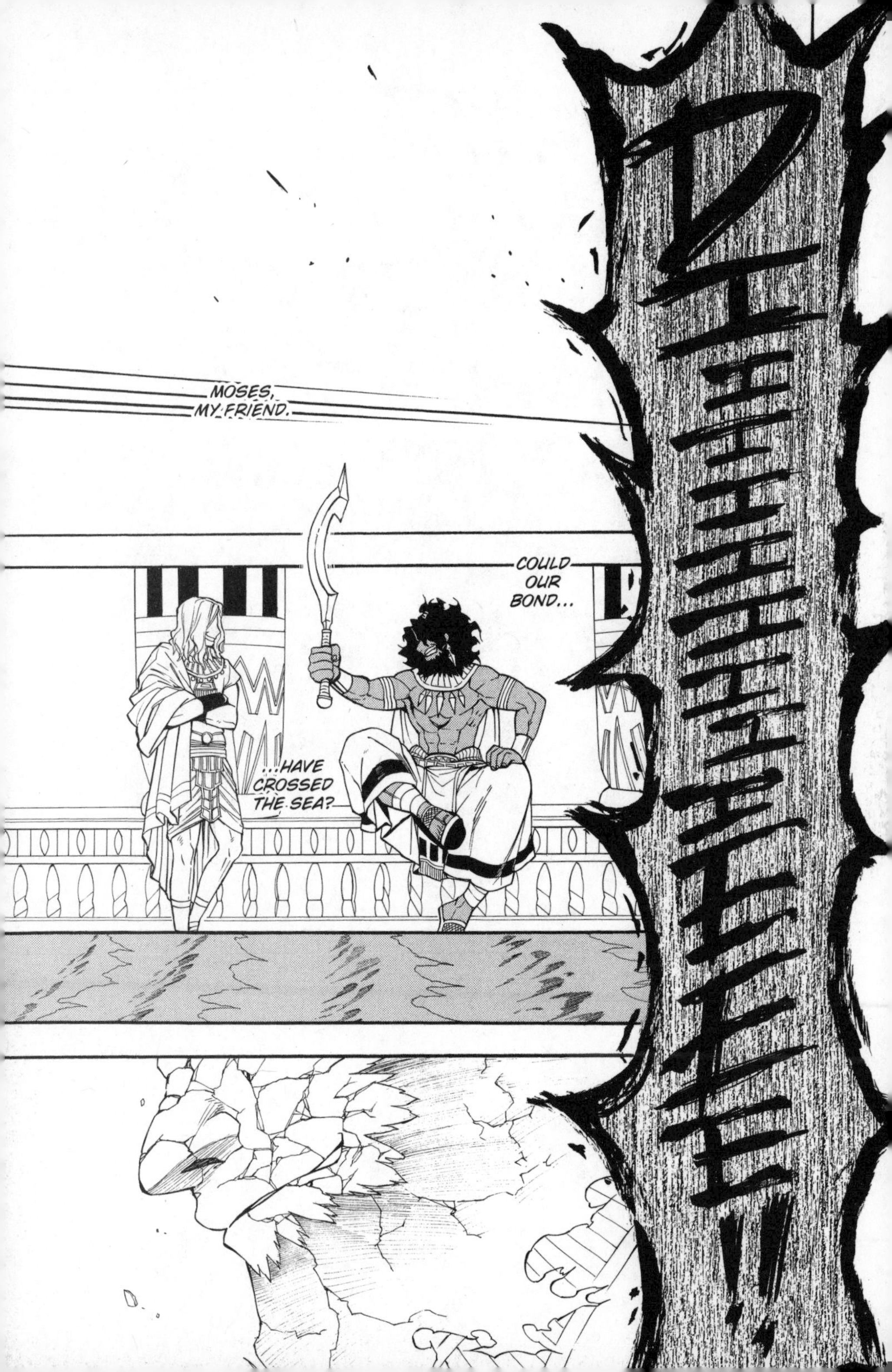
MOSES, MY FRIEND.
COULD OUR BOND...
...HAVE CROSSED THE SEA?

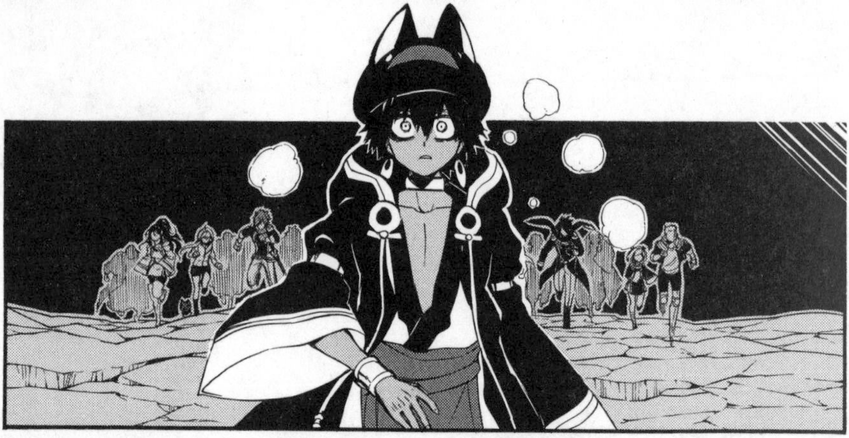
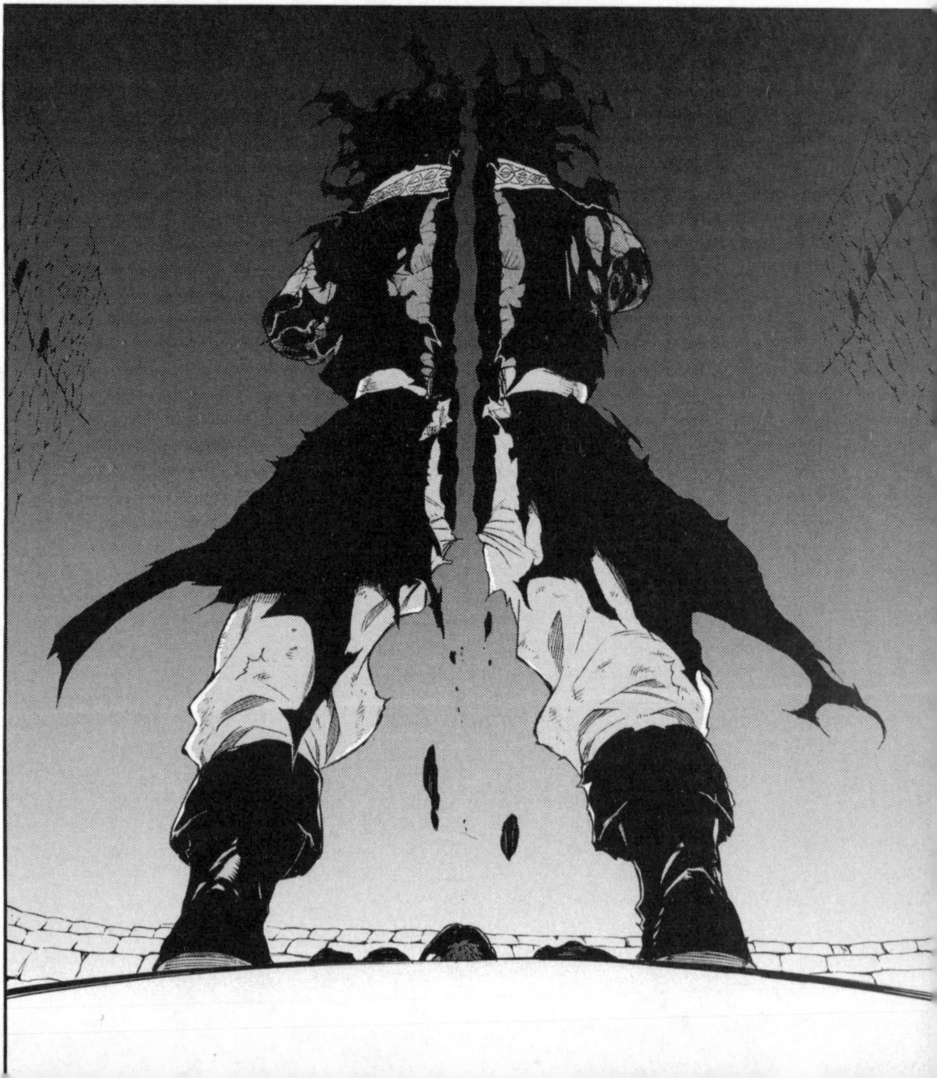

...SES...?

RAM...

WHAT IN THE GODS' NAMES HAPPENED HERE...!??

!!!!

HEE-HEE-HEE-HEE-HEE-HEE.

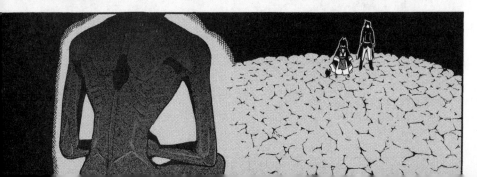

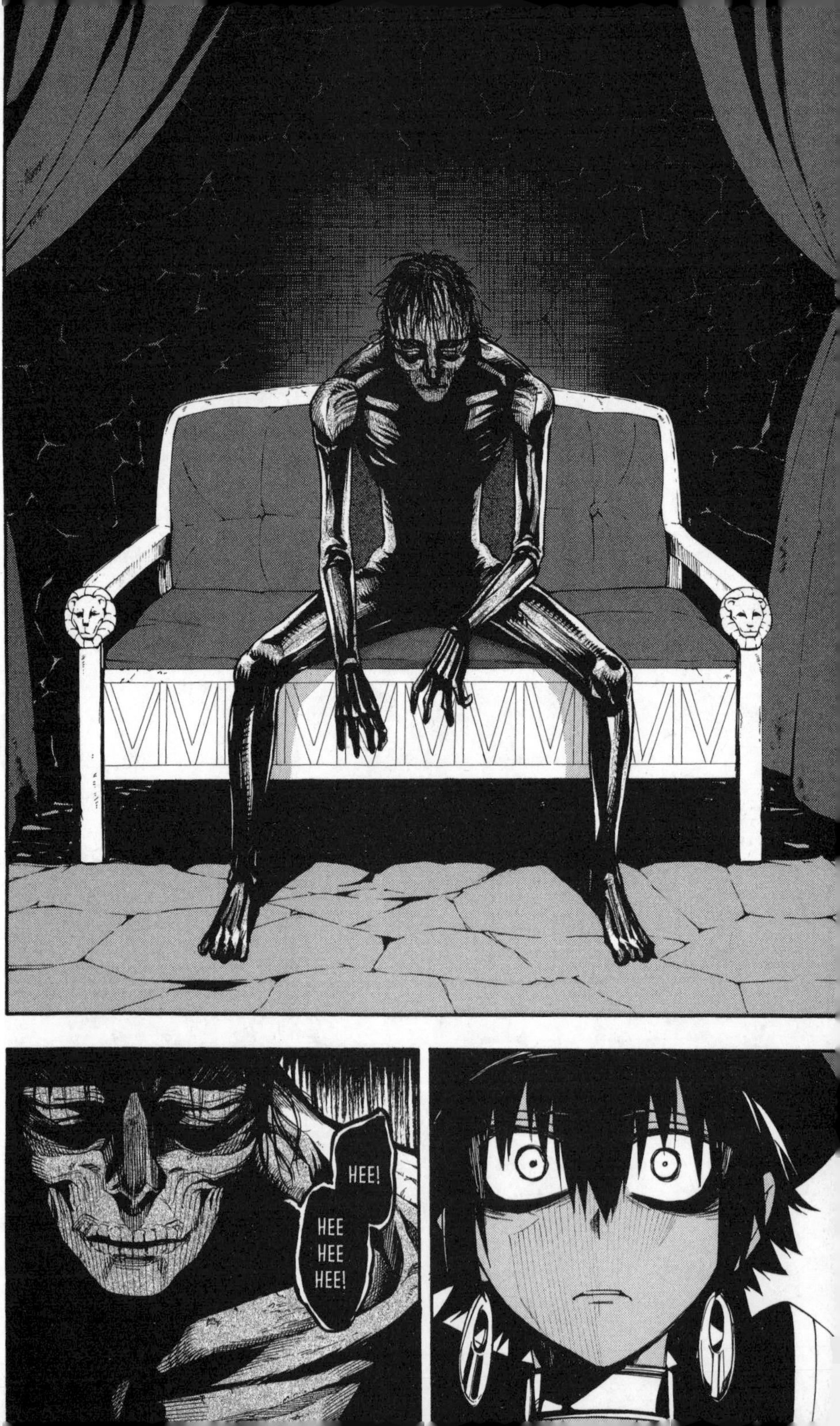
HEE!
HEE HEE HEE!

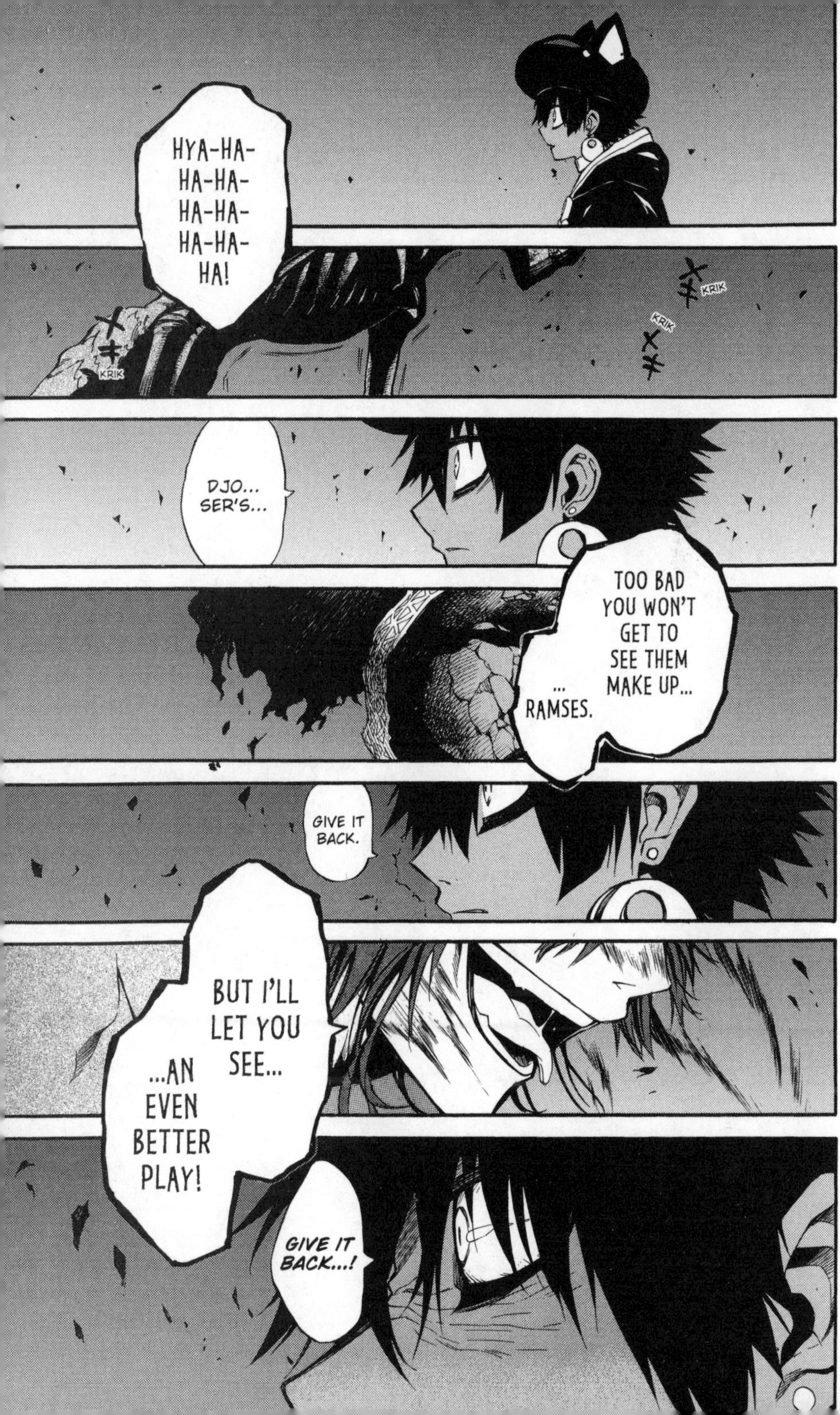
HYA-HA-HA-HA-HA-HA-HA-HA-HA!
KRIK
KRIK
KRIK
DJO... SER'S...
TOO BAD YOU WON'T GET TO SEE THEM MAKE UP...
... RAMSES.
GIVE IT BACK.
BUT I'LL LET YOU SEE...
...AN EVEN BETTER PLAY!
GIVE IT BACK...!

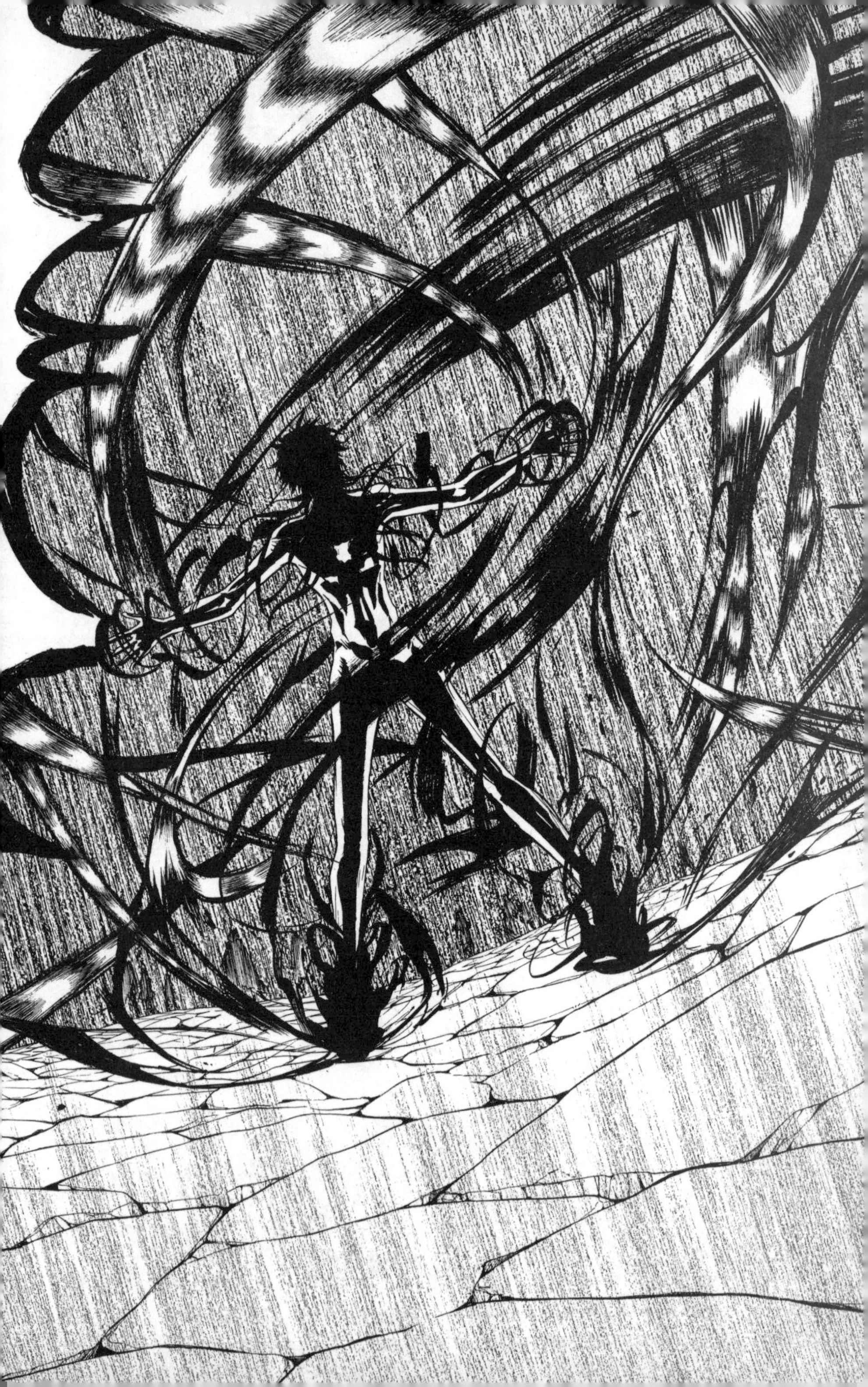

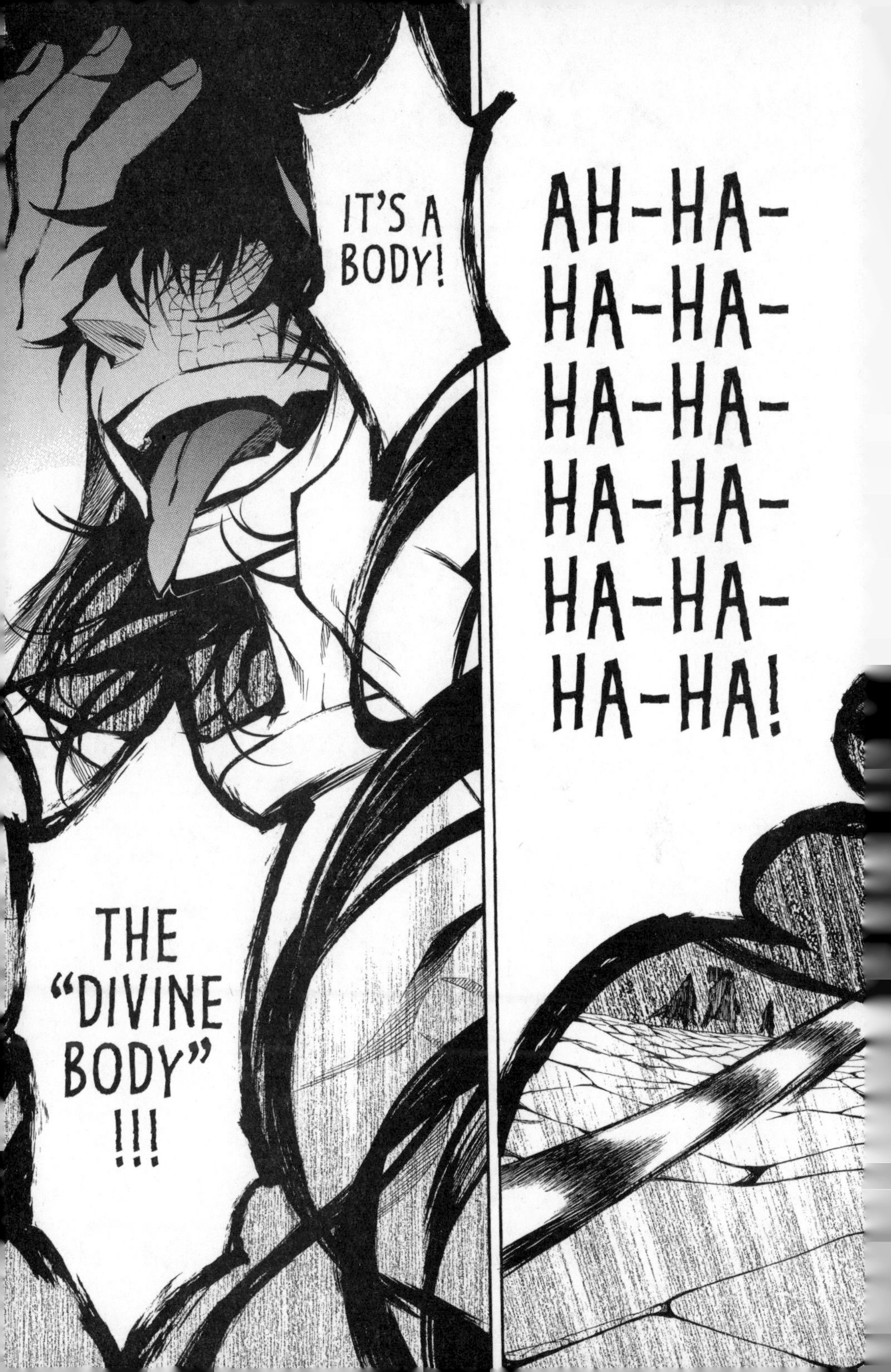
AH-HA-HA-HA-HA-HA-HA-HA-HA-HA-HA-HA-HA-HA-HA-HA!
IT'S A BODY!
THE "DIVINE BODY"!!!

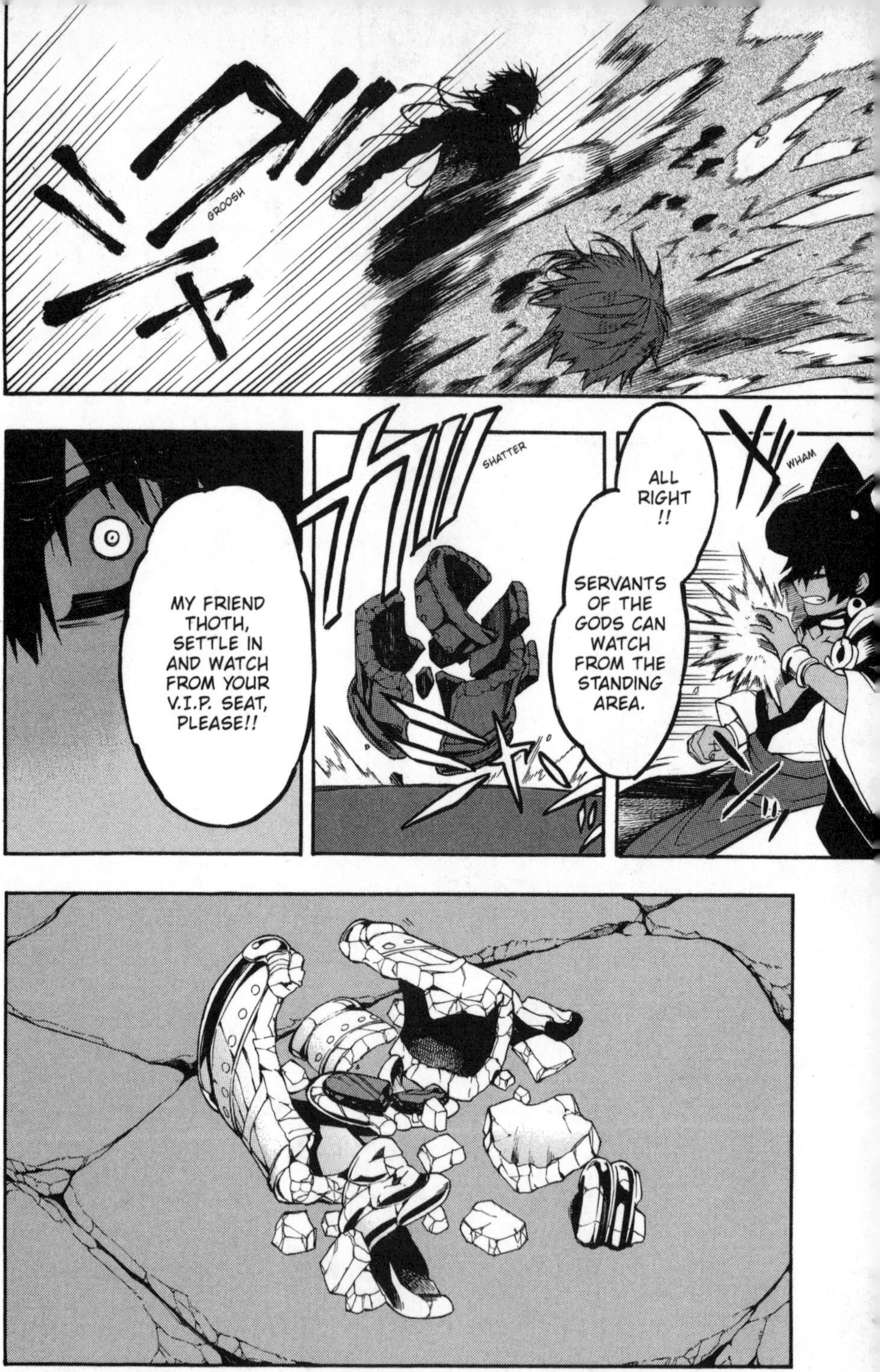
GROOSH
WHAM
ALL RIGHT !!
SERVANTS OF THE GODS CAN WATCH FROM THE STANDING AREA.
SHATTER
MY FRIEND THOTH, SETTLE IN AND WATCH FROM YOUR V.I.P. SEAT, PLEASE!!

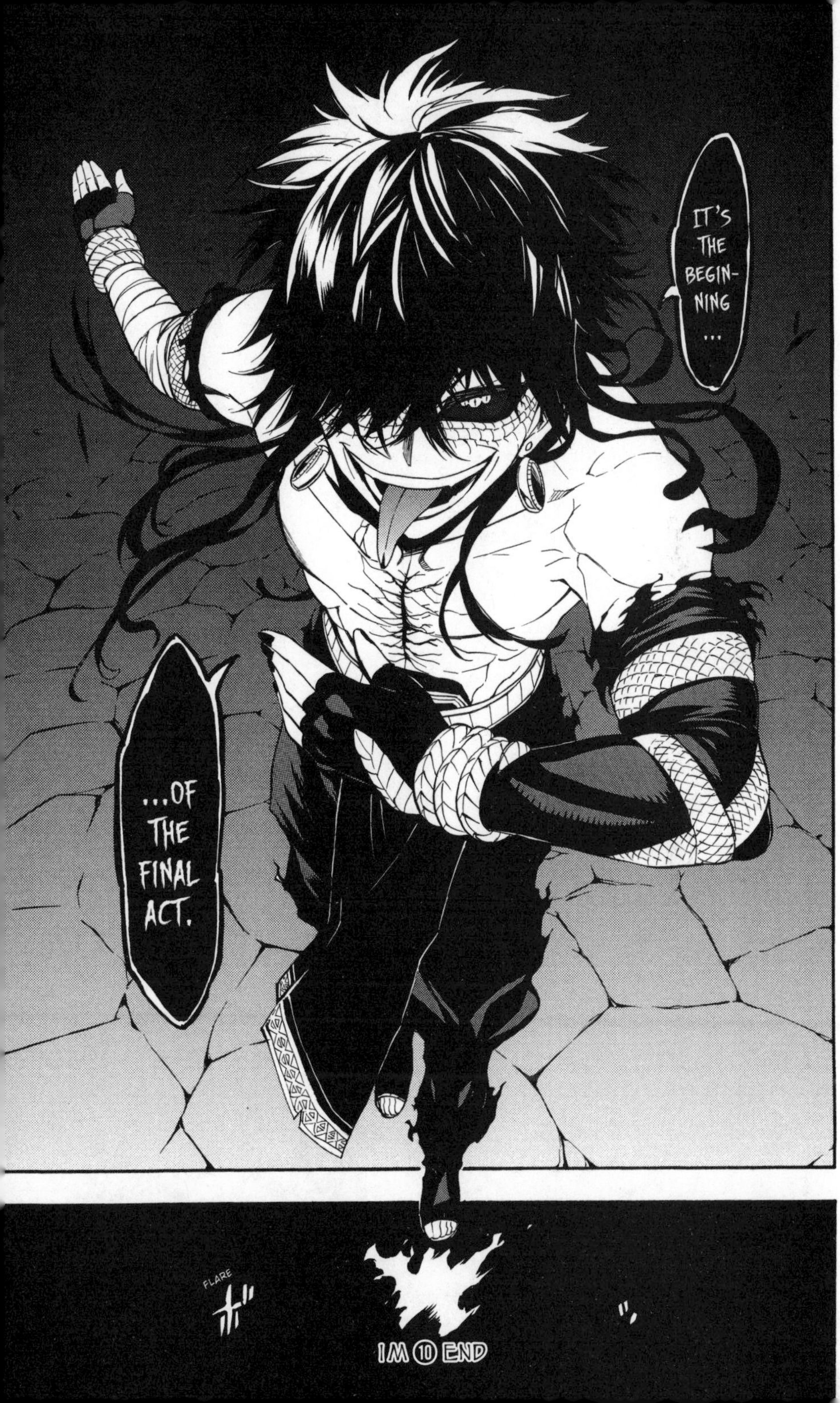
IT'S THE BEGIN- NING ...
...OF THE FINAL ACT.
FLARE
IM ⑩ END

Great Priest Imhotep

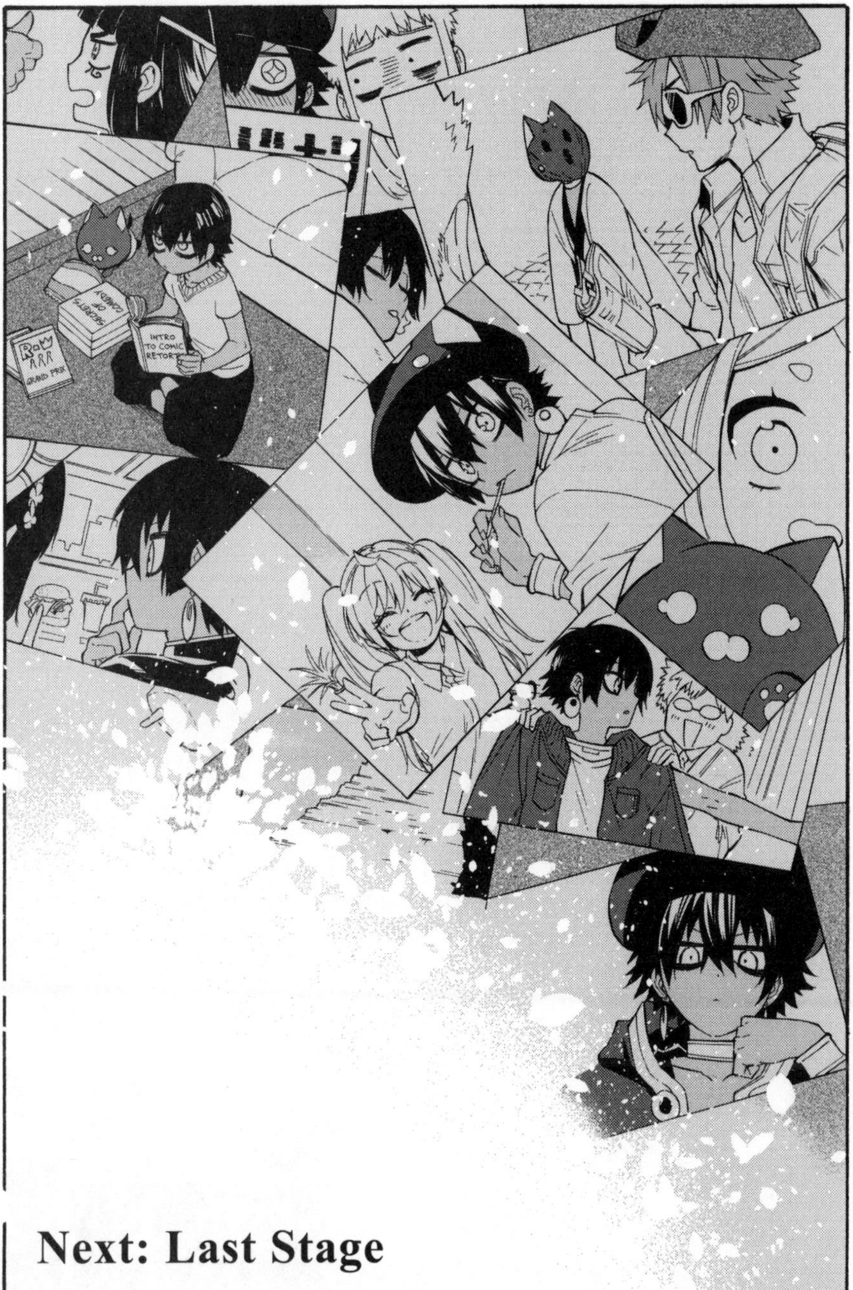
SECRETS OF COMEDY
INTRO TO COMIC RETORT
GRAND PRIX

Next: Last Stage

Great Priest Imhotep

HE'S NICE AND WARM!!

AKHE-NATEN-KUN!!!

CHAPTER 1 (FINAL CHAPTER)

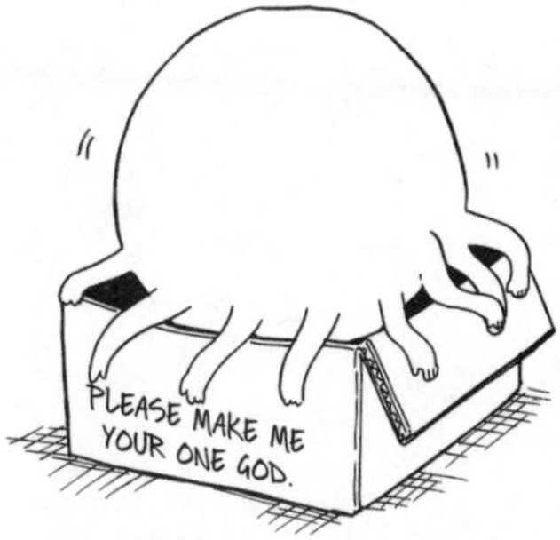
PLEASE MAKE ME YOUR ONE GOD.

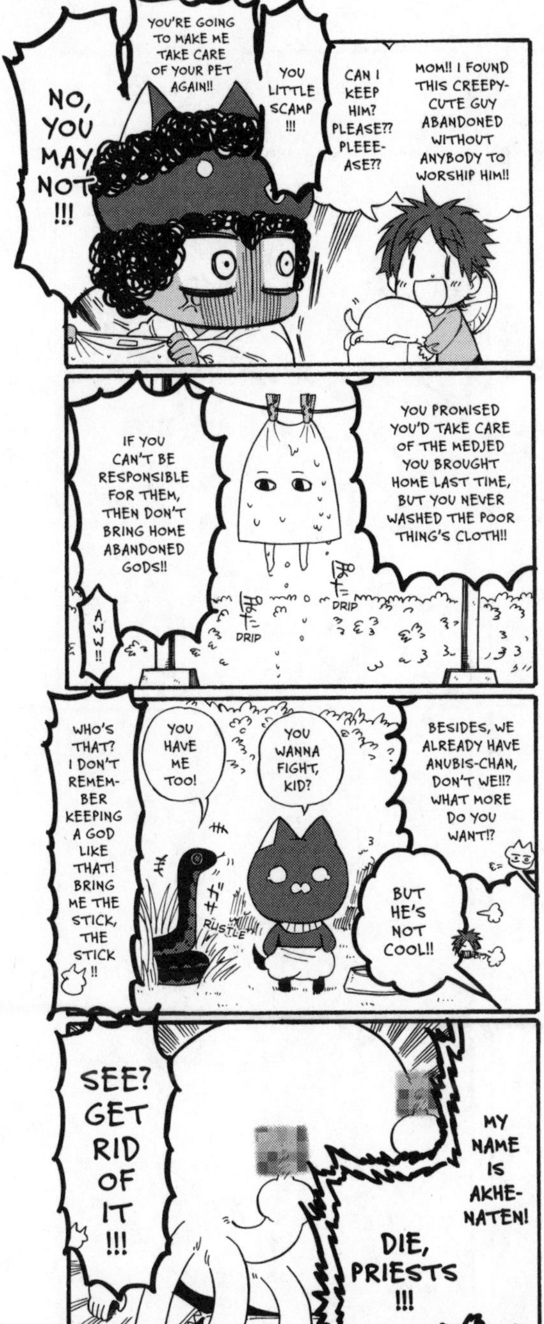
MOM!! I FOUND THIS CREEPY-CUTE GUY ABANDONED WITHOUT ANYBODY TO WORSHIP HIM!!
CAN I KEEP HIM? PLEASE?? PLEEE-ASE??
YOU LITTLE SCAMP!!!
YOU'RE GOING TO MAKE ME TAKE CARE OF YOUR PET AGAIN!!
NO, YOU MAY NOT!!!
YOU PROMISED YOU'D TAKE CARE OF THE MEDJED YOU BROUGHT HOME LAST TIME, BUT YOU NEVER WASHED THE POOR THING'S CLOTH!!
DRIP
DRIP
IF YOU CAN'T BE RESPONSIBLE FOR THEM, THEN DON'T BRING HOME ABANDONED GODS!!
AWW!!
BESIDES, WE ALREADY HAVE ANUBIS-CHAN, DON'T WE!!? WHAT MORE DO YOU WANT!?
BUT HE'S NOT COOL!!
YOU WANNA FIGHT, KID?
YOU HAVE ME TOO!
RUSTLE
WHO'S THAT? I DON'T REMEMBER KEEPING A GOD LIKE THAT! BRING ME THE STICK, THE STICK!!
MY NAME IS AKHENATEN!
DIE, PRIESTS!!!
SEE? GET RID OF IT!!!
EGYPT'S FAMOUS PRIEST-HATER

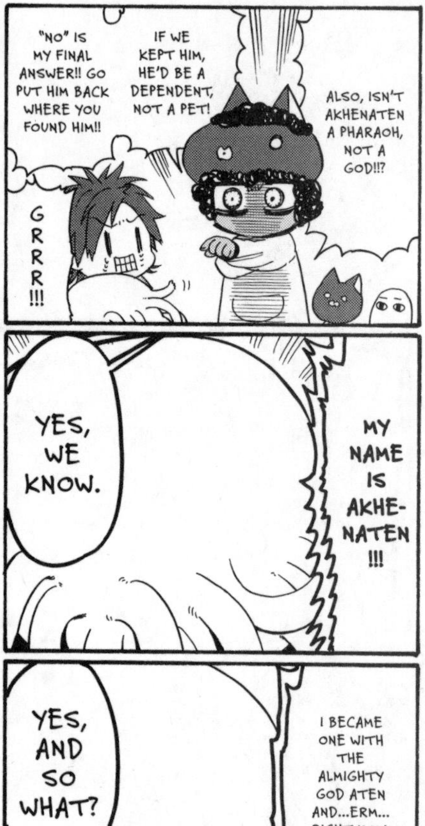
ALSO, ISN'T AKHENATEN A PHARAOH, NOT A GOD!!?
IF WE KEPT HIM, HE'D BE A DEPENDENT, NOT A PET!
"NO" IS MY FINAL ANSWER!! GO PUT HIM BACK WHERE YOU FOUND HIM!!
GRRR!!!
MY NAME IS AKHENATEN!!!
YES, WE KNOW.
I BECAME ONE WITH THE ALMIGHTY GOD ATEN AND...ERM... RIGHT NOW, I'M ACTUALLY ALSO (A MAGAI OF) THE GOD ATEN...!
YES, AND SO WHAT?
AND...! I THINK I COME WITH A LOT OF BENEFITS, MA'AM. CONCRETELY SPEAKING, UM...YOU KNOW, THAT... I CAN LIGHT THE WAY WHEN YOU NEED TO GO TO THE BATHROOM AT NIGHT, SO IF YOU WOULD USE ME, I COULD REDUCE YOUR ELECTRIC BILL. AND I'M CONFIDENT THAT I COULD BE A GOOD HOT WATER BOTTLE IN THE WINTER, SO PLEASE FIND IT IN YOUR HEART TO RECONSIDER BEFORE GETTING RID OF ME...
HE'S DESPERATE!!!

TRIGGERED BY PEOPLE PRETENDING HE DIDN'T EXIST (THIS PHARAOH WAS TRULY DAMNATIO MEMORIAE'D AWAY IN HISTORY)

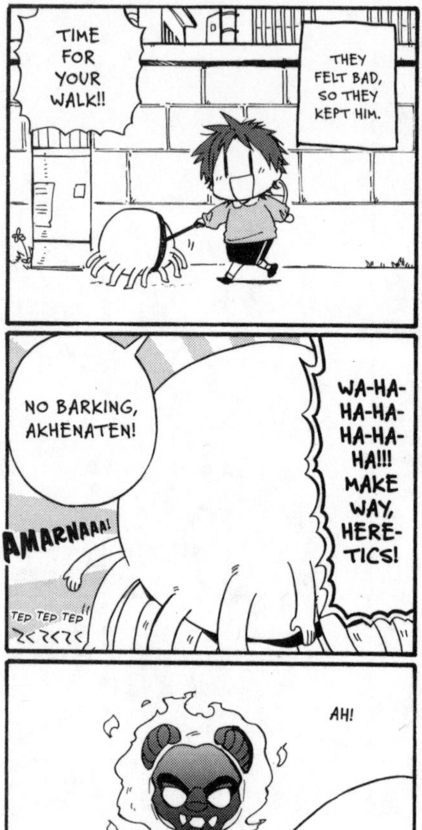
THEY FELT BAD, SO THEY KEPT HIM.
TIME FOR YOUR WALK!!
WA-HA-HA-HA-HA-HA-HA!!! MAKE WAY, HERETICS!
NO BARKING, AKHENATEN!
AMARNAAA!
TEP TEP TEP
てくてくてく
AH!
AW, GOOD FOR YOU!! YOU MADE A FRIEND!!
MEOW!
コロコロコロコロ
ROLL ROLL ROLL ROLL
WHAT'S YOUR PET AGAIN, HAWAKATA-SAN? A CAT?
A LION.

YUP, SEKHMET-SAN IS STRONG.

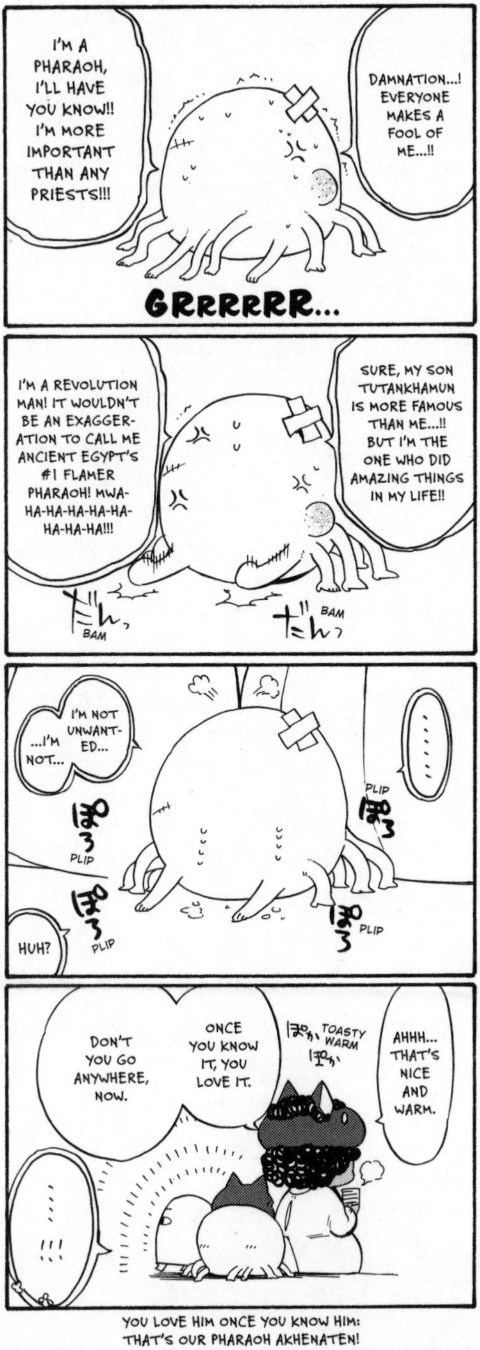
DAMNATION...! EVERYONE MAKES A FOOL OF ME...!!
I'M A PHARAOH, I'LL HAVE YOU KNOW!! I'M MORE IMPORTANT THAN ANY PRIESTS!!!
GRRRRRR...
SURE, MY SON TUTANKHAMUN IS MORE FAMOUS THAN ME...!! BUT I'M THE ONE WHO DID AMAZING THINGS IN MY LIFE!!
I'M A REVOLUTION MAN! IT WOULDN'T BE AN EXAGGER-ATION TO CALL ME ANCIENT EGYPT'S #1 FLAMER PHARAOH! MWA-HA-HA-HA-HA-HA-HA-HA-HA-HA!!!
BAM
BAM
......
PLIP
I'M NOT UNWANT-ED...
...I'M NOT...
PLIP
PLIP
PLIP
HUH?
AHHH... THAT'S NICE AND WARM.
TOASTY WARM
ONCE YOU KNOW IT, YOU LOVE IT.
DON'T YOU GO ANYWHERE, NOW.
......!!!

YOU LOVE HIM ONCE YOU KNOW HIM: THAT'S OUR PHARAOH AKHENATEN!

Special Thanks!

- Arisa Yukimiya
- Ui Kizuki
- Mai Kurozuki

SPECIAL HELP FROM:

- You Omura-sensei
- Shinonome-san
- Shikamori-san

My editor,
Yuuichi Shimomura-sama

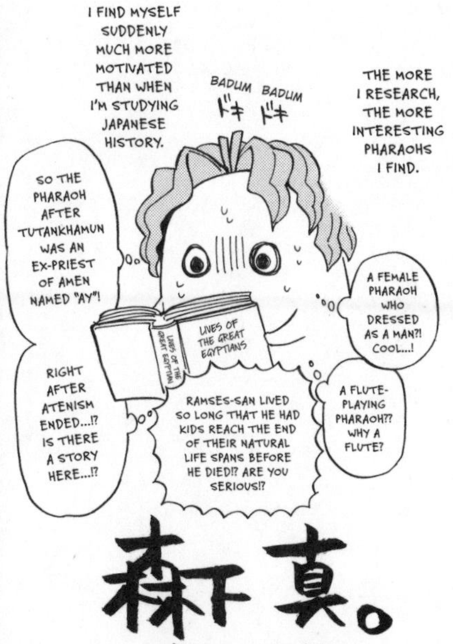
THE MORE I RESEARCH, THE MORE INTERESTING PHARAOHS I FIND.
I FIND MYSELF SUDDENLY MUCH MORE MOTIVATED THAN WHEN I'M STUDYING JAPANESE HISTORY.
BADUM BADUM
SO THE PHARAOH AFTER TUTANKHAMUN WAS AN EX-PRIEST OF AMEN NAMED "AY"!
A FEMALE PHARAOH WHO DRESSED AS A MAN?! COOL...!
LIVES OF THE GREAT EGYPTIANS
A FLUTE-PLAYING PHARAOH?? WHY A FLUTE?
RAMSES-SAN LIVED SO LONG THAT HE HAD KIDS REACH THE END OF THEIR NATURAL LIFE SPANS BEFORE HE DIED!? ARE YOU SERIOUS!?
RIGHT AFTER ATENISM ENDED...!? IS THERE A STORY HERE...!?

森下真。
Makoto Morishita

LET'S LEARN TOGETHER! ANCIENT EGYPT CREATION MYTHOLOGY!!

WE BROADLY CALL IT "EGYPTIAN MYTHOLOGY," BUT THE CREATION STORIES THAT WERE BELIEVED IN ANCIENT EGYPT ACTUALLY DIFFER QUITE A BIT DEPENDING ON THE TIME AND REGION! THIS TIME, WE'RE GOING TO GIVE YOU A SUPER ROUGH RUN-THROUGH OF THE MAIN THREE MYTHS!!

THE WAY EGYPTIAN MYTHOLOGY IS SO COMPLEX AND DIVERSE IS WHAT MAKES IT SO INTERESTING! PUZZLING OUT HOW THE MYTHOLOGY IS ARRANGED IN EGYPT-THEMED STORIES IS ANOTHER WAY TO ENJOY THEM TOO!! COMMIT THIS TO MEMORY, OKAY!?

① MYTH OF HELIOPOLIS...MAIN GODS: THE ENNEAD

THIS IS ANCIENT EGYPTIAN MYTHOLOGY'S BIGGEST CREATION STORY. IT'S SUN WORSHIP CENTERING AROUND THE SUN GOD, ATUM.

BUT THERE ARE TOO MANY DIFFERENT THEORIES RIGHT FROM THE GET-GO.

"ATUM CAME FROM THE PRIMORDIAL SEAS." "NO, ATUM CAME FROM THE HILL." "NO, NO, ATUM IS THE HILL." "ATUM ORIGINALLY HAD THE FORM OF A SNAKE." AND SO ON. SINCE IT'S THE BIGGEST MYTH, OF COURSE IT HAS LOTS OF SPIN-OFFS. MOST MYTHOLOGIES HAVE A CREATION STORY LIKE THIS!

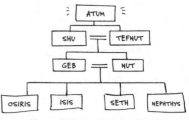

```
              ATUM
               |
       SHU ═══════ TEFNUT
               |
           GEB ═══ NUT
               |
   ┌───────┬───────┬───────┐
 OSIRIS  ISIS    SETH   NEPHTHYS
```

SEE VOLUME 7 FOR MORE ABOUT THE ENNEAD!

② MYTH OF MEMPHIS...MAIN GOD: PTAH

THIS WAS MEMPHIS'S PRIESTS OF PTAH'S RESPONSE WHEN THEY FOUND OUT THAT THE MYTH OF HELIOPOLIS HAD BLOWN UP: "OUR GOD, PTAH, BROUGHT LIGHT TO THE SUN!!! THEREFORE, PTAH IS THE TRUE OLDEST CREATION GOD!"

A MYTH THAT WAS CLEARLY PUSHED BECAUSE OF A SENSE OF COMPETITION.

MEMPHIS WAS, IN FACT, A CENTER OF RELIGION AND POLITICS BEFORE HELIOPOLIS EVER WAS. SO YEAH, THEY'D GET COMPETITIVE.

PTAH IS A DEIFICATION OF "THE POTENTIAL OF HUMANS." THOUGH HE ISN'T A MAJOR GOD, HE WAS MAINLY WORSHIPPED BY CRAFTSMEN!

A GOD FOR CREATORS!

③ MYTH OF HERMOPOLIS...MAIN GODS: THE OGDOAD

GOING BACK EVEN BEFORE ① AND ②, BEFORE THE BIRTH OF THE SUN (ATUM), THERE WERE EIGHT GODS WHO CREATED A CHAOTIC WORLD. THE EIGHT GODS CONTROLLED FOUR ATTRIBUTES—DEPTHS/ABYSS, INFINITENESS, INVISIBILITY, AND DARKNESS—AS FOUR MALE-FEMALE PAIRS.

IT SEEMS LIKE IT WOULD GET YOUNG HEARTS POUNDING, BUT THIS IS VERY SERIOUS MYTHOLOGY.

THIS IS ALSO THE ORIGIN OF THE AMEN PRIESTHOOD'S NAME. THE GOD AMEN WAS ONE OF THE OGDOAD—THE GOD OF INVISIBILITY!

REFERENCE: "ANCIENT EGYPT MAGAZINE: ANCIENT EGYPT'S GODS," WATARU MATSUMOTO

WHAT'S GOIN' ON??

EGYPT'S SUN GOD PROBLEM!

SUN GOD WORSHIP IS THE FIRST THING THAT COMES TO MIND WHEN YOU THINK EGYPTIAN MYTHOLOGY! BUT GET THIS—THEY HAVE **MORE THAN ONE** SUN GOD! WE'LL TALK ABOUT THE THREE MAIN ONES AND HOW TO TELL THEM APART.

① ATUM (FORM OF A HUMAN MAN)

THIS IS THE SUN GOD EVERYONE KNOWS. HIS NAME MEANS "COMPLETE ONE." SINCE HE'S COMPLETE, HE BEGOT OFFSPRING ALONE, YOU GUYS!

ATUM IS THE ONLY SUN GOD WITH CHILDREN!

ATUM IS ALSO THE ONLY ONE WITH A HUMAN FORM!

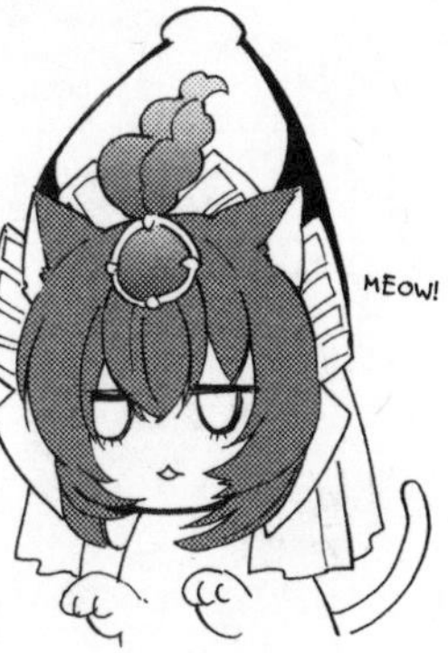
MEOW!
HE'S ALSO BEEN DRAWN AS A CAT WHEN FIGHTING APOPHIS.

② RA (FALCON HEAD)

I'M SURE THERE ARE PEOPLE WHO KNOW HIM, AT LEAST BY NAME? YES, HE IS

THE ORIGINAL SUN GOD!!

IF ATUM IS THE SUN GOD WHO BROUGHT THE FIRST LIGHT TO THE WORLD DURING ITS FORMATION, RA IS NOTHING LESS THAN

THE SUN ITSELF

THAT IS ABOVE OUR HEADS RIGHT NOW. BUT SINCE SOMETIMES HE'S FUSED INTO ONE GOD WITH ATUM, HE CAN ALSO BE CALLED "ATUM RA" ...IN ANY CASE, HE'S FUSED TOGETHER WITH DIFFERENT GODS, SO HE'S

COMPLICATED.

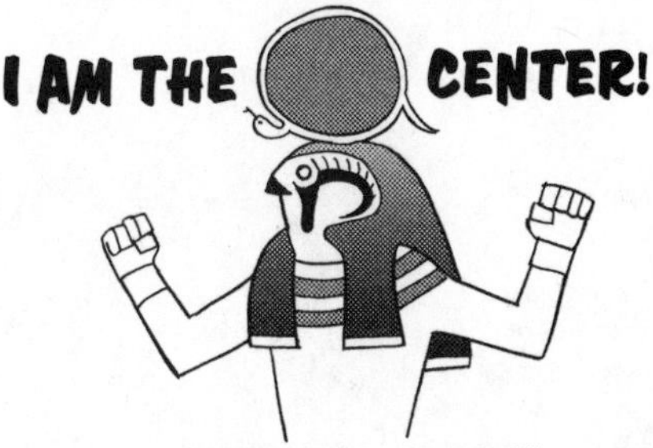
I AM THE CENTER!
EVERYONE, BECOME ONE WITH ME!!!

③ ATEN (CIRCLE)

THOSE HANDS? THEY'RE ACTUALLY RAYS OF LIGHT. IN THE NEW KINGDOM PERIOD, BECAUSE OF A FEUD WITH THE PRIESTS OF AMEN, WHO HAD TOO MUCH POWER, AMENHOTEP III BEGAN WORSHIPPING THIS SUN GOD WITHIN THE PALACE TO GAIN DISTANCE FROM THEM. LATER, HIS SON AMENHOTEP IV (PHARAOH AKHENATEN) WOULD REJECT ALL OTHER GODS, AND STAGE A RELIGIOUS REVOLUTION TO ATENISM (ATEN AS THE ONE TRUE GOD). THE **"AMARNA REVOLUTION"** (HUMAN HISTORY'S OLDEST RELIGIOUS REVOLUTION).

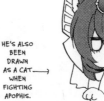

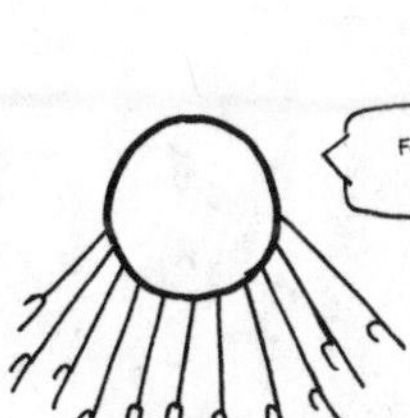
FOR A BRIEF MOMENT IN TIME, I WAS THE NATIONAL GOD.

BUT MOST OF THE PEOPLE DIDN'T ACCEPT ATENISM. IT WAS SO UNPOPULAR THAT THE FUTURE PHARAOHS TREATED IT AS AN EMBARRASSING MOMENT IN THEIR HISTORY. YOU GOTTA FEEL A LITTLE BAD FOR THIS SUN GOD.

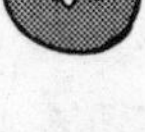

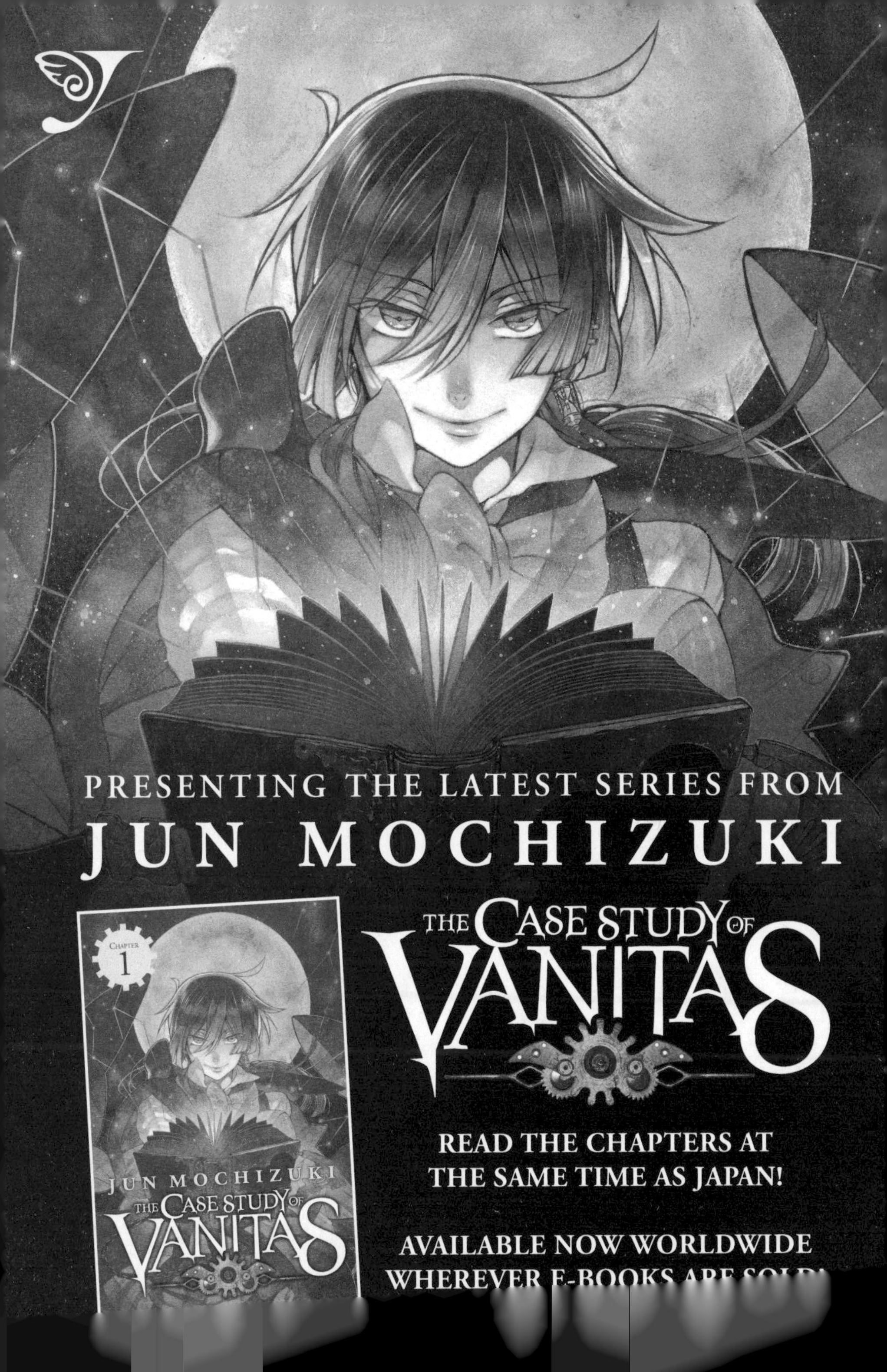
PRESENTING THE LATEST SERIES FROM
JUN MOCHIZUKI
THE CASE STUDY OF VANITAS
CHAPTER 1
JUN MOCHIZUKI
THE CASE STUDY OF VANITAS
READ THE CHAPTERS AT THE SAME TIME AS JAPAN!
AVAILABLE NOW WORLDWIDE WHEREVER E-BOOKS ARE SOLD!

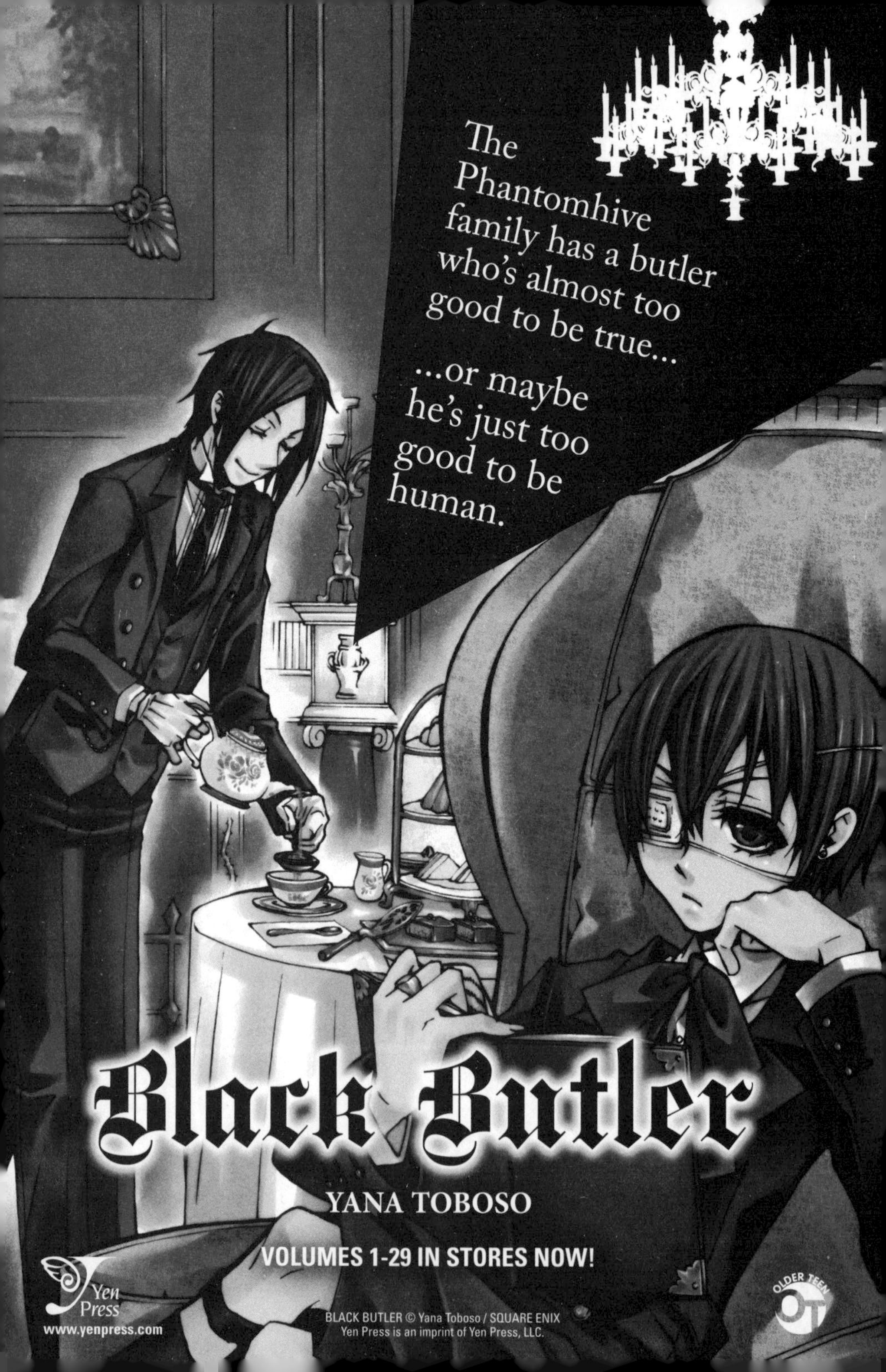
The Phantomhive family has a butler who's almost too good to be true...
...or maybe he's just too good to be human.
Black Butler
YANA TOBOSO
VOLUMES 1-29 IN STORES NOW!
Yen Press
www.yenpress.com
BLACK BUTLER © Yana Toboso / SQUARE ENIX
Yen Press is an imprint of Yen Press, LLC.
OLDER TEEN
OT

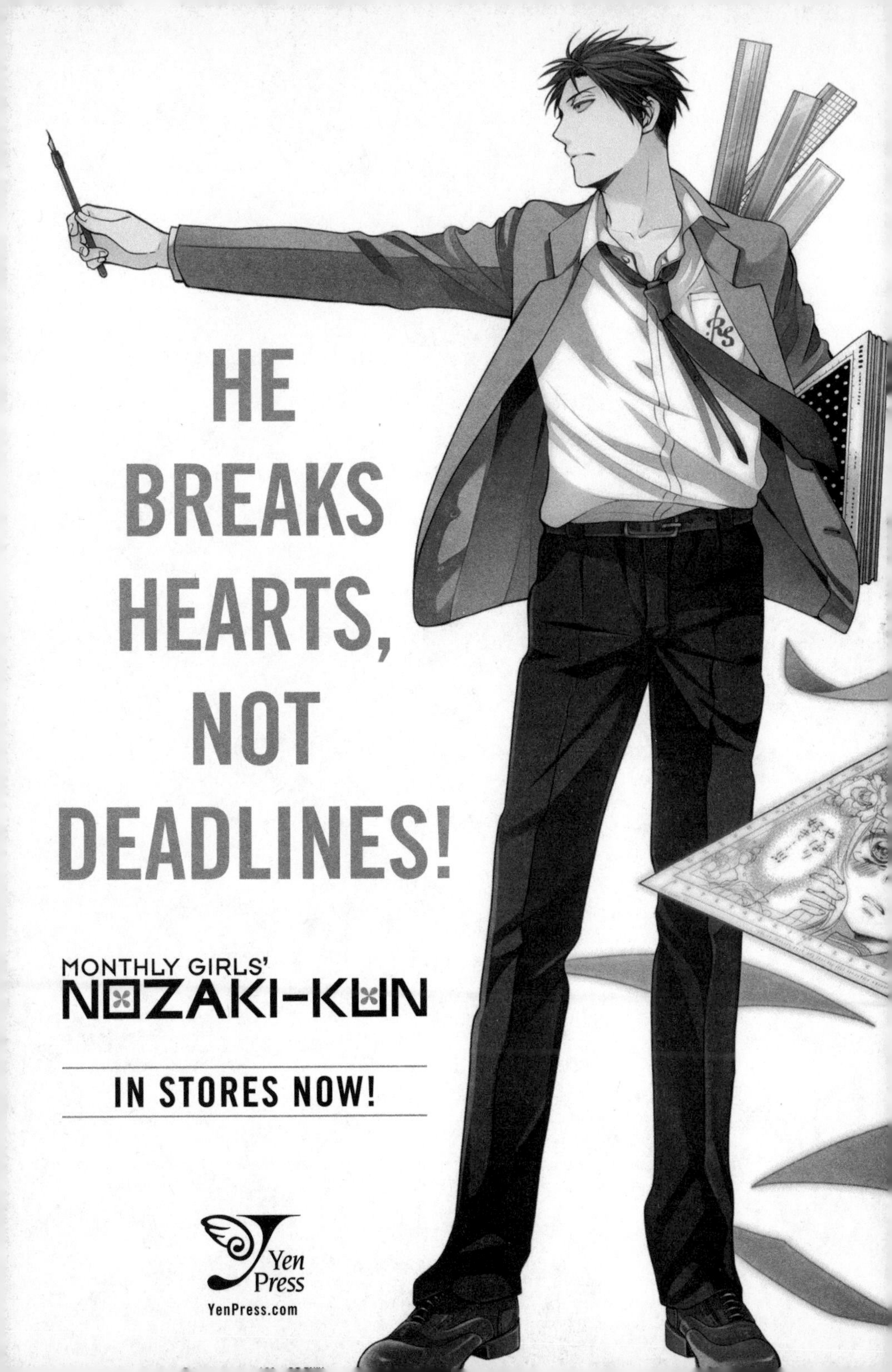
HE BREAKS HEARTS, NOT DEADLINES!
MONTHLY GIRLS'
NOZAKI-KUN
IN STORES NOW!
Yen Press
YenPress.com